MODERNISING LEGAL EDUCATION

Over the last decade, cost-pressures, technology, automation, globalisation, de-regulation and changing client relationships have transformed the practice of law. In the face of these changes, legal education has seemingly remained unmoved, reluctant to respond to the emerging professional environment or to look beyond doing what has always been done. Deciding what learning objectives a law degree ought to prioritise and how to best strike the balance between vocational and academic training, is a question of growing importance for students, regulators, educators and the legal profession. In response, this collection provides a range of perspectives on the suite of skills required by the modern lawyer and the various approaches to supporting their acquisition. Contributions report on a variety of curriculum initiatives, including role-play, gamification, virtual reality, project based learning, design thinking, data analytics, clinical legal education, apprenticeships, experiential learning and regulatory reform, and in doing so, offer a vision of what modern legal education might look like.

Catrina Denvir is a senior Lecturer at the Department of Business Law and Taxation, Monash University. She was previously Inaugural Director of the Legal Innovation Centre at Ulster University, having held research positions at the University of Sydney and UCL. She is a graduate of the University of Melbourne, the University of Cambridge, and holds a PhD in Law from University College London. Her research interests include technological innovation in legal services (including the use of artificial intelligence and intelligent systems in law), the role of law in everyday life, public understanding of the law/legal rights, professional ethics and identity, design of legal services, legal pedagogy, access to justice and research methodology.

T0382458

Modernising Legal Education

Edited by

CATRINA DENVIR

Monash University

CAMBRIDGE
UNIVERSITY PRESS

University Printing House, Cambridge CB2 8BS, United Kingdom

One Liberty Plaza, 20th Floor, New York, NY 10006, USA

477 Williamstown Road, Port Melbourne, VIC 3207, Australia

314-321, 3rd Floor, Plot 3, Splendor Forum, Jasola District Centre, New Delhi - 110025, India

103 Penang Road, #05-06/07, Visioncrest Commercial, Singapore 238467

Cambridge University Press is part of the University of Cambridge.

It furthers the University's mission by disseminating knowledge in the pursuit of education, learning and research at the highest international levels of excellence.

www.cambridge.org
Information on this title: www.cambridge.org/9781108468879
DOI: 10.1017/9781108663311

© Cambridge University Press 2020

First published 2020
First paperback edition 2022

A catalogue record for this publication is available from the British Library

Library of Congress Cataloging in Publication data
NAMES: Denvir, Catrina, editor.
TITLE: Modernising legal education / [edited by] Catrina Denvir.
DESCRIPTION: 1. edition. | New York : Cambridge University Press, 2020.
IDENTIFIERS: LCCN 2019033806 (print) | LCCN 2019033807 (ebook) | ISBN 9781108475754 (hardback) | ISBN 9781108663311 (epub)
SUBJECTS: LCSH: Law – Study and teaching.
CLASSIFICATION: LCC K100 .M63 2020 (print) | LCC K100 (ebook) | DDC 340.071/1–dc23
LC record available at https://lccn.loc.gov/2019033806
LC ebook record available at https://lccn.loc.gov/2019033807

ISBN 978-1-108-47575-4 Hardback
ISBN 978-1-108-46887-9 Paperback

Contents

Figures

Tables

About the Contributors

Julie Brannan is Director of Education and Training at the SRA. Before that she was a litigation partner at Herbert Smith (now Herbert Smith Freehills) and Director of the Oxford Institute of Legal Practice. At the SRA, she is leading the introduction of the Solicitors Qualifying Examination, a new standardised assessment for all intending solicitors.

Patrick Cahill is a solicitor at Onfido, a software company that helps businesses verify people's identities using a photo-based identity document, a selfie and artificial intelligence algorithms, with offices in the USA, UK, Portugal, Singapore and France. Patrick was previously Director of qLegal from 2013 to 2018 where he helped to establish the law clinic and develop a curriculum for postgraduate law students. He is a Visiting Fellow at the Centre for Commercial Law Studies and teaches on the Entrepreneurship Law Clinic module. His interests include models of legal advice delivery to start-ups and entrepreneurs and the interrelationship between law and emerging technologies.

Anna Carpenter is Professor of Law and Director of Clinical Programs at The University of Utah SJ Quinney College of Law. Her scholarship includes empirical and theoretical work on access to justice and the role of lawyers, non-lawyers and judges in the civil justice system. She also writes on legal and experiential education. For her empirical research on access to justice, she was named a Bellow Scholar. Her papers have been selected for the Junior Scholars Public Law Workshop and the New Voices in Civil Justice Workshop. Professor Carpenter previously held a Clinical Teaching Fellowship at Georgetown University Law Center in the Community Justice Project. She was also a Georgetown Women's Law and Public Policy Fellow. Prior to her academic career, Professor Carpenter worked as a legal services lawyer and as a federal policy analyst. She has a JD and an LLM in Advocacy from Georgetown University Law Center.

Elizabeth Chambliss is Henry Harman Edens Professor of Law and Director of the NMRS Center on Professionalism at the University of South Carolina School of

Law. Her research focuses on new models for legal services delivery and the development of legal and methodological standards for evidence-based lawyer regulation. She serves on the South Carolina Access to Justice Commission, the American Academy of Arts and Sciences Legal Services Design Project and the Editorial Advisory Board of Law & Society Review. She received her JD and PhD in sociology from the University of Wisconsin.

Jane Ching is a qualified solicitor and Professor of Professional Legal Education at Nottingham Law School, in the UK, working with colleagues in the Centre for Legal Education, of which she is co-director. Jane's PhD was on the learning of early career litigation solicitors. Between 2011 and 2013 she was also a member of the multi-institution research team which worked on the Legal Education and Training Review for England and Wales. She has worked with professional bodies and academic colleagues on professional legal education projects (including reviews of professional qualification frameworks) in Armenia, Canada, the CARICOM nations, England and Wales, Hong Kong, the Republic of Ireland, Mauritius and, currently, Mongolia.

Sylvie Delacroix is Professor in Law and Ethics at the University of Birmingham, She joined Birmingham from UCL where she was the founding Director of the UCL Centre for Ethics and Law, as well as the UCL Virtual Environments and the Professions Group. Prior to that Sylvie was the EG Davis Fellow at the Radcliffe Institute (Harvard), a lecturer in Kent and a post-doctoral researcher at Trinity College, Cambridge. Her research focuses on the intersection between law and ethics, with a particular interest in machine and professional ethics, agency and the role of habit within moral decisions. Sylvie's work has been funded by the Wellcome Trust, the NHS and the Leverhulme Trust, from whom she received the Leverhulme Prize. She has recently served on the Law Society of England and Wales' Commission on the use of algorithms in the justice system. She is a Fellow of the Alan Turing Institute.

Catrina Denvir is a senior lecturer at the Department of Business Law and Taxation, Monash University. She was previously Inaugural Director of the Legal Innovation Centre at Ulster University, having held research positions at the University of Sydney and UCL. She is a graduate of the University of Melbourne, the University of Cambridge, and holds a PhD in Law from University College London. Her research interests include technological innovation in legal services (including the use of artificial intelligence and intelligent systems in law), the role of law in everyday life, public understanding of the law/legal rights, professional ethics and identity, design of legal services, legal pedagogy, access to justice and research methodology.

Jeff Giddings is Professor of Law and Associate Dean (Experiential Education) at Monash University. He joined the Monash Law Faculty in 2017 after 22 years at

Griffith University in Brisbane, Queensland. Jeff remains an adjunct Professor of the Griffith Law School. He received an Australia National Teaching Fellowship in 2013 for the Effective Law Student Supervision Project. Jeff also received the Australian Award for University Teaching in Law and Legal Studies in 1999 along with multiple Griffith University teaching awards, including the inaugural Griffith Award for Excellence in Teaching. From 2013 to 2015, Jeff served as an International Scholar for the Academic Fellows Program of the Open Society Foundation, working extensively with the American University of Central Asia, Bishkek, Kyrgyzstan.

Genevieve Grant is an associate professor in the Faculty of Law at Monash University and Director of the Australian Centre for Justice Innovation. Genevieve's research interests include dispute resolution, civil justice, legal innovation and injury compensation and she has published widely in these fields. She teaches litigation and dispute resolution, legal ethics and pioneered the development of the Online Dispute Resolution course at Monash University.

Margaret Hagan is Director of the Legal Design Lab and a lecturer at Stanford Institute of Design (the d.school). Margaret graduated from Stanford Law School in June 2013. She served as a student fellow at the Centre for Internet & Society and president of the Stanford Law and Technology Association. Margaret holds an A.B. from the University of Chicago, an MA from Central European University in Budapest, and a PhD from Queen's University Belfast in International Politics.

Paresh Kathrani holds an LLB (Hons), LLM and PhD in Law. Currently Director of Legal Education and Training at the Chartered Institute of Arbitrators, Paresh was formerly a senior lecturer in Law at the University of Westminster, where he was a member of the Serious Games at Westminster group. Paresh's research focuses on lawtech in legal education and legal practice and he has worked on a number of EU funded projects, including a project with a start-up on how natural language processing can assist with triaging legal cases. He is currently leading alternative dispute resolution training at the Chartered Institute, including looking at how training delivery will change in the future.

Esther Lestrell is Research Fellow in the Law Faculty at Monash University and the Australian Centre for Justice Innovation. Esther graduated from Monash University with Honours in law and biomedicine, and her research interests span both fields. In 2017 Esther commenced a PhD with the Monash University Faculty of Pharmacy and Pharmaceutical Sciences at the Melbourne Centre for Nanofabrication.

Paul Maharg is a leading scholar in legal education whose work is focused on interdisciplinary educational innovation, the design of regulation in legal education, and the use of technology-enhanced learning. He joined Osgoode as Distinguished

Professor of Practice in May 2017. Prior to that he served as Professor of Law and Director of the Centre for Profession, Education and Regulation in Law (PEARL) at Australian National University College of Law. He also currently holds visiting Professorships at Hong Kong University Faculty of Law and Chinese University of Hong Kong Faculty of Law.

Rob Marrs is Head of Education at the Law Society of Scotland. He is primarily a policy advisor on all matters of legal education focusing on the route to qualification and continuing professional development. As well as this, he is heavily involved in the Society's work on new membership categories, widening access, equality diversity and public legal education. He sits on the advisory board of LawScotTech: an initiative to stimulate legal technology innovation in Scotland.

Andrew Moshirnia is a senior lecturer at Monash BLT. He is a magna cum laude graduate of Harvard Law School, where he, as a staff writer for the Berkman Center's Digital Media Law Project, analysed copyright infringement actions and takedown notices under the Digital Millennium Copyright Act. He clerked in Chicago for the Honorable Richard D. Cudahy of the US Court of Appeals for the Seventh Circuit and taught telecommunications law at DePaul as an adjunct professor. He later clerked in Los Angeles for the Honorable Mariana R Pfaelzer of the US District Court for the Central District of California. He worked as the Empirical IP Fellow at Chicago-Kent. He taught copyright law and legal writing for the Program in International Intellectual Property Law and was a member of the Chicago IP Colloquium faculty. Dr Moshirnia has a PhD in educational technology, with a concentration in statistics, from the University of Kansas.

Alexander Smith is Global Product Lead for iManage RAVN, which uses AI techniques to extract insight from data. In this role he heads up the product team, working closely with customers. Previously Alex was Innovation Manager at Reed Smith LLP, joining in 2016 to lead the Firm's Innovation Hub programme. Based in London, he managed activities in the Innovation Hub, Reed Smith's unique space for co-creation with clients, using service design and innovation techniques. As a user-centric design practitioner, Alex puts the client at the heart of everything he does. He has two decades of experience interacting with lawyers in law firms and in-house teams to design new products and technologies, primarily as Innovation & New Product Lead at LexisNexis.

Nigel Spencer is Senior Client Director at Saïd Business School, University of Oxford. Over a period of thirteen years he held Global Head of Learning roles in two international law firms, designing innovative leadership programmes including new legal Masters (MBA/MA) courses and practice-focused undergraduate law degrees. Nigel co-chaired the UK's national body of Legal Education professionals for a number of years and now sits on its Advisory Panel. Nigel also held Board roles at Higher Education Research Institutes and at the ACCA, and is a visiting

(Industry) Professor at the School of Law, Queen Mary University of London. At Oxford Nigel has developed a White Paper series of 'Practitioner Insights' on how strategic talent programmes can create competitive advantage for professional service firms. A qualified executive coach, Nigel is a member of Saïd Business School's Coaching Community, coaching on the School's MBA and executive development programmes.

Ian Walden is Professor of Information and Communications Law and Director of the Centre for Commercial Law Studies, Queen Mary University of London. Ian has been involved in law reform projects for a wide range of stakeholders and has sat on the boards of the Internet Watch Foundation (2004–09); the UK Council for Child Internet Safety (2010–12); the Press Complaints Commission (2009–14), and was a member of the RUSI Independent Surveillance Review (2014–15). Ian founded and is the academic lead for Queen Mary's qLegal initiative and is a principal investigator on the Cloud Legal Project. He has published widely in the field of information technology law.

Julian Webb is a Professor of Law at Melbourne University, he joined Melbourne Law School in 2014 having previously held chairs at the Universities of Warwick and Westminster in the UK. He was awarded his LLM and LLD degrees by the University of Warwick and is both a Fellow of the Royal Society of Arts (FRSA) and an Academic Bencher of the Honourable Society of the Inner Temple. Julian currently teaches legal ethics and legal theory on the JD programme and has particular research interests in the ethics and professional regulation of lawyers; legal technology and developments in the market for legal services; and legal education policy and pedagogy. Julian is an experienced empirical researcher and, between 2011 and 2013, led the research phase of a major national review of legal education and training in England and Wales undertaken by the Solicitors Regulation Authority, Bar Standards Board and ILEX Professional Standards, and was a consultant to the recent Comprehensive Review of Legal Education and Training undertaken on behalf of the Hong Kong government.

Jacqueline Weinberg is a lecturer, PhD Candidate and Clinical Supervisor in Monash Legal Practice Programs at the Faculty of Law, Monash University. Jacqueline received an Australian Postgraduate Award scholarship and commenced her PhD in 2016, which is focused on an exploration of ADR in clinical legal education. Her research areas are in ADR, student wellbeing and technology and the law, focusing on access to justice in clinical legal education.

Foreword

There is a sense, internationally, that legal education and training are approaching a crossroads. The work of law schools has faced, since the early 2000s, a particularly intense period of re-assessment, with major reviews and commissions taking place (with widely varying degrees of impact) in the UK, Canada, the USA, India and Hong Kong, to name but a few.[1] At the same time, concerns that radical reforms in jurisdictions like Japan, China and South Korea have had significant unintended consequences have added to a global sense of fluidity and uncertainty.[2]

The drivers of change in this process have been many. Commonly they include four significant (perceived) needs. First, to adapt national legal education systems for increasingly globalised and transnational legal education and legal services markets. Second, to respond to actual changes in the local market for law graduates, often framed in terms of an 'oversupply' problem. Third, to better align legal education systems with current perceptions of effective practice in higher and professional education (e.g., the widespread moves to outcomes-based education), and, fourth, perhaps most centrally, to better prepare students for the rapidly changing world of legal practice.

On the face of it, this collection responds most directly to the concerns of practice. It thus reflects, and reflects on, the significant challenges and opportunities wrought by market liberalisation and the disruption of existing business and workflow models in the legal sector; but it is also more than that. Whilst offering some excellent examples of what can be done, it does not lose sight of the larger systemic, regulatory and normative questions of what should be done. Unsurprisingly, the role of new technology[3] is writ large in this story, in terms both of how legal educators are

---

[1] For an overview of much of this activity, see Julian Webb, 'Preparing for Practice in the 21st Century: The Role of Legal Education and Its Regulation' in Bernhard Bergmans (ed.), *Jahrbuch der Rechtsdidaktik 2017/Yearbook of Legal Education 2017* (Berliner Wissenschafts-Verlag 2018).

[2] See, e.g., Carl F Minzner, 'The Rise and Fall of Chinese Legal Education' (2013) 36(2) Fordham International Law Journal 334.

[3] I use the term technology widely here to include not just 'legal tech' – the digital information and communication technologies that are largely dominating debates – but to also recognise that 'tools' like design thinking and legal project management are also new applied technologies in the legal space.

responding to the changing technologies of practice and using new (and less new) educational technologies to prepare students for a world beyond the classroom.

In reflecting on the value of this collection, I want to share a set of questions that kept recurring as I read. They are by no means the only questions, and they probably reflect the recent bias in my own work towards the policy and regulatory problems we face when we talk about modernising legal education and training.

First, what does it actually mean to *modernise* legal education? The *Oxford English Dictionary* defines modernisation as the 'process of adapting something to modern needs or habits'. As non-technical definitions go, this one offers a useful launch pad. There is in it a sense of the everyday experience we have of both responding to and sometimes resisting the pull of the new. But modernisation properly understood also brings with it a whole other lot of baggage. Modernisation uniquely references our pursuit of the *modern*, that cluster of values, technologies and institutions that constitute the material product of what we think of as the Enlightenment tradition: developed industrial and post-industrial Western society.

Modernisation thus paints a specific picture for us, one of liberalisation, progress and utility; in its most dominant versions it becomes a measure almost of civilisation itself.[4] To suggest that we are not modern is discomforting (sometimes a useful thing!), but more than that, to be less than modern is itself a mark of failure and a call for revolution. As Bruno Latour has observed:

> When the word 'modern', 'modernization', or 'modernity' appears, we are defining, by contrast, an archaic and stable past. Furthermore, the word is always being thrown into the middle of a fight, in a quarrel where there are winners and losers, Ancients and Moderns. 'Modern' is thus doubly asymmetrical: it designates a break in the regular passage of time, and it designates a combat in which there are victors and vanquished.[5]

This dualism is worrying. Modernisation requires its critics, but to refuse to be modern is also to risk setting oneself up as an anachronism. Despite its sometime conservatism, higher – including legal – education, is as both institution and experience a thoroughly 'modern' phenomenon. Its embeddedness in the wider political economy[6] means its modernity is also Janus-faced. It offers individuals the seductive opportunity to transform themselves, and perhaps their society; to satisfy their thoroughly modern desire to do, to know and to become,[7] but it also imbricates

---

[4] Michael Adas, *Machines as the Measure of Men: Science, Technology, and Ideologies of Western Dominance* (Cornell University Press 2014).

[5] Bruno Latour, *We Have Never Been Modern* (Harvard University Press 1993) 10.

[6] See, e.g., Harry W Arthurs, 'The Political Economy of Canadian Legal Education' (1998) 25 Journal of Law and Society 14; Margaret Thornton, 'The Law School, the Market and the New Knowledge Economy' (2007) 17(1–2) Legal Education Review 1.

[7] Richard Collier, '"Be Smart, Be Successful, Be Yourself … "?: Representations of the Training Contract and Trainee Solicitor in Advertising by Large Law Firms' (2005) 12(1) International Journal of the Legal Profession 51.

us as participants in the deepening interdependences between education, technoscience and the neoliberalisation of society. How do we modernise and yet stay critical? Perhaps the following questions help.

Second, *who are we modernising legal education for?* Legal education policy frequently finds itself at the push and pull of multiple stakeholders, with often competing interests.[8] This is a large part of what makes reform and innovation a socially, not just technically, complex problem. Who is proposing change and why, who benefits from innovation and at what cost to other stakeholders in the system, are important policy questions that should not be overlooked in evaluating change.

An obvious but no less significant third question flows from this: *who is the lawyer that is a (central) subject – and object – of our education and training activity?* At present legal education and training is being pulled between two forces. On the one hand there is the reality of an increasingly segmented and fractured legal services workforce, a declining proportion of which, in many systems, is regulated as such. On the other, is the institutional pressure from regulators and professional associations to maintain a homogeneous 'one size fits all' curriculum or competence framework for 'the profession'. How long is the latter position sustainable? What might or, more importantly, should take its place? Where would such legal education best be located, both in space and time – will the current front-loaded model of training be fit for these purposes?

Finally, *what, therefore, are the priorities for change?* Modern legal practice as currently conceived requires a broad and growing range of skills and competences. New competences (commercial awareness, resilience, understanding of new practice technologies, legal project management, etc.) tend to be viewed as purely additive, within an already crowded curriculum. What gives way and where? At present regulation has done very little to offer us a road map for the future.

Like any institution the law school requires adjustment, refinement, renewal. This volume is a welcome and often thought-provoking addition to that task; I hope it proves to be a fruitful part of the continuing conversation about what legal education might become.

Julian Webb

BIBLIOGRAPHY

Adas M, *Machines as the Measure of Men: Science, Technology, and Ideologies of Western Dominance* (Cornell University Press 2014)

Arthurs HW, 'The Political Economy of Canadian Legal Education' (1998) 25(1) Journal of Law and Society 14

---

[8] This is not a new insight: see Fiona Cownie (ed.), *Stakeholders in the Law School* (Hart 2010).

Collier R, '"Be Smart, Be Successful, Be Yourself … "?: Representations of the Training Contract and Trainee Solicitor in Advertising by Large Law Firms' (2005) 12(1) International Journal of the Legal Profession 51

Cownie F (ed.), *Stakeholders in the Law School* (Hart 2010)

Latour B, *We Have Never Been Modern* (Harvard University Press 1993)

Minzner CF, 'The Rise and Fall of Chinese Legal Education' (2013) 36(2) Fordham International Law Journal 334

Thornton M, 'The Law School, the Market and the New Knowledge Economy' (2007) 17(1–2) Legal Education Review 1

Webb, J, 'Preparing for Practice in the 21st Century: The Role of Legal Education and Its Regulation' in Bernhard Bergmans (ed.), *Jahrbuch der Rechtsdidaktik 2017/Yearbook of Legal Education 2017* (Berliner Wissenschafts-Verlag 2018)

Introduction

Catrina Denvir

Once characterised as a relatively stable profession, unfettered by the influence of modernity and strongly resistant to external forces, the legal services sector has in recent years exhibited marked change. Efforts to preserve profit margins increasingly eroded by the introduction of new fee models, the demand for increased billing transparency, rising client expectations, the adoption of technology and heightened market competition from high volume legal process outsourcers, have all contributed to the sector's evolution.[1] In what has been viewed as a clear shift towards corporatisation and commercialisation, the legal profession in a number of jurisdictions has moved away from the broader social mission on which it was founded and in which it existed as 'a branch of the administration of justice and not a mere money-getting trade'.[2] Free market ideologies have undermined 'justice and rights in the discourse of law', and in its place, the generation of profit has become the primary indicator of success.[3]

Whilst the commercialisation of law has been exacerbated in the UK as a result of the decline of the Keynesian welfare state and the introduction of the Legal Services Act 2007,[4] changes to the organisation of the profession and the recruitment of lawyers have occurred across a number of jurisdictions, including Europe, the USA, Canada and Australia,[5] partly as a function of globalisation and the internationalisation of the

---

[1]   See, e.g., Julian Webb, 'The LETRs (Still) in the Post: The Legal Education and Training Review and the Reform of Legal Services Education and Training—A Personal (Re)View' in Hilary Sommerlad and others (eds.), *The Futures of Legal Education and the Legal Profession* (Hart 2018); Julian Webb and others, 'Setting Standards: The Future of Legal Services Education and Training Regulation in England and Wales (Legal Education and Training Review)' (SRA, BSB and CILEX 2013) www .letr.org.uk/wp-content/uploads/LETR-Report.pdf accessed 17 August 2018; Hilary Sommerlad and others, 'The Futures of Legal Education and the Legal Profession' in Hilary Sommerlad and others (eds.), *The Futures of Legal Education and the Legal Profession* (1st edn, Hart Publishing 2015).

[2]   James W Jones, 'The Challenge of Change: The Practice of Law in the Year 2000' (1988) 41(4) Vanderbilt Law Review 683, 683. Jones was quoting Canon 12 of the 1908 Canons of Ethics set down by the American Bar Foundation at its' 31st Annual Meeting in Seattle, Washington.

[3]   Sommerlad and others (n 1) 4.

[4]   Ibid.

[5]   See, e.g., Margaret Thornton, 'The Law School, the Market and the New Knowledge Economy' (2007) 17(1–2) Legal Education Review 1; Margaret Thornton, 'Squeezing the Life out of Lawyers: Legal

legal services market. Reduced demand for qualified legal professionals[6] within an increasingly 'lean' profession[7] and continued growth in the number of law graduates has led to supply outstripping demand. The once straightforward, hierarchical and tournament-driven career path reflected in the Firm's pyramidal organisational structure, has become increasingly complex.[8] A 'thickening of the organisational middle', has resulted in a less linear and more differentiated path of career progression, based on performance rather than tenure. The resulting organisation model said to herald the 'death of "Big Law"',[9] has been described as both lattice-like[10] and diamond-shaped,[11] reflecting greater lateral movement of employees between firms and professions.

This has been accompanied by the proliferation of roles requiring lesser qualifications and justifying prolonged relegation to the lower ranks of a firm's hierarchy. Paraprofessional 'legal associate' positions in the offshore and near-shore service centres of large international law firms have emerged to target the population of legal graduates not yet admitted to practice, offering a much needed foot in the door for those unable to secure graduate training contracts or positions.[12] Untethered from the traditional partnership promotion route and the prospect of advancing to fee-earner status, legal associates support the work of fee-earners, undertaking the type of repetitive and time intensive document review, drafting and research tasks ordinarily the preserve of trainee lawyers or paralegals. This organisational expansion at the lower ranks has allowed firms to complete legal projects at lower cost, thereby preserving profit margins on fixed-fee work and supporting a shift away from the existing hourly billing model.

Practice in the Market Embrace' (2016) 25(4) Griffith Law Review 471; William D Henderson, 'From Big Law to Lean Law' (2014) 38(June) International Review of Law and Economics 5; Marc S Galanter and William D Henderson, 'The Elastic Tournament: The Second Transformation of the Big Law Firm' (2008) 60 Stanford Law Review 1867.

[6] Ray Worthy Campbell, 'The End of Law Schools: Legal Education in the Era of Legal Service Businesses' (2016) 85(1) Mississippi Law Journal 1.

[7] Larry E Ribstein, 'The Death of Big Law' (2010) 3 Wisconsin Law Review 749.

[8] Galanter and Henderson (n 5). It should be noted that the 'Tournament Model' is not a universally agreed upon description of the organisation of the law firm. Kordana for example proposes an alternative in the form of the 'Production-Imperative Model'. 'This model suggests that the type of work performed in law firms dictates their structure, that law firms hire associates to keep their costs down and profits up.' See further Kevin A Kordana, 'Law Firms and Associate Careers: Tournament Theory Versus the Production-Imperative Model' (1995) 104(7) Yale Law Journal 1907, 1908.

[9] Ribstein (n 7).

[10] Cathy Benko, Molly Anderson and Suzanne Vickberg, 'The Corporate Lattice: A Strategic Response to the Changing World of Work' (*Deloitte Insights*, 1 January 2011) www2.deloitte.com/insights/us/en/deloitte-review/issue-8/the-corporate-lattice-rethinking-careers-in-the-changing-world-of-work.html accessed 4 May 2019.

[11] Ibid.

[12] In England and Wales, a training contract involves (in part) a firm offering an individual a two-year training period with an approved training provider (Law Firm). This training period is compulsory component of the process of qualifying as a Solicitor. This will change from 2021 onwards due to changes introduced by the Solicitors' Regulation Authority, as is discussed in greater detail in Chapter 12.

This structural change has been facilitated by the dramatic expansion and diversification of higher education, which in the words of Sommerlad et al, has provided 'a supply of practitioners whose "difference" justifies their confinement to subordinate roles (including that of the salaried partner) and solidified the professions' stratification and commercialisation'.[13] Changes to the nature of legal work have operated to exacerbate the gap between graduate expectation and reality even further. The once clear delineation between those legal issues within the remit of the lawyer and those business matters falling outside of it, have been muddied by the expectation that a 'client-focused' lawyer will be just as capable at answering questions of an economic, scientific, financial, or political nature as they are at answering purely legal enquiries.[14]

These changes come in addition to the use of various forms of technology within legal practice, including that which purports to harness artificial intelligence (AI) to enable the efficient completion of high volume, repetitive tasks. The combined effect of these changes is the emergence of a profession where data is as relevant to legal decision-making as is doctrine;[15] where online systems are redefining dispute resolution and litigation;[16] where legal service delivery and project management go hand in hand;[17] and where legal professionals are not just expected to know the law, but to also present as innovators, design-thinkers and entrepreneurs.

As a consequence, those who exhibit familiarity with technology or its adjacent domains (e.g. science, engineering, maths) have become increasingly valued within the profession, particularly within large international law firms and legal outsourcers.[18] This has led to efforts to recruit a more diverse group of graduates into law, and the emergence of new training pathways that emphasise the acquisition of technical skills from other fields.[19] These developments hold very real implications for those individuals who intend to pursue a career in law and for those educators and educational institutions that play a role in supporting these ambitions and preparing these individuals for practice. For students, these changes mean that the skills and knowledge they require, the working environment into

---

[13] Sommerlad and others (n 1) 4.

[14] Jones (n 2).

[15] Daniel M Katz, 'Quantitative Legal Prediction – or – How I Learned to Stop Worrying and Start Preparing for the Data Driven Future of the Legal Services Industry' (2013) 62 Emory Law Journal 909.

[16] See, e.g., Pablo Cortés, 'The Online Court: Filling the Gaps of the Civil Justice System?' (2017) 36(1) Civil Justice Quarterly 109; Hazel Genn, 'Online Courts and the Future of Justice' (Birkenhead Lecture, London, 16 October 2017) www.ucl.ac.uk/laws/sites/laws/files/birkenhead_lecture_2017_professor_dame_hazel_genn_final_version.pdf accessed 28 February 2018; Ayelet Sela, 'Streamlining Justice: How Online Courts Can Resolve the Challenges of Pro Se Litigation' 1(26) Cornel Journal of Law & Public Policy 331; Victoria McCloud, 'The Online Court: Suing in Cyberspace' (2017) 36(1) Civil Justice Quarterly 34.

[17] See, e.g., Richard Susskind, *The End of Lawyers? Rethinking the Nature of Legal Services* (Oxford University Press 2008).

[18] This is discussed in further detail in Chapter 4.

[19] This is discussed in more detail in Chapters 1, 4 and 12.

which they enter and their likelihood of securing entry is no longer as straightforward as it once was.

This has given rise to a growing belief that in order to serve society 'legal education needs to engage with this changing market',[20] although a lack of answers as to what this engagement might look like, particularly from the profession,[21] continues to stifle progress. Despite some notable exceptions, in Europe as in other jurisdictions such as North America and Australia, legal education at the academic level has been slow to respond to the emerging professional environment, to incorporate knowledge from other disciplines or look beyond the teaching of legal doctrine and the legal method. As a result, 'although it is recognised that lawyers must perform a wide range of tasks in a range of different contexts, law schools continue to send the message that law is litigation'.[22] Instruction in a range of general and applied legal technologies remains a relative rarity in legal education as either a means or an end. Word processing software and legal research tools often demarcate the extent of a law student's exposure to technology at the undergraduate and vocational level. Opportunities to acquire skills beyond what regulations prescribe or what legal academics ordinarily teach remain relatively few and far between.

It is not just the content of a law degree that has seemingly failed to keep pace with the times, but also the method of delivery. Whilst experiential models of learning within the academic stage of legal education have become increasingly popular, they continue to be viewed as non-standard, leading to an educational model that exists largely detached from the application and experience of law in the real world. Although controversial, the claim that '[i]nnovation in legal education comes hard, is limited in scope and permission, and generally dies young', is not without substance.[23] As Thornton has observed, where legal educators were once encouraged to shift away from the pedagogically ineffective passive transmission of information via lecture towards more active forms of learning such as small-group seminars, expanding student numbers have seen an efficiency driven 'reversion to an unedifying chalk and talk pedagogy in most institutions'.[24] Though technology has been utilised in the 'massification' of legal education, there is reason to believe that it might deliver something more for students than death by PowerPoint.

In considering what technology and innovation can deliver for law students, whether as a tool to enhance existing teaching methods or as a subject of study in its own right, this book brings together a range of international perspectives. Authors include those working in the legal profession in large law firms and small technology start-ups; researchers, educators and clinicians drawn from the fields of law,

---

[20]   Campbell (n 6) 6.
[21]   Webb (n 1) 101.
[22]   Nancy L Schultz, 'How Do Lawyers Really Think?' (1992) 42(1) Journal of Legal Education 57, 59.
[23]   Sheldon Krantz and Michael Millemann, 'Legal Education in Transition: Trends and Their Implications' (2014) 94(1) Nebraska Law Review 1, 2 (quoting Shaffer and Redmount).
[24]   Thornton, 'The Law School, the Market and the New Knowledge Economy' (n 5).

business, design and education; as well as those working within professional representative, and regulatory bodies. These contributors draw on theoretical, empirical and reflective approaches to consider the modernisation of legal education and the role technology should play in this process. As such, this collection offers these authors an opportunity to provide practical insight into the specific initiatives on which they have led, the lessons learnt in the process of implementation, and the benefits derived or expected to follow as a result of their efforts. Intended to stimulate thinking around the various ways in which legal education can respond to changes occurring within the profession so as to better prepare students for their future careers, the work of this collection considers what aspects of legal education require modification and how this might be achieved.

In contemplating how legal education might respond to the changing nature of the profession, including the increasing commercialisation of legal services, the decline of social mission and the increased influence of technology, the contributions within this book directly and indirectly touch upon a number of issues. First among these is the range of skills that the law degree ought to bring under its remit. For, unlike other areas of legal study such as professional ethics where it is generally agreed that more must be done to incorporate such training within the academic stage of study, there is less consensus as to the need for law students to acquire technological skills, and less agreement as to what those skills might encompass. This is in part a function of the fact that the study of law incorporates both applied and general domains of knowledge.

Since inception, formal legal education has focused on teaching students what the law is, rather than how it is practised, rendering the law degree a 'three-year academic precursor to apprenticeship'.[25] Despite the seemingly clear purpose of the law degree as a mechanism by which to expose students to doctrine and the skills of critical analysis,[26] the academic study of law has routinely come under pressure to incorporate a broader range of vocationally relevant competencies.[27] As Webb explains, 'the intellectual battle lines are ... drawn increasingly sharply (at the extremes) between those academics who tend to see engagement with practice and employability skills as anti-academic and inconsistent with the liberal ideal, and those ... critical of the more theoretical and abstract drift of legal scholarship and law teaching'.[28] Although this collection does not reconcile this debate, it does highlight some models in which the objectives of liberal education and that of vocational education might more easily co-exist.

---

[25] Schultz (n 22). At 59
[26] Ibid.
[27] See, e.g., James Gray and Mick Woodley, 'The Relationship between Academic Legal Education and the Legal Profession: The Review of Legal Education in England and Wales and the Teaching Hospital Model' (2005) 2(1) European Journal of Legal Education 1; Harry T Edwards, 'The Growing Disjunction between Legal Education and the Legal Profession' (1992) 91(1) Michigan Law Review 34; Campbell (n 6); Webb (n 1).
[28] Webb (n 1) 110.

In Chapter 1 Smith and Spencer offer one such approach, describing their efforts to facilitate greater engagement between students and industry at the earlier stages of legal education. Identifying the range of skills required for future practice and the basis for this requirement, Smith and Spencer envisage the future lawyer occupying a much more proactive, solution- and client-orientated space than ever before. Focusing on the UK, but raising issues of global relevance, they observe, as have others, how the changing nature of legal practice requires lawyers exhibit greater commercial acuity.[29] Leveraging their extensive experience in practice, Smith and Spencer formulate a range of professional sub-specialisms they expect to emerge within legal services in the near future. In doing so, they build on similar work undertaken by Susskind over a decade ago,[30] producing career personas that better reflect the skills that support an increased 'client focus'. These professional roles belie an expectation of greater fluidity in the profession in which, in line with previous observations and predictions, loyalty to one firm is replaced with a greater degree of horizontal and lateral movement of professionals across the profession.[31]

Central to Smith and Spencer's vision for legal education is the development of a greater number and range of opportunities for students to acquire enhanced commercial acumen via industry-based work experience. It is a proposal that those familiar with the history of legal education in the UK will find reminiscent of the previous apprenticeship model,[32] albeit updated so as to facilitate greater integration between the academic and vocational elements of study. The model Smith and Spencer propose (a model that they themselves have piloted) is one that is contingent upon the cooperation of industry partners who have the resources and willingness to facilitate a vocational learning experience. This is a concept with which industry is familiar, given that many of the larger law firms in various jurisdictions have run summer internship schemes for decades. Nevertheless, with these opportunities unevenly distributed, and student numbers on the rise, there is a question of how experiential education of this nature can effectively scale.

It is this question that captures the attention of Giddings and Weinburg, who in Chapter 2, focus on how opportunities for clinical legal education might be expanded so as to even the playing field, providing access for those students who do not have existing networks and connections in the profession. In considering how legal education might exist, not as 'training for the hierarchy'[33] but as a 'vehicle for upward mobility',[34]

---

[29]   See, e.g., Webb and others (n 1).

[30]   See Susskind (n 17).

[31]   Jones (n 2); Galanter and Henderson (n 5).

[32]   See, e.g., John Flood, 'Legal Education in the Global Context: Challenges from Globalization, Technology and Changes in Government Regulation' (2011) University of Westminster School of Law Research Paper 11–16 http://ssrn.com/abstract=1906687 accessed 4 September 2018.

[33]   Duncan Kennedy, 'Legal Education as Training for Hierarchy' in D Kairys (ed.), *The Politics of Law: A Progressive Critique* (Pantheon Books 1990).

[34]   Robert B Stevens, 'Law Schools and Legal Education, 1879–1979: Lectures in Honor of 100 Years of Valparaiso Law School' (1980) 14(2) Valparaiso Law School 179, 182.

Giddings and Weinburg outline the 'Clinical Guarantee' introduced by Monash University in Australia. This describes the ambitious commitment the university has made to give all those students who wish to have hands-on work experience, the opportunity to acquire this experience. In detailing their plans for the full rollout of the programme over the next three years, Giddings and Weinburg reveal how strong institutional support, the use of technology and the leveraging of existing community-based clinical programmes, have positioned the University to make good on this promise and address the growing experience gap.

Marrying the need for broader technological and commercial awareness amongst law students (as raised in Chapter 1) with the demand for 'hands-on' experiential learning (as discussed in Chapter 2), in Chapter 3, Walden and Cahill detail the development of qLegal, a leading commercial clinical legal education programme based at Queen Mary University of London in which students provide supervised free legal advice to technology start-ups and entrepreneurs. Through the process of assisting clients with complex data protection issues, students acquire practical client management skills, as well as knowledge of an unfamiliar and often-changing area of law (data protection). In their Chapter, Walden and Cahill focus on the development of qLegal, its purpose, and the way in which it offers an opportunity for knowledge transfer between entrepreneurs and aspiring lawyers. In contrast to other clinical legal education programmes in the UK that have typically focused on dimensions of unmet civil justice need, Chapter 3 exemplifies a model for Clinical Legal Education (CLE) in which students can acquire the type of skills that are likely to resonate with prospective employers in the commercial law sector. Added to this, the example provided by qLegal demonstrates how knowledge of technology, the legislation governing its use, and its application in the real world, can be gained outside of the classroom.

Taken together, the observations made in Chapters 1, 2 and 3, provide insight into how work with real clients might enhance professional skills (including commercial acumen and client-mindedness) and expose students to various forms of technology. These examples share a common purpose, providing an opportunity for students to acquire 'the single most useful cognitive skill for a good lawyer', that is, 'the ability to learn from experience-from self and from others'.[35] Yet it is hard to overlook the fact that the value derived from these initiatives is principally measured in terms of the contribution they make to enhance student employability within the commercial law sector. This is a fact that will no doubt put some within and outside of the legal academy on edge, particularly those who believe that the extent of corporate influence in legal education has already gone too far. Although we have witnessed a shift away from the view of law as sacrosanct and have accepted (at least to some degree) the need to consider matters of commercial viability or the pragmatics of practice in the dispensing of advice,[36] there are those who oppose the academic study of law being reduced to

---

[35] Schultz (n 22).
[36] Thornton, 'The Law School, the Market and the New Knowledge Economy' (n 5).

a hurdle cleared en route to a lucrative commercial law career.[37] For these individuals, the law degree is an opportunity for broader intellectual development.[38]

For students who are paying fees at ever increasing rates, an increased vocational focus brings with it the prospect of enhancing employability, yet it also opens up content to the risk of corporatisation. Where some courses are viewed as prerequisites for gaining a lucrative business law job, 'the market gains an opportunity to determine curricula content'.[39] Opportunities for influence also proliferate in a climate of decreased public funding in which law firms and business enterprises 'are increasingly invited to financially support university-based legal education under a privatized model … gain[ing] leverage to influence the shape of legal education'.[40] As Thornton explains, this pressure has been amplified by the neoliberal transformation of higher education and market fundamentalism, which has operated to rebrand legal education as a private rather than a public good.[41] As a result, 'those aspects associated with social justice, theory and critique are perceived as having little "use value" within the market paradigm, thereby rendering them dispensable'.[42]

On this view, the concern regarding 'corporate creep' is understandable, yet even amongst those who seek to preserve the study of law as a liberal art or public good, there is some empathy with the view that legal education ought to encompass 'many more components than law schools have traditionally recognized'.[43] This includes, as I argue in Chapter 4, exposure to data-driven AI technologies. As with professional legal experience, the views put forth in Chapter 4 risk the allegation that embedding opportunities for quantitative and technological literacy within the legal curriculum serves too narrow a range of beneficiaries; prioritising skills that are of relevance to only a certain subset of the profession, rather than promoting the acquisition of knowledge and skills that may serve society more generally.[44]

Criticisms as to the influence of the legal profession on legal education are not new, nor are they concerns that ought to be easily dismissed. Nevertheless, they operate on the assumption that those on the receiving end of this influence lack the agency to incorporate vocational skills within the curriculum on their own terms. Although higher education institutions often see themselves as the objects of change

---

[37] Schultz (n 22) 57, 59.
[38] See further Burridge and Webb who describe the features of this intellectual development as including: (a) a varied curriculum;(b) reasoned debate; (c) independent thinking; and (d) pluralistic enquiry. Roger Burridge and Julian Webb, 'The Values of Common Law Legal Education Reprised' (2010) 42 The Law Teacher 263, 264.
[39] Susan B Boyd, 'Corporatism and Legal Education in Canada' (2005) 14(2) Social and Legal Studies 287, 288.
[40] Ibid.
[41] See Thornton, 'The Law School, the Market and the New Knowledge Economy' (n 5); Webb (n 1).
[42] Thornton, 'The Law School, the Market and the New Knowledge Economy' (n 5).
[43] Schultz (n 22) 59.
[44] E.g., study in legal philosophy, ethics, welfare law, access to justice or participation in traditional clinical legal education programmes that offer legal advice to underserved communities.

(as has been observed in the context of globalisation) they are also active participants in the process.[45] So whilst Chapter 4 identifies how these types of analytical skills may enhance student employability, it also identifies how the study of data-driven technology and its impact on 'communities, individuals, practices, disputes and behaviours' offers students the opportunity to 'test out a moral position' and 'develop their own notion of the good'.[46] Moreover, as Chapter 4 argues, exposing students to the impact and influence of new forms of data-driven technology in advance of their entry into the profession provides the intellectual space needed to assess the associated benefits and disadvantages of these tools with reference to something other than the economic gains they produce. Although concerns over the pernicious influence of corporatism in legal education deserve attention, the vocational and liberal goals of legal education do not have to be seen as mutually exclusive.

Similarly, when set within a larger series of learning outcomes, a curriculum that marries experiential learning with opportunities for critical analysis and reflection can offer students scope to contextualise and reconcile the way that law (and technology) is deployed in the real world. On this, Chapter 5's exploration by Grant and Lestrell of the delivery of an online dispute resolution module within an Australian law school operates as a case in point. Their Chapter describes the development and deployment of an experiential exercise in which students undertaking an Alternative Dispute Resolution (ADR) module are exposed to a dispute via both an Online Dispute Resolution (ODR) portal and more traditional face-to-face mediation role-play. Drawing from a short survey and reflective journals completed by the students, Grant and Lestrell interrogate the benefits and limitations of this approach in facilitating students' exposure to ODR. Further, they go some way towards realising the benefits that Chapter 4 anticipates can arise from exposing law students to technology in a range of settings, namely: greater awareness of the impact of technology on dispute processes and outcomes; recognition of appropriate conduct in online dispute resolution settings; and an appreciation of the challenges of computer-mediated communication. Thereby ensuring students perceive law and technology in a broader context and with reference to the power disparities and access to justice challenges that certain technologies may introduce.

As Chapter 4 argues and as Chapter 5 demonstrates, any effort to understand law through a broader lens, including that of technology, demands greater collaboration, and a shift away from what has been viewed as the 'unabashed disciplinary insularity of legal research'[47] and legal study more generally. Though pragmatic issues prevail, and the structure of higher education in law tends to militate against greater interdisciplinary work for a range of reasons, there are examples that buck the trend. Many of these examples are found in the USA and involve collaboration between computer scientists, empirical researchers, statisticians and scholars in

---

[45] Webb (n 1).
[46] Burridge and Webb (n 38) 266.
[47] Boyd (n 39) 289 (citing Arthurs 1983).

law.[48] However it is more often the case that students are simply given the option to study content delivered by experts in other domains, or delivered as part of degree programmes, meaning that they alone remain responsible for unifying separate epistemological foci and integrating their learning in a way that is of value to both disciplines.

The fragmentation of knowledge into ever increasing specialisms and the difficulty this poses for resolving complex problems that span different fields and stakeholders, have led some to advocate for 'integrative disciplines of understanding, communication, and action', as represented by the 'design thinking' paradigm.[49] This concept and its application to law is explored in detail by Margaret Hagan in Chapter 6, which provides a roadmap to producing interdisciplinary collaboration that 'involves critical, constructive, creative work by both faculty and students rather than a regime devoted primarily to the acquisition of information'.[50] Hagan's Chapter explores how this integration might take shape within legal education by drawing upon the development and evolution of the Legal Design Lab at Stanford University.

Profiling the objectives of the Lab and the design thinking courses, innovation sprints, and workshops it facilitates, Hagan's contribution explores the purpose, process and outcomes of this experiment in interdisciplinary legal education. This discussion provides evidence of the benefits that arise from exposing law students to ideas and concepts from other disciplines in an integrated fashion, and makes a persuasive case as to the value of design thinking within and outside of law. The lessons emerging from the Legal Design Lab highlight the potential for initiatives of this nature to deliver interdisciplinary education offerings which ' ... enhance teamwork and collaboration among the professions, thereby strengthening how one practices his or her discipline and how one thinks about what he or she does'.[51]

In a similar vein, Carpenter's contribution in Chapter 7 looks at how a broader suite of skills might be incorporated into legal education, not through the delivery of specific content as proposed in Chapter 4, but rather by adopting project-based learning methods. To this end, Chapter 7 identifies collaboration, design, project management, problem-solving and life-long learning as critical skills for future lawyers, many of whom will spend only part of their career in practice. In making a case for the value of project-based work in strengthening the range of 'hard' and 'soft' skills necessary in the working world (in and outside of law), Carpenter's pedagogical analysis identifies project-based learning as effective in placing students, rather than the teacher, at the centre of the learning experience. In what is a marked change from the existing model of legal education in which 'path-

---

[48] See Chapter 4 for further details.
[49] Richard Buchanan, 'Wicked Problems in Design Thinking' (1992) 8(2) Design Issues 5, 6.
[50] A Weinberg and C Harding, 'Interdisciplinary Teaching and Collaboration in Higher Education: A Concept Whose Time Has Come' (2004) 14(15) Washington University Journal of Law and Policy 14, 19 (citing Oliphant).
[51] Ibid 22.

dependent' thinking is a central focus, in the view of Carpenter, problem-based learning operates to 'move students from thinking focused on getting the "right" answer toward thinking that is creative, iterative, and reflective'.[52]

Cultivating students' capacity to engage in this form of thinking, is an objective that many other authors in this collection argue ought to represent a critical focus for legal education, particularly experiential legal education.[53] However, whilst Chapter 1 proposes that this model of thinking ought to be developed in a commercial law setting, both Hagan and Carpenter present these skills as transferable. This introduces the possibility that project-work conducted in conjunction with not-for-profit legal providers can allow students to acquire necessary skills, whilst simultaneously addressing the concern that legal education has become too insular, 'narrowing in a way that supports the market', and dissuading students from pursuing public interest employment.[54]

The clinical and experiential curricula described in Chapters 2, 5, 6 and 7 permits students to envisage a future in which skills and technologies are used not merely as tools to further the agenda of capitalism, but to support more transformative approaches to access to justice. Nevertheless, whilst university-based law clinics are generally seen as virtuous social contributions, less has been said about the use of legally underserved communities within clinical legal education. Whilst the majority of these clients are no doubt well served, there remain 'underlying moral questions in the use of actual clients as the means for the laudable end of lawyer training. The lives and welfare of real people are at risk in the in-house clinic setting.'[55] Evidently the servicing of clients and the educational enrichment of students are not incompatible objectives, but the balance is often difficult to strike or goes unaddressed. For this reason, it is reassuring that in Chapter 6, Hagan details the Legal Design Lab's efforts to respond to these concerns, so as to enhance benefit and minimise risk for participants. Whilst Grant and Lestrell's initiative described in Chapter 5 prompts greater consideration as to how the ethical issues associated with using 'real clients' might be addressed through simulation.

Maharg's discussion of the development of the seminal 'Ardcalloch' software in Chapter 8 also serves to reinforce the potential contribution that simulation might make to legal education delivery. Reflecting on the 'Ardculloch' project, its aims, the process by which it was developed and the assumptions (legal educational, technological and social) embedded within the software build, Maharg's Chapter exemplifies how exposure to aspects of clinical practice can be facilitated via technology. In tracing the history of legal education and defining technology with reference to both the object of communication and the social and cultural practices that

[52] Chapter 7, 138.
[53] Described by Stuckey as 'Cognitive', 'Performative' and 'Affective' skills. See further Roy Stuckey, 'Best Practices for Legal Education: A Vision and A Road Map' (Clinical Legal Education Association 2007) 122 https://clea.wildapricot.org/Resources/Documents/best_practices-full.pdf accessed 28 September 2018.
[54] Thornton, 'The Law School, the Market and the New Knowledge Economy' (n 5).
[55] James E Moliterno, 'In-House Live-Client Clinical Programs: Some Ethical Issues' (1999) 67(5) Fordham Law Review 2377, 2387.

accompany that object, Maharg observes the way in which content shifts according
to the technology used to deliver it.

Moshirnia touches upon a similar theme in Chapter 9, tracing how the engagement
philosophies underpinning the construction of role-play (or 'games') in classical legal
education are reconstructed in modern game-design. To this point he notes that both
forms of media share the notions of personae, heightened stakes, fantastical elements
and creative exploration and yet are separated by thousands of years. Evidently some
features sustain the transition from one technological medium to another; and yet, it is
also implicit in Moshirnia's discussion of the reticence of the academy to adopt game-
play that in the process of shifting content from the classroom to the computer (game),
content becomes coloured by the social and cultural practices and perceptions that
accompany that medium.

Similarly in Chapter 10, Kathrani adds to this discourse in his discussion of the
process of rendering legal problem questions within a computer game. Reviewing
a number of examples, including those using virtual reality technology, he observes
the way in which translating these tasks into simulations imports an authenticity that
a written problem question cannot. But whilst each form of technology brings with it
certain benefits that justify the view that it represents an evolution upon its written
antecedent, as Maharg observes in Chapter 8 it also brings with it a series of technocratic
traits that inhibit a more democratic or participatory approach to the development
process. For, whilst educators have control over 'analogue' mediums of transmission
such as classroom based role-play, written problem questions and hypotheticals, commercial games and complex virtual reality simulations draw upon specific forms of
expertise, experience and infrastructure that may be costly or difficult to acquire.

Nevertheless, it is possible to turn the lens of technocracy back on itself, using the
digital medium in a way that, in the words of Maharg, enables educators 'to create for
[their] students an environment that facilitates the learning of justice and reflexive
awareness of law and social [practice]'.[56] This is something that might feasibly be
achieved by drawing attention to these technocratic features directly (as discussed in
Chapter 4) or indirectly via reflections generated as a result of their participation in
online and offline activities (as demonstrated in Chapter 5). It is also possible if we use
technology to create rich experiences designed to break free of 'the dominant pedagogical form of legal rule [in which] factual proposition and problem resolution only
pretends a social relevance'.[57]

This potential is exemplified in Chapter 11, which explores how virtual reality
technology may assist in bringing the ethical realities of legal practice to life.
A myriad of criticisms have accompanied the teaching of ethics, ranging from alleged
gaps in provision, inconsistency in the quality of teaching[58] and insufficient emphasis
on fundamental principles, through to the delivery of training as though a box-ticking

---

[56]   See Chapter 8, 150.
[57]   Burridge and Webb (n 38) 267.
[58]   Webb and others (n 1).

exercise.[59] Most significant however are criticisms that relate to the substance of the teaching itself, and the view that the subject is too narrowly focused on rule-craft, adopting a 'highly instrumental, rule-based character'.[60] Seeking to address this challenge through technology, Delacroix and I demonstrate how virtual reality can allow students to explore the dissonance between their theoretical stance and the actual behaviour they adopt when faced with a (virtually) simulated ethical dilemma.

Taken together the contributions contained within the first eleven Chapters illustrate that there is much educators can do, with or without the involvement of technology. Yet what is also made clear is that educators cannot be expected to 'modernise legal education' single-handedly. At least some of the impetus and much of the apparatus required for change must be provided at the institutional level. This institutional support is discussed at various points in Chapters 8, 10 and 11, and ought to be accompanied by efforts to promote greater collaboration between disciplines, as identified in Chapters 4 and 6.

Yet there is also reason to believe that change requires the participation of a broader group of stakeholders. If 'black letter law is all [that] students want to hear, because that is all that is necessary to satisfy the admitting authorities' then it suggests that regulators have a role to play in the process of modernising legal education.[61] This is an issue addressed in the final two Chapters of this collection where it is approached from contrasting perspectives. In Chapter 12, Brannan and Marrs compare the approach to regulating for innovation taken by the Solicitors Regulation Authority (SRA) of England and Wales and by the Law Society of Scotland. The former has been inclined towards a minimalist approach leading to increased deregulation with the intention of leaving innovation to the market. Conversely for the Law Society of Scotland, the increased interest in technology has yielded opportunities to consolidate regulatory reach and to leverage emerging legal-adjacent roles to create new membership and accreditation types.

That these regulators exhibit contrasting views and approaches, and yet both arrive at what is a largely 'light-touch' regulatory response to digital innovation and technology, is interesting. It is an issue that Ching and Maharg help to explain in Chapter 13, which considers the relationship between regulatory culture and the creation, sustenance and dissemination of innovation, particularly digital education innovation. Their Chapter offers a critical analysis of the culture and context within which digital innovation is reported, analysed and recommended upon in regulatory reports and to this end they observe the relatively shallow and 'theory-lite' treatment of digital innovation, as well as the absence of consistent interdisciplinary input to date. Drawing on genre theory to

---

[59]   Richard Moorhead and others, 'The Ethical Capacities of New Advocates' (UCL Centre for Law and Ethics 2015) http://ssrn.com/abstract=2849698 accessed 24 September 2018.

[60]   Julian Webb, 'Taking Values Seriously: The Democratic Intellect and the Place of Values in the School Curriculum' in Michael Robertson and others (eds.), *The Ethics Project in Legal Education* (Routledge 2010).

[61]   Thornton, 'The Law School, the Market and the New Knowledge Economy' (n 5) 18.

produce a typology of reports, they observe the way in which different approaches to reporting deny the opportunity for direct comparison between reporting exercises. Ching and Maharg note that these failings inhibit the development of imaginative, theory-rich and persuasive accounts of digital cultures for legal education. In identifying these limitations and the way in which extensive reporting activity intended to support the development of legal education can often fall short of its potential, Ching and Maharg's work identifies why a report's methodology and terms of reference must be given greater attention if the report is intended to meaningfully contribute to legal education reform over the longer term.

This final Chapter identifies a number of recent enquiries into the state and future of legal education that have occurred in Australia, the UK, Canada and the USA over the last decade, and which have produced a range of complementary and conflicting proposals.[62] For example, both the Canadian Bar Association 'Futures' report[63] as well as the Legal Education and Training Review in England and Wales[64] have proposed the adoption of new models for legal education, emphasising: a focus on problem-solving and learning outcomes; easing restrictions on students in legal clinics; structured, consistent, rigorous pre-admission training; consistent knowledge and skills standards for certification; the creation of parallel legal programmes; and the improvement of continuing professional development.[65] On the whole, these recommendations point to a widening of the scope and breadth of legal education, and as such they stand in contrast to the positions put forth by other stakeholders. This includes the American Bar Foundation, which perceives a lesser role for the law degree as a route of entry into practice,[66] and the SRA, which recently announced regulatory changes in England and Wales, which do away with the requirement that those seeking to qualify as a solicitor must hold a degree or qualification in law.[67]

[62] See, e.g., the ABA's Commission on the Future of Legal Education; The Federation of Law Societies of Canada 'Taskforce on the Canadian Common Law Degree'; the Canadian Bar Association's 'Futures' Initiative; the Legal Education and Training Review in England and Wales; the SRA's Consultation on Legal Training; and the Law Society of NSW (Australia) Future of Law and Innovation in the Profession (FLIP) Inquiry.

[63] Canadian Bar Association, 'Futures: Transforming The Delivery Of Legal Services In Canada' (Canadian Bar Association 2014) www.cba.org/CBAMediaLibrary/cba_na/PDFs/CBA Legal Futures PDFS/Futures-Final-eng.pdf accessed 10 May 2019.

[64] Webb and others (n 1).

[65] Paul Maharg, 'Shared Space: Regulation, Technology and Legal Education in a Global Context' (2015) 6(1) European Journal of Law and Technology 1 http://ejlt.org/article/view/425/541 accessed 17 May 2019.

[66] Jay Conison, 'The Report and Recommendations of the ABA Task Force on the Future of Legal Education: Its Significance for Bar Admissions and Regulation of Entry into the Legal Profession' (2014) 83(4) The Bar Examiner 12.

[67] Solicitors Regulation Authority, 'A New Route to Qualification: The Solicitors Qualifying Examination (SQE) – A Summary of Responses and Next Steps' (Solicitors Regulation Authority 2017) www.sra.org.uk/documents/SRA/consultations/sqe-summary-responses.pdf accessed 31 October 2018.

Those working within the legal profession and legal education are likely to resist these changes, though not for the reasons that are likely to be alleged – that is, the wish to preserve the status quo and maintain control over entry to the profession. As the contributions to this collection reveal, the need for change is well recognised, and many, including those working in legal education, question the ability of the law degree to adequately prepare students for work in the modern professions (in or outside of law). As such, the issue is not whether change should occur, but rather whether the type of change proposed, particularly that planned by the SRA, is the best course of action. The longer legal education stands still, the greater the risk of the law degree being seen as an island rather than a stepping-stone. At the same time it is fair to question whether the proposed changes are likely to make it more difficult for law schools to garner the necessary financial and institutional capital upon which large-scale innovation depends.

It is clear from the contributions within this book that reaching consensus in relation to what legal education ought to do next and how it can acquire the capacity to do what it ought to do, continues to represent a work in progress. To this end, the initiatives discussed in this volume provide readers with food for thought as to the suite of skills required by the modern lawyer and the various responses that they and other stakeholders might take to better prepare law students for the world of work. In sharing the lessons, reflections and views, of early and established innovators, it is hoped that this collection inspires readers to consider what they themselves can contribute to advancing legal pedagogy and how they might build on the work exemplified in the Chapters that follow. If this book is successful in achieving this objective then we can expect many more such collections to emerge in the coming years as readers embark upon and document their own experiences of modernising legal education.

BIBLIOGRAPHY

Benko C, Anderson M and Vickberg S, 'The Corporate Lattice: A Strategic Response to the Changing World of Work' (*Deloitte Insights*, 1 January 2011) www2.deloitte.com/insights/us/en/deloitte-review/issue-8/the-corporate-lattice-rethinking-careers-in-the-changing-world-of-work.html accessed 4 May 2019

Boyd SB, 'Corporatism and Legal Education in Canada' (2005) 14(2) Social and Legal Studies 287

Buchanan R, 'Wicked Problems in Design Thinking' (1992) 8(2) Design Issues 5

Burridge R and Webb J, 'The Values of Common Law Legal Education Reprised' (2010) 42(3) The Law Teacher 263

Campbell RW, 'The End of Law Schools: Legal Education in the Era of Legal Service Businesses' (2016) 85(1) Mississippi Law Journal 1

Canadian Bar Association, 'Futures: Transforming The Delivery Of Legal Services In Canada' (Canadian Bar Association 2014) www.cba.org/cbamedialibrary/cba_na/pdfs/cba legal futures pdfs/futures-final-eng.pdf accessed 10 May 2019

Conison J, 'The Report and Recommendations of the ABA Task Force on the Future of Legal Education: Its Significance for Bar Admissions and Regulation of Entry into the Legal Profession' (2014) 83(4) The Bar Examiner 12

Cortés P, 'The Online Court: Filling the Gaps of the Civil Justice System?' (2017) 36(1) Civil Justice Quarterly 109

Edwards HT, 'The Growing Disjunction between Legal Education and the Legal Profession' (1992) 91(1) Michigan Law Review 34

Flood J, 'Legal Education in the Global Context: Challenges from Globalization, Technology and Changes in Government Regulation' (2011) University of Westminster School of Law Research Paper 11–16 http://ssrn.com/abstract=1906687 accessed 4 September 2018

Galanter MS and Henderson WD, 'The Elastic Tournament: The Second Transformation of the Big Law Firm' (2008) 60 Stanford Law Review 1867

Genn H, 'Online Courts and the Future of Justice' (Birkenhead Lecture, London, 16 October 2017) www.ucl.ac.uk/laws/sites/laws/files/birkenhead_lecture_2017_professor_dame_hazel_genn_final_version.pdf accessed 28 February 2018

Gray J and Woodley M, 'The Relationship between Academic Legal Education and the Legal Profession: The Review of Legal Education in England and Wales and the Teaching Hospital Model' (2005) 2(1) European Journal of Legal Education 1

Henderson WD, 'From Big Law to Lean Law' (2014) 38(June) International Review of Law and Economics 5

Jones JW, 'The Challenge of Change: The Practice of Law in the Year 2000' (1988) 41(4) Vanderbilt Law Review 683

Katz DM, 'Quantitative Legal Prediction – or – How I Learned to Stop Worrying and Start Preparing for the Data Driven Future of the Legal Services Industry' (2013) 62 Emory Law Journal 909

Kennedy D, 'Legal Education as Training for Hierarchy' in D Kairys (ed.), *The Politics of Law: A Progressive Critique* (Pantheon Books 1990)

Kordana KA, 'Law Firms and Associate Careers: Tournament Theory Versus the Production-Imperative Model' (1995) 104(7) Yale Law Journal 1907

Krantz S and Millemann M, 'Legal Education in Transition: Trends and Their Implications' (2014) 94(1) Nebraska Law Review 1

Maharg P, 'Shared Space: Regulation, Technology and Legal Education in a Global Context' (2015) 6(1) European Journal of Law and Technology 1 http://ejlt.org/article/view/425/541 accessed 17 May 2019

McCloud V, 'The Online Court: Suing in Cyberspace' (2017) 36(1) Civil Justice Quarterly 34

Moliterno JE, 'In-House Live-Client Clinical Programs : Some Ethical Issues' (1999) 67(5) Fordham Law Review 2377

Moorhead R and others, 'The Ethical Capacities of New Advocates' (UCL Centre for Law and Ethics 2015) http://ssrn.com/abstract=2849698 accessed 24 September 2018

Ribstein LE, 'The Death of Big Law' (2010) 3 Wisconsin Law Review 749

Schultz NL, 'How Do Lawyers Really Think?' (1992) 42(1) Journal of Legal Education 57

Sela A, 'Streamlining Justice: How Online Courts Can Resolve the Challenges of Pro Se Litigation' 1(26) Cornel Journal of Law & Public Policy 331

Solicitors Regulation Authority, 'A New Route to Qualification: The Solicitors Qualifying Examination (SQE) – A Summary of Responses and Next Steps' (Solicitors Regulation Authority 2017) www.sra.org.uk/documents/sra/consultations/sqe-summary-responses.pdf accessed 31 October 2018

Sommerlad H and others, 'The Futures of Legal Education and the Legal Profession' in Hilary Sommerlad and others (eds.), *The Futures of Legal Education and the Legal Profession* (1st edn, Hart Publishing 2015)

Stevens RB, 'Law Schools and Legal Education, 1879–1979: Lectures in Honor of 100 Years of Valparaiso Law School' (1980) 14(2) Valparaiso Law School 179

Stuckey R, 'Best Practices for Legal Education: A Vision and A Road Map' (Clinical Legal Education Association 2007) https://clea.wildapricot.org/resources/documents/best_practices-full.pdf accessed 28 September 2018

Susskind R, *The End of Lawyers? Rethinking the Nature of Legal Services* (Oxford University Press 2008)

Thornton M, 'The Law School, the Market and the New Knowledge Economy' (2007) 17(1–2) Legal Education Review 1

'Squeezing the Life out of Lawyers: Legal Practice in the Market Embrace' (2016) 25(4) Griffith Law Review 471

Webb J, 'Taking Values Seriously: The Democratic Intellect and the Place of Values in the School Curriculum' in Michael Robertson and others (eds.), *The Ethics Project in Legal Education* (Routledge 2010)

'The LETRs (Still) in the Post: The Legal Education and Training Review and the Reform of Legal Services Education and Training—A Personal (Re)View' in Hilary Sommerlad and others (eds.), *The Futures of Legal Education and the Legal Profession* (Hart 2018)

Webb J and others, 'Setting Standards: The Future of Legal Services Education and Training Regulation in England and Wales (Legal Education and Training Review)' (SRA, BSB and CILEX 2013) www.letr.org.uk/wp-content/uploads/letr-report.pdf accessed 17 August 2018

Weinberg A and Harding C, 'Interdisciplinary Teaching and Collaboration in Higher Education: A Concept Whose Time Has Come' (2004) 14(15) Washington University Journal of Law and Policy 14

1

Do Lawyers Need to Learn to Code?

A *Practitioner Perspective on the 'Polytechnic' Future of Legal Education*

Alexander Smith and Nigel Spencer[1]

The lawyer of the future will exist as a 'polytechnic' or 'many-skilled' professional, applying their legal expertise to a client's changing world in an increasingly agile way and within a range of organisational settings. For legal educators, there is a need to consider how education can best prepare future lawyers for this reality. The long view suggests that we should be looking to build core skills in legal, design and logic principles rather than learning specific technologies that may be rapidly superseded. But how can we develop these skills, and how we can balance the need to understand core academic principles of law against the need for applied, workplace experience? This chapter looks at the balancing process, focusing on the impact of changing roles in law firms and the demands of the in-house legal and law-advisory-organisation dynamic. It examines how legal education can instil within lawyers, both an understanding of the principles of law alongside an appreciation of the application of those principles in the workplace. It presents a vision of the roles and specialisations that are likely to emerge within the profession, and considers how the future work of lawyers will sit alongside alternative paths into the legal industry.

1.1 INTRODUCTION

As the legal sector is increasingly impacted by disruption and change caused by deregulation, new legal service providers and clients demanding 'more for less', there has been growing debate regarding the nature of the 'lawyer of the future', and the educational inputs which will best support those forging their careers in the legal sector.[2] This debate forms the focus of our chapter and centres around two key

---

[1] The authors would like to express their sincere thanks to the editor and to those who gave comments on earlier drafts of this chapter (in particular Lucy Dillon, Reed Smith LLP), together with the anonymous reviewers. Responsibility for the opinions expressed in the chapter remains with the authors.

[2] Many of the issues are well set out by Susskind in Richard Susskind, *Tomorrow's Lawyers: An Introduction to Your Future* (1st edn, Oxford University Press 2013) 109–65; Richard Susskind and

themes: first, the skills and knowledge that professional practice will demand from lawyers within the next ten years; and second, the form of educational and professional experience that best facilitates the acquisition of these skills and this knowledge.

As our chapter title pre-empts, one specific area of focus that has been the subject of continued professional interest is whether lawyers need to 'learn to code'. In addressing these claims, our chapter seeks to challenge the educational focus currently being considered in response to the market changes shaping the profession. Technology is becoming a key enabler of greater service efficiency in the repertoire of legal solutions offered to clients, yet technology knowledge alone is insufficient. We argue that educators at all levels should focus more on developing the broader skill-sets of students through experiential learning in client-facing settings.

Our educational vision sees lawyers exposed to a range of learning opportunities through which they can acquire the breadth of skills clients will expect from legal professionals in the years to come. To support our proposed approach to legal education, in this chapter we consider recent developments in the legal services market, and detail how we foresee these developments impacting the roles and skill-sets of lawyers. We identify a number of lessons to be learnt from previous educational innovations and make suggestions for others that have yet to be explored, but which, we anticipate, will be important in the future.

The present analysis is based upon our extensive experience of creating graduate/entry level educational programmes and knowledge tools for solicitors in the United Kingdom (UK) market, both in international private practice law firms and for in-house legal teams. Throughout the chapter we detail a number of short case studies of learning programmes developed at global law firm Reed Smith LLP ('Reed Smith'), including those which formed part of a future-focused innovation initiative resulting in the creation of an 'Innovation Hub' in the firm's London office.[3] Our aim in providing these real-world insights is to share what we have learnt as we have trialled various practical exercises, and also to reflect on which of these have been most effective in building the mindsets and skill-sets that will represent critical competencies for lawyers in the years to come.

Daniel Susskind, *The Future of the Professions: How Technology Will Transform the Work of Human Experts* (Oxford University Press 2015).

[3] The work at Reed Smith referenced here began in 2011 when one of the present authors (Spencer) joined the firm (becoming Global Director of Learning & Development) and created new commercially focused graduate programmes with Lucy Crittenden (Graduate Recruitment Manager). From early 2015, a project to create an 'Innovation Hub' in the firm was led by Roger Parker (Managing Partner, EMEA), Spencer and Lucy Dillon (Chief Knowledge Officer). Subsequently the other present author (Smith) joined the firm as Innovation Hub Manager to lead the Hub's work, with the 'Hub' opening officially in October 2016.

1.2 RECENT DEVELOPMENTS IN THE EDUCATION OF LAWYERS
IN THE UK

Whilst it has often been asserted that legal education is resistant to change,[4] over the last decade there have been a number of developments in the education of junior lawyers for the legal services market in the UK, specifically in the jurisdiction of England and Wales. Some of these developments have arisen as a result of the work of regulators, who over the course of the last few years have directed significant attention towards the current state and future direction of legal education. This attention has included a broad review of the training pathway for lawyers as part of the 'Legal Education Training Review' (LETR) commenced in 2011,[5] and the 'Training for Tomorrow' report produced by the Solicitor's Regulation Authority (SRA).[6] These reviews have led to the SRA's recent decision to enact wide-scale changes to legal education via the introduction of a Solicitors Qualifying Examination (SQE) as a precursor to qualification.[7]

However, many of the developments in education and training have been the product of other influences, coming at the request of the profession or as a result of educators pre-empting the needs of the profession. Economic recession, for example, has drastically re-shaped the client–firm relationship and prompted educators to address the long-standing criticism that legal education insulates students from the commercial realities of legal practice. Growing client demand for lawyers to graft more business knowledge onto their base of expertise in black-letter law, and the demand for enhanced commerciality has become a consistent theme in client feedback since the Global Financial Crises (GFC), and now forms a key factor in clients' decisions as to which firms to select for mandates or panel appointments.

In an effort to address this need and differentiate their offering, some forward-thinking firms and private sector education providers have experimented with integrating greater opportunities for students to acquire commercial knowledge throughout the educational pathway of aspiring lawyers. BPP University,[8] which

[4] Susskind (n 2) and Susskind and Susskind (n 2).
[5] Julian Webb and others, 'Setting Standards: The Future of Legal Services Education and Training Regulation in England and Wales (Legal Education and Training Review)' (SRA, BSB and CILEX 2013) www.letr.org.uk/wp-content/uploads/LETR-Report.pdf accessed 17 August 2018.
[6] Solicitors Regulation Authority, 'Training for Tomorrow: A Competence Statement for Solicitors' (Solicitors Regulation Authority 2014) www.sra.org.uk/sra/consultations/competence-statement.page accessed 8 November 2018.
[7] The changes were originally planned for 2020, however this has now been delayed to 2021. Solicitors Regulation Authority, 'SQE to be Introduced in Autumn 2021' (*Solicitors Regulation Authority*, 8 November 2018) www.sra.org.uk/sra/news/press/sqe-launch-2021.page accessed 26 May 2019.
[8] BPP provides courses for early career lawyers through its Law School, and was granted degree-awarding powers in 2007. It opened a Business School in 2008, and was granted the title of 'university' in 2013.

for many years has been a preferred supplier of the Legal Practice Course (LPC)[9] for a number of firms, created a full-year Master of Business Administration (MBA) programme in 2009 for graduate lawyers, working with one of the current authors (Spencer) and the firm Simmons & Simmons.[10] As part of this programme, students were given a range of new learning opportunities, including a Business Intelligence Project (BIP) module in which graduates applied their classroom business knowledge by leading a client project in the workplace.

These full-year, commercially focused educational courses later evolved into single-year combined programmes, as exemplified by the Masters of Arts/Legal Practice Course (MA/LPC) created by Reed Smith in conjunction with BPP. This latter programme integrated core MBA modules into the LPC, whilst retaining BIPs so as to expose students to the practical application of knowledge in client-facing settings.[11] Other innovative additions to the MA/LPC run by Reed Smith included reverse mentoring programmes whereby graduates were given the opportunity to bring knowledge from their MBA modules into group mentoring sessions at the firm, applying the business models they had learnt to the firm's clients, and discussing industry trends and strategies with more senior colleagues.[12] Reed Smith's MA/LPC programme went on to attract the attention of other law firms who subsequently enrolled their own legal trainees on a similar course at BPP.

Collaborative initiatives between the legal profession and providers of vocational study in law have coincided with industry efforts to facilitate new, more flexible

---

[9] The Legal Practice Course is a compulsory stage of vocational training that aspiring solicitors must complete in England and Wales. It follows the academic stage of training (Bachelor of Laws (LLB) or Graduate Diploma in Law (GDL) study) but precedes the two years of compulsory vocational training that intending solicitors must complete. For further information about the training pathway for lawyers in the England and Wales and a discussion of changes to this pathway, see Chapter 12.

[10] In 2009 Spencer held the position of global Head of Learning & Development at Simmons & Simmons and worked with Professor Chris Brady, Dean of the BPP Business School, to create a full-year MBA programme for graduate lawyers after completing their LPC. See Hilary Wilce, 'It's the UK's First MBA Delivered Entirely by a Private Organisation' *The Independent* (London, 1 October 2009) www.independent.co.uk/student/postgraduate/mbas-guide/hilary-wilce-its-the-uks -first-mba-delivered-entirely-by-a-private-organisation-1795527.html accessed 24 July 2018.

[11] Reed Smith created the shorter MA/LPC programme with BPP in 2012, see Peter Hardy, 'First for Reed Smith and BPP with September Launch of Unique Legal and Business Postgraduate Qualification: Bespoke MA (Legal Practice Course with Business)' (*Reed Smith*, 2 April 2012) www.reedsmith.com/en/ news/2012/04/first-for-reed-smith-and-bpp-with-september-launch accessed 7 November 2018.

[12] Nigel Spencer and Jon Stokes, 'Coaching and Mentoring as a Key Leadership Development Tool Across Legal Generations' in R Normand-Hochman (ed.), *Mentoring and Coaching for Lawyers: Building Partnerships for Success* (Globe Business Publishing 2014). See also the summary of Reed Smith's reverse mentoring initiative in the national Peer Awards for Excellence 2013: The Peer Awards, 'The 2014 Peer Awards' *The Independent* (London, April 2014) 1 http://thepeerawards.com/wp-content/uploads/2014/04/2014Indy.pdf accessed 24 July 2018; Reed Smith, 'Reed Smith Learning & Development Team Take Home Two Awards in the National Peer Awards for Excellence' (*ReedSmith*, 7 November 2013) www.reedsmith.com/en/news/2013/11/reed-smith-learning-development-team-take-home-tw accessed 24 July 2018.

educational pathways for those seeking to enter the legal profession.[13] In the recent past, the majority of those seeking positions as solicitors at major firms tended to pursue the traditional, degree-based route towards traineeship, from school to university and onto the LPC. Keen to offer more 'learn as you earn' routes to qualification, which did not depend on a university degree, education providers and employers in the legal sector became increasingly interested in the development of apprenticeship schemes. Legal services apprenticeships by the Chartered Institute of Legal Executives (CILEX) were introduced in 2013, followed by the approval of 'Trailblazer Apprenticeships' standards for the legal sector in 2015. These were developed by three regulators in partnership with a number of law firms and businesses with large in-house legal teams.[14] With an increased focus within the profession on the need to attract future solicitors from broader/more diverse talent pools (including more diverse socio-economic pools), this development was timely given that, in parallel, the level of student debt for a first degree in England rose to approximately £50,000.[15]

In recent years, the need for a broader skill-set to secure graduate level jobs (including a diminishing number of training contracts), and closer collaboration with legal employers, were two factors which also led to innovation in universities, prompting renewed emphasis on experiential learning and the importance of applied skills. These factors impelled more innovative law departments to experiment with the structure of law degrees, methods of teaching and the availability of clinical experience at both the graduate and undergraduate levels. At the undergraduate level, a Bachelor of Law (LLB) degree with a year in industry (at Reed Smith) has been pioneered at Queen Mary University of London (QMUL). This new degree has enabled students to gain a full year of workplace experience after a thorough grounding of core legal principles in years one to two, representing, in effect, a 'degree with apprenticeship' combined.[16] A second innovation at QMUL worthy of note has been the introduction of a skills-based degree module linked to

[13] The training pathways in the UK legal sector lead to the three branches of legal professionals: Barrister, Solicitor and Chartered Legal Executive.

[14] The Trailblazer apprenticeship standards were announced in 2015, and had been developed by three regulators: the Law Society, the Solicitors Regulation Authority and the Chartered Institute of Legal Executives (CILEx) working with an employer-led group, including Addleshaw Goddard, Barclays, Browne Jacobson, Burges Salmon, Clyde & Co, DAC Beachcroft, Dentons, DWF, Eversheds, Gateley PLC, Kennedys, Lewis Silkin, Mayer Brown, Olswang, Pannone LLP, The Royal Bank of Scotland, Simmons & Simmons, Stephenson Harwood, Thomas Eggar and Withers. See Lawcareers.net, 'Trailblazer Legal Apprenticeship Standards Receive Government Approval' (*Lawcareers.net*, 2015) www.lawcareers.net/Information/News/Trailblazer-legal-apprenticeship-standards-receive-government-approval-04092015 accessed 24 January 2018; Lynne Squires, 'Take an Alternative Route into a Career in Law' (*Apprenticeship News*) www.apprenticeshipsnews.co.uk/sectors/law/take-an-alternative-route-into-a-career-in-law accessed 24 July 2018.

[15] With fees of £9,000 per year for an undergraduate degree in the UK, and living expenses of £7,000–£8,000 per year, the anticipated student debt from a three-year degree totals approximately £50,000.

[16] Tim Moore, 'Routes into Law: Queen Mary Teams up with Reed Smith on "Degree with Apprenticeship in Law"' (*Legal Business*, 13 January 2015) www.legalbusiness.co.uk/blogs/routes-into-law-queen-mary-

periods students spend working in the award-winning Queen Mary Legal Advice Centre.[17] As with the other examples, this innovation has at its core the application of legal knowledge to practice, and the module's assessment incorporates practical examination methods such as role-play exercises to test the students' skills in action.

Elsewhere, technology-led innovations have been designed to enable students to gain greater applied experience. Historically such endeavours have been used to simulate high-street legal practice, for example, Strathclyde University's simulated town of 'Ardcalloch', which allowed students to play the role of lawyers in virtual law firms.[18] More recent initiatives, such as Exeter University's establishment of the 'virtual law firm' programme, have been directed at embedding commercial experience pervasively throughout the law degree.[19] This initiative enables students to work in a simulated office environment during their studies (ranging from office work-pods to a virtual boardroom), overseeing their own firm, and considering issues such as how a law firm delivers its services and how different departments in firms can best collaborate to deliver value for clients.[20] As Dr Sue Prince, Director of Education explains:

> Students study for all of their core modules as part of their 'virtual law firm', using these facilities, and each firm has a particular caseload to work through throughout the academic year (with cases on various aspects of subjects being studied in the first year). This encourages students to get a real sense of how law firms operate as well as developing teamwork, research, organisational and time management skills as part of the study of the law. The professional aspect of the pedagogical environment is enhanced through the input of each firm's own non-executive director: a mentor who is a solicitor from a local law firm. Each virtual law firm has to meet its mentor and prepare termly reports, which focus on setting objectives, organisation and timeliness.[21]

These technology-led innovations have also accompanied other initiatives in the UK, with Ulster University launching a Legal Innovation Centre in conjunction with the Law Firms Allen & Overy and Baker McKenzie, and a graduate programme

---

teams-up-with-reed-smith-on-degree-with-apprenticeship-in-law/ accessed 28 July 2018. For the benefits of this workplace-focused degree, see the feedback from students published on the QMUL website: QMUL School of Law, 'Courses – M130 Law in Practice' www.qmul.ac.uk/law/undergraduate/courses/m130-law-in-practice/ accessed 2 November 2018.

[17] See QMUL School of Law, 'Legal Advice Centre' www.lac.qmul.ac.uk/ accessed 2 November 2018.

[18] Karen Barton and Patricia McKellar, 'Transactional Learning: Ardcalloch Sheriff Court Is Open for Business' (2007) 1 Journal of Information, Law and Technology Article 3 https://warwick.ac.uk/fac/soc/law/elj/jilt/2007_1/barton_mckellar/ accessed 24 July 2018.

[19] Academic Development Team University of Exeter, 'Virtual Law Firms – ASPIRE Case Studies' (2013) https://as.exeter.ac.uk/tqae/academicdevelopment/assessmentandfeedback/work-integratedassessmentthecollaborateproject/casestudies/law/#d.en.485823 accessed 24 July 2018.

[20] Nick Birbeck and Sue Prince, 'Collaborate Project Case Study: Virtual Law Firms' (University of Exeter 2013) http://as.exeter.ac.uk/media/universityofexeter/academicservices/educationenhancement/collaborate/VLF_Case_Study_(2).pdf accessed 24 July 2018.

[21] Ibid 12.

in 'Legal Technology & Innovation' in 2017, while Edinburgh University has established a full Masters of Law (LLM) in 'Innovation, Technology and the Law'.[22] The growth of these initiatives designed to prepare students for the increasingly technological nature of practice reinforces the increased importance placed on cultivating a system of 'work-ready' graduates.

1.2.1 *Learning from Past Experimentation in Legal Education*

From our experience of creating and running a number of innovative in-house programmes over the past decade, we have arrived at two key observations. The first is the need to enable the application of learning and skill-building as early as possible to enhance workplace performance; the second is the need to have a core base of legal knowledge.

A core underlying principle of a number of experiments in legal education has been recognising the benefit of building in 'outside the classroom' experience right from the very start of a junior lawyer's career. In respect of our first observation, we have seen practical learning significantly fast-forward the development of young lawyers either as part of a formal apprenticeship with interwoven periods of working and learning, or in programmes where future lawyers have workplace episodes and client-facing workplace experience as early as possible.[23]

In particular, we have observed great benefits from ensuring that workplace episodes for early career lawyers have two features: a broad business focus, and the opportunity for clear leadership roles on client-facing projects. The broad business focus ensures that the junior lawyers frame their role as a true business adviser to clients rather than as a pure academic legal expert. The early opportunity to lead on client-facing projects means that they learn 'by doing' what it means to take responsibility for a project, building critical skills in a number of key areas, such as: asking good questions; listening to client needs; communicating effectively with senior stakeholders over a period of weeks; defining project scope; and producing a client-focused deliverable to meet tight deadlines.

Such early experiential episodes have largely not existed over the last three decades, yet feedback from early career lawyers exposed to such initiatives indicates their importance in building resilience and confidence in the application of

---

22 Ulster University, 'Legal Innovation Centre – Home' www.ulster.ac.uk/legalinnovation accessed 24 July 2018. The University of Edinburgh School of Law, 'DPT: Innovation, Technology and the Law (LLM) (Full-Time) (PTLLMINFTL1F)' www.drps.ed.ac.uk/17-18/dpt/ptllminftl1f.htm accessed 9 January 2019.

23 Over many years at Reed Smith, the performance of young lawyers who had such client-facing workplace experience was measured through self-assessment, feedback gained from a number of stakeholders and other performance metrics. Overall a faster 'speed to capability' was detected in the junior lawyers' initial years in the firm, and greater levels of confidence also, in comparison to earlier years when such workplace opportunities had not been available. In addition, the growth of client demand for graduates to run even more projects in their workplaces indicated the performance level, and value delivered by the junior lawyers in these workplace episodes.

knowledge and skill, and enhancing the performance of participants as they transition from their educational environment to the world of work. This is revealed in feedback offered by a graduate on the Reed Smith 'MA/LPC' programme who was involved in a client-facing business strategy project and who reported that:

> The [four-week client strategy] project was the best learning experience I can remember having taken part in, for several reasons. The project had to be excellent and, just as important, was a real-world task of genuine use to the client. Not only did this make the problem more engaging, it forced us to focus entirely on the client's needs. We were forced to constantly think: 'Is this relevant to the client's specific problem?' It was also useful in developing client relationship management skills. We kept in constant contact with the key stakeholders in the project, ensuring the scope and direction of the project was in line with their needs. We also had to manage differences and conflicts of opinion between individuals within the client. This taught us to ensure that everyone was heard (and perceiving themselves to have been heard) and his or her input valued.[24]

However, as per our second observation, we also observe that practical experience does not displace the continued need for a core base of legal knowledge. As Susskind acknowledges, the 'twist to the tale' is that despite new roles emerging as the legal sector evolves (which we explore in more detail below in Section 1.3), it remains important to qualify as a lawyer and have a strong base of legal black-letter law expertise.[25] This has been borne out of our own experiences and observations regarding the critical success factors associated with the wide range of innovative programmes we have created over the last decade. To succeed in these early workplace opportunities, young solicitors needed to possess core legal knowledge, which they then apply. We anticipate that this knowledge base will remain the foundation for educational pathways into the legal sector for the vast majority and therefore continues to represent a key area of learning.

1.3 EMERGING PROFESSIONAL ROLES AND DRIVERS OF CHANGE

In order to look forwards, to consider the skill-set and mindset which will be critical for the 'lawyer of the future', we must necessarily consider the market context shaping the profession. What are the current pressures and drivers for change, and what will clients demand of future lawyers? These demands will influence the organisations in which lawyers will work, their roles, the skill-set they will need to

---

[24] Oral feedback from student on the Reed Smith 2012–13 MA/LPC collected during a structured review of the programme to assess the learning benefits for students at the conclusion of the academic year. Students were asked to comment on both classroom and workplace elements of the course in feedback to the Learning & Development team to enable ongoing adjustments and improvements to be made to the new course.

[25] Susskind (n 2) 118–20.

acquire and, ultimately, the educational models, which will be needed to support their career pathways.

The market context can largely be distilled to a single theme: buyers of legal services are increasingly expressing varying degrees of dissatisfaction with the way legal services have traditionally been delivered. This has been characterised by increasing cost pressures, a need to minimise legal fees and to demand 'more for less' from external law firms. In response, law firms, law firm subsidiaries and alternative service providers are all experimenting, tweaking, changing or 'reinventing' the model for the legal profession in a way that maintains profit margins whilst also retaining clients.

For some firms this has involved introducing new non-partnership tiers into the organisational structure, outsourcing lower value and time-consuming tasks, shifting away from the hourly billing model, and embracing the efficiency gains found in technology adoption. Yet some gains are easier to achieve than others. It is no coincidence that the best capitalisation of legal technology has been in areas that have structured data and standardised data collection mechanisms. Activities such as corporate merger and acquisitions remain 'messy' from a data perspective, and common corporate law tasks, such as due diligence review, remain a manual and laborious process.

In the face of this ongoing pursuit of cost and process productivity, lawyers have had to adapt, seeking efficiencies in work, pursuing opportunities for automation and finding improved ways to serve their businesses and clients. This adaptation has included tentative steps to acquire a better understanding of change in the industries they service, and developing a toolkit of skills that will serve them well in the future.

These twin drivers of transformation and efficiency (which are at times conflicting and at times complementary) provide the context for our consideration of the legal roles likely to shape future practice. Drawing on our in-house experience and taking into account the continuing market, regulatory and client-driven changes since 2013, we highlight six potential roles, which we foresee emerging in the near future, and these role descriptions update and build upon some of the typologies previously described by Susskind.[26]

As a preface to this analysis, we have two preliminary observations. First, many recent initiatives have focused on the need for future lawyers to be able to code – hence the title of our chapter. Indeed authors such as Susskind have stressed the centrality of technology to many of the legal roles emerging in the future. However, it is important to consider technology as an enabler for people, business models and processes, not the driver of them. Technology adoption varies across organisations, is uneven in its distribution and is received with varying degrees of positivity by clients. Whilst it can produce greater efficiencies, technology can also exacerbate inefficiency by increasing service fragmentation.

[26] Ibid 109–20.

Second, given the differing market drivers and service requirements which each firm faces, we feel that it is important to always keep in mind the external world of the client, and their needs, in order to define what we believe will occupy the time of lawyers in the future legal services marketplace.

Keeping these two points in mind, below we outline six professional role constructs as follows: (a) the advisory role; (b) the transformation role; (c) the collaborative role; (d) the constant improver role; (e) the data-driven role; and (f) the preventative or predictive role. From this position we then work backwards to elucidate the skill-sets required to undertake these roles, and give our view on the educational implications that these skill-sets generate.

1.3.1 *The Advisory Role*

The ever-increasing complexity of the business and regulatory environment means that a senior partner's role as 'trusted advisor' to their key clients will remain in significant demand.[27] In fact, this role is only likely to grow as businesses, governments and other bodies increasingly adopt digitised processes, oversight mechanisms and methods of data collection/storage. The transformation of industry, working practices and the development of new types of goods and services will bring businesses face to face with a range of complex issues and associated consequences with regard to revenue-creation, share performance, business growth, regulatory compliance and public trust.

This is demonstrated by the 'fail fast and fail often'[28] approach exhibited within Silicon Valley, with digital corporate monoliths disrupting industries and generating complex legal issues as a result of corporate behaviour (and in some cases misbehaviour) and the implementation of new business models. This transformation of business begets increased regulation (with more to come) introduced by governments seeking to protect employee rights, promote ethical corporate behaviour and ensure corporate compliance with taxation schemes. In addition, as the Cambridge Analytica scandal demonstrates, problems with data protection and data misuse can cross international borders, bringing into play a range of jurisdictional issues.[29] Add to all these issues the impact of expected large-scale automation and we can see that there will be no shortage of work ahead for the right lawyers.

[27] For the definition of the 'trusted advisor' role, where consultants and advisors are seen as a highly valued source of trusted advice for their clients' most difficult challenges, see David H Maister, Charles H Green and Robert M Galford, *The Trusted Advisor* (Simon & Schuster 2000).

[28] See, e.g., Rory Carroll, 'Silicon Valley's Culture of Failure … and "The Walking Dead" It Leaves Behind' *The Guardian* (London, 28 June 2014) www.theguardian.com/technology/2014/jun/28/silicon-valley-startup-failure-culture-success-myth accessed 5 October 2018.

[29] Allegations relating to the actions of Cambridge Analytica and its impact on the outcomes of the UK's Brexit vote and the US presidential elections have been widely reported. For example, see Mark Scott, 'Cambridge Analytica Helped "Cheat" Brexit Vote and US Election, Claims Whistle-Blower' *Politico* (27 March 2018) www.politico.eu/article/cambridge-analytica-chris-wylie-brexit-trump-britain-data-protection-facebook/ accessed 8 November 2018.

This situation does not mean the legal industry should sit back and expect work to roll in. To acquire status as the 'trusted advisor' of new or transformative businesses, senior lawyers need to empathise with the emerging new leadership of organisations, the cadence of a workforce moving to an agile and iterative way of working, and to understand the role of data in advising on corporate risk, market risk and change.

The required skill-set for these needs will remain broad. The advisor will need to be an expert in areas such as technical architecture, user analytics, data protection, employment rights in the 'gig economy' and digitised risk in new systems. However, there will be an increased emphasis on how these advisors work with clients. Whilst maintaining a specific area of expertise, there will be an even greater need for lawyers to listen and ask insightful questions to understand the complexities of their clients' rapidly evolving worlds. The value of this expertise will lie in a lawyer's ability to tailor knowledge to a client's unique situation, as opposed to merely transmitting their knowledge.

These advisors will also be expected to be creative and persuasive, and capable of collaboration so that they can find solutions with other creative business and technology colleagues. Advice and value in the eyes of clients will look less like a memo, and will instead be orientated around facilitating thinking, for example, leading regular creative sessions in 'stand-up' meetings with the product and technology teams of their clients. As the role of trusted advisor changes so too will workplace expectations – future lawyers may even need to swap their suits for jeans and t-shirts!

1.3.2 *The Transformation Role*

In a rapidly transforming business environment, we will see the rise of the 'transformation lawyers' who specialise in advising their clients on long-term strategies to support decade-long projects. These projects will focus on the need to digitise or re-platform a client's operations in preparation for the increasingly data and technology driven future that is emerging. Such projects are well underway in financial services. However, we should expect to see transformation in other areas, including government work, transportation, shipping and infrastructure.

These projects involve vision, as well as long-term changes in leadership, corporate structure, workforce, revenue lines, financial and tax reporting. They also generate tension for regulators, especially in the realm of data and new technologies like artificial intelligence (AI). For some businesses and industries, the scope of legal work undertaken to facilitate transformation may be huge: from redefining the contractual core of the business to reflect new structures and commercial approaches, to supporting the transformation of a workforce's terms and conditions, to attracting and developing the right talent.

Lawyers in a transformative role will be strategic, long-term thinkers who understand the pace of change and appreciate the range of forces capable of disrupting industry. Expected to span multiple years, this large-scale work will demand specific skill-sets from legal advisors. The ability to 'think big', project manage and contextualise legal advice with reference to the human factors of making and embedding change, will all be critical. Transformation lawyers will also work closely with a client's leadership, innovation and change management structures, necessitating an understanding of the range of features (personal, economic, organisational, political, legal and historical) that shape these structures.

1.3.3 *The 'Blurred Lines' Collaborative Role*

As in-house legal teams work closer with their law firms to find efficiency, the shared understanding produced through these interactions gives rise to scope for collaboration. The increase in use of alternative fee arrangements, collaboration platforms and automation are leading to an increased need to 'process map' so as to understand the tasks, roles and hand-offs that are breaking down the traditional approach to instructing external counsel. In response, industry (legal and general) is slowly introducing a professional project management approach. However there is growing emphasis being placed on a collaborative approach where 'teams' of external (firm-based) and in-house (client-side) lawyers coordinate to undertake clear tasks and actions that are managed within a project and facilitated by a collaborative digital framework.

This places an increased onus on team participation, requiring lawyers to remain open and transparent in how work is carried out, sharing responsibility for the completion of that work and having clarity with regard to expectations. Whilst this may represent a change from the widespread view of lawyering as an individual 'sport', greater collaboration will yield benefits in terms of fostering closer working relationships with colleagues and clients, and promoting a mutual understanding of how to continuously improve the way in which work is completed. This way of working will increasingly blur the lines between external and in-house legal counsel, and will be accelerated by ongoing use of secondments in the industry (from firms to clients, and vice versa) and by the rise of 'New Law' efficiency providers. Lawyers will need to exhibit a mindset conducive to working in a multi-disciplinary project-managed team, and the requisite desire for teamwork and cooperation that underpins this style of working.

1.3.4 *The 'Constant Improver' Role*

Evolutionary change will be key to delivering ongoing enhancements to client services, and empowering lawyers to look for incremental efficiency gains instead of the next 'big thing' will be critical in driving innovation forward. These lawyers, legal engineers or 'T-shaped' lawyers (those with a technical legal skills-base, but who then broaden out their skills), will be key in facilitating the organic evolution of legal services, bringing knowledge of a range of technologies, working practices and

new approaches, deemed necessary to sustain improvement. An ability to understand processes, to exhibit a hands-on appreciation of the balance between people,
process, data and technology, and the ability to measure the benefits of change, will
be central to this role.

The industry has to take what may be considered 'innovative' today, and embed it
within their organisation so as to make it the 'new normal'. Lawyers who embrace
incremental change and look for small gains in the way in which legal work is
performed will be needed in order to sustain day-to-day innovation and improvement. We anticipate that the 'Constant Improver' role is likely to take the form of an
associate working with a junior in-house lawyer to build mutual insights. Skills
required for this role may be taught or fostered during legal education, though it is
expected that skills like project management, process mapping, service design and
a hands-on ability to work core legal technology, will all become integral to an
individual's on-boarding into a law firm.

1.3.5 *The 'Data-Driven' Role*

Client projects requiring detailed review work, ranging from mergers and acquisitions, due diligence, to regulatory reviews, or e-disclosure, are becoming exponen-
tially larger due to the increased volume of electronic data available. From
documents to messenger feeds, databases to electronic systems, there is so much
data to cover in legal work that technology is necessary. This shift has been
evidenced in litigation e-disclosure for a decade and will inevitably spread to other
parts of law.

For lawyers, the ability to understand the way various technological systems work,
what data they hold and to devise techniques to discover important information,
patterns and connections in that data, will be differentiating skills. Great lawyers in
the future will master these areas, leading to new business opportunities. For
example, these skills will enable them to turn a one-off review into an entire deal
life cycle, or to turn requests for one-off regulatory advice into a compliance
programme driven by data.

Data-driven decision-making will become the norm, necessitating that over the
next decade attention is paid to 'cleaning up' and organising data in a way that
facilitates the application of AI technologies. In the longer term, this will lead to the
emergence of new and more efficient processes, driven by digital legal assets such as
smart contracts, contract life cycle management, and data on the efficacy of litigation strategy.

1.3.6 *The Preventative or Predictive Lawyer*

The rise of the data-driven role (Section 1.3.5 above) will put information into the
hands of curious investigators, and forensic analysts, many of who may also act as the

lawyers of the future. These lawyers will have more avenues to explore opportunity, risk and strategy and to design ways to creatively solve a client's business problems. Increasingly, these business problems are digital in nature. Evidence of this is seen in data-driven scandals like Cambridge Analytica and recent election interference issues emerging in the USA and the UK, such that investigative journalists have abandoned the traditional aphorism 'follow the money' in favour of following the data.[30]

We are seeing this trend internally in law firms and 'New Law' business models with litigation, investigatory and now even transactional issues involving data hunts into social media feeds, instant messaging data, databases and business systems, as well as email and documents. Clients and businesses are also using e-disclosure technologies in-house, so as to limit the need for and the cost of purchasing external legal services.

As firms and clients start to share and blend datasets to provide a holistic view of legal and business processes, there will be increased opportunity for preventative lawyering to take hold. This will allow for lawyers to spot trends in data that indicate a legal risk and act to mitigate that risk in advance. These trends might signal widespread regulatory issues or may merely enable lawyers to proactively monitor compliance in line with corporate policy so as to spot mistakes early on.

The preventative lawyer will be a data-enabled 'Trusted Business Advisor'. They will be connected to the problem and have the data to hand to make decisions that affect business outcomes, including the ability to proactively avoid disputes. In other words, this role will facilitate the proactive use of law and the positive use of the governance frameworks that the law provides.

1.3.7 *The Overall Skill-Set of the 'Lawyer of the Future'*

As is clear from our emerging lawyer personas presented above, our analysis does not foresee a 'coding lawyer'. Instead we believe that future roles will build upon the foundations of the 'trusted advisor' role, with lawyers demonstrating a number of broad capabilities. These include:

- Enhanced commercial awareness and client empathy brought about by an understanding of the transformative processes shaping a client's industry.
- The ability to use law more proactively with clients, taking opportunities to be creative and to facilitate innovation and transformation.
- A mindset that is agile in nature, shows interest in agile-development principles, and demonstrates an openness to learn and interact with ideas of 'service design' and 'design thinking' in the organisations they serve.
- High levels of collaboration, communication and facilitation skills.
- An understanding of data (and appropriate/inappropriate use), to become someone with whom business colleagues and a new generation of product managers will want to interact.

[30] Ibid.

- Greater diversity in problem-solving for which a prerequisite will be to recruit in broader talent pools, so as to attract individuals with different voices, backgrounds, learning styles and preferences.

1.4 DEVELOPING FUTURE SKILL-SETS THROUGH WORKPLACE PRACTICE

To develop these future capabilities, we believe that legal educators will need to work closely with employers, in a way that builds on and strengthens the initiatives developed over the last decade and discussed above. Many of the skills we have identified as being central to the future work of lawyers are developed particularly effectively through client-facing workplace experiences. In order to foster a learning environment capable of transferring these skills, the educational and working worlds of young lawyers must be blended further, giving students synchronous opportunities to develop specific skills, and apply knowledge in practice.

As a guide to what some of these blended 'educational and workplace' experiences could look like, we set out below three examples of experimental approaches we have tried in the workplace of Reed Smith and its clients.

1.4.1 *Example One: Promoting an Earlier 'World View' Through Placements*

One conclusion from the skills inherent in the future 'personas' outlined above (and those skills identified by students themselves – see Figure 1.1) is that the recent experiments to create learning programmes which incorporate client-facing learning experiences and build broad commercial skills should be continued and enhanced. A prerequisite for this approach is for firms to have the openness to allow junior lawyers to work in front of and with clients from an early stage.

We have previously explained the way in which Reed Smith pioneered such client-facing project experience, running commercially focused projects for its graduates. In addition, the firm then added a six-month trainee 'seat' experience either at a client or a pro-bono organisation, as well as pioneering the introduction of 'Innovation Hours' for associates.[31] This gives associates time to create service innovations, working on a client's problem within a service design framework (see Example Two below) and focusing on the client outcome.

The fundamental educational philosophy of this overall approach is twofold. It frontloads opportunities for aspiring lawyers to develop a skill-set including leadership and accountability, as well as contributing to the creation of a mindset which

---

[31] In many private practice law firms solicitors are measured on a target number of 'billable hours' per year. The 'Innovation Hours' referenced here were units of time, which would count towards this target, but were time spent on innovation activities rather than chargeable client work.

FIGURE 1.1 Brainstorming the key characteristics for lawyers of the future during an Innovation Hub workshop with students

we believe is critical: working with a client to understand a problem, generate ideas and then co-design the solutions.

1.4.2 *Example Two: Rethinking Legal Services Delivery with* *'Service Design'*

'Service design' is currently the basis of change in many industries, including government digital services. Embracing this as a learning methodology has spearheaded the innovation strategy of Reed Smith, including the launch of the Innovation Hub, and hiring an Innovation Hub Manager with experience of product management and user-centric design.

The Hub regularly runs learning sessions where Reed Smith's lawyers and business teams examine and empathise with a problem or process, prioritise the areas that can be changed or improved, and then work out solutions that can be implemented. This educational approach works well where all parties are in the room and engaged in the process, and where it is understood that time spent at this stage leads to better outcomes rather than simply reverting to familiar yet often ineffective 'traditional' methods of solving a legal issue.

Whilst service design has its origins in the software world, the approach has features which, we believe, can enhance a lawyer's capabilities in communication and

FIGURE 1.2 Workshop outputs on 'persona development' for future lawyers at different career stages

iterative problem-solving (referenced also in Example One above), given that it encompasses a number of skills: spending time understanding the problem, empathising with the players in the problem, understanding processes, coming up with multiple ways to solve something (otherwise known as 'divergent solution solving') and prioritising areas to solve in collaboration with the beneficiary of a solution. An example of this approach is shown in Figure 1.2.

1.4.3 *Example Three: Drawing on Science Technology Engineering and Mathematics (STEM) Learning Methodologies*

A third client-orientated workplace learning experiment we have used has focused on differences in approaches to problem-solving and data analysis, and how these might lead to better client deliverables. Working with Legal

Cheek (a UK graduate/trainee online forum), in 2017 Reed Smith proactively participated in a programme to attract more Science, Technology, Engineering and Mathematics (STEM) students. The purpose was to explore how the approach of these students to legal problem-solving would align with the required 'future lawyer' skill-sets, as well as how it compared with the approach of traditional humanities students.

We selected the 'service design' learning methodology referenced above as the basis for an exercise in the Innovation Hub in the firm's London office. Students with STEM backgrounds were given a real legal task related to employment law contracts and were required to analyse data from a (hypothetical) client to present scenarios and options to the client. Interestingly, the STEM group used a logic-driven approach to create very visual data models, which powerfully enabled the client to explore the options in the advice.

We then repeated this exercise with a group of students from a purely humanities background and the results were very different. The analysis was much more 'legal', with students relying on approaches contingent upon legal argumentation and textual analysis of the contracts themselves.

From this experiment, we concluded that employers of future lawyers could benefit from broader talent recruitment approaches to bring in the 'data aware' skill-sets onto which legal expertise can then be grafted, and that legal educators could also usefully aim to develop elements of 'STEM mindsets' through their curricula.

1.5 CONCLUSION

Drawing on the analysis above and the benefits seen from our own trials of experiential learning, it is hard not to draw the conclusion that future commercial lawyers need to experience a tertiary education much more akin to an apprentice-ship. The client-informed mindsets we have repeatedly emphasised throughout this chapter can only be facilitated if a rebalancing towards practical education occurs through early workplace experience. Early (paid) experience would also improve access to the profession in the face of increasing student debt, and this broader access will in turn facilitate the more diverse mindsets and skill-sets clients are increasingly coming to expect. This shift means that universities should reflect deeply on how they can contribute towards the development of young lawyers who are 'polytechnic' or 'many-skilled'.[32] In particular, there is a need to focus on how an institution endeavours to produce 'many-skilled' graduates who exhibit creative thinking, recognise problems before they happen

---

[32] The word 'polytechnic' deriving from the two Greek words 'poly' ('πολύ', 'many') and 'technē' ('τέχνη', 'skill').

and who are capable of designing systems, processes and solutions that are built to work and not to fail.

It is our view that lawyers will not grasp these opportunities by learning to code, but rather by developing their interpersonal skills, comprehending the emerging user-centric business world, engaging with their curiosity and creative problem-solving skills, listening carefully to their clients' needs and openly engaging with the changing world within which their clients operate and the leadership dynamic that governs that operation. Data and collaboration technology will support lawyers in these tasks, but in line with emerging trends that technology will be no/low-code in three to five years. In other words, lawyers of the future will interact with the technology, not write it. For this reason, the sooner aspiring lawyers are exposed to the realities of this interaction via experiential learning, the better prepared they will be to face the future of legal practice.

BIBLIOGRAPHY

Academic Development Team University of Exeter, 'Virtual Law Firms – ASPIRE Case Studies' (2013) https://as.exeter.ac.uk/tqae/academicdevelopment/assessmentandfeed back/work-integratedassessmentthecollaborateproject/casestudies/law/#d.en.485823 accessed 24 July 2018

Barton K and McKellar P, 'Transactional Learning: Ardcalloch Sheriff Court Is Open for Business' (2007) 1 Journal of Information, Law and Technology Article 3 https://warwick .ac.uk/fac/soc/law/elj/jilt/2007_1/barton_mckellar/ accessed 24 July 2018

Birbeck N and Prince S, 'Collaborate Project Case Study : Virtual Law Firms' (University of Exeter 2013) http://as.exeter.ac.uk/media/universityofexeter/academicservices/educatio nenhancement/collaborate/vlf_case_study_(2).pdf accessed 24 July 2018

Carroll R, 'Silicon Valley's Culture of Failure . . . and "The Walking Dead" It Leaves Behind' *The Guardian* (London, 28 June 2014) www.theguardian.com/technology/2014/jun/28/ silicon-valley-startup-failure-culture-success-myth accessed 5 October 2018

Hardy P, 'First for Reed Smith and BPP with September Launch of Unique Legal and Business Postgraduate Qualification: Bespoke MA (Legal Practice Course with Business)' (*Reed Smith*, 2 April 2012) www.reedsmith.com/en/news/2012/04/first-for-reed-smith-and-bpp-with-september-launch accessed 7 November 2018

Lawcareers.net, 'Trailblazer Legal Apprenticeship Standards Receive Government Approval' (*Lawcareers.net*, 2015) www.lawcareers.net/information/news/trailblazer-legal-apprentice ship-standards-receive-government-approval-04092015 accessed 24 January 2018

Maister DH, Green CH and Galford RM, *The Trusted Advisor* (Simon & Schuster 2000)

Moore T, 'Routes into Law: Queen Mary Teams up with Reed Smith on "Degree with Apprenticeship in Law"' (*Legal Business*, 13 January 2015) www.legalbusiness.co.uk/blogs/ routes-into-law-queen-mary-teams-up-with-reed-smith-on-degree-with-apprenticeship-in -law/ accessed 28 July 2018

QMUL School of Law, 'Courses – M130 Law in Practice' www.qmul.ac.uk/law/undergradu ate/courses/m130-law-in-practice/ accessed 2 November 2018

'Legal Advice Centre' www.lac.qmul.ac.uk/ accessed 2 November 2018

Reed Smith, 'Reed Smith Learning & Development Team Take Home Two Awards in the National Peer Awards for Excellence' (*ReedSmith*, 7 November 2013) www.reedsmith.com/en/news/2013/11/reed-smith-learning-development-team-take-home-tw accessed 24 July 2018

Scott M, 'Cambridge Analytica Helped "Cheat" Brexit Vote and US Election, Claims Whistle-Blower' *Politico* (27 March 2018) www.politico.eu/article/cambridge-analytica-chris-wylie-brexit-trump-britain-data-protection-privacy-facebook/ accessed 8 November 2018

Solicitors Regulation Authority, 'Training for Tomorrow: A Competence Statement for Solicitors' (Solicitors Regulation Authority 2014) www.sra.org.uk/sra/consultations/competence-statement.page accessed 8 November 2018

'SQE to be Introduced in Autumn 2021' (*Solicitors Regulation Authority*, 8 November 2018) www.sra.org.uk/sra/news/press/sqe-launch-2021.page accessed 26 May 2019

Spencer N and Stokes J, 'Coaching and Mentoring as a Key Leadership Development Tool Across Legal Generations' in R Normand-Hochman (ed.), *Mentoring and Coaching for Lawyers: Building Partnerships for Success* (Globe Business Publishing 2014)

Squires L, 'Take an Alternative Route into a Career in Law' (*Apprenticeship News*) www.apprenticeshipnews.co.uk/sectors/law/take-an-alternative-route-into-a-career-in-law accessed 24 July 2018

Susskind R, *Tomorrow's Lawyers: An Introduction to Your Future* (1st edn, Oxford University Press 2013)

Susskind R and Susskind D, *The Future of the Professions: How Technology Will Transform the Work of Human Experts* (Oxford University Press 2015)

The Peer Awards, 'The 2014 Peer Awards' *The Independent* (London, April 2014) 1 http://thepeerawards.com/wp-content/uploads/2014/04/2014indy.pdf accessed 24 July 2018

The University of Edinburgh School of Law, 'DPT: Innovation, Technology and the Law (LLM) (Full-Time) (PTLLMINFTL1F)' www.drps.ed.ac.uk/17-18/dpt/ptllminftl1f.htm accessed 9 January 2019

Ulster University, 'Legal Innovation Centre – Home' www.ulster.ac.uk/legalinnovation accessed 24 July 2018

Webb J and others, 'Setting Standards: The Future of Legal Services Education and Training Regulation in England and Wales (Legal Education and Training Review)' (SRA, BSB and CILEX 2013) www.letr.org.uk/wp-content/uploads/letr-report.pdf accessed 17 August 2018

Wilce H, 'It's the UK's First MBA Delivered Entirely by a Private Organisation' *The Independent* (London, 1 October 2009) www.independent.co.uk/student/postgraduate/mbas-guide/hilary-wilce-its-the-uks-first-mba-delivered-entirely-by-a-private-organisation-1795527.html accessed 24 July 2018

2

Experiential Legal Education

Stepping Back to See the Future

Jeff Giddings and Jacqueline Weinberg

An experience gap has opened up in the development of legal professionals. The workplace-based experiences (traineeships and articles of clerkship) that were once pivotal to the progress of law graduates from student to practitioner are either no longer available or are much diminished in scope and scale. Graduates are expected to have accessed such experiences through other avenues. This is a particular challenge for those law graduates who lack the family and social connections to help them start their engagement with the profession. In response to these changing circumstances Monash University has instituted a Clinical Guarantee assuring every law student a place in its Clinical Legal Education (CLE) programme if they so choose. In this chapter, we describe the Clinical Guarantee initiative, our progress to date, the way in which we have used technology to support provision and the challenges we have faced during implementation. We conclude by emphasising the value of CLE as preparation for modern legal practice, and outlining our intention to measure that value through future evaluation work. This chapter tells an Australian story, but one which resonates with experiences in other jurisdictions.

2.1 INTRODUCTION

The content and organisation of professional work are changing rapidly. Professional work continues to evolve with globalisation,[1] the liberalisation of service markets, international outsourcing, the harnessing of new technology-driven work practices,[2]

---

[1]   Chris Carter, Crawford Spence and Daniel Muzio, 'Scoping an Agenda for Future Research into the Professions' (2015) 28(8) Accounting, Auditing & Accountability Journal 1198.
[2]   Aditya Johri, 'Engineering Knowledge in the Digital Workplace: Aligning Materiality and Sociality through Action' in Tara J Fenwick and Monika Nerland (eds.), *Reconceptualising Professional Learning: Sociomaterial Knowledges, Practices, and Responsibilities* (Routledge 2014).

the development of stronger client-driven frameworks,[3] an increased emphasis on working in interdisciplinary teams, greater professional mobility and the emergence of para-professions. In the midst of dramatic change in the nature of legal work and the structuring of the legal profession, legal educators face calls to better prepare graduates for a world of professional work that is much less certain.

Despite the inherent benefits of learning through practice in developing ethical awareness and professional judgement,[4] as well as acclimatising students to the modern functions of the profession, the opportunities for it are less uniformly available.[5] The traineeships and articles of clerkship that were once pivotal to the progress of law graduates from student to practitioner are either no longer available or are much diminished in scope and scale. As a result, graduates are expected to have found other avenues to gain hands-on experience. This assumption is con-venient for the profession but presents a serious challenge for many law graduates, especially those who lack the family and social connections to help them start their engagement with the profession.[6]

While law schools have traditionally characterised their education mission as to develop legal thinkers, governments and other stakeholders are increasingly focused on law schools producing graduates who are 'job ready'.[7] In 2008, a major review of Australian higher education and the government's response to this review acknowl-edged the need for universities to prepare graduates for the world of work.[8] In the decade since, clinical legal education (CLE)[9] and work-integrated learning (WIL)[10] have become increasingly popular in Australian universities. CLE refers to students

---

[3] Noel Semple, Russell G Pearce and Renee Newman Knake, 'A Taxonomy of Lawyer Regulation: How Contrasting Theories of Regulation Explain the Divergent Regulatory Regimes in Australia, England and Wales, and North America' (2013) 16(2) Legal Ethics 258.

[4] See, e.g., Daniel J Givelber and others, 'Learning through Work: An Empirical Study of Legal Internship' (1995) 45(1) Journal of Legal Education 1; Laura Grenfell and Cornelia Koch, 'Getting a Foot in the Door: Internships and the Legal Profession' (2018) 40(7) Bulletin 28.

[5] Andrew Stewart and Rosemary Owens, 'Experience or Exploitation? The Nature, Prevalence and Regulation of Unpaid Work Experience, Internships and Trial Periods in Australia' (University of Adelaide 2013) www.fairwork.gov.au/ArticleDocuments/763/UW-complete-report.pdf.aspx accessed 12 May 2019.

[6] See ibid. At 3.64, they quote a student who says that unpaid experience is almost a necessity for those without the right contacts in the legal industry. See also Grenfell and Koch (n 4). Further, see Fink's discussion of this in a US context where he observes that unpaid internships are a particularly effective barrier to mobility, operating as a class filter for those without affluence or connections. Eric M Fink, 'No Money, Mo' Problems: Why Unpaid Law Firm Internships Are Illegal and Unethical' (2013) 3 (Winter) University of San Francisco Law Review 435, 437–8.

[7] David Rigg, 'Embedding Employability in Assessment: Searching for the Balance between Academic Learning and Skills Development in Law: A Case Study' (2013) 47(3) The Law Teacher 404.

[8] Denise Bradley and others, 'Review of Australian Higher Education: Final Report' (Department of Education, Employment and Workplace Relations 2008) www.voced.edu.au/content/ngv%3A32134 accessed 12 May 2019.

[9] For details on the development and prominence of clinical legal education in Australia and else-where, see Jeff Giddings, *Promoting Justice through Clinical Legal Education* (Justice Press 2013).

[10] Adrian Evans and others, *Course Design for Clinical Teaching* (Australian National University Press 2017) ch 2.

engaging in closely supervised legal work for real clients with an emphasis on professional identity development and reflective practice. WIL is a broader term for activities that integrate academic learning with workplace experience. At Monash, WIL emphasises student development of employability skills including communication, teamwork, leadership, negotiation and problem-solving.[11]

Clinical programmes are now showcased by many law schools that rely on their clinic to address university requirements for student access to WIL, fostering community service and professional engagement. Clinics that specialise in addressing particular areas of law are increasingly prominent and new models are being developed. However, as existing avenues to acquire work experience diminish, universities face increased pressure to provide scalable opportunities for student engagement with clients and the world of legal work.

In this chapter we consider the value that experiential education (for example CLE and WIL) holds as a means by which to prepare students for twenty-first century legal practice. Drawing on our experience introducing a Clinical Guarantee at Monash University, we examine how educational institutions can build on existing effective CLE programmes so as to increase opportunities for students to acquire hands-on experience. In detailing the implementation of the Clinical Guarantee we describe the initiative, our progress to date, the way in which we have used technology to support provision and the challenges we have faced during implementation. We conclude by emphasising the value of CLE and WIL as preparation for modern legal practice, and outlining our intention to measure that value through future evaluation.

2.2 PROFESSIONAL SUPERVISION AND CLE

2.2.1 *The Changing Nature of Professional Supervision*

Historically, the distinctive feature of professional preparation has involved supervised practice experiences, following or combined with learning the foundations of professional knowledge. At its best, this involves the modelling of expert judgement and coaching of the learner so as to develop the blend of analytic and practical habits of mind demanded by professional practice.[12] The arrangements used by law firms to

---

[11]   CLE involves an intensive small group or solo learning experience in which each student takes responsibility for legal or law-related work for a client (whether real or simulated) in collaboration with a supervisor. Structures enable each student to receive feedback on their contributions and to take the opportunity to learn from their experiences through reflecting on matters including their interactions with the client, their colleagues and their supervisor as well as the ethical dimensions of the issues raised and the impact of the law and legal processes. See Giddings (n 9) 12–15. WIL is a curriculum design which combines formal learning with student exposure to real professional, work or other practice settings.

[12]   William Sullivan, *Work and Integrity: The Crisis and Promise of Professionalism in America* (2nd edn, Jossey Bass 2005).

manage their work and meet their professional responsibilities have always been underpinned by supervision arrangements. Senior lawyers traditionally take responsibility for the work of junior and trainee lawyers as well as paralegals. This supervision can be time-consuming and not fully recognised as part of professional work.[13] It is also not something for which professionals have traditionally been trained.[14] Nevertheless such experiences are vital. Supervisors can play a critical role in modelling professional practice to novices and this is particularly important for those who are 'first-in-family' in seeking to enter a profession.

CLE (whether in-house or involving external placements) and WIL can play an important role in exposing students to various professional environments and what it means to be a professional advisor, yet the ability to secure these experiences is rarely guaranteed. Dramatic increases in the size of law firms have meant that supervision, whilst more important than ever, is no longer uniformly available to law graduates. Some law graduates find themselves seeking to enter the legal profession with little in the way of direct experience of legal work.[15] The emergence of national firms and, over the past decade, the internationalisation and digitisation of legal practice, has further challenged traditional practical education and supervisory structures. This has led to the emergence of an experience gap, that is, a divide between the development needs of aspiring lawyers and the capacity and inclination of the legal profession to address those student needs.

The experience gap has been exacerbated by significant changes in the professional training law graduates must complete prior to admission to legal practice.[16] Across Australia the traditional articles of clerkship have been replaced with practical legal training (PLT) programmes (offered by law schools and private providers) and workplace traineeships. While these PLT programmes enjoy considerable educational strengths, the placement experiences offered to students vary considerably in terms of duration and nature, and have not been effectively integrated with other programme components.[17]

Professional apprenticeships in law can and, in our view, should include student experiences in law school-based clinical programmes with students engaged in the practice of their intended occupation and supported by structured experiences with the direct guidance of experienced practitioners. Such experiences enable development of the 'complex ensemble of analytic thinking, skilful practice and wise

---

[13] Jeff Giddings and Michael McNamara, 'Preparing Future Generations of Lawyers for Legal Practice: What's Supervision Got to Do With It?' (2014) 37(3) University of New South Wales Law Journal 1226.

[14] Givelber and others (n 4) 8.

[15] Giddings and McNamara (n 13).

[16] Ibid.

[17] Michael McNamara, 'Towards Effective Supervision for the Legal Profession: A Focus on Supervised Practice' (Griffith University 2018). Billett's 2015 study of WIL experiences found that educational processes should be enacted before and during work experiences. Further, the optimum point of engagement is after the student has engaged in the work experience. See Stephen Billett, *Integrating Practice-Based Experiences into Higher Education* (Springer Netherlands 2015).

judgment upon which every profession rests'.[18] Supervised practice is acknowledged as important in developing the dispositions required when taking responsibility for others' interests.[19]

Much of the recent innovation in legal education has involved developments in the digital domain. While useful, we need to avoid replacing student involvement in personal, hands-on, client-focused work. While the importance of experiential education in law is better recognised in the USA,[20] in light of the decreasing number of opportunities provided by the profession itself many Australian law schools have developed experiential learning opportunities (notably CLE). As a result of its more recent emergence, the pedagogy underpinning the development of CLE in Australia requires further refinement in order to make experiential education as effective as possible, particularly when the intention is to scale-up existing programmes.[21] In examining how we might leverage existing models of CLE to develop new practice-based learning opportunities we must necessarily consider what we are preparing law students for and how experiential learning can sensibly make a contribution to this end.

2.2.2 Clinical Education as Preparation for the Future of Law

In line with the changing nature of professional practice, law firms now expect new lawyers to be able to draw on a broader set of skills and understandings. In modern legal practice, 'the traditional conception of the lawyer as "rights warrior" no longer satisfies client expectations, which centre on value for money and practical problem solving rather than on expensive legal argument and arcane procedures'.[22] According to Macfarlane this requires renewed emphasis on negotiation skills, communication skills and skills to promote the lawyer-client relationship.[23] Further, the client's desire to be involved in the legal service provision process necessitates greater reliance on problem-solving strategies and more effort to directly include the client in face-to-face negotiation.[24]

---

[18] Sullivan (n 12) 195.
[19] Anthony Kronman, *The Lost Lawyer: Failing Ideals of the Legal Profession* (Belknap Press of Harvard University Press 1993).
[20] William M Sullivan and others, *Educating Lawyers: Preparation for the Profession of Law* (1st edn, Jossey-Bass 2007); Roy Stuckey, 'Best Practices for Legal Education: A Vision and A Road Map' (Clinical Legal Education Association 2007) https://clea.wildapricot.org/Resources/Documents/best_practices-full.pdf accessed 28 September 2018.
[21] Kingsford Legal Centre, 'Clinical Legal Education Guide' (Kingsford Legal Centre 2019) www.klc.unsw.edu.au/sites/klc.unsw.edu.au/files/2924 CLE guide-WEB.pdf accessed 12 May 2019.
[22] Julie Macfarlane, *The New Lawyer: How Settlement Is Transforming the Practice of Law* (University of British Columbia Press 2008) 23.
[23] Ibid.
[24] Richard Susskind, *Tomorrow's Lawyers: An Introduction to Your Future* (1st edn, Oxford University Press 2013) 135.

In order to respond to this environment, legal education needs to cultivate a new kind of lawyer who is trained not only in the use of coding and technology, but also in the skills that cannot be automated, including the very 'human' capabilities of creativity, empathy, compassion and emotional intelligence. It is in the cultivation of these skills where working with real clients under supervision demonstrates clear benefits over and above other forms of learning in developing students' proactive problem-solving, conflict management, communication and client awareness capabilities.

Proactive problem solving involves understanding client needs and interests, gathering and evaluating information, as well as identifying and working with those who can assist in advancing client interests.[25] Working with real clients under supervision gives students a clear opportunity to develop their capacity to identify alternatives, articulate the pros and cons of each alternative and then apply frameworks that assist the client to evaluate those alternatives. When combined with knowledge of alternative dispute resolution (ADR), this serves to reinforce that litigation is only one option and needs to be critically evaluated in the same exacting manner as other conflict management approaches.[26]

Understanding conflict resolution demands 'an extension of training beyond the analytical-adversarial paradigm of thinking like a lawyer to the affective and moral dimensions of human relationships, including professional relationships'.[27] It integrates emotions, values and attitudes in the analysis and practice of law.[28] Students who are encouraged to think like a lawyer within this humanising approach will be thinking about cooperative as well as adversarial options for dispute resolution.[29] Whilst ADR educators recognise the importance of teaching students about the dynamics of conflict,[30] there are few opportunities for students to acquire such knowledge in the absence of CLE and WIL.

Added to this is the role experiential education plays in helping build the communication skills of students. In line with the changing nature of professional practice, lawyers are expected to shift away from a default adversarial model towards a more flexible, conciliatory trajectory.[31] In doing so, they must become skilled in

---

[25] M Coper, 'Educating Lawyers for What? Reshaping the Idea of Law School' (2010) 29 (1) *Penn State International Law Review* 27, 29.

[26] Kathy Douglas, 'The Teaching of ADR in Australian Law Schools: Promoting Non-Adversarial Practice in Law' (2011) 22(1) Australasian Dispute Resolution Journal 49; Tom Fisher, Judy Gutman and Erika Martens, 'Why Teach ADR to Law Students – Part 2: An Empirical Survey' (2007) 17(2) Legal Education Review 67.

[27] Julie Macfarlane, 'The New Advocacy: Implications for Legal Education and Teaching Practice' in Roger Burridge, Abdul Hinett, Karen Paliwala and Tracey Varnava (eds.), *Effective Learning and Teaching in Law* (Routledge 2003) 167.

[28] Ibid.

[29] Ibid.

[30] Ben Waters, 'The Importance of Teaching Dispute Resolution in a Twenty-First-Century Law School' (2017) 51(2) The Law Teacher 227; Bernard S Mayer, *The Dynamics of Conflict Resolution: A Practitioner's Guide* (John Wiley & Sons 2000) 98–102.

[31] Kingsford Legal Centre (n 21).

helping clients to identify what is most important to them, what they believe they 'deserve' and the risks and rewards that accompany adopting certain positions.[32] Clinical experiences can highlight to students the gulf between abstract entitlement and what people with problems can realistically pursue through legal avenues. These experiences reveal the limits of legal remedies and the structural constraints that operate to dissuade pursuit of those remedies.

Taken together, participation in clinics and WIL enables students to build the problem-solving, conflict resolution and communication skills that underpin the client-orientated mentality required of practising lawyers. This comes in addition to a range of other benefits that 'rich, interactive and contextualised' learning experiences such as WIL and CLE[33] can bring in developing the interpersonal, written and oral communication, team work, self-management and professionalism skills of students, as well as the role WIL plays in improving student employment outcomes.[34]

Given these clear benefits, there is merit in considering how universities might harness the pedagogical value that CLE offers so as to address the emerging experience gap. This consideration necessarily demands we engage with a series of pragmatic issues, including: how initiatives to greatly increase the scale and scope of CLE can find wider faculty support; how technology might be harnessed to broaden the available opportunities for experiential learning; what challenges are likely to arise in the process of scaling-up; and what pre-conditions exist for the successful implementation and sustainability of new programmes. In the section that follows we consider these issues by drawing on the lessons we have learnt from the introduction of a Clinical Guarantee at Monash University.

2.3 MONASH UNIVERSITY: A CASE STUDY

2.3.1 *Offering a Clinical Guarantee at Monash University*

In recognition of the challenges involved in preparing our students for the modern legal profession, in 2018 Monash University Law Faculty introduced a Clinical Guarantee, which assures every law student an opportunity to participate in our clinical programme if they so choose. We are the first Australian law school to offer such an assurance and doing so has given rise to a number of opportunities and challenges. Monash is seeking to develop approaches to foster legal professionals and thinkers who will be adept in the emerging local and global professional

[32] Ibid.
[33] Brett Freudenberg, Mark Brimble and Craig Cameron, 'WIL and Generic Skill Development: The Development of Business Students' Generic Skills Through Work-Integrated Learning' (2011) 12(2) Asia-Pacific Journal of Cooperative Education 79, 81 (quoting McLennon).
[34] Ibid.

environments and has identified its clinical programme as playing a central role in preparing students for the future of work, including legal work.

The Monash clinical programme is the oldest and one of the most comprehensive in the country. The Monash model represents the start of the development of a distinctively Australian approach to clinic-based legal education, one that has maintained a strong community service focus while also developing significant aspects of clinical teaching, particularly in relation to professionalism and values. A range of Australian law schools have followed the Monash example of developing live-client clinics in a community legal aid setting with a mixture of funding sources.[35] Indeed the strength of the clinical programme at Monash is such that Monash was the lead institution for a collaborative project to develop 'Best Practices in Australian Clinical Legal Education' which ran from 2011 to 2012.[36]

The prospect of offering a Clinical Guarantee took some time to gather momentum, having been originally raised in 2016 by Professor Peter Joy, a law school visitor from Washington University in Saint Louis. Further impetus was generated by contributions from Professor Jay Pottenger at Yale Law School. Monash Law took a methodical approach to developing the Clinical Guarantee concept. With leadership from the Dean and Faculty Manager, the Faculty engaged external consultants to work closely with interested staff and external parties to develop a business case for the introduction of a Clinical Guarantee. Development of the business case by this external team gave the proposal greater credibility than if it had been developed by clinic advocates within the Faculty.

The Monash Law 2016–2020 Strategic Plan outlined a vision to provide 'the best experiential legal education in Australia' with the clinical programme central to that vision. The Business Case emphasised that the clinical programme was highly regarded by students and employers and a critical enabler of alumni engagement. Student evaluations highlighted the value of clinical experiences and the opportunity to engage in meaningful legal work on behalf of clients in need. There was also a wide range of anecdotal accounts from alumni as to the impact and value of their clinic experiences.

In planning, Monash Law identified that clinic-based learning enables students to build competencies, which are highly relevant to a wide range of future professions. Beyond law, the Business Case took an expansive view of the value of these competencies as important in fields such as:

- Banking and finance;
- Government agencies, not-for-profits and non-government organisations;
- Politics and community organising;

---

[35] Giddings (n 9) ch 6.
[36] See Adrian Evans and others, 'Best Practices Australian Clinical Legal Education' (Australian Government Office for Learning and Teaching 2013) https://ltr.edu.au/resources/PP10_1603_Monash_Evans_Report_2013.pdf accessed 12 May 2019.

- Professional services;
- Marketing and communications;
- Arts, media and publishing;
- Science and engineering; and
- Teaching and academia.

The offering of the Clinical Guarantee is seen as capable of embedding and further extending the faculty's reputation of producing highly valued, work-ready graduates. It was also seen as aligned with the broader university's 'Focus Monash' strategy with its emphasis on the university being excellent, international, enterprising and inclusive.[37]

Subsequently, in principle support was obtained from the faculty executive and broader leadership group and then from a faculty staff meeting. The faculty is implementing the guarantee across 2018–20. This involves a very substantial increase in the number of students able to participate in a clinical experience. In 2017, the existing set of clinical units enabled around 35 per cent of students to participate in a clinic. With expansion of those existing units and new options, participation increased to 40 per cent by the end of 2018 and is expected to reach 80 per cent by the end of 2020. In 2018, 287 students were able to participate in a clinical unit and 385 are projected to participate in 2019. The forecast for 2020 is to have 500 places available to students.

This expansion has been enabled by strong support from Monash University and its Law faculty with extension of one of its key clinic sites (Monash Law Clinics – Clayton); the opening of a new clinic site in the Melbourne CBD (Monash Law Clinics – Melbourne); as well as continuity arrangements that see more than 100 students each year involved in clinical experiences at a third site (Monash Legal Service – Springvale). This substantial infrastructure investment required to facilitate this expansion was the result of strong faculty leadership, most particularly by the Faculty Dean (Professor Bryan Horrigan) and Faculty Manager (Jane Prior). Strong support for investment was also engendered by the clinical programme's alignment with the priorities of the faculty and the university.[38]

2.3.2 *What the Guarantee Entails*

The Clinical Guarantee provides that all students will be offered the opportunity to take part in an appropriate clinic-based learning experience. The offering of particular places takes into account student capabilities and preferences, host organisation availability, as well as the level of student demand for particular opportunities. In allocating available places for any given teaching period, preference is given to students who are closer to completing their degree and who would not have another

---

[37] Monash University, 'Focus Monash' (Monash University 2015) www.monash.edu/__data/assets/ pdf_file/0004/169744/strategic-plan-print-version.pdf accessed 24 April 2019.
[38] See Giddings (n 9) ch 10.

opportunity to undertake a clinical experience prior to graduation. If a student declines the offer of a place in an appropriate clinic experience for which they have expressed an interest in participating, the Law faculty is not obliged to offer further clinical options to the student.

The guarantee focuses on student participation in units that attract academic credit. At present, this includes Professional Practice (double the standard credit points for an elective unit),[39] Professional Practice Family Law Assistance Program (FLAP) (double the standard credit points)[40] and Clinical Placements (that attract a standard credit point load).[41] The faculty drew on relevant research[42] and its experience in operating effectively integrated education-focused clinics to identify the following distinctive elements of a best practice clinical experience:

(a) It is an experience for which academic credit is awarded;
(b) Intensity, in that the experience requires regular and sustained participation;
(c) Duration, in that the experience extends across the course of a teaching period;
(d) Close supervision, focused on developing student awareness and skills in a professional context;
(e) Reflective practice is taught, modelled and practised; and
(f) It is integrated with a classroom component.

Both the practice and classroom components address the critical skills for future lawyers addressed earlier in this chapter.

In expanding these clinical offerings, Monash has built on areas of existing strength such as Family Law. It has also moved into new areas such as:

• Abolition of the death penalty (with the Capital Punishment Justice Project (formerly Reprieve Australia)[43] along with organisations in India, Indonesia, Pakistan and the Philippines);
• Climate defence (with Russell Kennedy Lawyers);[44]
• Human rights (with the Castan Centre for Human Rights);[45]

---

39 Monash University, 'LAW4328: Professional Practice' (*Unit Handbook*, 2019) www.monash.edu /pubs/2019handbooks/units/LAW4328.html accessed 26 April 2019.
40 Monash University, 'LAW4330: Family Law Assistance Program: Professional Practice' (*Unit Handbook*, 2019) www.monash.edu/pubs/handbooks/units/LAW4330.html accessed 11 May 2019.
41 Monash University, 'LAW 4803: Clinical Placement' (*Unit Handbook*, 2019) www.monash.edu/pubs/ 2019handbooks/units/LAW4803.html accessed 11 May 2019.
42 In particular, reference was made to the following sources: Evans and others (n 36); Evans and others (n 10); Giddings (n 9).
43 See further Capital Punishment Justice Project (CJPC), 'Home Page' (2016) www.reprieve.org.au/ accessed 25 April 2019.
44 See further Russell Kennedy Lawyers, 'Home Page' www.russellkennedy.com.au/ accessed 11 May 2019.
45 See further Monash University, 'Castan Centre for Human Rights Law' www.monash.edu/law/research/ centres/castancentre accessed 11 May 2019.

- Institutional law reform processes (with the Australian Law Reform Commission);[46]
- International trade law (with the Geneva-based group, TradeLab);[47]
- Modern slavery (with the Global Pro Bono Bar Association[48], Justice Mission International[49] and the Mekong Club[50]); and
- Start-ups and innovation (with Monash Innovation[51] and the Eastern Innovation Business Centre[52]).

These new clinics make use of a range of technologies in operating beyond standard models of face-to-face client services. The international and interstate clinics are all being facilitated through digital platforms to enable engagement with remote clients and to access external academic and professional expertise.

2.3.3 *Developing Virtual and Technology-Based Clinics*

Implementation of the Monash Clinical Guarantee has been informed by policy agendas that identify the potential for harnessing new technologies to deliver appropriate legal services to individuals and communities that struggle to access traditional services. In addition to developing a virtual clinic, Monash has introduced new technology-based clinics as a key part of broadening our offerings while also extending our existing strengths.

The Monash Virtual Clinic has been designed as a flexible framework for service delivery as well as for teaching students about access to justice, the changing nature of legal work and the parameters of professionalism. In 2016, the Victorian government released the 'Access to Justice Review August 2016 (A2JR)', which identified ways to help Victorians navigate the legal system and resolve everyday legal issues. It was acknowledged that the digital revolution means people now expect to be able to access information more easily, ask questions and resolve some problems more quickly than in the past.[53]

A2JR recognised the need to put community members at the centre of service design, that supporting practical access to justice means 'providing the right services,

---

[46]   See further Australian Law Reform Commission, 'Home Page' www.alrc.gov.au/ accessed 11 May 2019.
[47]   See further Tradelab, 'Home Page' (2019) www.tradelab.org/ accessed 4 March 2019.
[48]   See further Global Pro Bono Bar Association, 'Home Page' www.probonobar.org/ accessed 11 May 2019.
[49]   See further International Justice Mission, 'Home Page' www.ijm.org/ accessed 11 May 2019.
[50]   See further The Mekong Club, 'Home Page' (2017) https://themekongclub.org/ accessed 11 May 2019.
[51]   See further Monash University, 'Monash Innovation' (2016) www.monash.edu/research/infrastruc ture/platforms-pages/monash-innovation accessed 11 May 2019.
[52]   See further Eastern Innovation Business Centre, 'Home Page' https://eibc.net.au/ accessed 11 May 2019.
[53]   Victorian Department of Justice & Regulation, 'Access To Justice Review – Volume 1 – Report and Recommendations' (Department of Justice and Regulation 2016) https://engage.vic.gov.au/down load_file/844/612 accessed 24 April 2019; Victorian Department of Justice & Regulation, 'Access To Justice Review – Volume 2 – Report and Recommendations' (Department of Justice and Regulation 2016) https://engage.vic.gov.au/download_file/845/612 accessed 24 April 2019.

in the right places, at the right time and in the right way'.[54] This user focus highlighted the need to provide different responses, depending on whether the individual recognises the legal dimensions of their problem, their capacity to engage with the justice system and the type of legal problems that they face.

The Monash Virtual Clinic focuses on providing legal services to those who cannot attend Community Legal Clinics (CLCs) in person. Such clients may include those living in regional or remote areas, or those who cannot otherwise attend because of disadvantage and marginalisation. It operates similarly to more conventional services incorporating digital aspects in terms of the making of appointments, checks to identify and avoid conflict of interest concerns and the sharing of documents and information to prepare the client for their 'virtual appointment'. Clients need to have access to reliable Internet services in order to engage with the clinic.

In preparation for their appointment, the client is required to complete a number of documents available online via Google Docs, including the 'Client Agreement' and 'Authority to Act' forms. The client can upload relevant documents ahead of their appointment and the clinic has addressed a range of issues related to the appropriate digital storage of client information. The Zoom digital platform is used for client interviews. The interview rooms have been designed to enable technology-based service delivery. As with all our clinics, students are closely supervised by experienced practitioner-academics. Students take instructions and then pause the interview to confer with their supervisor, asking the client to stay near their computer. Once the supervisor and student agree on the advice to be provided to the client, the student returns to the interview room and conveys that advice.

The design of the Virtual Clinic has been informed by the Australian 'Best Practices in Clinical Legal Education Project'.[55] Students learn to apply legal principles to client problems. The clinic exposes students to the 'realities, demands and compromises of legal practice. In so doing, it provides students with real-life reference points for learning the law'.[56] It aligns with the 'pervasive ... aim ... to attune students to issues of social justice', providing an opportunity for students to analyse and reflect on the relationship between law and access to justice and the contributions that lawyers make.[57] It includes teaching about legal skills as well as the broader legal system, blending the development of doctrinal skills with practical application.[58]

The Virtual Clinic environment also directs students to tailor their communication and advice to the situation and context of each client as part of a 'client-centred

54 Victorian Department of Justice & Regulation, 'Access To Justice Review – Summary Report' (Department of Justice and Regulation 2016) https://engage.vic.gov.au/download_file/842/612 accessed 24 April 2019, 7.
55 Evans and others (n 36).
56 Ibid 2.
57 Evans and others (n 10) 75.
58 Ibid.

approach'.[59] Clinical pedagogy advocates for clinicians to teach students to focus on the 'importance of listening to the client and treating them as a person, not just a legal problem ... reflecting social justice values such as people's dignity and right to equality'.[60]

Through participation in the Virtual Clinic, students learn that access to justice issues attach to almost every client, enabling students to reflect on why the legal needs of clients and communities are not being met, or how they can be better met.[61] It brings together key elements, namely technology, access to justice, community service and clinical pedagogy.

2.3.4 *The Benefits and Challenges of Implementing a Clinical Guarantee*

The Clinical Guarantee offers significant opportunities to enhance student learning, foster alumni engagement and contribute to client and community service. It can also enable a range of practice and policy-related research activities. These benefits come in addition to the potential the Clinical Guarantee holds as a means by which to address the aforementioned experience gap that disproportionately affects students who do not have the family and social connections to facilitate engagement with the practising legal profession.

A key benefit of the guarantee is that it ensures clinical opportunities are available for all students at a time when placement opportunities are becoming both more important and more difficult for some students to access. The faculty has invested in building its capacity to offer increasing numbers of students an intensive in-house clinic experience. It has also engaged more systematically with the practising profession to broaden the range of professional placement opportunities available to students. Whether this type of initiative is capable of levelling the playing field for 'first in family' law students remains to be seen. What can be stated is that it provides a clear and well-supported pathway to professional engagement for those students who do not have existing connections to the profession. It also showcases the diversity of law-related professional work that students can pursue and reveals how their law studies at Monash are preparing them for such work.

In taking the Monash Clinical Guarantee forward, we have adopted a systematic, inclusive and strategic approach in both the planning and implementation processes. Inevitably, the successful implementation of the guarantee has also given rise to a number of challenges. It is important to consider the key elements that have enabled this project to progress where it might otherwise have stalled. For this reason, the key lessons we have learnt in the process of implementing the Clinical Guarantee are discussed below in the hope that our experiences will assist those wishing to rollout similar CLE projects.

[59]   Ibid 209.
[60]   Ibid 110.
[61]   Ibid 117.

1. Ensure clear vision and leadership

We have already referred to the leadership provided by senior Law faculty members both in proposing the Clinical Guarantee and in developing the framework for its implementation. The faculty also appointed Australia's first Associate Dean (Experiential Education) with the specific brief to lead the implementation of the Clinical Guarantee, working with an experienced Project Manager. This has helped ensure that the project is framed by a clear vision and led by a designated leadership team.

2. Provide adequate resourcing

The Law faculty relied on a comprehensive business case prepared by external consultants, SPP Consulting, in order to allocate strategic initiative funds to commence the implementation of the project. The business case provided an external benchmark for the project's resourcing needs, this justified the investment required and aided acceptance by the faculty's executive.

3. A comprehensive planning process

The scale of this project, more than doubling the number of available placements and diversifying the legal issues being addressed, necessitated a comprehensive planning process. The process of reaching shared understandings across the faculty revealed untested assumptions about the work of the clinical programme. Blending deep experience of the Monash clinical programme with knowledge of best practices elsewhere has been important in maintaining and building upon the strengths of the existing programme.

4. Undertake comprehensive consultation

We have already referred to the systematic approach taken to gaining Law faculty support for the Clinical Guarantee. The planning process continued with Faculty colleagues invited to open meetings to contribute their ideas. This consultation process was important in identifying existing networks that could be harnessed in the expansion of the clinical programme. Current students were also consulted in relation to the types of clinic-based experiences they were most interested in pursuing. This enabled us to design a programme that meets expressed need.

5. Raise awareness

The Law faculty has a strong interest in publicising the Clinical Guarantee initiative to the broad range of interested parties – to current and prospective students, the practising legal profession and other law-related professionals, the judiciary, legal professional associations and all tiers of government. The faculty is also seeking to strengthen links with other disciplines across the university. This has meant that even at this relatively early stage, the project has had an impact beyond its intention to offer a clinical guarantee: differentiating Monash from other education providers; supporting community and industry engagement; and facilitating opportunities for interdisciplinary collaboration.

6. Implement structures to support consistency and cohesion

The process of expanding and diversifying the opportunities available to students has placed pressure on existing arrangements. As the clinical programme becomes more central to the work of the faculty, it needs to be supported by structures designed to ensure suitable learning outcomes, involvement in relevant professional work and consistency in student and staff workloads as well as assessment arrangements.

7. Recognise turf sensitivities

In developing new clinic sites, we have been mindful of possible sensitivities on the part of other community legal service providers with concerns around possible competition for scarce funding resources. Our approach has been to seek to work with existing services, recognising their existing areas of service delivery and community networks.

8. Don't dilute the experience

Existing clinical staff were clear that scaling up the programme to offer a more diverse range of clinical opportunities should not dilute the existing clinical experiences. While this remains a key focus of the implementation, changes have been made to staff-student supervision ratios (increased from four to five per session) and we are considering ways in which to introduce consistency to the duration of the clinical period students experience.

9. Balance continuity with innovation

It is important to build on existing strengths and networks while also looking for new opportunities. Monash is fortunate to have the arrangements for new clinics informed by existing practices and expertise. While many students will be interested in experiences in emerging areas, it remains important to ensure that clients receive services in stable and sustainable ways. Making appropriate use of new technologies will also be important to diversifying and deepening the student experience.

10. Encourage ownership

It has been important to recognise and encourage colleagues to bring their existing expertise to the table and work with you to develop new clinical opportunities for students. It is particularly valuable when those colleagues have the motivation and energy to bring their ideas to fruition. The more energy and insight the clinical leadership can bring to those discussions, the more likely it is that the experience will be well designed. This has been the case for all of the new clinics developed as part of the Clinical Guarantee.

11. Build the classroom component

Some Monash clinical placements had developed with only a limited seminar programme and did not engage with issues around fostering effective and reflective practice. This has now changed with the introduction of seminars designed to prepare students for the world of professional work.[62] Where appropriate, the seminar programmes include material that students access and engage with online.

---

[62] The newly introduced seminar programme for the *Clinical Placement* unit includes an in-person Induction (addressing ethics, supervision and communication) and a series of online seminars (addressing 'The Work of Lawyers', 'Reflective Practice' and 'Law and Social Change').

12. Accept the uncertainty

Expanding the Monash clinical programme in the way required by the offering of a clinical guarantee has involved a significant level of uncertainty. Not everything can be planned well in advance and it is important to be flexible in how objectives are met. Colleagues need to be encouraged to 'not let the perfect become an enemy of the good'.

2.4 CONCLUSION: LOOKING TO THE FUTURE

As Australian developments are showing, CLE and experiential education can make an important contribution to developing law graduates who are effective, creative and reflective. A key characteristic that clinical programmes can foster is the capacity of students to respond to the evolving environments they will enter upon graduation. Clinics can introduce students to the dynamics of professional work. These include working with clients, working with supervisors and peers as well as understanding the dynamics of conflict and moving beyond an adversarial focus on litigation.

The modernising of legal education has seen an embrace of digital platforms but also a return to the power of learning from experience in professional settings. We see clinics and other forms of experiential learning as capable of playing an integral role in preparing students for the self-directed work that modern novices must undertake. The need to effectively address the complex set of factors referred to in this chapter necessitates a systematic process of engagement between key parties – universities, their students and academics, employers, industry groups and professional associations. It will be particularly important for law schools to engage with regulators and the practising profession and CLE is a valuable site for fostering this type of collaborative approach.

The Monash Clinical Guarantee has been presented in this chapter as an example of a project providing law students with the opportunity to engage with modern legal professional work. Evaluation of the project will involve both internal processes and engagement with external reviewers. Beyond delivering on the promise to provide every law student with the opportunity to participate in a clinic-based learning experience, evaluation will address issues such as the student experience, the development of new models for CLE and the integration of the clinical programme with the other activities of the law school (in both teaching and research).

The Clinical Guarantee project will consider the contribution of WIL experiences in substantive units as well as opportunities for students to participate in volunteer activities that scaffold their learning and prepare them to make the most productive use of clinic-based learning experiences. Already, a volunteer Street Law programme is being developed to provide mid-degree students with opportunities to be involved in various community education activities designed to enhance community understanding of law and legal processes. The Monash Clinical Program has lengthy experience in multidisciplinary clinic work, involving students studying social work and finance at Monash.[63] One of the objectives of the Clinical Guarantee is to deepen and broaden this multidisciplinary focus through a range of initiatives in the areas of health-justice partnerships, start-up, micro-business and small business legal services and seniors rights.

BIBLIOGRAPHY

Australian Law Reform Commission, 'Home Page' www.alrc.gov.au/ accessed 11 May 2019

Billett S, *Integrating Practice-Based Experiences into Higher Education* (Springer Netherlands 2015)

Bradley D and others, 'Review of Australian Higher Education: Final Report' (Department of Education, Employment and Workplace Relations 2008) www.voced.edu.au/content/ngv%3a32134 accessed 12 May 2019

Capital Punishment Justice Project (CJPC), 'Home Page' (2016) www.reprieve.org.au/ accessed 25 April 2019

Carter C, Spence C and Muzio D, 'Scoping an Agenda for Future Research into the Professions' (2015) 28(8) Accounting, Auditing & Accountability Journal 1198

Douglas K, 'The Teaching of ADR in Australian Law Schools: Promoting Non-Adversarial Practice in Law' (2011) 22(1) Australasian Dispute Resolution Journal 49

Eastern Innovation Business Centre, 'Home Page' https://eibc.net.au/ accessed 11 May 2019

Evans A and others, 'Best Practices Australian Clinical Legal Education' (Australian Government Office for Learning and Teaching 2013) https://ltr.edu.au/resources/pp10_1603_monash_evans_report_2013.pdf accessed 12 May 2019

Course Design for Clinical Teaching (Australian National University Press 2017)

Fink EM, 'No Money, Mo' Problems: Why Unpaid Law Firm Internships Are Illegal and Unethical' (2013) 3(Winter) University of San Francisco Law Review 435

Fisher T, Gutman J and Martens E, 'Why Teach ADR to Law Students – Part 2: An Empirical Survey' (2007) 17(2) Legal Education Review 67

Freudenberg B, Brimble M and Cameron C, 'WIL and Generic Skill Development: The Development of Business Students' Generic Skills Through Work-Integrated Learning' (2011) 12(2) Asia-Pacific Journal of Cooperative Education 79

Giddings J, *Promoting Justice through Clinical Legal Education* (Justice Press 2013)

Giddings J and McNamara M, 'Preparing Future Generations of Lawyers for Legal Practice: What's Supervision Got to Do With It?' (2014) 37(3) University of New South Wales Law Journal 1226

Givelber DJ and others, 'Learning through Work: An Empirical Study of Legal Internship' (1995) 45(1) Journal of Legal Education 1

Global Pro Bono Bar Association, 'Home Page' www.probonobar.org/ accessed 11 May 2019

Grenfell L and Koch C, 'Getting a Foot in the Door: Internships and the Legal Profession' (2018) 40(7) Bulletin 28

Hyams R, 'Multidisciplinary Clinical Legal Education: The Future of the Profession' (2012) 37(2) Alternative Law Journal 103

---

[63] Ross Hyams, 'Multidisciplinary Clinical Legal Education: The Future of the Profession' (2012) 37(2) Alternative Law Journal 103; Ross Hyams and Fay Gertner, 'Multidisciplinary Clinics – Broadening the Outlook of Clinical Learning' (2012) 17(1) International Journal of Clinical Legal Education 23.

Hyams R and Gertner F, 'Multidisciplinary Clinics – Broadening the Outlook of Clinical Learning' (2012) 17(1) International Journal of Clinical Legal Education 23

International Justice Mission, 'Home Page' www.ijm.org/ accessed 11 May 2019

Johri A, 'Engineering Knowledge in the Digital Workplace: Aligning Materiality and Sociality through Action' in Tara J Fenwick and Monika Nerland (eds.), *Reconceptualising Professional Learning: Sociomaterial Knowledges, Practices, and Responsibilities* (Routledge 2014)

Kingsford Legal Centre, 'Clinical Legal Education Guide' (Kingsford Legal Centre 2019) www .klc.unsw.edu.au/sites/klc.unsw.edu.au/files/2924 cle guide-web.pdf accessed 12 May 2019

Kronman A, *The Lost Lawyer: Failing Ideals of the Legal Profession* (Belknap Press of Harvard University Press 1993)

Macfarlane J, 'The New Advocacy: Implications for Legal Education and Teaching Practice' in Roger Burridge, Abdul Hinett, Karen Paliwala and Tracey Varnava (eds.), *Effective Learning and Teaching in Law* (Routledge 2003)

   The New Lawyer: How Settlement Is Transforming the Practice of Law (University of British Columbia Press 2008)

Mayer BS, *The Dynamics of Conflict Resolution: A Practitioner's Guide* (John Wiley & Sons 2000)

McNamara M, 'Towards Effective Supervision for the Legal Profession: A Focus on Supervised Practice' (PhD Thesis, Griffith University 2018)

Mekong Club, The 'Home Page' (2017) https://themekongclub.org/ accessed 11 May 2019

Monash University, 'Castan Centre for Human Rights Law' www.monash.edu/law/research/centres/castancentre accessed 11 May 2019

   'Focus Monash' (Monash University 2015) www.monash.edu/__data/assets/pdf_file/0004/169744/strategic-plan-print-version.pdf accessed 24 April 2019

   'Monash Innovation' (2016) www.monash.edu/research/infrastructure/platforms-pages/monash-innovation accessed 11 May 2019

   'LAW 4803: Clinical Placement' (*Unit Handbook*, 2019) www.monash.edu/pubs/2019handbooks/units/law4803.html accessed 11 May 2019

   'LAW4328: Professional Practice' (*Unit Handbook*, 2019) www.monash.edu/pubs/2019handbooks/units/law4328.html accessed 26 April 2019

   'LAW4330: Family Law Assistance Program: Professional Practice' (*Unit Handbook*, 2019) www.monash.edu/pubs/handbooks/units/law4330.html accessed 11 May 2019

Rigg D, 'Embedding Employability in Assessment: Searching for the Balance between Academic Learning and Skills Development in Law: A Case Study' (2013) 47(3) The Law Teacher 404

Russell Kennedy Lawyers, 'Home Page' www.russellkennedy.com.au/ accessed 11 May 2019

Semple N, Pearce RG and Knake RN, 'A Taxonomy of Lawyer Regulation: How Contrasting Theories of Regulation Explain the Divergent Regulatory Regimes in Australia, England and Wales, and North America' (2013) 16(2) Legal Ethics 258

Stewart A and Owens R, 'Experience or Exploitation? The Nature, Prevalence and Regulation of Unpaid Work Experience, Internships and Trial Periods in Australia' (University of Adelaide 2013) www.fairwork.gov.au/articledocuments/763/uw-complete-report.pdf.aspx accessed 12 May 2019

Stuckey R, 'Best Practices for Legal Education: A Vision and A Road Map' (Clinical Legal Education Association 2007) https://clea.wildapricot.org/resources/documents/best_practices-full.pdf accessed 28 September 2018

Sullivan W, *Work and Integrity: The Crisis and Promise of Professionalism in America* (2nd edn, Jossey Bass 2005)

Sullivan WM and others, *Educating Lawyers: Preparation for the Profession of Law* (1st edn, Jossey-Bass 2007)

Susskind R, *Tomorrow's Lawyers: An Introduction to Your Future* (1st edn, Oxford University Press 2013)

Tradelab, 'Home Page' (2019) www.tradelab.org/ accessed 4 March 2019

Victorian Department of Justice & Regulation, 'Access To Justice Review – Summary Report' (Department of Justice and Regulation 2016) https://engage.vic.gov.au/download_file/842/612 accessed 24 April 2019

'Access To Justice Review – Volume 1 – Report and Recommendations' (Department of Justice and Regulation 2016) https://engage.vic.gov.au/download_file/844/612 accessed 24 April 2019

'Access To Justice Review – Volume 2 – Report and Recommendations' (Department of Justice and Regulation 2016) https://engage.vic.gov.au/download_file/845/612 accessed 24 April 2019

Waters B, 'The Importance of Teaching Dispute Resolution in a Twenty-First-Century Law School' (2017) 51(2) The Law Teacher 227

3

Skills Swap?

Advising Technology Entrepreneurs in a Student Clinical Legal Education Programme

Ian Walden and Patrick Cahill

qLegal is a leading commercial clinical legal education programme at Queen Mary University of London in which postgraduate law students provide supervised pro bono legal advice to technology start-ups and entrepreneurs. Within qLegal, clients often present with complex data protection issues, which relate to their business or the technology that they are developing. Law students who participate in qLegal have to learn and develop skills to respond to the needs of technology entrepreneurs. This requires students to demonstrate practical client management skills, as well as familiarity with an area of law (data protection) that is in a constant state of evolution as new technologies arise. This chapter explores the relationship between the law, law students' skills development and technology entrepreneurs. In particular it focuses on the development of qLegal, its purpose and role as a clinical legal education programme. It explores the way in which qLegal offers an opportunity for knowledge transfer between entrepreneurs and aspiring lawyers. Further it examines how qLegal offers a means by which to test, expand and challenge students' understanding of the application of law in unfamiliar fact scenarios, where limited, as well as newly emerging case law, pushes students out of their comfort zone.

3.1 INTRODUCTION

Clinical legal education, 'learning by doing the types of things that lawyers do'[1] is a concept that has been enshrined in legal education in the USA for many years.[2] However, in the UK and Western Europe, legal education has historically centred on

---

[1] Hugh Brayne, Nigel Duncan and Richard H Grimes, *Clinical Legal Education: Active Learning in Your Law School* (Blackstone Press 1998) 13.

[2] William V Rowe, 'Legal Clinics and Better Trained Lawyers – A Necessity' (1916) 11(9) Illinois Law Review 591; J Wigmore, 'The Legal Clinic' (1917) 25 Illinois Law Review 35.

traditional lectures, with lecturers presenting legal concepts to students, with supplemental small-group teaching through seminars and tutorials. Institutions have therefore typically placed less emphasis on students developing important practical legal skills such as management of legal work, communicating with clients, interviewing and counselling clients, professional conduct and ethics, negotiation, litigation and practical legal research; despite these skills having been identified as fundamental to lawyering.[3] The reasons for this dearth of skills-based learning are varied, they include the influence of the 'qualifying' law degree, a determination amongst academics to maintain the distinction between legal studies and the practice of law, and institutional divisions between universities and providers of professional qualifications.[4]

Yet in recent years there has been a well-documented rise in the number of legal clinics established within educational institutions in the UK. In 1996, it was reported that only 23 per cent of 79 institutions[5] surveyed in the UK 'offered a live-client clinic'.[6] Nearly a decade later in 2005, Marson wrote that 'Few law schools within the United Kingdom (UK) university sector have integrated clinics established as legal practices that offer live client work to the student body.'[7] However, by 2018 the picture appeared very different, with the LawWorks Clinics Network[8] reporting that there were some 95 universities in the UK hosting a legal clinic or some form of clinical programme.[9]

Traditionally, university clinics in Europe have provided legal advice to individuals who do not qualify for legal aid or cannot afford a legal adviser. More often than not, these clients have nowhere else to go to receive legal advice. The advice provided by universities to these individuals, in line with the primary focus of university clinics worldwide, could be viewed as contributing to the wider objectives of upholding the rule of law and providing access to justice. In the UK, the demand for legal advice has been amplified by recent changes in legal aid provision, as implemented by the Legal

---

[3]   Brayne, Duncan and Grimes (n 1) provides a broad understanding of lawyers and their work.

[4]   The qualifying law degree contains training in the seven foundations of legal knowledge, specified by the Solicitors Regulation Authority and the Bar Standards Board.

[5]   Institutions that acquired university status since 1992 and those who retained polytechnic or collegial status. Only 5 per cent of old universities surveyed had a live client clinic at that time.

[6]   A live client clinic is defined as 'where real clients with actual problems are advised and/or represented'. This is in contrast to a simulated clinic with actors. See Richard Grimes, Joel Klaff and Colleen Smith, 'Legal Skills and Clinical Legal Education - A Survey of Undergraduate Law School Practice' (1996) 30(1) The Law Teacher 44, 64.

[7]   James Marson, Adam Wilson and Van Hoorebeek, 'The Necessity of Clinical Legal Education in University Law Schools: A UK Perspective' (2005) 7 International Journal of Clinical Legal Education 29.

[8]   LawWorks operates as part of the largest national pro bono charity in the UK and 'provide[s] a free consultancy service to guide advice agencies, law firms and law schools in developing and maintaining a legal advice clinic'. It is a charity committed to enabling access to justice through free legal advice. It promotes, encourages and supports pro bono activity across England and Wales, using its experience and understanding to ensure pro bono is targeted where it can be most effective and have the greatest impact. See further LawWorks, 'Find a Legal Advice Clinic Near You' www.lawworks.org.uk/legal-advice-individuals/find-legal-advice-clinic-near-you accessed 23 January 2019.

[9]   E-mail Correspondence between the authors and LawWorks, 18 July 2018.

Aid, Sentencing and Punishment of Offenders Act 2012. This reduction in legal aid provision has had an insurmountable negative effect on access to justice and seen a subsequent increase in demand for pro bono assistance from legal clinics.[10]

Despite the important and worthwhile social justice work of law clinics, law schools in Europe have branched out into other fields, developing law clinics for businesses, start-ups and entrepreneurs. This growth has been aided by funding from the European Commission, under the Seventh Framework Programme,[11] to the ICT Law Incubators Network (iLINC).[12] Spearheaded by the Centre for Commercial Law Studies at Queen Mary University of London (QMUL), the need for more diverse forms of pro-bono legal assistance has also been precipitated by the burgeoning business and start-up technology sector across Europe.[13] Clinics established to meet this demand for commercial law advice[14] provide an opportunity for students to put their theoretical knowledge of the law into practice, whilst obtaining a wider commercial understanding of the context in which these businesses operate. Aside from enhancing skills acquisition, these clinics are also a vital means of enhancing student employability. Whilst the skills that students learn are transferable, they are of particular relevance to those interested in practising commercial law or entering into a business-related career.

---

[10] See LawWorks, 'LawWorks Clinics Network Report: April 2016 – March 2017' (2017) www.lawworks.org.uk /about-us/news/lawworks-clinics-network-report-april-2016-march-2017 accessed 23 January 2019.

[11] Regulation (EC) No 1906/2006 of the European Parliament and of the Council of 18 December 2006 laying down the rules for the participation of undertakings, research centres and universities in actions under the Seventh Framework Programme and for the dissemination of research results [2006] OJ L 391

[12] The iLINC Network originally comprised five academic institutions, Queen Mary University of London (UK), University of Amsterdam (Netherlands), Katholieke Universiteit Leuven (Belgium), Hans Bredow Institute (Germany) and Brooklyn Law School (USA) but has some eighteen active network partners. Its main objective is to facilitate the provision of free legal support to start-ups while, at the same time, offering postgraduate law students the opportunity to engage in professional practice in the fast-moving and highly exciting world of technology start-ups. This way iLINC is helping to create both the companies and the lawyers of tomorrow. See iLINC, 'ILINC – The ICT Law Incubators Network' www.ilincnetwork.eu/ accessed 23 January 2019.

[13] The client group that receives legal advice from commercial law clinics has grown substantially in the past decade. In the UK nearly 660,000 companies were established in 2016, up from 608,000 in 2015, according to think-tank 'The Centre for Entrepreneurs', see Andy Bounds, 'Number of UK Start-Ups Rises to New Record' *The Financial Times* (London, 12 October 2017). The number of self-employed increased from 3.3 million people (12 per cent of the labour force) in 2001 to 4.8 million (15.1 per cent of the labour force) in 2017 see Office for National Statistics, 'Trends in Self-Employment in the UK' (*Office for National Statistics*, 7 February 2018) www.ons.gov.uk/employmentandlabourmarket/peo pleinwork/employmentandemployeetypes/articles/trendsinselfemploymentintheuk/2018-02-07 accessed 23 January 2019. In East London alone in 2012, there were an estimated 3,000 technology companies which employ an estimated 50,000 people (James Silver, 'East London's 20 Hottest Tech Startups' *The Guardian* (London, 8 July 2012) www.theguardian.com/uk/2012/jul/08/east-london-20-hottest-tech-companies accessed 23 January 2019).

[14] Commercial law includes intellectual property, data protection, financing, corporate transactions or other commercial focussed pathways.

One such clinic, qLegal, is based at the Centre for Commercial Law Studies, QMUL. In this chapter we focus on the establishment, development and work of the clinic. We commence by providing contextual background regarding the genesis of the clinic, before turning to examine the composition of the clinic, the work conducted and the skills students develop through participation in a range of activities.[15] We conclude by reflecting on the way in which qLegal, as an atypical form of clinical legal education, makes a contribution to the evolution of legal education and the innovation sector more broadly.

3.2 CLINICAL LEGAL EDUCATION AT QLEGAL

3.2.1 *Context*

QMUL has a long tradition of clinical legal education, having founded a social justice focused Legal Advice Centre in 2006 within the Department of Law, before going on to found qLegal in 2013 within the Centre for Commercial Law Studies.[16] The Centre for Commercial Law Studies was established in 1980 and specialises in teaching commercial law to postgraduate law students, primarily through its LLM programme, with students coming from over eighty countries.[17] qLegal was established to offer these postgraduate students the opportunity to provide free legal advice to technology start-ups and entrepreneurs, the majority of which are based in Tech City, around Shoreditch and the 'Silicon Roundabout'.[18] The proximity of the University to this area, combined with the need for free legal advice for early stage start-ups (as recognised by the European Commission) were catalysts for founding the clinic.

The type of client that can obtain advice from qLegal is based on thresholds contingent upon the start up's level of development and revenue. This allows us to focus on providing assistance to those most in need, as well as (rather more pragmatically) helping ensure that we meet our insurance requirements. The scope of legal advice provided by qLegal links to the modules taught on various postgraduate programmes at the Centre for Commercial Law Studies (discussed further below in Section 3.2.2). This provides students with an opportunity to advise clients on legal issues that closely align with their theoretical knowledge and studies.

Initially students participated in qLegal as an extracurricular activity, this enabled them to show commitment to the activity and distinguish it from their academic

---

[15] For other examples of commercial law clinics see Elaine Campbell, 'Recognizing the Social and Economic Value of Transactional Law Clinics: A View from the United Kingdom' (2016) 65(3) Journal of Legal Education 580.

[16] QMUL School of Law, 'Legal Advice Centre' www.lac.qmul.ac.uk/ accessed 2 November 2018.

[17] Queen Mary University of London (QMUL), 'Centre for Commercial Law Studies' www.qmul.ac.uk /ccls/ accessed 23 January 2019.

[18] A term used to describe the East London hub in which there are many co-working spaces, accelerators, office space and technology companies, particularly at an early stage of the business cycle.

qualifications.[19] However, with the burgeoning interest in clinical legal education as an academic discipline, as well as demand from students, qLegal has recently transitioned to a credit-bearing module on QMUL's LLM programme.[20] Students now have a choice between participating in the programme as an extracurricular activity or as a credit-bearing module.

3.2.2 *The qLegal Model*

For the extracurricular version of qLegal, thirty-six postgraduate students are selected from an online application form to participate in all three strands of the clinic's services: Advice,[21] Small Print Workshops[22] and Media Items.[23] The application form does not ask for academic results and instead students are selected for the clinic using a marking criterion which focuses on six main areas: motivation, teamwork, qualities of the role, independent thought, drafting and spelling, punctuation, grammar, tone and sentence structure.[24] Once selected, students attend a training session which provides an induction to the clinic and students are also required to participate in a number of sessions which are designed to build students' legal skills so as to equip them for the work that they will undertake.[25]

In addition to the extracurricular model of delivery, qLegal selects a further twelve students to work with the clinic as part of a credit-bearing 'Entrepreneurship Law Clinic' module. As part of the module, students advise start-ups and entrepreneurs through written advice, workshops and media items. Students also attend weekly classes with the qLegal Director and visiting lawyers from partner law firms and technology companies. The classes focus on helping students develop legal skills, including: drafting, research, interviewing, presenting, teamwork and approaching

---

[19] QMUL qLegal, 'QLegal – Student Area' www.qlegal.qmul.ac.uk/students/ accessed 23 January 2019.

[20] QMUL School of Law, 'Entrepreneurship Law Clinic' www.law.qmul.ac.uk/postgraduate/courses/ modules/llm/items/qllm407-entrepreneurship-law-clinic.html accessed 2 November 2018.

[21] Clients come to qLegal for advice on a range of issues including patent, trademark, commercial and corporate advice. Students have the opportunity to counsel clients with a partner, supervised by a qualified lawyer, and then research and draft advice.

[22] This is public legal education or Streetlaw. Students work in a group to help draft a workshop on a specific area of law, which they present to an audience of tech start-ups and entrepreneurs. Students are trained on public speaking, receive feedback on their performance and their work is supervised remotely by a qualified lawyer. Student groups may present on intellectual property, commercial or company law.

[23] Students work in a group on media items, which are uploaded to the qLegal website so tech start-ups and entrepreneurs can access it. Students are supervised remotely by a qualified lawyer or by the qLegal team. Student groups may write a news article on smart cities, produce a podcast on law tech start-ups or update the qLegal resources.

[24] See Queen Mary University of London (QMUL), 'Application Marking Criteria' www .qlegal.qmul.ac.uk/students/ accessed 23 January 2019.

[25] qLegal training includes interviewing, drafting, corporate structure, intellectual property, introduction to a shareholder agreement, data protection, practical law training, research, public speaking, overview of legal issues faced by start-ups and industry training from lawyers.

a case through problem-based learning. The module is legal practice focused, although previous practical legal experience is not required of the students. The module is set in the wider context of the development of the European start-up ecosystem and includes an exchange visit with students at the University of Amsterdam start-up law clinic.[26]

Throughout the module, students approach a number of practical legal and ethical issues and counsel and manage the cases of clients in the technology sector. The learning outcomes are specific to each class and are very closely related to student assessment tasks and the work conducted for clients. The mode of assessment reflects the multitude of skills being taught through the module and includes a 3,750-word essay (50 per cent), an assessed group viva (discussion) on clinic work (40 per cent) and two client files (10 per cent). The split of assessment relates to university requirements and the fact that the client file work that students undertake is externally supervised. The group viva includes questions that relate to client files, with which students must be familiar.

3.2.3 *Work Conducted*

Students undertake a range of work during their engagement with qLegal and activities are centred around the provision of written advice, small printed workshops and the creation of media (or 'public legal education') items.

3.2.3.1 Written Advice

Students work in pairs and are supervised by the qLegal Director and external counsel from participating law firms, patent and trademark firms and in-house teams.[27] External counsel are specialists in data protection, regulatory, technology, commercial and corporate law. Clients are booked in for an appointment, and students and supervisors receive a client case summary in advance of their appointment that summarises the client details and provides a brief overview of the case and the objectives of the client. Students then prepare questions for the client interview based on the case summary provided. The supervisors and students meet for fifteen minutes before the appointment to discuss their interview questions and the format of the appointment. The client appointment lasts around forty-five minutes, during which time the students lead questioning, with supervisors clarifying any particular questions at the end of the interview.

---

[26]   CLINIC at University of Amsterdam was established as part of the iLINC Network. See Clinic Law Incubator, 'Juridische Helpdesk Voor Media-, IE-, IT- En Privacyrecht' www.clinic.nl/ accessed 23 January 2019.

[27]   qLegal is staffed by a professor (academic lead), a director (solicitor) and coordinator. It is supported by a number of law firms and patent and trademark attorneys.

Students do not provide any form of legal advice to the client during the course of the interview; instead, a post-interview meeting between the students and supervisors takes place after the appointment so as to prepare students to draft a client's advice. Students then have twenty-one days to draft an advice letter outlining the client's legal issue/s and the steps that the client should take in order to resolve their legal issue/s. This note of advice is then reviewed and approved by the supervisor and qLegal Director, and legal advice is provided only in written form and not orally. The period of time in between the interview and the delivery of the advice gives students the opportunity to form a team, clarify outstanding questions, undertake research, build rapport with their supervisor and gain confidence with the legal problem, as well as develop the skills used in drafting written advice. An example of how this process operates and the client's impression of this process is detailed in Figure 3.1 below, which outlines qLegal's work in relation to the client 'Immersive Rehab'.

3.2.3.2 'Small Print' Workshops

Students work in teams of four in preparing workshops that are facilitated internally at the university and externally with qLegal partners.[28] Students are provided with workshop outlines based on topics that have arisen from requests received from clients and other sources, such as 'The Patent Process in the UK and EU: From Invention to Protection', 'Setting Up a Business in the UK: The Legal Essentials' and 'Law for Start-ups/Navigating the Maze: Law and Funding for Start-Ups'. The workshop outlines provide suggestions for the content of the workshop, layout, title, time, date and location of the workshops and deadlines. Through their participation, students engage in knowledge creation and dissemination, as well as learning associated organisational skills. The completed draft workshops are sent to the students' supervisor and reviewed remotely. Telephone meetings are used to cover any points raised by the supervisor. The benefit of remote supervision is that dual qualified supervisors from outside of the UK can supervise students, and students benefit from learning how to communicate professionally via different electronic methods.

Once the workshop content is reviewed and agreed with a supervisor, students practise the workshop with the qLegal team over a number of days, focusing on public speaking and presentation skills. Students then deliver their workshop to an audience of start-ups who hear about workshops through social media, qLegal workshop hosts (university entrepreneurship programmes, accelerators and incubators), word of mouth and the qLegal mailing list and newsletter. If there are questions from attendees after the workshop, the students can answer these directly (if they have the requisite knowledge) or refer them for a client appointment.

---

[28] Morrison & Foerster LLP, Hewlett-Packard Company (HP), Ropes & Gray LLP, Orbrys and Kilburn & Strode LLP.

Immersive Rehab was introduced to qLegal by one of the qLegal student advisers. Immersive Rehab develops interactive games in virtual reality, with the games aiding a patient's physical rehabilitation by providing an accessible solution to people who have neurological limitations.

Immersive Rehab came to qLegal for advice on whether they would constitute a data controller under the legal meaning of the term. Two qLegal advisers and a supervising lawyer worked with the client to assess whether the business was responsible for the data that providers generate through use of the product and the purposes for which the data was used. The advisers undertook a forty-five-minute fact finding interview with the client and asked further questions by e-mail.

After researching and drafting a letter of advice, they advised Immersive Rehab to make it clear, in the terms and conditions and privacy policy (signed by their providers), that the client is not the data controller, or data processor of data if the client does not record or process data. The letter also detailed the distinction between 'personal' and 'sensitive data' in order to convey for the client's business and providers, the different legal implications associated with different data types. The letter also detailed that if the client wanted their own customers to be able to access their own data directly through the client's app, the client would need to assess whether they had assumed the role of data controller. The letter concluded that the criteria to determine whether the client could be considered a data controller would turn on whether the client was responsible for deciding the means and purposes for which the information is processed.

In response to the advice provided, a representative from Immersive Rehab commented that 'Everything was very well written, and I plan on going back to consulting the letter from time to time, when facing any issues again. I really appreciate all the attention from qLegal and would definitely recommend your services to any start-ups, as a good source of quick, easy and accessible professional legal advice.'

3.2 QLEGAL WORKSHOP ON DATA PROTECTION FOR EHEALTH SMALL-MEDIUM ENTERPRISES (SMES)

European eHealth business support.

qLegal hosted a workshop at the eHealth Summer University, Castres, France on 'How to secure an e-health App relating to personal data? What are the rules to comply with?'

This talk introduced participants to the new online data and privacy landscape and explored how European data protection laws impact the collection and processing of data. qLegal advisers provided a detailed understanding of how to adhere to data protection standards whilst maintaining a start-up's commercial goals. Material included: an overview of the European data protection and online privacy standards, compliance requirements, fines, current and most common data protection mistakes and unfit privacy practices, and what start-ups should do in order to protect their current or potential business.

3.2.3.3 Media Items

Media items encompass the range of different methods of online advice provided by students, including toolkits, news articles, podcasts, videos and partner profiles. These are produced by students and then uploaded to the qLegal website. Given the volume of enquiries that qLegal receives, media items serve as a method of triaging these enquiries from potential clients, as well as fulfilling a public legal education function. For example, if a client makes an enquiry in relation to general intellectual property rights, they would be directed to the qLegal website to read the Intellectual Property Rights Toolkit. Other toolkits cover topics such as confidentiality, licensing intellectual property, patents, trademarks and UK company structure.

Students work in teams to prepare media items and are provided with a clear outline and suggestions for content in advance. The qLegal supervisory team supports them throughout this process. If the media item has a legal focus, the teams of students send their draft to a supervisor and over an agreed time the students and supervisor work to amend the draft until the media item is approved and published.

As a result, media item activities give students the opportunity to develop their research and drafting skills over a longer period of time and without the pressure of client deadlines. Media items also ensure that students are familiar with applying the law in a practical context, and encouraged to refine content so that it is clear, accessible, understandable and precise.

3.2.4 *Skill Development: Advising Technology Entrepreneurs*

Whilst the activities undertaken by students as part of their qLegal work are intended to build a wide range of skills, the strength of qLegal as a pedagogical model is in its capacity to support students to provide legal advice. The 'real-life' provision of legal advice fosters the attainment of two interconnected educational outcomes: (i) acquisition of the skills required to interact with a client, from initial contact to the provision of advice; and (ii) acquisition of knowledge about the legal issues that the client is seeking input on. These two domains are closely related, not least because the ability to interact with a client when initially approached and to discern what sort of advice that client is actually seeking, requires a base level of legal knowledge. However, it also requires the ability to communicate, empathise and anticipate client needs. The client may not be clear or may not understand exactly what sort of advice they need, with requests often containing a range of issues jumbled together, including many non-law related concerns. This reflects the existing empirical evidence, which indicates that the public tends to misunderstand the application of their rights and the law, and do not necessarily recognise legal problems as 'legal' issues.[29]

It is the task of qLegal staff to sift through a request to identify the distinct issues of concern, identifying matters that qLegal are capable of providing advice on and those for which it is not the appropriate advice provider. For those latter issues, qLegal attempts to signpost the requestor of advice to other potential sources of assistance or to other services. Having identified the distinct issues requiring advice, a decision may need to be made about the number of sessions that the client can be offered. Given limited resources and the desire to offer services to as many clients as possible, some clients may have to be told that qLegal is only able to advise on one or two of the range of issues that may have been raised.

Managing this process and the expectations of the client can be challenging. To this end, qLegal staff members and supervisors provide training to assist students to recognise when a client is asking questions outside of the agreed client summary document (available in each client file). The summary document provides an

---

[29]   See, e.g., Nigel J Balmer and others, 'Knowledge, Capability and the Experience of Rights Problems' (PLENET 2010); Pascoe Pleasence, Nigel J Balmer and Catrina Denvir, 'Wrong About Rights: Public Knowledge of Key Areas of Consumer, Housing and Employment Law in England and Wales' (2017) 80 (5) Modern Law Review 836.

overview of the client's business, their aims and objectives, as well as the legal issue/s that students can assist with. Students and supervisors are instructed to hand out a qLegal business card if other issues arise and a staff member can then provide further support to the client in identifying their next steps, with regard to additional issues.

In terms of the legal issues encountered by start-ups and entrepreneurs, a wide variety of matters may arise, although given the commercial focus, there tends to be less diversity than that likely to be experienced in a social justice advice environment. Since qLegal was established, there remain four key areas of law on which advice is sought, these include intellectual property, business structure, contracts and data protection.

Intellectual property issues range from non-disclosure agreements, designed to protect clients when discussing their ideas with others, to understanding the different forms of legal protection available (e.g. trade mark, patent and copyright) and how to obtain those that require some formal process to acquire (e.g. registration), as well as avoiding infringements of the intellectual property rights of others.[30] Queries in relation to business structure often emerge from the need to formalise relationships between the various friends, family and co-workers that have supported the client and the start-up during the early stages of development. This requires a client to decide between embarking on those agreements as a company, sole trader or partnership.[31] Contract matters tend to focus on the drafting of or agreement to standard terms and the validity of these terms and conditions in light of existing consumer protection rules. Whilst data protection matters are increasingly critical to the work of qLegal, and queries emerging in this context often relate to the extent to which start-ups can use personal data of users, and the requirements governing use as laid down by domestic law and EU Community law (including the EU General Data Protection Regulations (GDPR) which have recently entered into force).[32]

As law postgraduates, most qLegal students will have had some level of exposure to these areas of law during their undergraduate studies. However, because they are postgraduate students, qLegal advisers may be specialising in different areas of commercial law, or have experience in a foreign jurisdiction where the rules and laws differ. As such, each adviser has to obtain relevant knowledge in the course of advising a client. Advisers are expected to carry out preliminary legal research in order to produce a series of pertinent questions to ask the client during interview.

---

[30] Free and open source software is a particular area of risk, as clients tend to consider that such software can be freely used, which is not the case. See Noam Shemtov and Ian Walden (eds.), *Free and Open Source Software: Policy, Law, and Practice* (Oxford University Press 2013).

[31] See QMUL qLegal, 'UK Company Structure' www.qlegal.qmul.ac.uk/resources/ accessed 23 January 2019.

[32] Regulation (EU) 2016/679 of the European Parliament and of the Council of 27 April 2016 on the protection of natural persons with regard to the processing of personal data and on the free movement of such data, and repealing Directive 95/46/EC (General Data Protection Regulation – GDPR) [2007] OJ L 119/1.

Prior to the interview the supervising solicitor reviews the questions to confirm that the relevant issues have been covered. Following the interview, the supervising solicitor discusses the outcome of the meeting and the proposed structure of the advice. Over the next days, the students continue to research the topic and write the draft advice for review and approval by the supervising solicitor.

While students will generally have studied contract, corporate law and intellectual property law previously, the area where students often have little experience is that of data protection. Although the UK has had data protection law since 1984, this area of law has become increasingly important, as the digital economy has developed. Personal data has become the 'oil of the digital era',[33] underpinning the giants of the Internet economy, especially the likes of Google, Facebook and Amazon. In keeping with this trend, a great many of the business ideas brought to qLegal involve the collection and use of personal data, and clients often approach data collection with the view that the more data they can collect, the better. Personal data is also relevant when seeking business investment. Traditionally, the key issue for a potential corporate investor would have been ownership of the underlying intangible assets via the operation of intellectual property laws. However, as personal data has become increasingly valued, investors are differentiating between potential investments based on the scope of data a start-up might feasibly collect, and the extent to which that collection is compliant with data protection law.

In response to the increasing use and abuse of personal data, legislators have recently extended the scope of data protection law, enhancing the rights of data subjects, increasing the obligations of controllers and strengthening the enforcement regime. In May 2018, the GDPR came into force across the EU with maximum fines of 4 per cent of total worldwide annual turnover or €20 million.[34] While qLegal clients would not be exposed to penalties of that scale, the importance of data protection law has risen proportionally. In order to fulfil their obligations, qLegal advisers must get to grips with this (often rapidly changing) area of law, however data protection law generates challenges for student advisers that differ from the issues raised in other areas of law.

In providing advice, first students have to analyse the nature of the conduct being carried out by the business to determine whether it is acting as a 'controller', 'joint controller' or 'processor' in respect of the personal data being processed. Having determined the client's status, advisers must consider the direct implications for the contractual relationships between the client and his suppliers (as potential processors) and customers (as data subjects), as well as the way in which the business interacts and communicates with its customers (e.g. website cookies). They must then consider compliance obligations, such as the principle of data minimisation

---

[33]   The Economist, 'The World's Most Valuable Resource Is No Longer Oil, but Data' *The Economist* (6 May 2017) www.economist.com/leaders/2017/05/06/the-worlds-most-valuable-resource-is-no-longer -oil-but-data accessed 23 January 2019.

[34]   General Data Protection Regulation, art 83(5).

and data protection by design and default. This can have a direct impact on how the product or service is developed given that trying to retrofit compliance can have extensive resource implications.

These tasks have to be undertaken with reference to the provisions in the legislation itself, as well as the interpretive guidance issued by the supervisory authority, which in this case is the Information Commissioner (ICO).[35] Guidance is also framed by a degree of uncertainty, since the risk-based approach to data protection compliance means that a client has to assess and evaluate the risks for each processing activity they perform and amend practices and procedures accordingly.[36] The client therefore has a degree of flexibility and discretion when making determinations as to the level of risk and what measures it should take to meet its compliance obligations, which introduces a degree of ambiguity into the process. Taken as a whole, data protection represents a substantial compliance burden for many start-ups and entrepreneurs, as well as a complex area of law for student advisers to get to grips with.

A further challenge for student advisers is obtaining an adequate understanding of the environment within which the client is operating, particularly in respect of the technologies and services the client is using as this has clear implications for the provision of legal advice. In terms of environment, the complex and layered ecosystem in which a start-up may be situated has to be carefully mapped out for the benefit of the advisers as well as the client. For example, the client may operate from a website or eCommerce platform hosted by a service provider but may not be aware of where data is geographically located; an issue which has important implications under both intellectual property and data protection law.[37] Clients will also often use acronyms or terms of art unfamiliar to students, meaning that students have to research both the legal issues and the associated technologies involved.

3.3 THE CONTRIBUTION QLEGAL MAKES TO LEGAL EDUCATION

Since its inception in 2013, qLegal has almost doubled the number of places offered on its programmes, from thirty-six students in the first year, to over sixty by 2018–19 (including postgraduate students studying at QMUL in Paris). Student interest in the programme is reflected in the increase in student applications each year and in 2017 we received over 260 student applications in respect of fifty-four places. In response to this growth, qLegal has recruited a full-time coordinator and two part-time administrators to support the programmes.

---

[35] Information Commissioner's Office, 'Home' https://ico.org.uk/ accessed 23 January 2019.
[36] The term 'risk' is used seventy-five times in the GDPR, sometimes qualified by other terms: 'significant', 'serious', 'high', 'immediate' or 'increased'. The primary threshold in the substantive provisions are those processing activities that are considered to result in 'high risk' to the rights and freedoms of data subjects.
[37] Under Intellectual Property law, a licence may be restricted to use in a certain territory; while under the GDPR, controls are placed on the flow of personal data outside of the European Economic Area.

Knowledge of qLegal and the opportunities it offers has often been cited by students in their initial applications and end-of-year testimonials, and for some qLegal actually led them to study at QMUL. Through participating in qLegal, student advisers gain a deeper understanding of start-ups' legal issues and grow their commercial awareness, most notably through client interviews and internships, where they work closely with practising lawyers. Students appreciate the opportunity to learn about different career paths (e.g. private practice and in-house) and the varieties of legal practice. Exposure to a diverse range of cases, supervisors and clients also help qLegal students decide whether they want to practise law and if so, what area of law they might wish to pursue.

Former students have described the way in which their experience at qLegal has impacted their educational experience and professional pathway. Many students describe how their participation in qLegal has advanced their graduate job search, and how their experience has generated great interest from interviewers. Several students have also found that their qLegal work with particular start-ups has led to ongoing employment with that start-up. Whilst most qLegal students do complete the process of becoming a lawyer and, or, return to practice in their home countries, their proximity to early stage businesses broadens their perspectives as to the range of possible careers that they could pursue.

qLegal has received funding from a variety of sources, including the Legal Education Foundation (LEF), the Higher Education Innovation Fund (HEIF), public engagement funding from QMUL, as well as the European Commission under the FP7 (i.e. iLINC project) Horizon 2020 frameworks (i.e. eHealth Hub). The qLegal initiative has had a significant impact on the university itself in terms of widening participation, promoting student entrepreneurship and facilitating local community engagement. It has also operated to promote the development of commercial clinical legal initiatives across the higher education sector, and strengthened emerging networks in the UK through activities such as hosting of the first national commercial law clinic roundtable in 2017.[38]

3.4 CONCLUDING REMARKS

qLegal was established to provide postgraduate students with a broad clinical legal education experience, one that reflects the skills used in professional practice and the experiences faced by practitioners day-to-day. The approach taken by qLegal in providing opportunities for students to advise through different models, one-to-one and one-to-many, is a valuable learning opportunity for students to understand the process of advising different audiences. This approach is also helpful for the technology companies as recipients of advice, who may be at different stages of development and require differing types of digestible advice.

[38] Followed by Sheffield University in 2018 and Manchester University in 2019.

qLegal advocates and delivers opportunities for students to fail, learn, develop and grow. This includes harnessing students' skills, strengths, weaknesses and interests. These may cover a combination of presenting in public, networking, marketing, research, coding, public relations, drafting, teamwork, professional skills or commercial awareness. As highlighted in this chapter, the types of legal issues faced by start-ups and entrepreneurs, especially data protection compliance, add another layer of challenge and opportunity for students to learn and enhance their future employment prospects.

Since qLegal was founded in 2013, it has not only developed an effective service for clients and a unique learning experience for students, but it has also been involved in helping other universities develop similar schemes. Through the iLINC network, qLegal has shared lessons with similar clinics in Europe and the USA, fostering an international network that we expect will provide many more opportunities for skill swaps between future lawyers and those building the technologies of the future.

BIBLIOGRAPHY

Balmer NJ and others, 'Knowledge, Capability and the Experience of Rights Problems' (PLENET 2010)
Bounds A, 'Number of UK Start-Ups Rises to New Record' *The Financial Times* (London, 12 October 2017) www.ft.com/content/cb56d86c-88d6-11e7-afd2-74b8ecd34d3b accessed 16 January 2019
Brayne H, Duncan N and Grimes RH, *Clinical Legal Education: Active Learning in Your Law School* (Blackstone Press 1998)
Campbell E, 'Recognizing the Social and Economic Value of Transactional Law Clinics: A View from the United Kingdom' (2016) 65(3) Journal of Legal Education 580
Clinic Law Incubator, 'Juridische Helpdesk Voor Media-, IE-, IT- En Privacyrecht' www.clinic.nl/ accessed 23 January 2019
Grimes R, Klaff J and Smith C, 'Legal Skills and Clinical Legal Education - A Survey of Undergraduate Law School Practice' (1996) 30(1) The Law Teacher 44
iLINC, 'ILINC – The ICT Law Incubators Network' www.ilincnetwork.eu/ accessed 23 January 2019
Information Commissioner's Office, 'Home' https://ico.org.uk/ accessed 23 January 2019
LawWorks, 'Find a Legal Advice Clinic Near You' www.lawworks.org.uk/legal-advice-individuals/find-legal-advice-clinic-near-you accessed 23 January 2019
'LawWorks Clinics Network Report: April 2016 – March 2017' (2017) www.lawworks.org.uk/about-us/news/lawworks-clinics-network-report-april-2016-march-2017 accessed 23 January 2019
Marson J, Wilson A and Van Hoorebeek, 'The Necessity of Clinical Legal Education in University Law Schools: A UK Perspective' (2005) 7 International Journal of Clinical Legal Education 29
Office for National Statistics, 'Trends in Self-Employment in the UK' (*Office for National Statistics*, 7 February 2018) www.ons.gov.uk/employmentandlabourmarket/peopleinwork/employmentandemployeetypes/articles/trendsinselfemploymentintheuk/2018-02-07 accessed 23 January 2019

Pleasence P, Balmer NJ and Denvir C, 'Wrong About Rights: Public Knowledge of Key Areas of Consumer, Housing and Employment Law in England and Wales' (2017) 80(5) Modern Law Review 836

QMUL qLegal, 'QLegal – Student Area' www.qlegal.qmul.ac.uk/students/ accessed 23 January 2019

'UK Company Structure' www.qlegal.qmul.ac.uk/resources/ accessed 23 January 2019

QMUL School of Law, 'Entrepreneurship Law Clinic' www.law.qmul.ac.uk/postgraduate/courses/modules/llm/items/qllm407-entrepreneurship-law-clinic.html accessed 2 November 2018

'Legal Advice Centre' www.lac.qmul.ac.uk/ accessed 2 November 2018

Queen Mary University of London (QMUL), 'Application Marking Criteria' www.qlegal.qmul.ac.uk/students/ accessed 23 January 2019

'Centre for Commercial Law Studies' www.qmul.ac.uk/ccls/ accessed 23 January 2019

Regulation (EC) No 191906/2006 of the European Parliament and of the Council of 18 December 2006 laying down the rules for the participation of undertakings, research centres and universities in actions under the Seventh Framework Programme and for the dissemination of research results [2006] OJ L 391

Regulation (EU) 2016/679 of the European Parliament and of the Council of 27 April 2016 on the protection of natural persons with regard to the processing of personal data and on the free movement of such data, and repealing Directive 95/46/EC (General Data Protection Regulation – GDPR) [2007] OJ L 119/1

Rowe WV, 'Legal Clinics and Better Trained Lawyers – A Necessity' (1916) 11(9) Illinois Law Review 591

Shemtov N and Walden I (eds.), *Free and Open Source Software: Policy, Law, and Practice* (Oxford University Press 2013)

Silver J, 'East London's 20 Hottest Tech Startups' *The Guardian* (London, 8 July 2012) www.theguardian.com/uk/2012/jul/08/east-london-20-hottest-tech-companies accessed 23 January 2019

The Economist, 'The World's Most Valuable Resource Is No Longer Oil, but Data' *The Economist* (6 May 2017) www.economist.com/leaders/2017/05/06/the-worlds-most-valuable-resource-is-no-longer-oil-but-data accessed 23 January 2019

Wigmore J, 'The Legal Clinic' (1917) 25 Illinois Law Review 35

4

Scaling the Gap

Legal Education and Data Literacy

Catrina Denvir

Over the last decade artificial intelligence (AI), in the form of data-driven tools designed to support legal task completion, has occupied a growing position within the field of law. As a result, the capacity to use particular forms of word processing software, navigate the Internet or send electronic correspondence is no longer enough. Modern forms of literacy demand a user exhibits a broader range of skills, including the ability to understand, apply, visualise and infer patterns from data. This chapter considers the range of current initiatives developed to address the technology skills and awareness gap amongst law students, and identifies the subject areas that ought to take priority in future curriculum development. It argues that exposure to data analysis and data-driven technologies represents a necessary component of students' preparation for entry into the professions on the basis that this knowledge: (i) enhances student employability in an increasingly competitive graduate job market; and (ii) equips graduates to meet their wider civic responsibilities to uphold the rule of law and promote access to justice.

4.1 INTRODUCTION

Over the last decade artificial intelligence (AI) in the form of data-driven tools designed to support legal task completion, has occupied a growing position within the delivery of private legal services and the exercise of administrative functions by the public sector.[1] As a result, whilst technological literacy was once understood as the capacity to use particular forms of word processing software, navigate the Internet or send electronic correspondence, modern forms of literacy demand a user exhibits a broader range of skills, including the ability to understand, apply, visualise and infer patterns from data.

---

[1] See, e.g., Daniel M Katz, 'Quantitative Legal Prediction – or – How I Learned to Stop Worrying and Start Preparing for the Data Driven Future of the Legal Services Industry' (2013) 62 Emory Law Journal 909.

Although lawyers have been said to possess an unflagging confidence in their ability to get to grips with a wide variety of subject matter,[2] technology, specifically those forms of technology which employ data-driven analytical methods, presents one area where a lack of foundational training is problematic. This is not just because the analytical process employed by data-driven methodologies contrasts so strikingly with the methods of analysis and inference taught in law school. It is also because a lack of knowledge in this domain constitutes a serious deficiency in an individual's ability to evaluate the impact and efficacy of these tools within legal practice and across society more generally.

This chapter makes a case for the incorporation of these modern technological literacy skills within legal education. It commences by considering the role of the lawyer and the way in which technology and data analysis has come to influence this role. Second, it identifies the potential impact arising from a failure to address the aforementioned skills deficiency. In doing so, it looks at impact with reference to issues of graduate employability as well as the broader societal implications at play. Finally, it considers the range of current initiatives developed to address the data literacy gap amongst law students, and identifies the subject areas that ought to take priority in future curriculum development. It argues that exposure to the process, potential and pitfalls of data analysis and data-driven decision-making systems, not only represents a necessary component of students' preparation for entry into the professions, it also equips students to fulfil their wider civic obligations to uphold the rule of law and promote access to justice.

4.2 TECHNOLOGY AND THE WORK OF THE LAWYER

For over five decades researchers have attempted to apply techniques from the field of AI to the practice of law and the process of legal decision-making.[3] Expert systems have regularly featured in research and scholarship since the 1980s, whilst neural networks have been developed for law since the 1990s. Throughout this period, interest in the field has not remained consistent: peaks and troughs have followed broader societal trends.[4] In line with these trends, at various points during this period

---

[2] Richard Susskind, *Tomorrow's Lawyers: An Introduction to Your Future* (1st edn, Oxford University Press 2013) 72.

[3] See, e.g., Graham Greenleaf, 'Legal Expert Systems — Robot Lawyers? An Introduction to Knowledge-Based Applications to Law' (Australian Legal Convention, Sydney, August 1989) www2 .austlii.edu.au/cal/papers/robots89/ accessed 29 May 2018; Kevin Ashley and others, 'Legal Reasoning and Artificial Intelligence: How Computers Think Like Lawyers' (2001) 8(1) The University of Chicago Law School Roundtable Article 2 http://chicagounbound.uchicago.edu/roundtable/vol8/iss1/2 accessed 29 May 2018; Philip Leith, 'The Application of AI to Law' (1988) 2(1) AI & Society 31.

[4] See Philip Leith, 'Fundamental Errors in Legal Logic Programming' (1986) 29(6) The Computer Journal 545; Leith, 'The Application of AI to Law' (n 3); Philip Leith, 'Correspondence: The Emperor's New Expert System' (1987) 50(128) Modern Law Review 128; Antonis C Kakas and Fariba Sadri (eds.), *Computational Logic: Logic Programming and Beyond: Essays in Honour of Robert A Kowalski* (1st edn, Springer-Verlag 2002); Greenleaf (n 3).

there has been a push for legal educators to consider the role that technology and AI should play as a subject of focus within the legal curriculum. This has included calls for law, technology and society to occupy a larger position within the overall law degree;[5] insistence that the 'segmented and ad hoc approach to the use of computers in law teaching' must be replaced with a 'full program [designed to] integrate computers fully into the learning and teaching activities of the faculty';[6] and regular support for broader coverage of technology, including the development of skills to enable the organisation and manipulation of data.[7]

Notwithstanding these calls, the prospect of including coverage of technology within the legal curriculum does not hold universal appeal. Throughout modern legal education a debate has persisted between those who believe law schools should be teaching students the full range of skills they will need in practice, and those who believe educators should focus on the instruction of the substance of the law and its doctrinal and critical analysis.[8] For some this is an issue of roles and responsibility, with teaching applied skills considered a vocational matter. For others, resistance to greater interdisciplinary interaction may reside in the belief that law should be studied internally as a 'pure system . . . unrelated to other social systems',[9] including that of technology.

Whilst the effort to maintain a distinction between the academic and vocational study of law has sustained the existence of an academic profession, the extent to which the status quo serves the interests of students is less clear. As Schultz has observed, 'Few seem to recognize that we cannot really teach students how lawyers think without teaching them at the same time what lawyers do.'[10] This, according to Schultz, involves: (1) dealing with uncertainty in a wide variety of situations on behalf of a wide range of stakeholders; and (2) public service in the form of assisting and representing individuals in order to secure justice under the law.[11]

For those familiar with the propensity of technology to succumb to reoccurring 'hype cycles',[12] the recent surge of support exhibited in favour of a renewed focus on technology within legal education,[13] may be easily dismissed as a passing fad. For

---

[5] Robert S Redmount, 'The Future of Legal Education: Perspective and Prescription' (1985) 30(3) New York Law School Law Review 561, 575.

[6] RP Jones and J Van Wyk, 'Computers in Legal Education' (1989) 4(1) International Review of Law, Computers & Technology 1, 2.

[7] Mark Levin, 'Legal Education for the Next Generation: Ideas from America' (2000) 3(1) Asian-Pacific Law & Policy Journal 1, 17.

[8] Nancy L Schultz, 'How Do Lawyers Really Think?' (1992) 42(1) Journal of Legal Education 57.

[9] Werner Schäfke, Juan A Mayoral Díaz-Asensio and Martine Stagelund Hvidt, 'Socialisation to Interdisciplinary Legal Education: An Empirical Assessment' (2018) 52(3) Law Teacher 273, 274.

[10] Schultz (n 8) 57.

[11] Schultz frames these as three roles, separating out 'assistance' and 'representation' but for the purposes of brevity these separate roles have been combined under (2). See Schultz (n 8).

[12] Gartner, 'Gartner's 2016 Hype Cycle for Emerging Technologies' (16 August 2016) www.gartner.com /newsroom/id/3412017 accessed 1 July 2017.

[13] Nick Holborne, 'University Pioneers Legal Tech Course for Law Degree Students' (*Legal Futures*, 7 June 2018) www.legalfutures.co.uk/latest-news/university-pioneers-legal-tech-course-for-law-degree-

others, the way in which technology has weaved itself into the fabric of everyday life to become indistinguishable from it, means that neither of the functions Schultz describes can be divorced from its influence.[14] This becomes clear when considering the role of the lawyer and the extent to which technology has shaped this role.

4.2.1 Managing Uncertainty

The changing nature of legal practice has led to the increased use of technology to overcome and quantify ambiguity, and to manage its associated risks. If 'risk is uncertainty about the outcome', then it follows that the more (quality) data you have the greater your ability to predict the relative likelihood of a particular outcome.[15] In transactional contexts, a lawyer operates to mitigate risk by procuring for a client as much information as is possible to inform a particular decision (e.g. agreeing to the terms of a particular deal). Risk is also lowered by using standardised forms and drafting documents, which 'might be thought of as elaborately tailored insurance policies listing the various adverse contingencies that conceivably might arise should the deal "go wrong", defining these events precisely, specifying security arrangements, and stipulating what expediting or remedial actions should be taken'.[16] In the advisory context, efforts to handle uncertainty may involve canvassing risks that arise in the legal and the business operations environment. In a regulatory context it might involve preemptive auditing and developing compliance policies so as to safeguard against the risk of being unprepared for the occurrence of external audits. Whilst in the litigation context, managing uncertainty may involve assessing the likelihood of success at court vis-à-vis benefit, and gathering information via the discovery process to enhance material advantage.

Across all of these activities, lawyers have always dealt with large amounts of information, yet it is only relatively recently that much of this information has taken a digital format. The potential for this digital data to inform the process of legal or business decision-making has led to growth in the range and availability of technologies employing statistical and machine learning methods specifically designed to support data analysis. These allow for the quantification of uncertainty via probabilistic methods – evidence which can then be set out using data visualisations or more complex techniques such as decision trees (which assign probabilities to

students accessed 20 May 2019; Susskind (n 2); Monica Goyal, 'Do Lawyers and Law Students Have the Technical Skills to Meet the Needs of Future Legal Jobs?' (*Slaw*, 29 June 2017) www.slaw.ca/2017/06/29/do-lawyers-and-law-students-have-the-technical-skills-to-meet-the-needs-of-future-legal-jobs/ accessed 20 July 2018.

[14] Mark Weiser, 'The Computer for the 21st Century' (1991) 265(3) Scientific American 94.
[15] Michael Lewis, *The Fifth Risk: Undoing Democracy* (Penguin 2018) 178.
[16] Robert A Kagan and Robert Eli Rosen, 'On the Social Significance of Large Law Firm Practice' (1985) 37(2) Stanford Law Review 399, 415.

concatenating events).[17] The increased uptake of these technologies may be viewed as an effort to respond to an increasingly risk-adverse corporate environment in which expectations around detailed reporting and auditing mechanisms, clear chains of accountability, and transparent decision-making have shaped corporate leadership. Yet these tools also serve a more commercially orientated purpose by enhancing the efficiency of legal service delivery, as can be seen with reference to e-discovery software.

During the process of disclosure, lawyers handling litigation must demonstrate that they have performed a reasonable search of materials. This process involves in-depth document review in which materials are identified as responsive or unresponsive to a disclosure request, and responsive materials are redacted to uphold legal privilege. Information received from the other party to a dispute must also be reviewed so as to provide evidence to substantiate one's own claims or undermine the claims of the opposing party. In an effort to offset the cost of manual (human) review, which has increased in line with the growth of (digital) data, systems employing machine learning techniques including Natural Language Processing (NLP) functionality have been developed to facilitate computer assisted human review (CAHR) and human-aided computer review (HACR) modalities. These tools rank the potential relevance of documents subject to review based on a set of simply coded (not relevant =0, relevant =1) training documents, as well as dynamically re-ranking documents in response to a user's interaction with the materials during review.

Due diligence, contract review and lease review processes have also benefitted from data-driven machine learning implementations. In the absence of automation, legal documents are reviewed in a linear manual fashion. Commercial software packages such as Ravn, Kira, Brainspace and Drooms, permit rapid extraction of insights ('entity recognition') across a range of material. In the case of lease review, this is achieved by extracting entities from individual lease documents, such as property postcode, percentage return, weekly rent, loan amount outstanding, duration of the loan or duration of tenancy. These key pieces of information can then be organised in a spreadsheet and when analysed globally, can provide insight into the features of the entire portfolio under consideration (e.g. the number of leases, average income and duration, and the total estimated value of the portfolio). This enables the accurate pricing of assets, the identification of unusual contract clauses and/or the investigation of transaction risks in advance of agreement.

Further, these tools allow legal review work to be priced on the basis of comprehensiveness and breadth versus depth. So, a due diligence exercise may produce 10,000 documents that require review to obtain an understanding of

[17] Robert Eli Rosen, '"We're All Consultants Now": How Change in Client Organizational Strategies Influences Change in the Organization of Corporate Legal Services' (2002) 44(3 & 4) Arizona Law Review 637, 659; Katz (n 1).

content and liabilities. Typically, not all 10,000 documents would be reviewed, especially not in instances where the cost of manual review would render the exercise prohibitively expensive. Data-driven NLP techniques make it possible to review 10,000 documents using automated intelligent search queries that quantify patterns in language.[18] This allows a review exercise to be limited to a random subset of the documents and makes it possible to quantify the risk that the remaining unseen documents contain clauses, conditions or material that are substantively different from that already reviewed.

In light of this potential, data-driven systems have been developed for a range of different purposes, such as:

- Prediction – including predicting the characteristics of winning a case, the success of certain cases by judge, the likely quantum of damages a court or jury would award,[19] the likely interpretation of an ambiguous term[20] or the number of hours required for the purpose of fixed fee quotes for project work;[21]
- Classification – including dynamically ranking documents for review according to their predicted relevance (as derived from a user's interaction with a set of initial documents or a marked up set of sample documents);[22]
- Extraction – to accelerate the process of extricating relevant information from a cache of documents to provide a global snapshot of the material;[23]
- Monitoring – to ascertain which staff teams work most efficiently together on projects, to assign new work in a way that maximises staff capacity, or to detect unusual access patterns in relation to confidential files.[24]

Accompanying the proliferation of these technologies is a growing expectation that those entering the legal workforce will have the capacity to use such tools, and moreover, to consider how new variations of these tools might be developed to

---

[18] It should be noted that not all techniques are exclusively data-driven and many will also employ rules-based methods.

[19] See, e.g., Lex Machina, 'About' https://lexmachina.com/about/ accessed 1 August 2018; LexPredict, 'Predicting the Supreme Court' www.lexpredict.com/portfolio/predicting-the-supreme-court/ accessed 21 April 2019; Papis Wongchaisuwat, Diego Klabjan and John O McGinnis, 'Predicting Litigation Likelihood and Time to Litigation for Patents', *Proceedings of the 16th International Conference on Artificial Intelligence and Law* (ACM Press 2017); Matt Dunn and others, 'Early Predictability of Asylum Court Decisions', *Proceedings of the 16th International Conference on Artificial Intelligence and Law* (ACM 2017); Judicata, 'About' www.judicata.com/about accessed 1 August 2018.

[20] Lawrence M Solan and Tammy A Gales, 'Corpus Linguistics as a Tool in Legal Interpretation' [2017] BYU Law Review 1311.

[21] See, e.g., Clocktimizer, 'Home Page' www.clocktimizer.com/ accessed 21 April 2019.

[22] See, e.g., Kira Systems, 'About' www.kirasystems.com/about/ accessed 22 January 2018; iManage, 'RAVN' https://imanage.com/product/ravn/ accessed 22 January 2018.

[23] See, e.g., Brainspace, 'Home Page' www.brainspace.com/ accessed 22 January 2018.

[24] iManage, 'Home' https://imanage.com/ accessed 6 February 2018.

address existing inefficiencies.[25] Whilst the spread of these tools has, to date, been confined to large corporate law firms in the service of large corporate clients, or in-house legal departments within large corporations, a range of technologies that rely on the same type of design principles have spread beyond this section of the legal services industry. The emergence of new forms of technology to assist in the completion of legal work has been accompanied by forms of technology employed by state actors to assist in the fulfilment and oversight of a range of bureaucratic and regulatory tasks. As a result, variations on the types of technologies described above have become inextricably linked to the role a lawyer plays in securing justice under the law for a range of stakeholders.

4.2.2 *Securing Justice under the Law*

As technology has become increasingly available, a range of automated decision-making tools within the public and private sphere have emerged. These have been employed to determine access to goods and services, to monitor compliance with the law, to allocate public sector resources and to support judicial decision-making. Recent examples include the use of data-driven technology to identify welfare fraud in Australia[26] and the Netherlands;[27] to detect illegal poaching activities; to collate information on workplace injuries;[28] to respond to child welfare risks; to assess the personality of job applicants; to apply 'deception detection' to screen non-EU nationals at EU borders; to evaluate the job search activity of the long-term unemployed for the purpose of welfare-benefit sanctioning; to score and assess loan applicants; to calculate car insurance premiums based on driver behaviour;[29] to identify tax law abuse;[30] to monitor terrorism; to predict reoffending in the context of

[25] See, e.g., Christopher Niesche, 'Technology Focus Gives Law Students an Edge' *The Australian* (Sydney, 1 June 2017) www.theaustralian.com.au/business/legal-affairs/technology-focus-gives-law-students-an-edge/news-story/88b483fda973429d5eeefd9b4e30c55a accessed 20 April 2019.

[26] Administrative Review Council, 'Automated Assistance in Administrative Decision Making: Report to the Attorney-General' (Administrative Review Council 2004) www.arc.ag.gov.au/Documents/AAADMreportPDF.pdf accessed 19 May 2018; Amie Meers and others, 'Lessons Learnt about Digital Transformation and Public Administration: Centrelink's Online Compliance Intervention' (Commonwealth Ombudsman 2017) www.ombudsman.gov.au/__data/assets/pdf_file/0024/48813/AIAL-OCI-Speech-and-Paper.pdf accessed 19 February 2018.

[27] Matthias Spielkamp (ed.), 'Automating Society Taking Stock of Automated Decision-Making in the EU' (AW AlgorithmWatch gGmbH 2019) www.algorithmwatch.org/automating-society accessed 7 March 2019.

[28] See further Partnership for Public Service & IBM Center for The Business of Government, 'The Future Has Begun. Using Artificial Intelligence to Transform Government' (Partnership for Public Service & IBM Center for The Business of Government 2018) www.businessofgovernment.org/blog/future-has-begun-using-artificial-intelligence-transform-government accessed 20 May 2019.

[29] Spielkamp (n 27).

[30] See, e.g., Erik Hemberg and others, 'Tax Non-Compliance Detection Using Co-Evolution of Tax Evasion Risk and Audit Likelihood', *Proceedings of the 15th International Conference on Artificial Intelligence and Law* (ACM 2015).

parole decisions;[31] to predict custody risk;[32] and to detect crime hot-spots for a range of purposes, including resource management.[33]

In a range of circumstances, the use of these technologies in society has the capacity to overlap with the role of the lawyer tasked with securing justice under the law for a client. Indeed, efforts to introduce automated decision-making systems into government processes have resulted in significant concerns that these systems may operate as an impediment to access to justice and undermine the operation of the rule of law.[34] One example is Australia's Department of Human Services (DHS) 'Online Compliance Intervention' system which launched in July 2016. This system was designed to automate the investigation and debt raising process where DHS detected a discrepancy between the amount of Pay-As-You-Go (PAYG) income reported to DHS by an individual in receipt of welfare benefits, and the amount of PAYG income reported to the Australian Tax Office (ATO). The system resulted in an exponential increase in the number of discrepancies identified (from 20,000 – per year under human oversight, to 20,000 per week under the automated system). Sustained public criticism emerged as to the transparency, fairness and usability of the system (dubbed 'Robodebt' by the media) and the vulnerable user-group subject to debt notifications, resulting in a detailed senate inquiry. Of particular importance was the validity and comprehensiveness of the data relied upon to establish 'guilt', the margin of error and number of false positives identified by the system, and the procedural changes the design of the system introduced by stealth.[35]

In the context of a lawyer's duty to secure justice under the law for a client, it is relevant to note that automated debt notifications present a significant legal issue and are, by their nature, adverse decisions. Those said to have under-reported income in order to over-claim welfare benefits are subject to a range of civil and criminal legal consequences. Similarly, an individual's exposure to legal sanctions on the basis of protected characteristics as a result of the application of data-driven AI systems has also caused unease. It has been generally recognised that data can encode biases due to the human decisions made to create it and algorithms reliant on this data can act to institutionalise this bias. This has been revealed in relation to criminal risk prediction software used in the USA, which has been shown to

---

[31] See further Bernard E Harcourt, *Against Prediction: Profiling, Policing, and Punishing in an Actuarial Age* (University of Chicago Press 2007); Richard A Berk, *Criminal Justice Forecasts of Risk: A Machine Learning Approach* (Springer Science & Business Media 2012).

[32] For example, England and Wales has recently reported using historical police records to inform custody risk decisions. See further Chris Baraniuk, 'Durham Police AI to Help with Custody Decisions' *BBC News* (London, 10 May 2017) www.bbc.co.uk/news/technology-39857645 accessed 29 May 2018.

[33] See, e.g., Shotspotter, 'Technology' www.shotspotter.com/technology accessed 1 August 2018; Movidius, 'Intel Movidius' www.movidius.com/ accessed 1 August 2018; PredPol, 'Predict Crime' www.predpol.com/ accessed 1 August 2018.

[34] Sarah Marsh, 'Ethics Committee Raises Alarm Over "Predictive Policing" Tool' *The Guardian* (London, 21 April 2019) www.theguardian.com/uk-news/2019/apr/20/predictive-policing-tool-could-entrench-bias-ethics-committee-warns accessed 21 April 2019.

[35] See further Meers and others (n 26).

routinely assign higher levels of risk to black subjects.[36] Such examples reinforce the fact that without opportunities to acquire a broader range of technological literacy skills, lawyers will not be alive to these risks, nor will they have the capacity to identify when particular technological tools directly or indirectly undermine the operation of justice.

4.3 THE NEED FOR ENHANCED TECHNOLOGICAL LITERACY

Technological and numerical literacy is of relevance for law students and graduates for two key reasons. The first of these relates to issues of graduate employability and the effects of market exigencies. The second relates to the role that lawyers perform in guarding against incursions upon the rule of law, and in fulfilling their duties in a way that protects the interests of their clients and contributes to the broader access to justice agenda. These issues are each explored in turn.

4.3.1 *Employability and Market Pressures*

Those who tend to support the incorporation of a broader suite of analytical skills within legal education do so 'as a response to the demand for law school graduates to be capable of dealing with complex problems in both scientific and professional environments'; some of which arise as a result of the use of technology and some of which can only be solved with the use of technology.[37] In line with an increasingly competitive market for legal services, market pressures 'make themselves felt, because the legal profession is in horizontal competition with adjacent professions, which actually draw on more than one discipline and do not leave the demand for professionals to exhibit a broader range of skills to "learning on the job"'.[38]

Recent examples exemplify the need for law graduates to possess a broader suite of skills and to bring more to the profession than just knowledge of the law. In England and Wales, law firms are increasingly recruiting Bachelor of Laws (LLB) and Graduate Diploma in Law (GDL) graduates in roughly equal numbers, having exhibited a clear preference for graduates of the former qualification over the preceding decades.[39] In the USA there has been a slow but steady growth in the number of Science, Technology, Engineering and Mathematics (STEM) graduates

---

[36] Julia Angwin and others, 'Machine Bias' *ProPublica* (23 May 2016) www.propublica.org/article/machine-bias-risk-assessments-in-criminal-sentencing accessed 29 May 2018.

[37] Schäfke, Mayoral Díaz-Asensio and Hvidt (n 9) 274.

[38] Ibid 275.

[39] Catherine Baksi, 'Late to Law: Studying Another Degree First Is a Sensible Option' *The Guardian* (London, 16 January 2018) www.theguardian.com/law/2018/jan/16/late-to-law-studying-another-degree-first-is-a-sensible-option accessed 31 October 2018.

applying to the JD,[40] and more recently, active efforts by law school admissions officers to recruit higher numbers of STEM graduates.[41] This has been accompanied by developments such as the STEM Future Lawyers Network established in the UK in 2017,[42] events intended to encourage STEM students to consider a career in law,[43] as well as the emergence of legal technology training contracts in England and Wales.[44]

The value of importing greater breadth into the teaching of law at the higher degree level also takes on renewed importance given radical changes to the education and training pathway for lawyers in England and Wales set to be introduced in 2021.[45] These changes fundamentally decouple the process of qualifying as a solicitor from the obtainment of a degree in law. Students will no longer have to possess a higher degree in law (an LLB, a JD or a GDL) and instead will be expected to sit and pass a Single Qualifying Examination (SQE) in two-parts, alongside accumulating twenty-four months of work experience. Whilst we might expect that a law degree will offer some students better preparation to pass the SQE, the changes are likely to challenge the dominance of the law degree as the main route of entry into the legal profession.

Failure by legal educators to respond to the profession's need for graduates with a broader range of analytical skills, will signal the diminishing esteem placed on those who graduate with a law degree but who do not demonstrate broader competencies. Whilst such issues are important in the context of the rising cost of education and increasing competition for entry into the profession, the need for legal professionals to demonstrate broader literacy in technology and data analysis is also a social justice issue. This need arises as a result of the potential ramifications that data-driven tools present for the rule of law, the discharging of regulatory responsibilities, access to legal services, fairness of legal outcomes or the exercise of individual liberty.

[40] Tiffane Cochran and India Heckstall, 'From the Bachelor's to the Bar Using College Completion Data to Assess the Law School Pipeline' (AccessLex Institute 2016) www.accesslex.org/sites/default/files/2017-04/bachelors_to_the_bar.pdf accessed 28 October 2018.

[41] Claire E Parker, 'To Keep Pace with Tech, Law School Seeks STEM Students' *The Crimson* (Cambridge MA, 6 May 2016) www.thecrimson.com/article/2016/5/6/HLS-admissions-STEM-recruiting/ accessed 20 May 2019.

[42] See further STEM Future Lawyers Network, 'Home Page' (2017) https://stemfuturelawyers.co.uk accessed 31 October 2018.

[43] See, e.g., STEM Future Lawyers Network, 'Why STEM Students Make Great Lawyers' (2018) https://stemfuturelawyers.co.uk/event/why-stem-students-make-great-lawyers/16 accessed 31 October 2018.

[44] Lex 100, 'Clifford Chance Launches Law Tech Training Contract' (*Lex 100*, 1 August 2018) www.lex100.com/index.php/news/news-2/1562-clifford-chance-launches-law-tech-training-contract accessed 31 October 2018.

[45] Solicitors Regulation Authority, 'A New Route to Qualification: The Solicitors Qualifying Examination (SQE) – A Summary of Responses and Next Steps' (Solicitors Regulation Authority 2017) www.sra.org.uk/documents/SRA/consultations/sqe-summary-responses.pdf accessed 31 October 2018; Solicitors Regulation Authority, 'SQE to be Introduced in Autumn 2021' (*Solicitors Regulation Authority*, 8 November 2018) www.sra.org.uk/sra/news/press/sqe-launch-2021.page accessed 26 May 2019.

4.3.2 *Knowledge and the Public Good*

Tools designed to help lawyers manage risk, or to help individuals determine their entitlements or obligations in respect of a particular benefit, increasingly feature in the day-to-day work of lawyers and other professionals working in business, social welfare and government. It is concerning therefore that the extent to which lawyers are likely to be familiar with the underlying assumptions, methods and processes by which output is derived, is at best uncertain and at worst highly unlikely. Familiarity with certain forms of software that exercise a decision-making function does not displace the need for familiarity with the process by which that software operates.

Whilst the increased prominence of data-driven techniques across society amplifies the relevance of technological and numerical literacy for all, within law this understanding is crucial because data-driven technologies increasingly govern the space between the law and its application in the real world.[46] Given the intrinsically quantitative nature of these tools, including and especially those tools that are designed to parse natural language or predict the likelihood of certain outcomes, we might question the appropriateness of a law degree that pays no heed to the value that accompanies greater familiarity with these technologies and a more detailed understanding of their numerical underpinnings.

Without instruction in these forms of technology and their underlying assumptions, law graduates cannot be expected to identify their failings or understand their limitations. This is true of those tools deployed within legal practice that are intended to enhance the efficiency of task completion, as well as tools implemented in a range of other settings where they touch upon dimensions of law or the exercise of legal rights and responsibilities. Given the importance of such knowledge in enabling lawyers to effectively discharge their duties, this capacity for critical reflection must necessarily be built into the academic stage of legal training. As such, it is worth considering who is responding to the need for data-literate graduates and the focus for emerging curricula in legal technology.

4.4 TECHNOLOGY INSTRUCTION WITHIN LEGAL EDUCATION: A PROPOSED APPROACH

It has long been recognised that familiarity in quantitative methods of the type used in data analysis is relatively rare within legal education. As Schlegel observes, most legal academics 'neither under[stand] nor [know] how to use the quantitative and

---

[46] See, e.g., Mireille Hildebrandt, 'Law as Information in the Era of Data-Driven Agency' (2016) 79(1) The Modern Law Review 1; Mireille Hildebrandt, 'A Vision of Ambient Law' in Roger Brownsword and Karen Yeung (eds.), *Regulating Technologies: Legal Futures, Regulatory Frames and Technological Fixes* (Hart 2008); Mireille Hildebrandt, *Smart Technologies and the End(s) of Law: Novel Entanglements of Law and Technology* (Edward Elgar 2015).

statistical methods . . .'.[47] This is also true of technology more generally where it has been said that law schools are not equipped to teach these types of skills.[48] Others have also observed the failure of the legal academy to take technology seriously, as exemplified by the lack of established posts in the field. As a consequence, despite technology and law 'becoming more vital and central to the task of legal scholarship in a technologically determined society' it remains largely neglected.[49]

Whilst this criticism is true of the majority of educational providers, outliers do exist and there is some evidence of momentum gaining in support of change, though much of this is concentrated in the USA. For example, Staudt and Medeiros's efforts at Chicago-Kent University to 'add a new type of clinical course that teaches law students how to use and deploy technology to assist law practice'[50] has since seen it rolled out to a further seven law schools around the USA, including Georgetown, Michigan State and Columbia Universities.[51] This initiative joins a number of other offerings at Chicago-Kent Law School, which for a number of years has been at the forefront of legal technology education, including providing specialised courses on legal analytics intended to build the quantitative skills of students and introduce them to the R data analysis environment.[52] Further examples are recorded in Linna's Law School Innovation index, which documents those US institutions addressing the current data-literacy skills gap. To date, twenty-one schools, including Duke, Harvard, Yale, Stanford, Georgetown and Columbia universities have introduced courses in empirical methods, whilst sixteen provide courses in data analytics.[53] Other universities, such as Michigan State, offer 'Quantitative Analysis for Lawyers' within a broader suite of technology, analysis and practice orientated courses.[54]

Changes to degree programmes and the development and delivery of new modules have been accompanied by the growth of the university incubator movement, which offers students and graduates with legal technology ideas, access to support for early-stage development. Such initiatives demonstrate the first steps taken by law

---

[47]   A Weinberg and C Harding, 'Interdisciplinary Teaching and Collaboration in Higher Education: A Concept Whose Time Has Come' (2004) 14(15) Washington University Journal of Law and Policy 14, 20.

[48]   Stephanie Kimbro, 'What Should Be in a Digital Curriculum: A Practitioner's Must Have List' in Marc Lauritsen and Oliver Goodenough (eds.), *Educating the Digital Lawyer* (Lexis Nexis e-Books 2012).

[49]   Philip Leith, 'It and Law, and Law Schools' (2000) 14(2) International Review of Law, Computers and Technology 171, 173.

[50]   Ronald W Staudt and Andrew P Medeiros, 'Access to Justice and Technology Clinics: A 4% Solution' (2013) 88(3) Chicago-Kent Law Review 695.

[51]   Sheldon Krantz and Michael Millemann, 'Legal Education in Transition: Trends and Their Implications' (2014) 94(1) Nebraska Law Review 1.

[52]   Daniel Martin Katz and Michael J Bommarito, 'Legal Analytics Course' (2016) www.legalanalyticscourse.com/ accessed 18 May 2019.

[53]   Daniel W Linna Jr and Jordan Galvin, 'Law School Innovation Index' (*Legal Tech Innovation*, 2017) www.legaltechinnovation.com/law-school-index/ accessed 31 October 2018.

[54]   See further Michigan State's LegalRnD Centre which convenes a number of courses. LegalRnD, 'Home Page' (Michigan State University) http://legalrnd.org/ accessed 18 May 2019.

schools in the USA to build the capacity required to support the delivery of 'experiential technology projects, and [the] empirical bases to evaluate them'.[55] Although few are purely focused on data analytics or the intricacies of certain forms of AI, these examples, when taken in conjunction with the proliferation of 'Legal Apps' courses on offer, provide evidence that change is afoot.

In addition, whilst not specifically addressing the need for skills in data analysis, a number of educational institutions have taken steps to encourage greater disciplinary breadth from students. This includes moves by the University of Melbourne to deliver law as a JD degree (in a shift away from the existing undergraduate model of legal education within Australia); the requirement set down by the University of Sydney that an LLB must be studied for in conjunction with another Bachelor degree in the Arts, Sciences or Engineering fields; and the development of combined degrees in Law and Computer Science that have emerged in Scotland (at Strathclyde University and Edinburgh University).

Outside of these examples a more mixed picture emerges as to the place of technology and data within legal education as well as the pace of progress. For, although some have called for a more sociolegal understanding of technology within the legal curriculum, less emphasis has been placed on students' need to understand legal technology as a means to organise, store, extract, analyse and predict from data.[56] Similarly there has been little consensus as to the need for students to be familiar with the techniques by which insights from data might be harnessed, so as to minimise legal uncertainty, quantify legal risk, determine access to legal entitlements, monitor legality of behaviour or accelerate the completion of legal tasks.

Amidst the ongoing debate as to whether legal education is expected to turn out 'lawyer scriveners' or 'lawyer statesmen', it seems not to have been recognised that the study of technology offers a valuable contribution to both of these objectives.[57] As Krantz and Milleman observe 'Legal educators have a leadership role to play in protecting the public from overreaching and exploitation that inevitably come with rapid development of new commercial products.'[58] This is a role that is discharged, in part, by teaching students how to evaluate data-driven technologies. For this reason, whilst a certain degree of familiarity with existing technologies ought to be seen as a prerequisite for entry into legal education (notably familiarity with a range of office software), other areas of study represent a priority for future curriculum development. These areas of study include:

---

[55] Krantz and Millemann (n 51) 25.
[56] Redmount (n 5); Abdul Paliwala, 'Creating an Academic Environment: The Development of Technology in Legal Education in the United Kingdom' (1991) 5(1) International Review of Law, Computers & Technology 136.
[57] Deborah L Rhode, 'Legal Education: Professional Interests and Public Values' (2001) 34(1) Indiana Law Review 23, 23 (paraphrasing Twinning).
[58] Krantz and Millemann (n 51) 26.

- Basic Statistics (e.g. sampling, research design, data collection, variables, probability, distributions, correlation and regression);
- Data Analysis (e.g. cleaning and manipulating data, data protection, data limitations, statistical and machine learning methods, visualisation, natural language processing, data ethics, and the hazards of data use);
- Computational Legal Reasoning (e.g. case-based, rules-based and quantitative approaches, legal semantics and linguistics, legal theory);
- Legal Software (e.g. tools used within the private and public legal sectors, software evaluation, barriers to software implementation in the legal work environment, and software integration);
- Project Management and Design (e.g. design thinking, client project management, agile development, and working within multidisciplinary teams).

Whether at the academic or vocational stage, students ought to benefit from exposure to a range of subject areas that are increasingly becoming fundamental to all forms of professional work. Certainly, some of these subjects such as legal project management and digital legal tools could be provided as optional modules, other topics such as data and analysis in law, basic statistics and computational legal reasoning might sensibly form an element of foundation learning if a student does not have a record of prior study.

Identifying these fields as priority areas does not address the issue of capacity within law schools to deliver such a programme. However, the nature of these subject areas reveals the ways in which law schools may work to develop stronger interdisciplinary relationships across faculties within higher education. Many subjects would not necessarily need to be convened specifically for law students — first year statistics courses run by other departments would suffice for law students to gain a broad understanding, provided students were given an opportunity to apply their learning to the legal domain. The same is true of project management and design courses, which could retain a general focus whilst offering a range of case studies which contextualise content for students from different faculties. Opportunities for joint-delivery across faculties also emerge in respect of data analysis. Whilst computational legal reasoning would sensibly be offered by someone with requisite legal expertise, this subject could attract interest as an optional module if made available to students undertaking studies in other disciplines.

Other subjects such as advanced office skills might form part of prerequisite private study as exemplified by the European Computer Driving License Scheme, or could be taught pervasively throughout other traditional law subjects. For example, students could be required to review key cases in contract law, and produce a data table with extracted facts organised in a structured manner. This pervasive approach also presents as possible with respect to computational legal reasoning, as exemplified by Ashley's work at the University of Pittsburgh, developing a range of

rule and case-based systems to introduce law students to the basics of legal argumentation with cases.[59]

The value of studying these topics lies not just in their capacity to better prepare
students for certain careers in law. Whilst such subjects provide a competitive
advantage in the job market, they also fulfil a much more significant purpose.
They provide students with the tools to evaluate, critically, the role of these technologies in society and in practice. Learning about these technologies in an impartial environment uncoloured by the economic pressures of legal practice and the
motivations that often dictate their implementation in the real world, will produce
graduates capable of critically and ethically reflecting on the merits and impact of
use. In doing so, this will better position graduates to uphold their duties to their
clients, the profession, the rule of law and the public at large.

4.5 CONCLUSION

The fact that the law degree remains epistemologically narrow stands in contrast to
the widely held belief that a law degree provides solid preparation for a career in
a range of different fields. Many of those who study law do so with no intention of
going into practice, but although advocates identify a range of different virtues
instilled by the study of law, it has never been fully explained how a graduate's
ability to answer a problem question or recite various aspects of legislation offers
adequate preparation for a career outside of law. Instead, it is perhaps the status of
a law degree rather than its content that continues to sway prospective employers.
That being the case we might expect that the growing importance of data literacy
across all professions will, in the absence of response by the legal academy, prompt
students and employers to reconsider the position the undergraduate law degree
holds as the primary route of entry into the profession. In jurisdictions where law is
taught at the graduate level, such as the USA, we might expect a different sort of
response, one that sees a growing number of science/engineering/computing graduates vis-à-vis liberal arts graduates studying for the JD.

Beyond issues of employability, wider-ranging implications emerge. A lack of
knowledge with regard to how data and technology is used to make decisions within
law, and an inability to assess the opportunities and limitations that attach to that
use, poses a real risk for the capacity of legal professionals to fulfil their professional
and civic responsibilities. The importance of these risks as well as their centrality to
the real-world implementation of all of the concepts covered as part of the legal
education 'core', suggests that this is foundational knowledge that cannot and should
not be left to acquisition by osmosis. The increasingly complex technologies that
have and will continue to transform the legal profession (and society at large) are not

---

[59] See further Kevin Ashley, *Artificial Intelligence and Legal Analytics New Tools for Law Practice in the
Digital Age* (Cambridge University Press 2017).

impartial objects. Without the requisite training in the types of data analysis and methods that underpin data-driven AI implementations, lawyers will find themselves increasingly unable to evaluate the value of these tools or assess the risk/benefit they pose to the process of managing uncertainty or securing justice under the law. Were that to occur it would produce an outcome antithetical to the 'public good' argument regularly invoked in support of the academic study of law, and represent a significant failing by the legal academy.

BIBLIOGRAPHY

Administrative Review Council, 'Automated Assistance in Administrative Decision Making: Report to the Attorney-General' (Administrative Review Council 2004) www.arc.ag.gov.au/documents/aaadmreportpdf.pdf accessed 19 May 2018

Angwin J and others, 'Machine Bias' *ProPublica* (23 May 2016) www.propublica.org/article/machine-bias-risk-assessments-in-criminal-sentencing accessed 29 May 2018

Ashley K, *Artificial Intelligence and Legal Analytics New Tools for Law Practice in the Digital Age* (Cambridge University Press 2017)

'Legal Reasoning and Artificial Intelligence: How Computers Think Like Lawyers' (2001) 8 (1) The University of Chicago Law School Roundtable Article 2 http://chicagounbound.uchicago.edu/roundtable/vol8/iss1/2 accessed 29 May 2018

Baksi C, 'Late to Law: Studying Another Degree First Is a Sensible Option' *The Guardian* (London, 16 January 2018) www.theguardian.com/law/2018/jan/16/late-to-law-studying-another-degree-first-is-a-sensible-option accessed 31 October 2018

Baraniuk C, 'Durham Police AI to Help with Custody Decisions' *BBC News* (London, 10 May 2017) www.bbc.co.uk/news/technology-39857645 accessed 29 May 2018

Berk RA, *Criminal Justice Forecasts of Risk: A Machine Learning Approach* (Springer Science & Business Media 2012)

Brainspace, 'Home Page' www.brainspace.com/ accessed 22 January 2018

Clocktimizer, 'Home Page' www.clocktimizer.com/ accessed 21 April 2019

Cochran T and Heckstall I, 'From the Bachelor's to the Bar Using College Completion Data to Assess the Law School Pipeline' (AccessLex Institute 2016) www.accesslex.org/sites/default/files/2017-04/bachelors_to_the_bar.pdf accessed 28 October 2018

Dunn M and others, 'Early Predictability of Asylum Court Decisions', *Proceedings of the 16th International Conference on Artificial Intelligence and Law* (ACM 2017)

Gartner, 'Gartner's 2016 Hype Cycle for Emerging Technologies' (16 August 2016) www.gartner.com/newsroom/id/3412017 accessed 1 July 2017

Goyal M, 'Do Lawyers and Law Students Have the Technical Skills to Meet the Needs of Future Legal Jobs?' (*Slaw*, 29 June 2017) www.slaw.ca/2017/06/29/do-lawyers-and-law-students-have-the-technical-skills-to-meet-the-needs-of-future-legal-jobs/ accessed 20 July 2018

Greenleaf G, 'Legal Expert Systems — Robot Lawyers? An Introduction to Knowledge-Based Applications to Law' (Australian Legal Convention, Sydney, August 1989) www2.austlii.edu.au/cal/papers/robots89/ accessed 29 May 2018

Harcourt BE, *Against Prediction: Profiling, Policing, and Punishing in an Actuarial Age* (University of Chicago Press 2007)

Hemberg E and others, 'Tax Non-Compliance Detection Using Co-Evolution of Tax Evasion Risk and Audit Likelihood', *Proceedings of the 15th International Conference on Artificial Intelligence and Law* (ACM 2015)

Hildebrandt M, 'A Vision of Ambient Law' in Roger Brownsword and Karen Yeung (eds.), Regulating Technologies: Legal Futures, Regulatory Frames and Technological Fixes (Hart 2008)

    Smart Technologies and the End(s) of Law: Novel Entanglements of Law and Technology (Edward Elgar 2015)

    'Law as Information in the Era of Data-Driven Agency' (2016) 79(1) The Modern Law Review 1

Holborne N, 'University Pioneers Legal Tech Course for Law Degree Students' (*Legal Futures*, 7 June 2018) www.legalfutures.co.uk/latest-news/university-pioneers-legal-tech-course-for-law-degree-students accessed 20 May 2019

iManage, 'Home' https://imanage.com/ accessed 6 February 2018

    'RAVN' https://imanage.com/product/ravn/ accessed 22 January 2018

Jones RP and Van Wyk J, 'Computers in Legal Education' (1989) 4(1) International Review of Law, Computers & Technology 1

Judicata, 'About' www.judicata.com/about accessed 1 August 2018

Kagan RA and Rosen RE, 'On the Social Significance of Large Law Firm Practice' (1985) 37 (2) Stanford Law Review 399

Kakas AC and Sadri F (eds.), *Computational Logic: Logic Programming and Beyond: Essays in Honour of Robert A. Kowalski* (1st edn, Springer-Verlag 2002)

Katz DM, 'Quantitative Legal Prediction – or – How I Learned to Stop Worrying and Start Preparing for the Data Driven Future of the Legal Services Industry' (2013) 62 Emory Law Journal 909

Katz DM and Bommarito MJ, 'Legal Analytics Course' (2016) www.legalanalyticscourse.com/ accessed 18 May 2019

Kimbro S, 'What Should Be in a Digital Curriculum: A Practitioner's Must Have List' in Marc Lauritsen and Oliver Goodenough (eds.), *Educating the Digital Lawyer* (Lexis Nexis e-Books 2012)

Kira Systems, 'About' www.kirasystems.com/about/ accessed 22 January 2018

Krantz S and Millemann M, 'Legal Education in Transition: Trends and Their Implications' (2014) 94(1) Nebraska Law Review 1

LegalRnD, 'Home Page' (Michigan State University) http://legalrnd.org/ accessed 18 May 2019

Leith P, 'Fundamental Errors in Legal Logic Programming' (1986) 29(6) The Computer Journal 545

    'Correspondence: The Emperor's New Expert System' (1987) 50(128) Modern Law Review 128

    'The Application of AI to Law' (1988) 2(1) AI & Society 31

    'It and Law, and Law Schools' (2000) 14(2) International Review of Law, Computers and Technology 171

Levin M, 'Legal Education for the Next Generation: Ideas from America' (2000) 3(1) Asian-Pacific Law & Policy Journal 1

Lewis M, *The Fifth Risk: Undoing Democracy* (Penguin 2018)

Lex 100, 'Clifford Chance Launches Law Tech Training Contract' (*Lex 100*, 1 August) www.lex100.com/index.php/news/news-2/1562-clifford-chance-launches-law-tech-training-contract accessed 31 October 2018

Lex Machina, 'About' https://lexmachina.com/about/ accessed 1 August 2018

LexPredict, 'Predicting the Supreme Court' www.lexpredict.com/portfolio/predicting-the-supreme-court/ accessed 21 April 2019

Linna Jr DW and Galvin J, 'Law School Innovation Index' (*Legal Tech Innovation*, 2017) www.legaltechinnovation.com/law-school-index/ accessed 31 October 2018

Marsh S, 'Ethics Committee Raises Alarm Over "Predictive Policing" Tool' *The Guardian* (London, 21 April 2019) www.theguardian.com/uk-news/2019/apr/20/predictive-policing-tool-could-entrench-bias-ethics-committee-warns accessed 21 April 2019

Meers A and others, 'Lessons Learnt about Digital Transformation and Public Administration: Centrelink's Online Compliance Intervention' (Commonwealth Ombudsman 2017) www.ombudsman.gov.au/__data/assets/pdf_file/0024/48813/aial-oci-speech-and-paper.pdf accessed 19 February 2018

Movidius, 'Intel Movidius' www.movidius.com/ accessed 1 August 2018

Niesche C, 'Technology Focus Gives Law Students an Edge' *The Australian* (Sydney, 1 June 2017) www.theaustralian.com.au/business/legal-affairs/technology-focus-gives-law-students-an-edge/news-story/88b483fda973429d5eeefd9b4e30c55a accessed 20 April 2019

Paliwala A, 'Creating an Academic Environment: The Development of Technology in Legal Education in the United Kingdom' (1991) 5(1) International Review of Law, Computers & Technology 136

Parker CE, 'To Keep Pace with Tech, Law School Seeks STEM Students' *The Crimson* (Cambridge MA, 6 May 2016) www.thecrimson.com/article/2016/5/6/hls-admissions-stem-recruiting/ accessed 20 May 2019

Partnership for Public Service & IBM Center for The Business of Government, 'The Future Has Begun. Using Artificial Intelligence to Transform Government' (Partnership for Public Service & IBM Center for The Business of Government 2018) www.businessofgovernment.org/blog/future-has-begun-using-artificial-intelligence-transform-government accessed 20 May 2019

PredPol, 'Predict Crime' www.predpol.com/ accessed 1 August 2018

Redmount RS, 'The Future of Legal Education: Perspective and Prescription' (1985) 30(3) New York Law School Law Review 561

Rhode DL, 'Legal Education: Professional Interests and Public Values' (2001) 34(1) Indiana Law Review 23

Rosen RE, '"We're All Consultants Now": How Change in Client Organizational Strategies Influences Change in the Organization of Corporate Legal Services' (2002) 44(3 & 4) Arizona Law Review 637

Schäfke W, Mayoral Díaz-Asensio JA and Hvidt MS, 'Socialisation to Interdisciplinary Legal Education: An Empirical Assessment' (2018) 52(3) Law Teacher 273

Schultz NL, 'How Do Lawyers Really Think?' (1992) 42(1) Journal of Legal Education 57

Shotspotter, 'Technology' www.shotspotter.com/technology accessed 1 August 2018

Solan LM and Gales TA, 'Corpus Linguistics as a Tool in Legal Interpretation' [2017] BYU Law Review 1311

Solicitors Regulation Authority, 'A New Route to Qualification: The Solicitors Qualifying Examination (SQE) — A Summary of Responses and Next Steps' (Solicitors Regulation Authority 2017) www.sra.org.uk/documents/sra/consultations/sqe-summary-responses.pdf accessed 31 October 2018

'SQE to be Introduced in Autumn 192021' (*Solicitors Regulation Authority*, 8 November 2018) www.sra.org.uk/sra/news/press/sqe-launch-2021.page accessed 26 May 2019

Spielkamp M (ed.), 'Automating Society Taking Stock of Automated Decision-Making in the EU' (AW AlgorithmWatch gGmbH 2019) www.algorithmwatch.org/automating-society accessed 7 March 2019

Staudt RW and Medeiros AP, 'Access to Justice and Technology Clinics: A 4% Solution' (2013) 88(3) Chicago-Kent Law Review 695

STEM Future Lawyers Network, 'Home Page' (2017) https://stemfuturelawyers.co.uk accessed 31 October 2018

'Why STEM Students Make Great Lawyers' (2018) https://stemfuturelawyers.co.uk/event/why-stem-students-make-great-lawyers/16 accessed 31 October 2018

Susskind R, *Tomorrow's Lawyers: An Introduction to Your Future* (1st edn, Oxford University Press 2013)

Weinberg A and Harding C, 'Interdisciplinary Teaching and Collaboration in Higher Education: A Concept Whose Time Has Come' (2004) 14(15) Washington University Journal of Law and Policy 14

Weiser M, 'The Computer for the 21st Century' (1991) 265(3) Scientific American 94

Wongchaisuwat P, Klabjan D and McGinnis JO, 'Predicting Litigation Likelihood and Time to Litigation for Patents', *Proceedings of the 16th International Conference on Artificial Intelligence and Law* (ACM Press 2017)

5

Bringing ODR to the Legal Education Mainstream

Findings from the Field

Genevieve Grant and Esther Lestrell[1]

The field of dispute resolution has long been at the forefront of modernising legal education. Continuing this tradition, this chapter presents findings from an evaluation of an exercise introduced into the core law school curriculum at Monash University in Australia. In our compulsory litigation and dispute resolution units, we built an experiential exercise in which students resolved a dispute using both an online dispute resolution (ODR) platform and more traditional face-to-face mediation role-play. Students completed a short survey about their experience of the portal (n=64, response rate 30 per cent) and provided their reflective journals about the exercise for analysis (n=55). Drawing on the findings, we consider the benefits and limitations of this approach for facilitating students' exposure to ODR. We explore themes including student understanding of ODR's impacts on dispute processes and outcomes; appropriate conduct in dispute resolution settings; and the challenges of computer-mediated communication. We also identify means by which experiential activities can draw students' attention to power disparities and access to justice challenges in ODR to develop their critical thinking about the rapid developments in this field.

5.1 INTRODUCTION

Legal technology and online platforms are becoming ever more prominent in dispute resolution discourse and practice. As legal services and the profession innovate and transform, there is a growing need to consider the ways these developments can be addressed via our preparation of future lawyers in legal education. This chapter presents findings from an evaluation of an online dispute resolution (ODR)

[1] The authors acknowledge the support provided for this research by Mr Ross Paull and Mr Nitzan Karni of Guided Resolution, together with our Monash colleague Ms Nicole Mollard. Additionally, we thank the students who participated in the evaluation and the Monash University Faculty of Law for the Unit Enhancement Funding which made the intervention possible.

activity implemented within a litigation and dispute resolution course at Monash University. In partnership with Guided Resolution (GR), a pioneering Australian conflict management system developer, we trialled and assessed the use of GR's ODR platform as part of a mediation role-play activity. Through a survey of students and analysis of their reflective journals about the activity, we gauged student perceptions and assessed the value of this method of incorporating ODR in legal education settings. We use these findings to interrogate the benefits and limitations of our approach for facilitating students' exposure to, and critical thinking about, ODR.

We begin with a brief overview of the need for dispute resolution teaching in legal education, the Australian context and the central role experiential activities have come to play in this field. We then provide evidence of the growing profile of ODR, and the paucity of ODR-related content in units offered in Australian law schools. As an illustration of one way to remedy this gap, the chapter sets out the experiential exercise we introduced in teaching dispute resolution at Monash University. We present findings from our evaluation and make observations about key learnings.

5.2 SITUATING DISPUTE RESOLUTION IN LEGAL EDUCATION

The argument has long been made that legal educators should allocate more time to Alternative Dispute Resolution (ADR), collaborative learning and problem-solving. The benefits of such a shift include the capacity for education to reflect the reality of modern legal practice and the skills employers expect law graduates to have.[2] Despite this, as Douglas and others have observed, debate continues as to the appropriate place and status of ADR in the law degree and there are significant barriers to increased ADR teaching.[3] Though leading experts argue that ADR should constitute a mandatory, stand-alone unit,[4] practices vary between institutions. The majority of Australian law schools feature a limited amount of ADR content in what are otherwise decidedly litigation-focused courses.[5]

---

[2] See, e.g., James Duffy and Rachael Field, 'Why ADR Must Be a Mandatory Subject in the Law Degree: A Cheat Sheet for the Willing and a Primer for the Non-Believer' (2014) 25(1) Australian Dispute Resolution Journal 9; Treyor CW Farrow, 'Dispute Resolution, Access to Civil Justice and Legal Education' (2004) 42(3) Alberta Law Review 741; Jordan Goldberg, 'Online Alternative Dispute Resolution and Why Law Schools Should Prepare Future Lawyers for the Online Forum' (2014) 14(1) Pepperdine Dispute Resolution Law Journal 1; Ben Waters, 'The Importance of Teaching Dispute Resolution in a Twenty-First-Century Law School' (2017) 51(2) The Law Teacher 227.

[3] See generally Kathy Douglas, 'The Teaching of ADR in Australian Law Schools: Promoting Non-Adversarial Practice in Law' (2011) 22(1) Australasian Dispute Resolution Journal 49.

[4] Duffy and Field (n 2); Lillian Corbin, Paula Baron and Judy Gutman, 'ADR Zealots, Adjudicative Romantics and Everything in between: Lawyers in Mediations' (2015) 38(2) University of New South Wales Law Journal 492.

[5] Kathy Douglas, 'The Role of ADR in Developing Lawyers' Practice: Lessons from Australian Legal Education' (2015) 22(1) International Journal of the Legal Profession 71.

Recent regulatory developments in the Australian setting have given added impetus to the case for ADR in the curriculum. Admission to practise as an Australian Lawyer requires study of eleven areas of knowledge, known as the 'Priestly 11'.[6] Until December 2016, the list of necessary elements in the prescribed area of knowledge most closely connected to dispute resolution, Civil Procedure, made no reference to ADR. Following a review of the academic admission standards, 'Alternative Dispute Resolution' is now identified as a required component of the rebranded Civil Dispute Resolution area of knowledge. Accordingly, dispute resolution is required content for all Australian law degree programmes where graduates seek admission to practice. Less clear, however, is the extent to which the ADR content of law degree units has evolved to address the increasing prominence of technology and the practices and approaches known collectively as ODR.

5.3 THE MAINSTREAMING OF ODR

ODR is the 'application of information and communications technology to the prevention, management, and resolution of disputes'.[7] ODR encompasses a spectrum of developments and approaches, spanning supportive, replacement and disruptive technologies in justice systems.[8] With origins in e-commerce, ODR has expanded rapidly across the public and private sectors, encompassing a wide range of disputes between citizens and government.[9] Indicators of the institutionalisation of ODR mechanisms are proliferating,[10] including the United Nations Commission on International Trade Law (UNCITRAL) model rules for online arbitration;[11] the ODR platform established as a mandatory step for consumer disputes in European Union states;[12] the Civil Resolution Tribunal in British Columbia, which deals with strata disputes and

---

[6]   Law Admissions Consultative Committee, 'Prescribed Academic Areas of Knowledge' (Law Council of Australia, December 2016) www.lawcouncil.asn.au/resources/law-admissions-consultative-committee/documents-about-present-admission-policies accessed 23 January 2019.

[7]   Ethan Katsh and Colin Rule, 'What We Know and Need to Know about Online Dispute Resolution' (2015) 67 South Carolina Law Review 329, 329.

[8]   Tania Sourdin, 'Justice and Technological Innovation' (2015) 25(2) Journal of Judicial Administration 96; Tania Sourdin, *Alternative Dispute Resolution* (5th edn, Thomson Reuters 2015). Note that Sourdin differentiates replacement and disruptive technologies from supportive technologies (which can 'assist to inform, support and advise people involved in ADR'), suggesting that the latter are less associated with ODR. See Sourdin, *Alternative Dispute Resolution* 386.

[9]   Noam Ebner and John Zeleznikow, 'No Sheriff in Town: Governance for Online Dispute Resolution' (2016) 32(4) Negotiation Journal 297.

[10]   Ibid.

[11]   United Nations Commission on International Trade Law, 'Report of Working Group III (Online Dispute Resolution) on the Work of Its Thirty-Third Session (New York, 29 February – 4 March 2016)' (United Nations 2016) 49th Session http://undocs.org/EN/A/CN.9/868 accessed 11 March 2016.

[12]   Regulation (EU) No 524/2013 of the European Parliament and of the Council of 21 May 2013 on Online Dispute Resolution for Consumer Disputes and Amending Regulation (EC) No 2006/2004 and Directive 2009/22/EC [2013] OJ L 165.

small claims through a compulsory online platform;[13] and the United Kingdom's mammoth and multifaceted court modernisation programme.[14]

In Australia, the pace has been slower but the growth of ODR is still apparent, with first-tier consumer complaints handling and family dispute resolution presenting initial areas for experimentation.[15] Further steps forward have been supported by recent and current major inquiries. The Productivity Commission's 2014 Access to Justice Arrangements inquiry report recommended more extensive incorporation of technologies into court services,[16] and Victoria's 2016 Access to Justice Review recommended that an ODR platform be developed to handle small civil claims before the Victorian Civil and Administrative Tribunal (VCAT).[17] The review of the family law system being undertaken by the Australian Law Reform Commission in 2017–19 is exploring whether ODR should play a greater role in the resolution of family disputes, and the appropriate safeguards.[18] Taken together, these developments represent a trend to which legal educators must respond.

5.4 THE CURRENT PROFILE OF ODR IN LEGAL EDUCATION

Alongside the calls for legal educators to teach more ADR,[19] demands are increasing for law schools to better prepare graduates for the resolution of disputes in online forums.[20] Importantly, just as varieties of ODR have been in operation since at least the mid-1990s,[21] there has long been experimentation with online experiential learning in dispute resolution education, particularly for negotiation training.[22]

[13] See generally Shannon Salter, 'Online Dispute Resolution and Justice System Integration: British Columbia's Civil Resolution' (2017) 34(1) Windsor Yearbook of Access to Justice 112.

[14] HM Courts and Tribunals Service, 'HMCTS Reform Programme Projects Explained' (*gov.uk*, 2018) www.gov.uk/guidance/hmcts-reform-programme-projects-explained accessed 22 January 2019.

[15] Sourdin, *Alternative Dispute Resolution* (n 8) 392.

[16] Productivity Commission, 'Access to Justice Arrangements' (Commonwealth of Australia 2014) ch 17 www.pc.gov.au/inquiries/completed/access-justice/report accessed 23 January 2019.

[17] Victorian Department of Justice & Regulation, 'Access To Justice Review – Volume 2 – Report and Recommendations' (Department of Justice and Regulation 2016) 281 https://engage.vic.gov.au/down load_file/845/612 accessed 24 April 2019.

[18] Australian Law Reform Commission, 'Review of the Family Law System' (Australian Law Reform Commission 2018) 48, 63 www.alrc.gov.au/sites/default/files/dp86_review_of_the_family_law_sys tem_4.pdf accessed 22 January 2019.

[19] See, e.g., Tom Fisher, Judy Gutman and Erika Martens, 'Why Teach ADR to Law Students – Part 2: An Empirical Survey' (2007) 17(2) Legal Education Review 67; Farrow (n 2) 742; Goldberg (n 2); Waters (n 2).

[20] Goldberg (n 2).

[21] Ebner and Zeleznikow (n 9) 298.

[22] See, for example, Gail A Lasprogata, 'Virtual Arbitration: Contract Law and Alternative Dispute Resolution Meet in Cyberspace' (2001) 19(1) Journal of Legal Studies Education 107; Lucille M Ponte, 'The Case of the Unhappy Sports Fan: Embracing Student-Centered Learning and Promoting Upper-Level Cognitive Skills Through an Online Dispute Resolution Simulation' (2006) 23(2) Journal of Legal Studies Education 169; Andrea M Seielstad, 'Enhancing the Teaching of Lawyering Skills and Perspectives through Virtual World Engagement' (2012) 7(1) University of

Examples include chat room negotiations with live interaction;[23] the use of wikis to supplement face-to-face negotiation and role-play design;[24] and exploration of online role-plays for mediator accreditation.[25]

For innovations of this kind to reach large numbers of students and maximise their impact, they must make their way into the core legal curriculum. To determine how many of Australia's thirty-eight universities with accredited law schools offered units with ODR-specific content in 2016, we examined unit descriptions published online.[26] Our review indicated little overt engagement with ODR in Australian legal education. Only four out of thirty-eight universities offered units that made reference to ODR, and only two of the six units offered were at an undergraduate level, where the majority of students are enrolled. None of the units were compulsory for admission to practice. One university offered an elective unit in which students practised and participated in ODR, albeit with a cross-border mediation focus. Others investigated specific ODR settings (such as a postgraduate internet law unit dealing with domain name disputes), or referred to ODR in passing, such as including it in a list of potential content or methods students should be able to critically analyse and evaluate. While the lack of explicit reference to ODR may have been the product of a gap between advertised unit descriptions and actual content (as is the case for the Monash intervention described in this chapter), this review suggests it is likely that there is limited attention to ODR in current law school offerings, especially in core units.

5.5 THE MONASH ODR INTERVENTION

To explore the benefits of incorporating ODR in our dispute resolution teaching, we developed, piloted and implemented an experiential activity in our core litigation and dispute resolution units in the Law Faculty at Monash University. Monash is one of Australia's largest universities, and the Law Faculty is consistently ranked amongst the top 100 in the world. The faculty offers two courses leading to admission to practise as an Australian Lawyer: the undergraduate Bachelor of Laws and postgraduate Juris Doctor degrees. Both programmes include a litigation and

Massachusetts Law Review 40; Ian Macduff, 'Using Blogs in Teaching Negotiation: A Technical and Intercultural Postscript' (2012) 28(2) Negotiation Journal 201.

[23] Noam Ebner and others, 'You've Got Agreement: Negoti@ting via Email' (2009) 31(2) Hamline Journal of Public Law & Policy 427.

[24] Michele Ruyters, Kathy Douglas and Siew Fang Law, 'Blended Learning Using Role-Plays, Wikis and Blogs' (2011) 4(4) Journal of Learning Design 45.

[25] Kathy Douglas, 'Mediation Accreditation: Using Online Role Plays to Teach Theoretical Issues' (2007) 18(2) Australasian Dispute Resolution Journal 92.

[26] A university law school is accredited if the degree offered satisfies the theoretical component of educational training required for admission to practice in the relevant state or territory. Universities with accredited law schools were identified, and the search terms 'online dispute resolution' and 'ODR' were entered into course information searches on university public websites. Details of the units reviewed are held on file by the authors and are available on request.

dispute resolution unit that satisfies the admission to practise requirement, and is typically taken in the later years of the course. The units cover ADR and litigation content and in recent years they have been revised to include an experiential mediation activity.[27]

We adopted a blended learning design for the exercise, bringing together online and face-to-face interaction in a role-play.[28] Students worked in small groups to resolve a dispute using negotiation and mediation, first using an ODR portal and then in a more traditional face-to-face mediation and debriefing session. The factual scenario involved a contractual dispute between two parties: a publishing company and an author with an overdue manuscript. Each party was represented by one or two lawyers.[29] Students were assigned to participate in the role-play as one of the parties, a party lawyer, or a mediator. Each participant was provided with common facts about the dispute; the parties and their lawyers were also provided with party-specific confidential facts. The exercise consisted of three components:

1. Students used the GR ODR portal to identify alternatives, issues and interests and communicate about these with the opposing party. They were required to work together to use the portal to understand the ground rules of the mediation and to identify issues, interests and alternatives in a structured and stepped process. Students were encouraged to watch short explanatory videos imbedded in the portal (to clarify each stage, along with key terms and concepts) before entering data, and were referred to supporting reading on mediation. Students were instructed to aim to reach the stage of developing options in the portal in preparation for the in-class mediation. Those playing the mediator role were able to see the parties' issues, interests and alternatives in the portal, and could use this information to prepare for exploring options in the in-class mediation. At any stage participants could download a summary of the information exchanged in the portal.

2. Students participated in an in-class, face-to-face mediation, followed by a debriefing session.

3. Students prepared a reflective journal (500 words) about their experiences in the ODR portal and in mediation. The reflective journal was worth 10 per cent of the marks available in the unit. Consistent with recommendations by Rundle and Hiller regarding the need for clear communication about reflection activities,[30] we had trialled and refined the task instructions over two prior teaching periods.

---

[27] Douglas, 'The Role of ADR in Developing Lawyers' Practice: Lessons from Australian Legal Education' (n 5) 75.

[28] See Ruyters, Douglas and Law (n 24) 45.

[29] On the need for attention to lawyer roles in mediation role-plays, see Douglas, 'The Teaching of ADR in Australian Law Schools: Promoting Non-Adversarial Practice in Law' (n 3) 54–6.

[30] Olivia Rundle and Sarah Hiller, 'Teaching Self-Reflection to Law Students in a Dispute Resolution Unit' (2012) 23(3) Australasian Dispute Resolution Journal 169, 178. See also Ruyters, Douglas and Law (n 24).

The task drew on Ryan and Ryan's '4 Rs' reflective model, which encourages students to report (and respond), relate, reason and reconstruct in relation to their experience.[31]

We piloted the intervention with two streams of postgraduate litigation and dispute resolution students (n=40) in January 2016, before implementing it in the undergraduate unit in Semester 1 2016. The study received ethics approval from the Monash University Human Research Ethics Committee.[32]

5.6 EVALUATION SAMPLE AND SURVEY RESPONSES

There were 207 students enrolled in the unit and sixty-five participated in the study (response rate 32 per cent; all but two participants answered all survey questions). Key participant characteristics are presented in Table 5.1 below. Just over half of the participants were female (56 per cent), closely corresponding to the unit's proportion of female enrolled students (54 per cent). Participants were engaged in a range of degree programmes, with Arts/Law (58 per cent) and Commerce/Law (19 per cent) being the most common. Two thirds of participants reported that they intended to practise as a lawyer on completion of their studies (64 per cent), with most others undecided (33 per cent).

Students were asked a small number of binary questions about their perceptions of the GR Portal (Table 5.2) and its impact on their experience in the exercise. Overwhelmingly, they reported that the portal was easy to use (95 per cent), it assisted them with preparation for the in-class component of the exercise (91 per cent) and that the online aspect of the task gave them insight into how parties might experience ODR (89 per cent).

5.6.1 *Insights from Student Reflections*

Participating students' reflective journals were analysed to identify commentary relating to the portal-based component of the exercise. Journals submitted by students who provided consent for the analysis were reviewed for ODR-related terms (technology, ODR, online, portal) by one author. Of the fifty-six journals provided for the study, twenty-four (43 per cent) made reference to the portal. It is a surprising finding that fewer than half of the reviewed journals discussed the portal. Possible explanations include the constraints of the word limit, and the likelihood that the in-person component of the exercise was more impactful for students and was therefore more likely to be the subject of their journals. It is also possible that for this cohort of students, the use of a portal in the learning environment is familiar and not especially

---

[31] Mary Ryan and Michael Ryan, 'Theorising a Model for Teaching and Assessing Reflective Learning in Higher Education' (2013) 32(2) Higher Education Research & Development 244.

[32] Approval number CF16/1314–2016000693.

TABLE 5.1 *Respondent characteristics (n=65)*

Characteristic	n (%)
Female	36 (56%)
Course	
Arts/Law	37 (58%)
Commerce/Law	12 (19%)
Law (single degree)	9 (14%)
Engineering/Law	3 (5%)
Music/Law	2 (3%)
Other	1 (2%)
Intention to practise as lawyer	
Yes	41 (64%)
No	2 (3%)
Unsure	21 (33%)

TABLE 5.2 *Using the portal*

Question	n (%)
Was the ODR portal easy to use?	
Yes	62 (95%)
No	3 (5%)
Did the portal help you to prepare for the in-class mediation exercise?*	
Yes	58 (91%)
No	6 (9%)
Did the portal give you insight into how parties might experience ODR?	
Yes	58 (89%)
No	7 (11%)

worthy of comment, given their extensive digital interactivity and exposure to online platforms in this and other facets of their lives.

The ODR-related journal content was extracted and read through by each author to independently identify preliminary themes and codes. The authors then worked together to compare findings, develop a consensus-based coding framework and discuss connections between themes.[33] Key themes were identified for further analysis

---

[33] See Jane Forman and Laura Damschroder, 'Qualitative Content Analysis' in Liva Jacoby and Laura A Siminoff (eds.), *Empirical Methods for Bioethics: A Primer (Advances in Bioethics, Volume 11)* (Emerald Group Publishing Limited 2007) 39, 41, 43.

and those findings are presented here. They are efficiency and preparation; communication, interaction and emotion; access to justice; and the gaps between expectations and experience.

5.6.1.1 Efficiency and Preparation

Students were enthusiastic about the way their use of the portal enabled them to
efficiently prepare for the face-to-face mediation. The online exchange of information enabled them to collaboratively clarify issues and prioritise interests. This
'was fundamental in facilitating the mediation process' (Respondent 22), 'provided a very good platform that meant both parties went into the mediation with
a good understating of what each party sought from the process' (Respondent 34)
and ensured that 'each party was on the same page' (Respondent 52).

The online component prepared the students for the face-to-face mediation by
engaging them with the facts, legal problems and relational priorities of the parties
outside of class time. As a result, students readily determined the 'issues, interests and
agenda of both parties' prior to meeting in-class for the mediation (Respondent 34).
Further, parties began building mutual trust that was beneficial when subsequently
engaging in person. One student observed:

> Our pre-tutorial discussions were conducted online and I felt that this platform
> was a useful way to engage with the process as it set out the 'mediation diamond' in
> discrete, manageable steps ... I had assumed it would be a long, drawn-out
> discussion that would wildly pinwheel through a bunch of different issues before
> settling on some contract or arrangement. However, the mediation proceeded
> quicker than I anticipated, due to the previous preparation on the portal.
> (Respondent 38)

Students were also very positive about the combination of online and face-to-face
components of the exercise:

> In my view, the combination of both an online and face-to-face mediation worked
> very well, as the online component enabled me to be prepared for the actual
> mediation, and the face-to-face component made the mediation more personable
> and allowed me to gauge the other party's reaction when issues were being dis-
> cussed. In essence, the online component and the face-to-face mediation comple-
> mented each other. (Respondent 20)

These findings lend support to the broader evidence base indicating the advantages
of blended modes of learning;[34] from a more prosaic perspective, it suggests that
ODR activities may provide opportunities to maximise student preparation and the

---

[34]   See generally Semiral Oncu and Hasan Cakir, 'Research in Online Learning Environments:
Priorities and Methodologies' (2011) 57(1) Computers & Education 1098; Ruyters, Douglas and Law
(n 24).

use of the limited in-class time available for the task. On these counts, the portal was highly successful.

Importantly, however, the efficiency gains from online preparation and interaction may impact upon the face-to-face role-play in unanticipated ways. A perceptive student noted, for example, that the exchange of information in the portal obviated the need for the mediator to meet separately with the parties to develop rapport and credibility, as the mediator had become aware of the parties' interests through the portal information. As the student observed, this represented a missed opportunity for the mediator to develop the parties' trust and confidence in the mediation process (Respondent 40). Implications of this kind should be considered in the planning and development of ODR-based activities.

5.6.2 *Communication, Interaction and Emotion*

Unlike the discussion of efficiency, where most students agreed that use of the online portal enhanced their preparation for and participation in the face-to-face mediation, students had varying views on the benefits and suitability of online communication. The reasons for their evaluations differed, as did their level of capability and comfort in the online setting.

5.6.2.1 Asynchronous Communication and Managing Emotions

Students identified the asynchronous exchange of information as beneficial because they had 'time to research, for example, industry standards for payment negotiations' (Respondent 46), and were able to reflect on the other party's interests and concerns in advance (Respondent 53). The role of emotion was also the subject of student commentary: some referred to the benefit of collaborating on the portal being that it prompted a group to 'debate what would be raised by whom and how to present a well-organised front to the other party, thereby controlling emotions and maintaining composure' (Respondent 46). Students perceived being able to control emotion as a benefit, though some also speculated whether the lack of emotional stake they had in the dispute made the process (including the use of the portal) unrealistic.

5.6.2.2 Online versus Face to Face Communication

Some students indicated surprise at the differing qualities of their online and in-person communication experiences: 'Even though the issues were previously established through ODR, actual negotiation discussions took much longer than I thought as everyone had a lot more to verbally elaborate in person on the underlying emotive rationales rather than just recounting plain facts' (Respondent 30). Others were sceptical about the relative value of communicating online, maintaining that face-to-face communication achieves heightened understanding for the parties:

If I was to complete the ADR again, I would probably try and work on the pre-mediation issues and options in real life with the other party, as opposed to doing it all online. Face to face communication ensures that these issues are clear to both parties, which would make the subsequent in-class mediation more efficient as both parties are well informed as to what the other wants. Apart from that, the mediation was a success with each party leaving satisfied with their client's outcome. (Respondent 23)

The discomfort some students feel communicating online is consistent with previous studies investigating student experiences negotiating and interacting professionally online.[35] Non-verbal cues are considered a crucial supplement to verbal communication.[36] The immediacy and ubiquity of social media has changed the way people communicate in text, and to combat the lack of non-verbal cues, emotion icons (emoticons) have evolved to perform some of the non-verbal communication work of face-to-face interaction.[37] Questions remain, however, about the extent to which online and social media communication can translate into effective professional communication in the ODR context. Our findings add weight to the argument that being familiar with technology socially does not necessarily equate to confidence or competence using technology professionally. This highlights a gap in legal education and suggests that teaching law students the genre of online professional communication may be beneficial.[38]

5.6.3 *Student Initiative and Capability*

Students reported communicating online in a within-portal chat facility as well as contemporaneously using Skype to work with their group members as they progressed through the portal steps. These accounts speak to the initiative students demonstrated in engaging in technology-supported collaborative work. In contrast, one student reported experiencing a lack of communication from and with the other party in the portal, with resultant frustration about 'the mystery surround[ing] the other party's position' (Respondent 43). Playing the role of a lawyer, this student reported disappointment with the lack of face-to-face preparation they undertook with their client: without in-person communication, the student felt that they 'could not be sure that we were on the same page'.

This evidence suggests that student capabilities vary, both with technology and problem-solving through group work challenges, and that support may be required to better prepare students for engaging in group work and collaboration. These

---

[35] See, e.g., Seielstad (n 22) 73; Macduff (n 22).

[36] See, e.g., Claire Holland and Donnalee Taylor, 'Was That Said With a Smile?: Factors Influencing Effective Online Negotiations' (2016) 27 Australian Dispute Resolution Journal 103.

[37] Ibid 108–10.

[38] Kylie Burns and Lillian Corbin, 'E-Professionalism: The Global Reach of the Lawyer's Duty to Use Social Media Ethically' [2016] Journal of the Professional Lawyer 153.

findings are further evidence that mere equality of exposure or accessibility to technology does not equate to equality of confidence or competence in using the technology.[39] There is clearly potential pedagogical benefit in helping students work though such challenges, however, not least because communication breakdowns and opposing party non-response are common features of dispute resolution practice.

5.6.4 Power and Access to Justice

Four students commented on the impact of the portal on power dynamics and access to justice considerations, including the potential for online mechanisms to 'level the playing field' between differently resourced disputants. One student identified that some members of the community are unable to access the internet, and so the use of ODR as a substitute for other mechanisms would heighten the risk of perpetuating power imbalances (Respondent 9). Others identified the positive potential of online mechanisms, one observing that 'power imbalances are not always easily remedied' in the absence of 'external supervision and institutional structures (like the court system)':

> This is where I believe online processes are helpful. It allows issues and desired outcomes to be asserted without confrontation, and further negotiated in person, each party aware of the position of the other ... It was easy and efficient to organise a time to meet with the Student/Lawyer over Skype and discuss the issues, following the prompts. In a real dispute, this would favour those who live remotely or without funds for face-to-face meetings prior to mediation. (Respondent 44)

Similarly, two students referred to the expedited exchange of ideas through the portal as being beneficial for the less advantaged disputant in the scenario (an impoverished and unwell novelist) for its cost savings, convenience and scope to enhance access to justice. One of these students also described the benefits of the 'impersonal' quality of the portal as 'favourable for disadvantaged parties [who] are easily intimidated or where the issues are emotionally charged' (Respondent 28).

The relative paucity of evidence of students' critical thinking about power and access to justice in connection with the portal was disappointing, but may in part reflect the timing of the exercise in the early weeks of the unit, and the limited number of words students had to work with in their reflective journals. As ODR becomes more mainstream, providing students with opportunities to consider the range of access to justice implications, benefits and disadvantages of the use of this and other legal technology will be critical.[40] In one of the pilot teaching periods we paired the ODR activity with a research task that required students to prepare a submission on the access to justice implications of ODR for small civil claims to

---

[39] See the similar findings discussed in Macduff (n 22).
[40] On these issues, see Victorian Government Department of Justice and Regulation (n 17) 271–81.

the Victorian Government inquiry on the topic.[41] Having students engage with the research evidence on the impact of online forums on access to justice in tandem with the experiential exercise was a more effective means to engage their critical thinking on this issue than the experiential exercise alone.

5.6.5 *Gaps between Expectation and Experience*

The final key theme in students' reflections was the gap between their expectations in the exercise and their actual experience, and the role the portal played in this. These expectations had been developed through students' preparatory reading, previous study and preconceptions about what dispute resolution entails 'in the real world'.

A student who had undertaken previous negotiation study in their law degree based on the Harvard Model was disconcerted by the extent to which 'the transparency of the module took away a substantial negotiation practice': 'I felt this removed the most challenging part of negotiation – trying to work out what the other side wants in order to find a mutually satisfactory outcome – and perhaps is why I didn't find this task challenging compared to tasks in [my previous studies]' (Respondent 33). In contrast, another participant commented that: 'The online portal was a useful tool for outlining the process by which the in class mediation would follow' (Respondent 22).

This evidence highlights an opportunity for better explanation of what ODR offers in addition to more traditional methods of dispute resolution. In particular, students should be provided with access to the emerging ODR-specific literature in preparation for their participation in these activities, as opposed to resources that focus on face-to-face modes of interaction.

Other students indicated that they had expected their colleagues to be candid and transparent in the information entered into the portal, but didn't find this occurring in practice. One such student noted that

> Everyone was protective over their interests and this resulted in difficulty communicating freely. The content in ODR was vague as some information were not disclosed. For example, we were not aware of [the other party's] illness until the mediator encouraged the sharing of information. This begs the question: will mediation work when parties are unwilling to communicate constructively? (Respondent 56)

This same student connected their concern to their previous learning in Evidence Law, contrasting cross examination and admissibility rules with the ADR setting, where the student suggested (erroneously) that: 'No evidence is required to prove any allegations. It is informal and there is no judge to rule. Although technologies are transforming the ADR processes whereby it is less confronting and easier to

---

[41]   Victorian Department of Justice & Regulation (n 17).

communicate in ODR than in-person, I think the challenge of encouraging parties to communicate candidly would still remain.'

Another student experienced considerable teamwork 'as it was a role-play and the participants engaged in good faith' (Respondent 40), but believed it was unrealistic and that real-life parties to ADR would not so willingly engage. Observations of this kind highlight the need to ensure that students participating in ODR are made aware of the extension of lawyers' ethical duties and obligations to ODR and ADR settings.[42]

5.7 CONCLUSION

The legal profession and institutions have embraced ADR, and ADR and litigation are increasingly incorporating online mechanisms. In the future lawyers will be expected to competently interact with their peers, external bodies and their clients both face-to-face and online. Teaching ODR is an obvious way of combining contemporary dispute resolution with online communication skills in an effort to prepare law graduates for practice. Accounts of efforts to incorporate ODR in legal education settings provide useful examples and an evidence base for law schools seeking to ensure that the curriculum reflects the technological developments shaping civil dispute resolution policy and practice.[43]

Our evaluation demonstrated that student perceptions of the online portal were overwhelmingly positive. The study findings identify a number of learning opportunities in the gaps between student expectation and experience, but also in their preconceptions of appropriate conduct in ADR and ODR in practice. The mix of online and face-to-face role-play was generally well received and given the constraints of time and resources in a combined litigation and dispute resolution unit, the blended learning exercise was relatively successful and has been retained as a permanent fixture in our core litigation and dispute resolution units.

Of greater concern is the limited opportunity our experiential ODR activity provided for fostering students' critical thinking about the impacts of legal technology on access to justice. While many of the benefits of incorporating ODR into dispute

---

[42] See, e.g., Bobette Wolski, 'The Truth about Honesty and Candour in Mediation: What the Tribunal Left Unsaid in Mullins' (2012) 36(2) Melbourne University Law Review 706; Bobette Wolski, 'On Mediation, Legal Representatives and Advocates' (2015) 38(1) University of New South Wales Law Journal 5.

[43] See, for example, Martha E Simmons and Darin Thompson, 'The Internet as a Site of Legal Education and Collaboration Across Continents and Time Zones: Using Online Dispute Resolution as a Tool for Student Learning' (2017) 34(1) Windsor Yearbook of Access to Justice 222; Daniel Rainey, 'Teaching Online Dispute Resolution: Results from a Survey of Students' (*Mediate*, 2 August 2010) www.mediate.com/articles/RaineyD1.cfm accessed 23 January 2019; Ian Macduff, '"Stand by Your Devices"; or "Access through the [Virtual] Looking Glass"' (*Kluwer Arbitration Mediation Blog*, 26 February 2016) http://mediationblog.kluwerarbitration.com/2016/02/26/stand-by-your-devices-or-access-through-the-virtual-looking-glass/ accessed 23 January 2019.

resolution teaching mirror the benefits of having regard for ADR,[44] there are specific considerations about computer-mediated communication, access to justice and power in the online environment that warrant attention.[45] This is especially the case in view of the risk that the comfort law students may experience with technology could make them less likely to question its effects. We were disappointed with the extent of student engagement on these issues, but acknowledge that the time constraints of a busy core unit may have played a role in limiting the opportunity for reflection. Creating space for consideration of the quality, equity and access to justice implications of ODR in its various guises will be important for future analysis of ODR's performance by our graduates. Admittedly, capitalising on the greater amount of time available in an elective unit may be necessary to enable more in-depth analysis to occur. To facilitate that, we subsequently developed Australia's first elective unit dedicated to ODR, with the specific learning objectives of exploring 'the evaluation of ODR, including its suitability for varieties of disputes and disputants, its impact on access to justice and practical approaches for assessing the performance of ODR systems'.[46]

BIBLIOGRAPHY

Armstrong S, 'Is Robotic or Online Dispute Resolution the Future?' (*The Australian Dispute Resolution Research Network*, 19 July 2016) https://adrresearch.net/2016/07/19/is-robotic-or-online-dispute-resolution-the-future/ accessed 22 January 2019

Australian Law Reform Commission, 'Review of the Family Law System' (Australian Law Reform Commission 2018) www.alrc.gov.au/sites/default/files/dp86_review_of_the_family_law_system_4.pdf accessed 22 January 2019

Burns K and Corbin L, 'E-Professionalism: The Global Reach of the Lawyer's Duty to Use Social Media Ethically' [2016] Journal of the Professional Lawyer 153

Corbin L, Baron P and Gutman J, 'ADR Zealots, Adjudicative Romantics and Everything in between: Lawyers in Mediations' (2015) 38(2) University of New South Wales Law Journal 492

Douglas K, 'Mediation Accreditation: Using Online Role Plays to Teach Theoretical Issues' (2007) 18(2) Australasian Dispute Resolution Journal 92

'The Teaching of ADR in Australian Law Schools: Promoting Non-Adversarial Practice in Law' (2011) 22(1) Australasian Dispute Resolution Journal 49

'The Role of ADR in Developing Lawyers' Practice: Lessons from Australian Legal Education' (2015) 22(1) International Journal of the Legal Profession 71

Duffy J and Field R, 'Why ADR Must Be a Mandatory Subject in the Law Degree: A Cheat Sheet for the Willing and a Primer for the Non-Believer' (2014) 25(1) Australian Dispute Resolution Journal 9

---

[44] See Sue Armstrong, 'Is Robotic or Online Dispute Resolution the Future?' (*The Australian Dispute Resolution Research Network*, 19 July 2016) https://adrresearch.net/2016/07/19/is-robotic-or-online-dispute-resolution-the-future/ accessed 22 January 2019; Carrie Menkel-Meadow, 'Is ODR ADR? Reflections of an ADR Founder from 15th ODR Conference, the Hague, the Netherlands, 22–23 May 2016' (2016) 3(1) International Journal of Online Dispute Resolution 4.

[45] Waters (n 2) 243–4.

[46] Monash University, 'LAW5460 – Online Dispute Resolution' (Unit Handbook, 2018) www.monash.edu/pubs/2018handbooks/units/LAW5460.html accessed 23 January 2019.

Ebner N and others, 'You've Got Agreement: Negoti@ting via Email' (2009) 31(2) Hamline Journal of Public Law & Policy 427

Ebner N and Zeleznikow J, 'No Sheriff in Town: Governance for Online Dispute Resolution' (2016) 32(4) Negotiation Journal 297

Farrow TCW, 'Dispute Resolution, Access to Civil Justice and Legal Education' (2004) 42(3) Alberta Law Review 741

Fisher T, Gutman J and Martens E, 'Why Teach ADR to Law Students – Part 2: An Empirical Survey' (2007) 17(2) Legal Education Review 67

Forman J and Damschroder L, 'Qualitative Content Analysis' in Liva Jacoby and Laura A Siminoff (eds.), *Empirical Methods for Bioethics: A Primer (Advances in Bioethics, Volume 11)* (Emerald Group Publishing Limited 2007)

Goldberg J, 'Online Alternative Dispute Resolution and Why Law Schools Should Prepare Future Lawyers for the Online Forum' (2014) 14(1) Pepperdine Dispute Resolution Law Journal 1

HM Courts and Tribunals Service, 'HMCTS Reform Programme Projects Explained' (*gov.uk*, 20 June 2018) www.gov.uk/guidance/hmcts-reform-programme-projects-explained accessed 22 January 2019

Holland C and Taylor D, 'Was That Said With a Smile?: Factors Influencing Effective Online Negotiations' (2016) 27 Australian Dispute Resolution Journal 103

Katsh E and Rule C, 'What We Know and Need to Know about Online Dispute Resolution' (2015) 67 South Carolina Law Review 329

Lasprogata GA, 'Virtual Arbitration: Contract Law and Alternative Dispute Resolution Meet in Cyberspace' (2001) 19(1) Journal of Legal Studies Education 107

Law Admissions Consultative Committee, 'Prescribed Academic Areas of Knowledge' (Law Council of Australia, December 2016) www.lawcouncil.asn.au/resources/law-admissions-consultative-committee/documents-about-present-admission-policies accessed 23 January 2019

Macduff I, 'Using Blogs in Teaching Negotiation: A Technical and Intercultural Postscript' (2012) 28(2) Negotiation Journal 201

"'Stand by Your Devices"; or "Access through the [Virtual] Looking Glass"' (*Kluwer Arbitration Mediation Blog*, 26 February 2016) http://mediationblog .kluwerarbitration.com/2016/02/26/stand-by-your-devices-or-access-through-the-virtual -looking-glass/ accessed 23 January 2019

Menkel-Meadow C, 'Is ODR ADR? Reflections of an ADR Founder from 15th ODR Conference, the Hague, the Netherlands, 22–23 May 2016' (2016) 3(1) International Journal of Online Dispute Resolution 4

Monash University, 'LAW5460 – Online Dispute Resolution' (Unit Handbook, 2018) www .monash.edu/pubs/2018handbooks/units/law5460.html accessed 23 January 2019

Oncu S and Cakir H, 'Research in Online Learning Environments: Priorities and Methodologies' (2011) 57(1) Computers & Education 1098

Ponte LM, 'The Case of the Unhappy Sports Fan: Embracing Student-Centered Learning and Promoting Upper-Level Cognitive Skills Through an Online Dispute Resolution Simulation' (2006) 23(2) Journal of Legal Studies Education 169

Productivity Commission, 'Access to Justice Arrangements' (Commonwealth of Australia 2014) www.pc.gov.au/inquiries/completed/access-justice/report accessed 23 January 2019

Rainey D, 'Teaching Online Dispute Resolution: Results from a Survey of Students' (*Mediate*, 2 August 2010) www.mediate.com/articles/raineyd1.cfm accessed 23 January 2019

Rundle O and Hiller S, 'Teaching Self-Reflection to Law Students in a Dispute Resolution Unit' (2012) 23(3) Australasian Dispute Resolution Journal 169

Ruyters M, Douglas K and Law SF, 'Blended Learning Using Role-Plays, Wikis and Blogs' (2011) 4(4) Journal of Learning Design 45

Ryan M and Ryan M, 'Theorising a Model for Teaching and Assessing Reflective Learning in Higher Education' (2013) 32(2) Higher Education Research & Development 244

Salter S, 'Online Dispute Resolution and Justice System Integration: British Columbia's Civil Resolution' (2017) 34(1) Windsor Yearbook of Access to Justice 112

Seielstad AM, 'Enhancing the Teaching of Lawyering Skills and Perspectives through Virtual World Engagement' (2012) 7(1) University of Massachusetts Law Review 40

Simmons ME and Thompson D, 'The Internet as a Site of Legal Education and Collaboration Across Continents and Time Zones: Using Online Dispute Resolution as a Tool for Student Learning' (2017) 34(1) Windsor Yearbook of Access to Justice 222

Sourdin T, *Alternative Dispute Resolution* (5th edn, Thomson Reuters 2015)

'Justice and Technological Innovation' (2015) 25(2) Journal of Judicial Administration 96

United Nations Commission on International Trade Law, 'Report of Working Group III (Online Dispute Resolution) on the Work of Its Thirty-Third Session (New York, 29 February – 4 March 2016)' (United Nations 2016) 49th Session http://undocs.org/en/a/cn.9/868 accessed 11 March 2016

Victorian Department of Justice & Regulation, 'Access To Justice Review – Volume 2 – Report and Recommendations' (Department of Justice and Regulation 2016) https://engage.vic.gov.au/download_file/845/612 accessed 24 April 2019

Waters B, 'The Importance of Teaching Dispute Resolution in a Twenty-First-Century Law School' (2017) 51(2) The Law Teacher 227

Wolski B, 'The Truth about Honesty and Candour in Mediation: What the Tribunal Left Unsaid in Mullins' (2012) 36(2) Melbourne University Law Review 706

'On Mediation, Legal Representatives and Advocates' (2015) 38(1) University of New South Wales Law Journal 5

Regulation (EU) No 524/2013 of the European Parliament and of the Council of 21 May 2013 on Online Dispute Resolution for Consumer Disputes and Amending Regulation (EC) No 2006/2004 and Directive 2009/22/EC [2013] OJ L 165

6

Design Comes to the Law School

Margaret Hagan

This chapter documents how the Legal Design Lab at Stanford University has integrated design thinking into law school technology curriculum. In this chapter we profile the objectives of the lab and explore the work the lab has undertaken to introduce new opportunities for skill acquisition through design thinking courses, innovation sprints, and workshops. We explore the purpose, process, and outcomes of these new experiments in legal education, and overview the interdisciplinary methods we have developed, brought from design schools and human-computer interaction programmes. We detail examples of the specific types of classes, sprints, and workshops run, how we define learning outcomes, and how we evaluate student performance. Further, we explore the way in which we leverage technology to provide students with opportunities to acquire user research, mapping, rapid proto-typing, and improved communication skills. Drawing on lessons observed over the life of the Design Lab, we conclude by reflecting on our experience of integrating design thinking into a law school programme and argue for the importance of design thinking as an aspect of technology training within and outside of law.

6.1 INTRODUCTION

The domain of 'legal design' has come into focus over the past several years, as a new track for innovative legal education. There have been Legal Design Summits in Helsinki and Stanford, in which people working in these nascent fields have come together to define methodologies, share use cases, and set an agenda for the future.[1] Legal design classes have been taught at universities across the United States, including Stanford, Northeastern University, Michigan State Law School,

---

[1] See Nora Al Haider, 'The Legal Design Summit Recap: Uncharted Territory' (*Medium*, 1 January 2018) https://medium.com/legal-design-and-innovation/the-legal-design-summit-recap-uncharted-territory-77d8795315cc accessed 23 January 2019; Margaret Hagan, 'The State of Legal Design: The Big Takeaways of the Stanford Law + Design Summit' (*Medium*, 2017) https://medium.com/legal-design-and-innovation/the-state-of-legal-design-the-big-takeaways-of-the-stanford-law-design-summit-ee363b5bf109 accessed 23 January 2019.

Vanderbilt Law School, and Brigham Young University.[2] While not as prominent as legal informatics or legal technology programmes in law schools, legal design offers a promising new way of training law graduates and existing professionals in how to foster innovation within the legal system.

Legal design is a particular application of a broader human-centred design approach to innovation in which 'innovation is powered by a thorough understanding, through direct observation, of what people want and need in their lives and what they like or dislike about the way particularly products are made, packaged, marketed, sold and supported'.[3] Legal design applies the principles and methodologies from this broad approach to the particularities of the legal system. Its driving principle is that the legal system should be more human-centred, that is to say, more accessible, effective, affordable, comprehensible, and empowering.

Legal design crosses into legal technology and informatics often because automation, artificial intelligence, standardised data, and digital services prove to make the legal system more human-centred. However, unlike legal technology and informatics approaches, legal design does not advocate for using technology as a solution without a strong use case, grounded in people's needs, routines, and values. Legal design solves problems in the legal system by starting with an intense focus on the people involved and what opportunities or problems they have. It then considers what solutions might serve users best, and although this might include a new technology, it might also include a new paper document, a new legal strategy, a new service or organisation, or a policy or rule change.

Since inception Stanford Legal Design Lab has been at the forefront of educational innovation in law: integrating human-centred design methodologies into the legal curriculum and establishing a new design track within the law degree. As the first lab of its kind, it is a case study in the process of widening student skills through interdisciplinary and cross-faculty collaboration, and a demonstration of the way in which innovation in legal education can catalyse wider innovation across the profession. Tracing the development of the lab over the last five years, this chapter reflects upon its dual aims, as both: (i) an exemplar of innovation in curriculum development, demonstrating how design can develop law students' capacity for problem-solving and leadership; and (ii) an engine for research and development leading to the creation of innovative solutions which effect structural change for the

---

[2]   See Margaret Hagan, 'Justice Innovation with Law School Design Labs' (ABA *Dialogue*, 15 June 2018) www.americanbar.org/groups/legal_services/publications/dialogue/volume/21/spring-2018/iolta-design -labs/ accessed 23 January 2019 (for an overview of Law School Design Labs); Margaret Hagan, 'The Rise of the Law School Labs' (*Open Law Lab*, 13 September 2017) www.openlawlab.com/2017/09/13/ the-rise-of-the-law-school-labs/ accessed 23 January 2019 (a more visual encapsulation of what these labs are doing); Dan Jackson, 'Human-Centered Legal Tech: Integrating Design in Legal Education' (2016) 50(1) The Law Teacher 82 (how design is used in a law school lab); Martha F Davis, 'Institutionalizing Legal Innovation: The (Re)Emergence of the Law Lab' (2015) 65(1) Journal of Legal Education 190 (a fuller description of law school labs).

[3]   Tim Brown, 'Design Thinking' (2008) 6 Harvard Business Review 84, 86.

benefit of society. Taken together, the work of the lab contributes to the growing recognition of human-centred legal design as vital to both the study and practice of law.

In this chapter, we outline the development and growth of the lab from initial inception. First, we detail the emergence of the lab and the purpose to which work is directed. We then explore the educational dimensions of the lab's work, including, the various events and courses convened, the organisation of teaching, the assessment of students, and the development of the curriculum. Third, we document the research and development work undertaken at the lab, and evaluate the contribution the lab makes to the wider research environment of the school and university. Finally, we consider the challenges that the lab has faced and discuss how this has shaped our emerging priorities.

6.2 THE LEGAL DESIGN LAB AT STANFORD UNIVERSITY

6.2.1 *Establishment and Influences*

The Legal Design Lab has been in operation since September 2013 at Stanford University. It evolved first as the Programme for Legal Tech and Design at Stanford Institute of Design, was then adopted by Stanford Law School as the Legal Design Initiative, before becoming the Legal Design Lab. It now straddles both the Law School and the Institute of Design (d.school) as an interdisciplinary programme with one director, one lead technologist, a post-JD fellow, and approximately twelve research scholars and fellows working on various projects.

The Legal Design Lab is an experiment in how design methodologies, particularly those drawn from human-centred design (which might also be termed 'design thinking', 'user experience design', or 'service design'), can be introduced into legal education and practice. It has three core competencies:

i Educating students from the law school and across the university in design-driven innovation in the legal system.
ii Conducting research into new designs and technologies for the legal system.
iii Developing these designs and technologies in-house to be implemented or transferred to a partner.

The first of these competencies are directed at the development of legal education, whilst the second and third competencies are intended to support the broader human-centred legal design eco-system, particularly within the access to justice space.

Design in the law school has been predated by design work in many other schools and disciplines including medicine, education, and business.[4] The Stanford d. school method of teaching had grown out of use cases focused on consumer product

---

[4]   See the course catalog from Stanford Institute of Design's past archive of classes profiling the range of domains that design work is being applied to in academic explorations Stanford Institute of Design, 'Class Archive' https://dschool.stanford.edu/class-archive/ accessed 23 January 2019.

design and industrial design. In this context, design was a method to develop products that would please a single user-type, or increase sales. In order to translate design to the legal context and develop it as a method of finding feasible, promising concepts to resolve policy and social issues, the lab drew on a range of influences.

Our initial experiments in how to use design methodologies for more complex, abstract, and social systems such as law, were informed by reference to theory and practice. Richard Buchanan's work on design as a method of resolving wicked challenges in policy and social systems which framed design as a rhetorical approach, and not strictly a craft to manufacture pleasant objects or communications, proved especially informative.[5] This led the lab to adopt a definition of design as a systematic, ethical, and exploratory method of addressing problems that are particularly difficult to 'solve' and that involve a range of competing stakeholders and interests.

In operationalising Buchanan's vision of design as a tool for social innovation, the lab drew inspiration from design work being taught in other policy-making fields. This included the work of Ezio Manzini and the DESIS Network, focused on better environmental and municipal policy-making through participatory, exploratory design, which pointed at ways that creative, human-centred methodologies could be brought into social science research and experimentation.[6] It also included the work of Lucy Kimbell whose teaching in the UK in the design field and close collaboration with the national policy lab to develop methods for policy-makers and government officials provided practical guidance on adapting design for a legal setting.[7]

Given that the problems to which we apply design are complex and involve a wide range of stakeholders, we adopt a participatory methodology and actively engage with relevant stakeholders. As a result, most of the work of the lab (across our teaching, research and development activities) involves partnership with other organisations. This includes public sector legal organisations such as state courts,

---

[5]   See, e.g., Richard Buchanan, 'Wicked Problems in Design Thinking' (1992) 8(2) Design Issues 5; Richard Buchanan, 'Human Dignity and Human Rights: Thoughts on the Principles of Human-Centered Design' (2001) 17(3) Design Issues 35; Richard Buchanan, 'Strategies of Design Research: Productive Science and Rhetorical Inquiry' in Ralf Michel (ed.), *Design Research Now* (Birkhäuser Basel 2007). Note that Buchanan's work drew from and was influenced by theoriests such as John Dewey, Horst Rittel, and Herbert Simon. See Horst WJ Rittel and Melvin M Webber, 'Planning Problems Are Wicked Problems' in Nigel Cross (ed.), *Developments in Design Methodology* (Wiley 1984); John Dewey, 'Having an Experience', *Art as Experience* (Perigee Books 1939).

[6]   See Ezio Manzini and Francesca Rizzo, 'Small Projects/Large Changes: Participatory Design as an Open Participated Process' (2011) 7(3–4) CoDesign 199; Christian Bason and others, *Public and Collaborative: Exploring the Intersection of Design, Social Innovation and Public Policy* (Ezio Manzini and Eduardo Staszowski eds., DESIS Network 2013).

[7]   Lucy Kimbell and Joe Julier, 'The Social Design Methods Menu in Perpetual Beta' (Field Studio 2013) www.lucykimbell.com/stuff/Fieldstudio_SocialDesignMethodsMenu.pdf accessed 20 January 2019; Lucy Kimbell, 'Applying Design Approaches to Policy Making: Discovering Policy Lab' (University of Brighton 2015) https://researchingdesignforpolicy.files.wordpress.com/2015/10/kimbell_policylab_report .pdf.

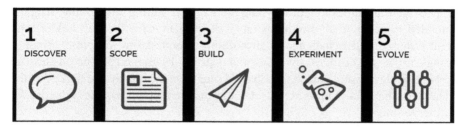

FIGURE 6.1 The Lab's 'Design Cycle' framework

court self-help centres, legal aid groups, non-profit advocacy organisations, and legal start-ups focused on serving segments of the community who otherwise struggle to afford legal services. It also includes collaboration with corporate law firms, legal departments, and innovation units in technology companies with an interest in legal and social services.

6.2.2 *The Structure of 'Design'*

Drawing on standard practice, the lab structures its training and research/development work around the unit of the 'design cycle'.[8] The design cycle is the pattern of how a designer approaches a challenge area to arrive at resolution. Although a component of standard design practice, the cycle is not practised too strictly to allow for adaption to the idiosyncrasies of a particular context. The basic framework of the design cycle refined by the lab for use in legal design, involves the stages detailed in Figure 6.1 above.

As shown in Figure 6.1, the 'Design Cycle' covers five stages of progression, commencing with 'Discovery' work to understand the challenge area given to the team. This involves speaking to the users, service providers, experts, and observers involved, observing the challenge directly, gathering data about behaviour and outcomes, and researching past attempts to address the challenge and the efficacy of these attempts.

This is followed by the 'Scoping' stage, which is intended to make sense of the information gathered, and to help the team decide which people and opportunities are of focus. During this stage the teams clarify the 'real problem', and detail the attributes of the people involved and the dynamics at work. This scoping exercise involves mapping the process, systems, and stakeholders, ranking the various ways to frame the problem, and producing a guiding design brief and set of user personas.

---

[8] Read more about the design cycle as documented in the toolkit for social innovation, IDEO, 'Design Kit: The Human-Centered Design Toolkit' (2015) www.ideo.com/post/design-kit accessed 23 January 2019.

The brainstorming and prototyping that occurs during the 'Build' stage, is intended to generate an ambitious range of ideas to serve the stakeholders and resolve the reframed challenge. Brainstorming is undertaken without constraints, using creative provocations, analogies, and matrices. From there, proposed ideas are sorted into clusters and ranked. Feedback is sought on the quality and ranking of the ideas and a handful of ideas are selected to generate rough prototypes intended for further testing.

This groundwork facilitates the 'Experiment' and 'Evolve' stages, in which teams test their first prototypes and then use the feedback to scrap or refine concepts. This is repeated for several cycles and with each cycle the prototype gains in fidelity, detail, and contextualisation. Gradually, and with many experts and users giving their input, the prototype grows into something that can be piloted.

'Pilot', 'Scale', and 'Investment' follow if the testing has indicated that the concept has sufficient promise. If a legal organisation is willing to carry out the pilot, then we work with them to hand off the prototype and provide a suggested pilot and testing plan. Alternatively, the lab may create the pilot and carry out the operational logistics and evaluation in conjunction with a partner. If this early pilot indicates the prototype is proving useful, usable, and engaging to the stakeholders, without producing any unexpected negative consequences, then the design cycle concludes with handover to a unit who will take it forward.

The teaching of design and the research and evaluation projects conducted by the lab are all orientated around this model. For short events, a design cycle can last forty-five minutes (with minimal methodologies used, and no discussion of pilots and scale). More robust cycles last anywhere from eighteen weeks to two years, during which time ideas may progress to the development of full pilots and working implementations. The design cycle is an important tool for teachers and students, it gives structure to a problem-solving approach that is new and that can appear messy and uncomfortable to the uninitiated.

6.2.3 *Target Objectives*

The lab experiments with various offerings in order to determine which might have the greatest educational and justice impact, and this impact is evaluated with reference to three target objectives.

(i) Increase the reach and diversity of student participants
   To engage a diverse group of participants, including those from disciplines outside of law, those within law but who do not typically consider themselves technology or innovation focused, and those from outside of the university who are pursuing different professional tracks (including technologists, data scientists, lawyers, and journalists, and others who are interested in social systems).

(ii) Enhance student training

To make design methodologies relevant to students' professional developments, irrespective of whether participants intend to go into corporate practice, public interest work, further study, entrepreneurship, or legal technology companies.

(iii) Make a positive contribution to the wider community

By supporting the development of an innovation ecosystem and contributing to the improvement of access to justice. To this end, the lab hopes that the prototypes and implementation plans that emerge from its sessions have lives beyond the university.

Progress against objectives is measured through student feedback. Students produce qualitative assessments in addition to the standard school-wide Likert scale evaluations of the class based on general factors. In these qualitative assessments, we ask students to map out the main lessons and insights deriving from their involvement that they expect to find useful in their career one year from now. This helps us to understand their key learning outcomes and professional aspirations. We also track the level of ongoing student engagement with the work of the lab following completion of a class. Students are offered the opportunity to join the Legal Design Lab as a fellow, to attend meetings, to continue working on the class projects, and to receive further training. A student's decision to opt into further work with the lab is taken as an indicator of success. Progress on the other objectives is measured via feedback sessions with partners, and inferred by a partner's ongoing willingness to collaborate with the lab through testing designs, engaging staff in lab workshops, and piloting. We also document the diversity of student involvement and the variety of partners who engage with the work of the lab.

6.3 WEAVING DESIGN INTO LEGAL EDUCATION

6.3.1 *Learning Objectives*

The lab is focused on experiential education and providing students with exposure to current legal practice and client needs. In that way it is similar to a law school clinic: students in the lab's programmes work with real organisations and people, to understand their problems and work on crafting new solutions. But unlike a clinic, the lab does not focus exclusively on training students in how it is that lawyers serve clients, instead training is focused on a variety of other tools and methods to use when considering how a service could be delivered or a problem could be solved. To this end, the lab has piloted different activities in order to interest students in learning more about human-centred design as a way to enhance their innovation, leadership, and professional skills.

6.3.2 Models of Delivery

The lab trains students through a range of events: several-hour workshops, day-long sprints and hackathons, several-session pop up classes, and full-quarter or multiple-quarter courses.

6.3.2.1 Workshops

The smallest events – workshops offered at lunch or dinner – serve to introduce law students, who are often over-committed with classes and obligations, to the lab's offerings through a focused and rapid design cycle. Rather than listen passively to a lecture, a workshop requires students to actively collaborate in teams and brainstorm new ideas for reform. Smaller events have included: a court design night, to contemplate problems and propose solutions to common issues experienced by the public when accessing courts; testing and iteration sessions for an eviction web application designed to help the public handle eviction notices; and a workshop on how to improve the career counselling support for students who intend to pursue public interest law.[9]

These small events are also designed to encourage non-law students to engage with the law school. The goal is to recruit a diverse set of students, with skills in engineering, education, business, management, data science, and beyond, to work on legal system problems with lawyers. This allows us to foster the development of a particular hybrid of human-centred design, one that draws on lawyers' ability to research policy landscapes, draft new systemic solutions like legislation and policies, analyse risk, and facilitate conversations around ethics. These lawyering skills, when paired with the skills brought by those in other disciplines, enables a more harmonious combination of creativity and human-centred thinking to the design cycle. In this ambition, the lab has seen some success: shorter sessions usually attract an even mix of law and non-law students, whilst longer classes tend to have a heavier representation of law students, although one-third of the class are typically based in disciplines other than law.

6.3.2.2 Design Sprints and Hackathons

Our design sprints and hackathons have an organisational partner, such as legal aid organisations, court self-help leadership, academic clinics, or other groups that are interested in open access innovation. Partners typically approach the lab to discuss opportunities for working together, and the ideas are solidified during a pre-planning stage where we work with an organisation to scope a particular design brief that

---

[9]   More documentation and images from these events are on the Legal Design Lab's site under the Workshops section, including, for example, the Court Design Night around guardianship system redesign Legal Design Lab, 'Guardianship Navigator Project: Court Innovation Design Night' www .legaltechdesign.com/guardianship-navigator/process-events/ accessed 23 January 2019.

captures the challenges that they face. Partner organisations facilitate the participation of other subject matter experts and 'users', whilst the lab team advertises the sprint, recruits facilitators and coaches, and coordinates a one or two-day event. The student and volunteer participants who attend are put on teams to work intensively together, and are supplied with material describing the current system, past attempts to improve it, the challenge statements that various stakeholders have framed, and any other resources of use. The organisational partner ensures that the teams' work is rooted in real use cases and constraints, and that there is an interested party who might implement the proposals generated.

6.3.2.3 Pop-Up Classes

Pop-up classes take the model of the design sprint and stretch it to three to five sessions. The students who attend pop-up classes do not receive credit for their work, but they are more carefully selected and recognised as having been trained in legal design, a skill that they can then list on their CV. Pop-up classes are framed around a very specific design brief with a partner so that the structure can ensure teams are able to focus quickly in a limited time frame. Recent example topics include: how plea bargain contracts in San Francisco might be made more comprehensible to defendants; how eviction notices in Arizona can be designed to encourage tenants to defend their housing rights; and how grandmothers in California who are trying to secure legal custody for their grandchildren might navigate the guardianship procedure more easily.

Students in pop-up classes benefit from more detailed coaching and relationship building with the lab staff, so that they can understand how to improve their work. The outcomes tend to be more refined than that of a sprint because the classes involve more consultations with experts, testing with users, and subsequent rounds of improvement. For the lab, pop-up classes are useful as a pilot to test out a new partnership with an organisation or a particular challenge brief. If a topic and a partner work well for three or five sessions, then the lab can commit to working with them over nine or eighteen weeks during a full class. The ideas and research generated during the pop-up then feed into the full quarter class' work, with student teams picking up where the previous team left off.

6.3.2.4 Full-Quarter Classes

The lab's full-quarter classes stretch the design cycle, from a few sessions to nine or eighteen weeks of work. Teams learn a wider range of methodologies for each stage of the design cycle, and the teaching team sets higher expectations around the number of stakeholders consulted, the amount of research conducted, and the degree of refinement or prototyping and testing carried out. In the full-quarter setting, teams also progress further through the design cycle, iterating through several rounds of prototyping and testing, rather than only one. These repeated rounds increase the quality of their prototypes and implementation plans, which are then submitted as final deliverables.

Teams are expected to create something that partner organisations can implement and test. This requires that students build a relationship with their partner to understand their dynamics and constraints, so that the proposal they make for a new technology, service, or policy is rooted in a realistic vision of what can succeed. At the same time, students are encouraged to think of themselves as lab-based experimenters rather than consultants. They are allowed and encouraged to deviate from instructions given to them by partners. With the luxury of a university-based lab project, they can propose solutions that are radical, contentious, and ambitious. The university environment affords more time and support to experiment with solutions and grants teams the organisational autonomy and the scope to synthesise many different groups' points of view.

6.3.2.5 Fellowships

In the past year the lab has also added student fellowship positions, structured through the university's research assistantship tracks, to provide greater opportunity for those who want to build more skills and portfolio pieces in legal design. Between twelve and twenty students who have completed pop-up or full-quarter classes and who would like to continue with their own project or contribute to one of the lab's ongoing projects are selected to join the lab as fellows for a school year, with the possibility of further extension. Fellows are drawn from various schools (including law, computer science, and social science) and degree programmes at the undergraduate and postgraduate level. In addition to the student fellows, the lab also has one full-time salaried post-JD fellow who works on a particular legal design challenge for an entire calendar year. The full-time fellow typically has been trained in design methodologies, has a licence to practise law, and has proposed a particular challenge or solution to work on for the duration of the fellowship. The fellow can attract collaborators by running events and classes, hiring student fellows and finding other partners to work with.

The fellowship track scales up the lab's capacity to run more events, carry out more research, and generate more high-fidelity designs. The capacity-building efforts of the lab also serve to bolster the development of legal design as a field in its own right, and offer the type of institutional support required to enable the field to flourish. Both the student fellowships and the full-time fellowships offered to graduates also serve students. These opportunities strengthen the position of those who wish to apply to the growing number of 'legal innovation' jobs in the market and operate as an important bridge to practice. They also allow the lab to identify talent and to develop the skills of those who may wish to continue working with us in the future. Full-time fellows have tackled a range of issues: from coordinating dispersed housing legal service providers in the San Francisco Bay

Area,[10] to developing better ways to prevent and resolve consumer contract issues (like landlord-tenant contracts, or homeowner-cleaner contracts).

6.3.3 Student Assessment

Those who enrol in workshops, sprints, hackathons, pop-up classes, and full-quarter classes are graded as part of a team, based on how well they understand their partner's context, how they design for it, and the ambition and creativity of their solutions. The goal is to create feasible proposals, to stretch traditional bureaucracies' notion of what constitutes 'innovation', and to set a more forward-thinking agenda about what it is possible to achieve within the legal system. Often at the beginning of a project, partners have either a general wish for 'innovation' without thinking about the particular improvements that can be made, or they think only in terms of the most popular 'innovation' solutions appearing in the media. The team's task is to bring this general wish for innovation into more concrete, feasible, and appropriate plans for what can be done to solve people's problems.

The students are also graded based on the quality of their teamwork so as to prioritise learning outcomes around collaboration, interdisciplinary working styles, and endurance in dealing with messy, complex problems. The evaluation process is continuous throughout the class. The teams have regular in-person design reviews in the class with their peers and the teaching team, as well as delivering presentations and submitting written descriptions of their process, decisions, and feedback. The submissions are submitted collectively, although individual students will sometimes write up further reflections and proposals on their own. This helps the teaching team to understand how the team is operating, how much work they are putting into their design cycle, and how thoughtful and researched their decision-making is.

Importantly, assessment also considers the amount of 'iteration' the teams have exhibited in their projects. The teaching team encourages the students not to settle with the first prototype they create. We observe that many student teams commit to this first prototype, settling on it as the 'solution' and then devote the rest of the class to detailing it or establishing how to pilot it. We see this as a lost opportunity to make more significant and more ambitious refinements of the concept. As such, we grade students on how many critiques they can gather in response to their concept, what strategies they devise to respond to the critiques they judge to be the most meaningful, and how they perform new rounds of brainstorming and proto-typing to create something that shows ingenuity in devising ways to respond to criticism.

[10] Jane Wong, 'Unifying Legal Aid in the Bay Area' (*Medium*, 7 January 2018) https://medium.com/legal-design-and-innovation/unifying-legal-aid-in-the-bay-area-67eec111634e accessed 23 January 2019.

6.4 DESIGN AS A RESEARCH AND DEVELOPMENT TOOL

Like many other university departments and centres, the Legal Design Lab is charged with both a research and teaching function. In contrast to the traditional doctrinal research that tends to occupy the research agenda within many law schools,[11] the Legal Design Lab functions as an exploratory incubator. Although many of the projects that emerge from pop-up, short, or longer events are sacrificial designs, which may ultimately benefit students (in building skills) more than end users, the expectation is that all stakeholders will gain from the process. As such, the learning and experimentation process produces relevant inspiration and case studies for innovation units inside courts, legal aid groups, foundations, legal departments, and firms, as well as solutions that can be piloted, or adapted and run straight away.

The lab contributes to the broader design and policy evidence base, bridging the gap between the academy and practice by generating new initiatives for more rigorous evaluation and randomised control trials. This contribution is further supported by our commitment to making our work product as open as possible and documenting our experiences, so that insights can be shared and effect a wider impact on the legal system. It also establishes a virtuous circle in which the research and development work of the lab is informed by the teaching and public engagement work conducted, whilst the lab's teaching and public engagement work is continuously informed by the findings emerging from our research and development.

The design lab serves a useful purpose inside a research university such as Stanford by generating and vetting new ideas that may go towards improving outcomes in the real world. The design lab informs the development of further research, operating as a feeder of ideas for new initiatives to be empirically studied, determining if these initiatives positively impact the legal system and the people using it, and contributing to the conduct of high impact research. This allows researchers from elsewhere in the law school or university to structure more rigorous evaluations and provides evidence to support larger research funding grant applications.

This can be seen in relation to two recent projects that the lab has nurtured. The first of these was a conversational text-messaging platform designed to distribute legal information and procedure in short, digestible phone messages. This prototype was developed to allow legal organisations to automate sending messages to litigants and clients, warning of important deadlines, hearings, rejections of filings, or confirmations of correct procedures easily, without the need for new technical systems or increased technical capacity from staff. The second emergent prototype has led to the development of a step-by-step guide to navigating legal processes, integrating tasks, deadlines, contextual knowledge, and strategic warnings and advice, designed

[11] See, e.g., Peter H Schuck, 'Why Don't Law Professors Do More Empirical Research' (1989) 39(3) Journal of Legal Education 323.

to allow a person to manage their own journey through the system, with or without legal assistance. The guide provides an overview of the process, helping individuals feel in control of the sequence of phases and tasks.

In the fourth year of the lab, these two concepts were chosen to prototype at a higher fidelity. After initial observational soft pilots of both of these software products, the prototypes are now proceeding through more rigorous research study. The Messenger platform is being tested through randomised control trials, to determine if the text messages impact appearance rates at hearings and legal meetings. The step-by-step guide platform is being built out with more content around restraining orders and guardianships, so that it might be tested observationally to determine how litigants fare while using it in comparison to a paper-based guide. These software efforts will continue in-house in the lab, though they are being transitioned into standalone platforms that can be used openly and with minimal support from lab staff.

In addition to developing tools and feeding into the development of research-led policy, the design lab nurtures enduring relationships with legal organisations that can then translate into research commitments and agreements. Because the design process involves so much communication with outside organisations, incorporation of their feedback and priorities, and visits to their sites, typically it results in a very strong relationship with a sense of trust and appreciation between parties. This relationship can be very useful in transitioning to a research agreement, which might involve the sharing of data, integration of technology systems, borrowing staff time, and agreement to data collection and participant randomisation. In these ways, a design lab can be a very useful preparatory partner for empirical researchers in the university to determine what possible new initiatives they might study and the partners they might work with. It also provides the lab with an audience to raise the profile of human-centred design in law, to encourage the profession's engagement with the driving principles of design, and to enhance the growth and acceptance of the field within legal education, the legal academy, and professional practice.

6.5 CHALLENGES AND FUTURE PRIORITIES

Whilst there are clear contributions that methods drawn from design offer legal education and research/development, there are also a number of complexities that we have had to navigate. For those who wish to establish similar initiatives in other institutions, these challenges and our response to them may prove informative. In exploring these challenges, how we handled them, and how they have shaped our priorities going forward, we look at three examples in particular. These include the ethical constraints emerging from the incubator model; the allocation of scarce staff resources across a myriad of possible projects; and scaling projects so that they have a life beyond the lab.

6.5.1 Addressing Ethics

One major adaptation the Legal Design Lab has made over the last few years has been to develop a stronger approach to ethical research. During its initial time at the d.school, there was a focus on agile, immediate user-research that favoured speed and volume over protocols. Most research undertaken at the d.school is completed in class settings, and so does not go through institutional review for ethical concerns. That also means that most students are not trained explicitly in ethical social science work.

In response, the lab has developed training materials for our students and for professionals to assist them in understanding how research ethics should guide and limit their work. This includes a short, informal book with resources on how to secure consent, pass institutional review board procedures (which the lab does for all its research work on access to justice and legal services development), and deal with highly sensitive topics that might emerge during design work.[12] Though ethical and formal procedures are often excused during initial design work, the lab has developed this curriculum and resources so that the practices of ethical, sensitive, and community-oriented research remain central to our work. As design work continues to weave its way into law and policy education, a focus on ethical training and institutional review should be prioritised as one of the most difficult but necessary areas of further work.

6.5.2 Allocating Resources and Building Capacity

We have developed a handful of projects in earnest, as research and development projects inside the lab. Though many of the student and workshop initiatives (as concepts and early prototypes) hold promise, we attempt to constrain how we commit the lab's limited central resources when committing to take a concept through to implementation. First because it is better for the organisation to take leadership in developing innovation inside their own teams, to ensure sustainability, and second, the lab would soon lose its effectiveness and its quality if there were no explicit limits on what projects we invested resources into for implementation. The design process, especially when run repeatedly during small and large events, produces a wealth of ideas for new solutions. The danger in pursuing all projects is that the lab would overstretch its limited staff time and financial resources and would not produce strong research or well-developed new solutions.

To define the limits and priorities of the design work done in the law school, the lab has limited the themes of the projects it concentrates on. After two years of open work, in which various partners and students could propose events and projects as long as they pertained to new legal services or legal system reform, the lab put limits on which topics it would direct resources toward. Whilst short events still retain an

---

[12]   Margaret Hagan, *Ethical Design Engagement with Your Community* (Legal Design Lab, 2018).

open and occasionally random spirit, longer sprints, pop-ups, full-quarter classes, and longer research and development work is now restricted to topics, which fit annual themes and which contribute to the target outcomes previously discussed.

This has permitted coverage of three to four themes per year. In recent years, innovation in the civil courts has consistently been a theme, and a range of other themes have featured, including privacy design, consumer contract patterns, models of legal innovation units in law firms, creating a better legal internet, and building a better lawyer in law schools.

6.5.3 *Scaling-Up*

Initially the lab was focused on determining how to run partner-based classes and create new innovations that gave students rich learning experiences, strong portfolio pieces, and served as pilot-ready models for legal organisations to test in practice. While this initial mode of work was beneficial for students and the partners they worked with, it was not built for scale. In the next few years, the Legal Design Lab will run a new set of experiments to define its own agenda and how it trains its students. Our new round of experiments, development, and offerings will be oriented around building innovation cultures and promoting more scale in innovation work. This includes more training of legal professionals in this mode of work, so that our partners are better able to act and continue the projects that law school and innovation labs begin.

With the desire to scale up our activities and promote wider appreciation for innovation via design comes the need for more procedural and outcome data about the legal system, to facilitate the customisation and automation that users of the system request. This means establishing policies, privacy and ethics protocols, and standard agreements that courts and legal aid groups can follow. Hence, one of our themes has extended into promoting open justice data efforts, to provide the data required to build an ecosystem of legal innovation.

6.6 CONCLUSION

The establishment of the Legal Design Lab at Stanford University has been an ambitious initiative on two fronts. The first being our attempt to change the shape of legal education, to widen student horizons and to stimulate opportunities for interdisciplinary collaborations and exchange. Our success in doing so is attributed to the level of institutional autonomy that we have been given to experiment with new events, curriculum, and partnerships; the cross-disciplinary resources that existed throughout the university to support design and innovation efforts; and the commitment of staff, faculty, partners, and students to work on ambitious initiatives many of which did not align with the existing metrics that govern career advancement in a collaborator's professional track.

The challenges that we have faced in innovating legal education and which are touched upon above, are magnified by our commitment to orientating our work (both teaching and research) towards projects that make a contribution to access to justice. Whilst this increases the public impact of our work, it also amplifies our responsibility to ensure that the collaborations that we facilitate benefit all of those with a stake in the process, including and especially, the potential end beneficiaries.

Having spent the last five years making the transition from programme to lab, we expect the next five years will see us focus on promoting the growth of legal design by building networks with other labs, training a greater number of legal professionals in design work, and refining our own approach through continuous experimentation and evaluation of our teaching and research. We expect that the growing interest in design will help build momentum for the wider inclusion of these methods for innovation in legal education and legal service delivery. This will serve to produce students who are better prepared for the future of law and who exhibit a desire to shape that future and the innovations yet to come.

BIBLIOGRAPHY

Al Haider N, 'The Legal Design Summit Recap: Uncharted Territory' (*Medium*, 1 January 2018) https://medium.com/legal-design-and-innovation/the-legal-design-summit-recap-uncharted-territory-77d8795315cc accessed 23 January 2019

Bason C and others, *Public and Collaborative: Exploring the Intersection of Design, Social Innovation and Public Policy* (Ezio Manzini and Eduardo Staszowski eds, DESIS Network 2013)

Brown T, 'Design Thinking' (2008) 6 Harvard Business Review 84

Buchanan R, 'Wicked Problems in Design Thinking' (1992) 8(2) Design Issues 5
   'Human Dignity and Human Rights: Thoughts on the Principles of Human-Centered Design' (2001) 17(3) Design Issues 35
   'Strategies of Design Research: Productive Science and Rhetorical Inquiry' in Ralf Michel (ed.), *Design Research Now* (Birkhäuser Basel 2007)

Davis MF, 'Institutionalizing Legal Innovation: The (Re)Emergence of the Law Lab' (2015) 65(1) Journal of Legal Education 190

Dewey J, 'Having an Experience', *Art as Experience* (Perigee Books 1939)

Hagan M, 'The Rise of the Law School Labs' (*Open Law Lab*, 13 September 2017) www.openlawlab.com/2017/09/13/the-rise-of-the-law-school-labs/ accessed 23 January 2019
   'The State of Legal Design: The Big Takeaways of the Stanford Law + Design Summit' (*Medium*, 26 September 2017) https://medium.com/legal-design-and-innovation/the-state-of-legal-design-the-big-takeaways-of-the-stanford-law-design-summit-ee363b5bf109 accessed 23 January 2019
   Ethical Design Engagement with Your Community (*Legal Design Lab*, 2018) www.legaltechdesign.com/2018/02/short-book-ethical/ accessed 23 January 2019
   'Justice Innovation with Law School Design Labs' (*ABA Dialogue*, 15 June 2018) www.americanbar.org/groups/legal_services/publications/dialogue/volume/21/spring-2018/iolta-design-labs/ accessed 23 January 2019

IDEO, 'Design Kit: The Human-Centered Design Toolkit' (2015) www.ideo.com/post/design-kit accessed 23 January 2019

Jackson D, 'Human-Centered Legal Tech: Integrating Design in Legal Education' (2016) 50 (1) The Law Teacher 82

Kimbell L, 'Applying Design Approaches to Policy Making: Discovering Policy Lab' (University of Brighton 2015) https://researchingdesignforpolicy.files.wordpress.com /2015/10/kimbell_policylab_report.pdf

Kimbell L and Julier J, 'The Social Design Methods Menu in Perpetual Beta' (Field Studio 2013) www.lucykimbell.com/stuff/fieldstudio_socialdesignmethodsmenu.pdf accessed 20 January 2019

Legal Design Lab, 'Guardianship Navigator Project: Court Innovation Design Night' www .legaltechdesign.com/guardianship-navigator/process-events/ accessed 23 January 2019

Manzini E and Rizzo F, 'Small Projects/Large Changes: Participatory Design as an Open Participated Process' (2011) 7(3–4) CoDesign 199

Rittel HWJ and Webber MM, 'Planning Problems Are Wicked Problems' in Nigel Cross (ed.), *Developments in Design Methodology* (Wiley 1984)

Schuck PH, 'Why Don't Law Professors Do More Empirical Research' (1989) 39(3) Journal of Legal Education 323

Stanford Institute of Design, 'Class Archive' https://dschool.stanford.edu/class-archive/ accessed 23 January 2019

Wong J, 'Unifying Legal Aid in the Bay Area' (*Medium*, 7 January 2018) https://medium .com/legal-design-and-innovation/unifying-legal-aid-in-the-bay-area-67eec111634e accessed 23 January 2019

7

Developing 'NextGen' Lawyers through Project-Based Learning

Anna Carpenter

Today, technology is driving disruptive change in the legal profession and the public is demanding lawyers offer more value and choice in how legal services are delivered. Given these pressures, tomorrow's legal profession will be fundamentally different from the profession we know today. Against this backdrop, this chapter argues the next generation of lawyers need at least five categories of multidimensional knowledge and skills: collaboration; design; project management; problemsolving; and lifelong learning. The prevailing, traditional legal education model was not designed to teach these multidimensional skills. This chapter describes some of traditional legal education's deficiencies, introduces the pedagogy of problem-based learning, and advocates a particular form of this pedagogy: project-based learning that involves real clients or community partners. Through project-based learning – a student-centred, active, and experiential learning model – students learn the fundamentals of law and legal practice while gaining the multidimensional knowledge and skills needed to navigate disruptive change. Project-based learning can prepare law students to actively shape the future of the profession – as opposed to merely reacting to change – by harnessing technology and interdisciplinary insights to improve legal systems and create better legal service models for the public.

7.1 INTRODUCTION

The prevailing model of legal education was developed in an age of horses, carriages, and oil lamps – a time when law was inaccessible for the vast majority of the population and lawyers had complete control over legal service delivery and the organisation of legal systems. Technological advancement began stripping this control away thirty years ago. Today, any person with a smartphone holds a legal library in the palm of their hand.

Unfortunately, most law students are still educated within a system that assumes law and legal advice are under the sole control of elite, law-trained professionals. Law students are taught to expect their clients will want to pay by the hour for bespoke, full-scope legal services. In reality, people and organisations are demanding more value and more choice in how they receive legal services and interact with the justice system. Where lawyers have not responded to these demands, forces outside the profession are driving disruptive change. Case-in-point: an eighteen-year-old non-lawyer created an application that, as of writing, has helped people in cities across the globe appeal parking tickets, saving them millions of dollars.[1] Our interconnected, information-rich, and technologically enhanced world has generated tremendous pressure to reform the legal profession. We have every reason to predict this pressure will intensify over time. Given our trans-formative moment and uncertain future, this volume calls for reform and modernisation of the law school curriculum, a curriculum that has remained largely static for the past century and a half. This chapter offers one pedagogical prescription for what ails legal education today: project-based learning. It ima-gines a future where lawyers work together with those not legally trained, leveraging technology to add value for their clients and enhance access to justice; a future where lawyers have skills to design and build better ways of delivering legal services and organising legal systems. To achieve these ambi-tious goals, this chapter argues future lawyers will need five categories of multi-dimensional knowledge and skills: collaboration (including with other lawyers and across disciplines), design, project management, problem-solving, and life-long learning. Finally, it argues project-based learning can help students develop these skills.

Project-based learning is a student-centred, experiential pedagogy that falls under the broader umbrella of problem-based learning.[2] Many different forms of the latter are commonly used in secondary and higher education settings around the world.[3] Problem-based pedagogical models, including project-based learning, are on the rise in law school clinical and experiential programmes, but are rare in legal

---

[1] Wikipedia, 'Joshua Browder' (2018) https://en.wikipedia.org/wiki/Joshua_Browder accessed 20 May 2019.

[2] For a seminal work on problem-based learning, see Howard S Barrows, 'Problem-Based, Self-Directed Learning' (1983) 250(22) JAMA: The Journal of the American Medical Association 3077. For a project-based learning in law school, see Anna E Carpenter, 'The Project Model of Clinical Education: Eight Pedagogical Principles to Maximize Student Learning and Social Justice Impact' (2013) 20(1) Clinical Law Review 39; Sameer M Ashar, 'Law Clinics and Collective Mobilization' (2008) 14(2) Clinical Law Review 355; Katherine R Kruse, 'Biting Off What They Can Chew: Strategies for Involving Students in Problem-Solving beyond Individual Client Representation' (2002) 8(2) Clinical Law Review 405. For problem-based learning in law school, See, e.g., Barbara J Flagg, 'Experimenting with Problem-Based Learning in Constitutional Law' (2002) 10 Washington University Journal of Law & Policy 101; Gabriël A Moens, 'The Mysteries of Problem-Based Learning: Combining Enthusiasm and Excellence' (2007) 38(2) University of Toledo Law Review 623; Myron Moskovitz, 'Beyond the Case Method: It's Time to Teach with Problems' (1992) 42(2) Journal Legal Education 241; Suzanne Kurtz, Michael Wylie and Neil Gold, 'Problem-Based Learning an Alternative Approach to Legal Education' (1990) 13(2) Dalhousie Law Journal 797.

[3] Cindy E Hmelo-Silver, 'Problem-Based Learning: What and How Do Students Learn?' (2004) 16(3) Educational Psychology Review 235.

education's core curriculum.[4] This chapter calls for project-based learning, particularly where it involves real clients and community partners, to become a bigger part of the law school curriculum.

Project-based learning, like other problem-based approaches, turns the traditional legal education model on its head. In most of legal education, a teacher transmits substantive knowledge to students and asks them to apply that knowledge to a problem in the context of a high stakes exam.[5] In contrast, project-based learning places students at the centre, requiring they direct their own learning experience in an active manner. The teacher is a guide and facilitator, not the 'sage on the stage'. In project-based learning, students work in teams to solve complex, real-world problems for real clients or partners. Through project work, students learn substantive law and how to practise law. In addition, they begin developing the multidimensional knowledge and skills that will help tomorrow's lawyers actively shape the future of the profession, improve legal systems, and increase the public's access to justice.

In this chapter, I first offer a conceptual framework for thinking about the future of the legal profession. Then, based on that framework, I discuss the five key categories of multidimensional knowledge and skills future lawyers will need. Next, I critique traditional legal education and make the case that it cannot (as currently designed) prepare tomorrow's lawyers to thrive and provide high-quality legal services and systems in the future. Finally, I introduce project-based learning, discussing its theoretical roots, value, and practical application in a law school setting.

7.2 A PROFESSION UNDER PRESSURE AND A PUBLIC IN NEED OF BETTER LEGAL SERVICES AND SYSTEMS

This chapter is grounded in two assumptions about the present and the future of the legal profession and legal systems. First, external and internal forces – driven by technological development – have, and will continue to, place serious disruptive pressure on the market for legal services and the organisation of legal systems.[6]

---

[4] For examples of project-based learned in legal education, see Columbia Law School, 'Columbia Law Expands Experiential Offerings' (2019) www.law.columbia.edu/news/2018/08/new-clinics-experiential -education accessed 20 May 2019; The University of Arizona, 'Innovation for Justice: Unlock Change' (2019) https://law.arizona.edu/innovation-for-justice accessed 20 May 2019. For problem-based learning, see University of York, 'Problem Based Learning' www.york.ac.uk/law/postgraduate/llmpro grammes/llm-international-corporate-commercial/problem-based-learning/ accessed 20 May 2019; Flagg (n 2).

[5] Whilst educational theory has developed significantly in recent years, much of the law curriculum remains content-driven and delivered traditionally, predominantly through lecture format. Students are, in the main, treated as empty vessels to be filled by the eminent academics of the day. Richard H Grimes, *Re-Thinking Legal Education under the Civil and Common Law: A Road Map for Constructive Change* (Routledge 2018); James E Moliterno, 'The Future of Legal Education Reform' (2013) 40(2) Pepperdine Law Review 423.

[6] Richard Susskind, *Tomorrow's Lawyers: An Introduction to Your Future* (1st edn, Oxford University Press 2013); Gillian K Hadfield, *Rules for a Flat World: Why Humans Invented Law and How to Reinvent It for a Complex Global Economy* (Oxford University Press 2017).

Second, the public needs and wants more effective, efficient ways to solve legal problems and interact with the legal system.[7] Given these forces, it is likely that change will be the most important constant in the legal profession moving forward.

Internal and external pressures on the legal profession are growing. The market for legal services is increasingly competitive, commoditised, and democratised.[8] The traditional bespoke, full-service model is falling away and being replaced by self-help services, limited scope services, non-lawyer services, and in-house legal departments.[9] Even in the USA's protectionist legal profession, regulatory change is slowly opening up the delivery of legal services to non-lawyers.[10]

The practice of law and the operation of legal systems will continue to be transformed by technological development whether lawyers guide the transformation or not. New platforms, services, applications, and devices have already given people more ways to access legal services and the courts.[11] Entrepreneurial lawyers and entrepreneurs without legal training are using technology and design to innovate legal services delivery, finding new ways to offer discrete legal products that used to be exclusively available via the bespoke, full service model.[12] In this new environment, if the legal profession is to continue to add value for clients and advance justice, lawyers and legal systems must evolve and innovate.

The public needs and wants more effective, efficient ways to prevent and solve legal problems.[13] Clients, particularly corporate clients, are demanding more value from lawyers.[14] As our world has grown more legally complex, the cost of legal services has increased.[15] Many people who need legal services cannot pay for

[7] Hadfield (n 6); Rebecca L Sandefur, 'What We Know and Need to Know About the Legal Needs of the Public' (2016) 67(2) South Carolina Law Review 443.

[8] Susskind (n 6); Hadfield (n 6); Carole Silver, 'Getting Real About Globalization and Legal Education: Potential and Perspectives for the US' (2013) 24(2) Stanford Law and Policy Review 457; Laura Snyder, *Democratizing Legal Service: Obstacles and Opportunities* (Lexington Books 2016).

[9] Susskind (n 6).

[10] A few American states have already created, or are in the process of creating, frameworks that allow limited forms of non-lawyer practice. Brooks Holland, 'The Washington State Limited License Legal Technician Practice Rule: A National First in Access to Justice' (2013) 82 SUPRA 75; Bob Ambrogi, 'Utah Nears Licensing of Paralegals to Practice Law in Limited Circumstances' (Law Sites Blog, 2018) www.lawsitesblog.com/2018/08/utah-nears-licensing-paralegals-practice-law-limited-circumstances.html accessed 12 March 2019; Jason Tashea, 'California Bar Task Force to Consider Regulatory Changes on Nonlawyer Ownership of Legal Services Firms' ABA Journal (Chicago, 27 July 2018) www.abajournal.com/news/article/california_bar_task_force_to_propose_regulatory_changes_affecting_nonlawyer accessed 20 May 2019.

[11] Bob Ambrogi, 'The 20 Most Important Legal Technology Developments of 2018' (Law Sites Blog, 2018) www.lawsitesblog.com/2018/12/20-important-legal-technology-developments-2018.html accessed 12 March 2019.

[12] Ibid; Bill Henderson, 'Legal Services and the Consumer Price Index (CPI) (042)' (Legal Evolution, 2018) www.legalevolution.org/2018/01/legal-services-consumer-price-index-cpi-cost-going-up-wallet-share-going-down-042/ accessed 20 May 2019.

[13] Deborah L Rhode, *The Trouble with Lawyers* (Oxford University Press 2015).

[14] Susskind (n 6).

[15] Hadfield (n 6).

them, and many businesses are refusing to continue absorbing astronomical legal fees.[16]

And it turns out that money is not even the biggest barrier to legal services.[17] Instead, most people with civil legal problems simply do not understand their problems to be legal in nature. Most people who have civil legal problems never seek the advice of a lawyer or court and instead use self-help or do nothing at all.[18] Lawyers have failed, to date, to deliver legal services effectively and efficiently to vast swaths of the public. Instead, in what is a regulatory and market failure, lawyers predominantly serve large corporate clients, leaving most people without access to the services they need, in a form they can use, and at a price they can afford.[19]

Courts are also under pressure. The public is fed up with the cost, inefficiency, and confusion of interacting with justice systems.[20] Civil cases are expensive to litigate. As a result, people with meritorious claims (but without the means to pay for litigation) are effectively barred from using the courts.[21] Meanwhile, businesses have largely abandoned the state courts, turning instead to private arbitration and only using the courts when absolutely necessary to obtain and enforce a civil judgment.[22] Criminal cases move slowly, leaving defendants and victims of crime in limbo.[23] Across the economy, people and organisations are increasingly using privatised systems to resolve disputes where they have a choice.[24]

Lawyers who can use design, technology, and interdisciplinary collaboration to create new ways of delivering legal services more effectively, and at a lower cost, stand to profit on a grand scale. This is particularly true if the services are

[16] William D Henderson, 'Three Generations of US Lawyers: Generalists, Specialists, Project Managers' (2011) 70(2) Maryland Law Review 373; Susskind (n 6).
[17] Catherine R Albiston and Rebecca L Sandefur, 'Expanding the Empirical Study of Access to Justice' [2013] Wisconsin Law Review 101.
[18] Sandefur (n 7).
[19] Elizabeth Chambliss, 'Marketing Legal Assistance' (2019) 148(1) Daedalus 98; Ben Barton, 'A Comparison Between the American Markets for Medical and Legal Services' (2016) 67(5) Hastings Law Journal 1331; Gillian K Hadfield and Deborah L Rhode, 'How to Regulate Legal Services to Promote Access, Innovation, and the Quality of Lawyering' (2016) 67(5) Hastings Law Journal 1191.
[20] Examples from a few nations: National Centre for State Courts, 'Civil Justice Initiative: The Landscape of Civil Litigation in State Courts' (National Centre for State Courts 2015) www.ncsc.org/~/media/Files/PDF/Research/CivilJusticeReport-2015.ashx; Jane Miller, 'Australia's Family Law Crisis Reaches Tipping Point' (InDaily, 2018) https://indaily.com.au/opinion/2018/03/22/australias-family-law-crisis-reaches-tipping-point/; Benjamin Perrin, Richard Audas and Sarah Péloquin-Ladany, 'Canada's Justice Deficit : The Case for a Justice System Report Card' (Macdonald-Laurier Institute 2016) www.macdonaldlaurier.ca/report-card-criminal-justice-system/.
[21] National Centre for State Courts (n 20).
[22] Ibid.
[23] See, e.g., Perrin, Audas and Péloquin-Ladany (n 20).
[24] Judith Resnik, 'The Privatization of Process: Requiem for and Celebration of the Federal Rules of Civil Procedure at 75' (2014) 162(7) University of Pennsylvania Law Review 1793; Gillian K Hadfield, 'Privatizing Commercial Law' (2001) 24(1) Regulation Magazine 40.

systematised, packaged, or commoditised and marketed to a broad base of consumers.[25] The public will benefit through greater access at a lower cost.

A logical conclusion that flows from these realties is that the legal profession will be in a state of constant evolution and change as lawyers (along with competitors outside the profession) struggle to rethink legal services delivery and redesign legal systems. It is hard to overstate exactly how dramatic this shift is, and will be, for a profession so deeply rooted in the values of tradition and precedent. Lawyers are trained to pay attention to the lessons of the past in an attempt to mitigate risk in the future. But this backward-looking tendency has led the legal profession and legal education to spend far too long rooted in static modes of thinking and working – a tendency based on the sometimes explicit, but more often unstated, assumption that the future will look exactly like the past. It won't.

7.3 KNOWLEDGE AND SKILLS FOR THE FUTURE

To thrive as a profession and serve the public's needs, future lawyers will not only need the core knowledge and skill already emphasised in legal education, but also a new toolbox of knowledge and skills designed for an evolving world. If we accept inevitable change for the legal profession, it follows that we should do all we can to prepare our law students for a world and a professional life marked by innovation and disruption. Legal education needs pedagogical models designed to help future lawyers navigate, shape, and lead reform in the profession and the justice system.

Many of tomorrow's lawyers will need the traditional knowledge and skills transmitted through the existing law school curriculum. Many will need to know how to practise law.[26] However, many future lawyers will not practise law in any traditional sense, or they may practise for a portion of their career, and move into different roles at other points.[27] A subset of law graduates should become tomorrow's law-trained entrepreneurs, technologists, project managers, problem-solvers, creators, designers, and builders.[28] Today's lawyers are already facing the complex problem of how to deploy technology to reimagine, redesign, and rebuild the new ways that legal services will be provided to clients, as well as the way people interact with law and legal systems. The pressure to innovate will only grow as time goes on. These massive, related reform projects will require law-trained minds, to be sure, but also minds that can draw on a broader range of multidimensional skills, including

---

[25] Susskind (n 6).
[26] National Association for Law Placement ('NALP'), which reports that the percentage of graduates pursuing non-conventional legal careers has almost doubled, from 7.99 per cent to 14.8 per cent see National Association for Law Placement, 'What Do We Know about JD Advantage Jobs?' NALP Bulletin (Washington, DC, November 2017) www.nalp.org/1117research accessed 20 May 2019.
[27] Susskind (n 6).
[28] Ibid.

collaboration within the field and with other disciplines, design, project management, problem-solving, and lifelong learning.[29] Below, I briefly discuss each.

7.3.1 *Collaboration*

In our already deeply interconnected world, people and organisations must work together and share information more than ever before.[30] In a profession as dependent on interpersonal interaction as law, those who collaborate effectively are likely to come out ahead. Future lawyers will not only need to collaborate with other lawyers but also know how to work with people who are not law-trained.[31] They will need to know how to assess the limits of their own expertise, when to call on the help of thinkers and creators in other fields. The ability to collaborate across disciplines is already critical in the profession, and it will only become more so. Today, only a small slice of law school courses (most of them experiential) explicitly teach collaboration concepts and skills.[32] Even fewer courses help students learn how to work with people from other fields.[33]

7.3.2 *Design*

Design has the potential to transform the way legal services are provided and to improve how people interact with legal systems.[34] The practice of design is fundamentally about making services, products, and things that are 'useful, useable, and engaging' for the people who use them.[35] User-centred design is an approach that, as the name suggests, places the user at the centre of a product development process. For decades, user-centred design has been a foundational practice in the development of new technological tools and systems across many fields and sectors of the

---

[29] Daniel H Pink, *A Whole New Mind: Moving from the Information Age to the Conceptual Age* (Riverhead Books 2005); Susskind (n 6).

[30] Pink (n 29); Richard Susskind and Daniel Susskind, *The Future of the Professions: How Technology Will Transform the Work of Human Experts* (Oxford University Press 2015).

[31] Susskind (n 6).

[32] There are many notable exceptions to this general statement. For an overview of some US-based collaboration work in law schools, see Renee Newman Knake, 'Cultivating Learners Who Will Invent the Future of Law Practice: Some Thoughts on Educating Entrepreneurial and Innovative Lawyers' (2012) 38(3) Ohio Northern University Law Review 847. See also, Janet Weinstein and others, 'Teaching Teamwork to Law Students' (2013) 63(1) Journal of Legal Education 36.

[33] Weinstein and others (n 32).

[34] Margaret Hagan, one of the leaders in this field, discusses design and its role on the profession in Chapter Six. See also Stephanie Dangel, Margaret Hagan and James Bryan Williams, 'Designing Today's Legal Education for Tomorrow's Lawyers: The Role of Legal Design, Technology and Innovation' in Antoine Masson (ed.), *Legal and Judicial Innovation: Methodology and Perspectives* (Springer-Verlag 2018); Margaret Hagan, 'Participatory Design for Innovation in Access to Justice' (2019) 148(1) Daedalus 120.

[35] Dangel, Hagan and Williams (n 34).

economy. In recent years, design thinking and user-centred design have finally found a foothold in the legal sector.[36]

Historically, lawyers have designed legal systems and legal service delivery models with a primary focus on the needs and interests of lawyers, as opposed to those of clients or the public. But this dynamic is changing. Innovators are proving that legal systems and services can be designed in more effective, usable, consumer-centred ways. For example, the 'Innovation for Justice Program' at The University of Arizona is developing easy-to-read guides for landlord/tenant law.[37] The Australian Taxation Office employed user-centred design and design thinking to reshape the organisation and reform the entire national taxation system.[38] The California court system has used design to rethink how people experience its self-help centres.[39]

7.3.3 *Project Management*

Until recently, most lawyers had never uttered the phrase 'project management', let alone practised it.[40] For decades, the billable hour has driven the way lawyers manage and process client work.[41] Concepts like efficiency, prioritisation, resource-allocation, and long-range planning have not, until recently, shaped how law firms are organised and managed and how legal services are delivered.[42] Today, legal project management is still in a nascent stage and is more common in large law firms than in smaller practices.[43] But since the great recession, clients (particularly large corporate clients) have begun demanding more attention to project management.[44]

Applying project management to legal practice and the development of legal services and products requires more sophisticated, intentional, and value-focused tools than most in the profession use today. Legal project management is an iterative, disciplined practice of predicting, planning, budgeting, executing, evaluating, and communicating about a legal product or service.[45] Effective project management

---

[36] See Stanford University, 'The Legal Design Lab' https://law.stanford.edu/organizations/pages/legal-design-lab/#slsnav-our-mission accessed 20 May 2019.

[37] See The University of Arizona (n 4).

[38] Alan Preston, 'Designing the Australian Tax System' in Richard J Boland Jr. and Fred Collopy (eds.), *Managing as Designing* (Stanford University Press 2009).

[39] Margaret Hagan, 'A Human-Centered Design Approach to Access to Justice: Generating New Prototypes and Hypotheses for Intervention to Make Courts User-Friendly' (2018) 6(2) Indiana Journal of Law and Social Equality 199.

[40] James Mullan, 'Legal Project Management: Passing Fad or Here to Stay?' (2012) 12(3) Legal Information Management 214.

[41] Susan Raridon Lambreth and David A Rueff Jr., *The Power of Legal Project Management: A Practical Handbook* (American Bar Association 2014).

[42] Ibid.

[43] JB Ruhl, 'The Rise of Legal Project Management' (2015) 19(4) The Young Lawyer 6.

[44] Ibid; Erin J Cox, 'An Economic Crisis Is a Terrible Thing to Waste: Reforming the Business of Law for a Sustainable and Competitive Future' (2009) 57(2) UCLA Law Review 511; Lambreth and Rueff Jr. (n 41); Susskind (n 6).

[45] Lambreth and Rueff Jr. (n 41).

can make lawyers' work easier and more satisfying, while increasing value and transparency for clients. It can also support the development of new legal service delivery models and ways of organising legal systems.

Many fields outside of law have been using project management practices to increase the efficiency and value of their work for decades. In the face of growing pressure from clients and market forces external to the profession, project management practices are increasingly infiltrating the legal profession.[46] But given that few law schools teach project management today, the vast majority of lawyers have never been exposed to the concept.

7.3.4 *Problem-Solving*

Legal education scholarship emphasises the importance of problem-solving skills.[47] This literature also sharply critiques how problem-solving is currently taught in law schools.[48] Problem-solving should be a bigger part of the law school curriculum and professors should constantly improve the way to teach it. Law teachers should also expand how we think about and teach the lawyer's problem-solving role.

The traditional view of problem-solving in legal education is focused on individual clients and matters.[49] The problem-solving work of practising lawyers typically begins with meeting a client and gathering information about the client's short- and long-term goals and interests, and the challenges they face. Clients present lawyers with messy, human situations and it's our job to help them find strategic, practical, affordable solutions.[50] This traditional mode of individual client-and-case-focused problem-solving will continue to be a critical skill for future lawyers.

If the next generation of lawyers is to provide valuable services and access to justice, they will have to tackle broader, systemic problems. The problem-solving

---

[46]   See, e.g., Cox (n 44); Lambreth and Rueff Jr. (n 41); Susskind (n 6).

[47]   See, e.g., Paul Brest, 'The Responsibility of Law Schools: Educating Lawyers as Counselors and Problem Solvers' (2006) 58(3/4) Law and Contemporary Problems 5; Stephen Nathanson, 'The Role of Problem Solving in Legal Education' (1989) 39(2) Journal of Legal Education 167; Janet Weinstein and Linda Morton, 'Stuck in a Rut: The Role of Creative Thinking in Problem Solving and Legal Education' (2003) 9(2) Clinical Law Review 835; Janeen Kerper, 'Creative Problem Solving vs. the Case Method: A Marvelous Adventure in Which Winnie-the-Pooh Meets Mrs. Palsgraf' (1998) 34(2) California Western Law Review 351.

[48]   Brest (n 47); Nathanson (n 47); Weinstein and Morton (n 47); Kerper (n 47).

[49]   Janet Reno, 'Lawyers as Problem-Solvers: Keynote Address to the AALS' (1999) 49(1) Journal of Legal Education 5.

[50]   Susskind (n 6); Michael Hunter Schwartz, 'Teaching Law by Design: How Learning Theory and Instructional Design Can Inform and Reform Law Teaching' (2001) 38(2) San Diego Law Review 347; Morrison Torrey, 'You Call That Education?' (2004) 19(1) Wisconsin Women's Law Journal 93; John O Sonsteng and others, 'A Legal Education Renaissance: A Practical Approach for the Twenty-First Century' (2007) 34(1) William Mitchell Law Review 303; Erwin Chemerinsky, 'Rethinking Legal Education' (2008) 43(2) Harvard Civil Rights-Civil Liberties Law Review 595; Lauren Carasik, 'Renaissance or Retrenchment: Legal Education at a Crossroads' (2011) 44(3) Indiana Law Review 735; Grimes (n 5); Moskovitz (n 2); James E Moliterno, 'Legal Education, Experiential Education, and Professional Responsibility' (1997) 38(1) William and Mary Law Review 71.

lawyers of the future will need to know how to solve complex, systemic challenges in collaboration with one another, experts from other disciplines, clients, and their communities. Thus, legal educators should offer law students more than just individual, client-focused problem-solving skills. We should give them the opportunity while they are learning in our schools, to tackle real-world challenges, drawing on tools from inside and outside of law to do the hard work of solving complex, ill-defined problems.

7.3.5 *Lifelong Learning*

The next generation of lawyers will need to be lifelong learners.[51] Future lawyers will need to know when and how to teach themselves new legal subject matter, processes, ways of thinking, systems, and most critically, technology.[52] It is practically unquestionable that today's law students need to learn to navigate, leverage, and maximise the value of technology.[53] But as we have seen over the past few decades, as computing power increases, computers become smarter, and the limits of technology will continue to expand. The lawyers of tomorrow will need to know how to keep up.[54]

Legal educators should bear the responsibility of teaching law students how to be effective learners and integrate ongoing learning into their careers.[55] The theory of self-regulated learning is a common frame for thinking about lifelong learning. Self-regulated learners are 'metacognitively, motivationally, and behaviorally active participants in their own learning process'.[56] Meta-cognition is the act of thinking about thinking, of a person understanding and managing how she learns. Broadly, the purpose of self-regulated learning is to enhance a person's control and management of their own learning. Self-regulated learners understand that they must drive their own learning, rather than wait to learn in reaction to a teacher's prompting.[57]

7.4 TRADITIONAL LEGAL EDUCATION

Picture a typical law school classroom anywhere in the world. Chances are, your mind reveals students seated neatly in rows, facing a teacher at the front of the room.

---

[51]   Barry J Zimmerman, 'Becoming a Self-Regulated Learner: An Overview' (2002) 41(2) Theory Into Practice 64; Michael Hunter Schwartz and Paula J Manning, *Expert Learning for Law Students* (3rd edn, Carolina Academic Press 2018); Elizabeth M Bloom, 'Teaching Law Students to Teach Themselves: Using Lessons from Educational Psychology to Shape Self-Regulated Learners' (2013) 59(2) Wayne Law Review 311.
[52]   Susskind (n 6).
[53]   This is discussed in depth in a number of chapters throughout this collection, see specifically Chapters 1 and 4.
[54]   Susskind (n 6).
[55]   Schwartz and Manning (n 51); Bloom (n 51).
[56]   Barry J Zimmerman, 'A Social Cognitive View of Self-Regulated Academic Learning' (1989) 81(3) Journal of Educational Psychology 329.
[57]   Schwartz and Manning (n 51).

Maybe they are taking notes. Maybe they are just listening. Occasionally, the teacher will ask a question and a few students will raise their hands. Perhaps the teacher will have a conversation with the student, pressing her to refine her thinking and get to the right answer. At some point, there will be a high-stakes exam.[58]

Even in the face of expansions in experiential learning in law – for example, labs, internships, clinics, and simulations – most law students are still educated in a passive, lecture-based, teacher-as-expert format, concluding with an all-or-nothing exam.[59] For decades, scholars, lawyers, judges, and the public have widely and roundly criticised this model.[60] And yet, little has changed.

The traditional legal education model was designed in and for a time far different than the one we live in today. To use the USA as an example: today's lawyers (with the exception of clinics and other experiential models) learn through the lecture-based 'case study' model that was refined and promoted 150 years ago by Harvard law school dean Christopher Columbus Langdell.[61] Langdell's method, a 'scientific' approach to the study of law using the raw material of appellate decisions, is still the foundation of legal education in the USA.[62]

The traditional legal education model is good at some important things.[63] Current law students learn legal rules and the skills of legal analysis and argument. They are steeped in the importance of precedent and how to interpret appellate decisions. They are asked to research legal issues, to analyse issues from all sides, and to practise writing memos for lawyers and briefs for courts. They engage in critical thinking, becoming expert at poking holes in others' arguments.[64]

However, legal education exhibits clear weaknesses in its capacity to impart other important skills. Students trained in the traditional model in the USA, using the 'case study' and 'Socratic' methods, can become habituated to stay quiet unless called upon and to exhibit deference to authority. Students learn there are negative consequences for those who deviate from expected norms and path-dependent

---

[58] Grimes (n 5).
[59] Susskind (n 6); Schwartz (n 50); Torrey (n 50); Sonsteng and others (n 50); Chemerinsky (n 50); Carasik (n 50); Grimes (n 5); Moskovitz (n 2); Moliterno (n 50).
[60] See, e.g., ibid; Robert J Derocher, 'What's Going on in Legal Education?' [2012] American Bar Association Bar Leader www.americanbar.org/groups/bar_services/publications/bar_leader/2011_12/spring/legaled/ accessed 20 May 2019; New York Times Editorial, 'Legal Education Reform' New York Times (New York, 25 November 2011) A18 www.nytimes.com/2011/11/26/opinion/legal-education-reform.html accessed 20 May 2019; Judith C Areen, '2016 James P While Lecture on Legal Education: Legal Education Reconsidered' (2017) 50(4) Indiana Law Review 1087.
[61] See Moskovitz (n 2); Moliterno (n 5); Judith Welch Wegner, 'Reframing Legal Education's "Wicked Problems"' (2009) 61(4) Rutgers Law Review 867.
[62] Moskovitz (n 2).
[63] Christine Cerniglia Brown, 'The Integrated Curriculum of the Future: Eliminating a Hidden Curriculum to Unveil a New Era of Collaboration, Practical Training, and Interdisciplinary Learning' (2015) 7(1) Elon Law Review 167.
[64] William M Sullivan and others, *Educating Lawyers: Preparation for the Profession of Law* (1st edn, Jossey-Bass 2007); Jerome M Organ, 'Legal Education and the Legal Profession: Convergence or Divergence' (2012) 38(3) Ohio Northern University Law Review 885.

modes of thinking. Many come to focus on individual success without concern for how others will fare. Team-based work is generally not encouraged or required.[65] Students are not given opportunities to solve real-life problems.[66]

Given the heavy focus on learning legal doctrine, students' view of law and legal analysis may be divorced from ethical, moral, and social values.[67] They learn to avoid uncertainty at all costs and provide the expected response to any question or problem. They are most comfortable with the critical mode of thinking, which encourages breaking ideas apart without concern for how to build something new. Today's law students are trained in a very narrow and specific mode of communication about law: how to communicate about law and legal processes with other lawyers, mainly law professors, but also law firm partners and judges.[68]

Legal educations' deficiencies are not a 'bug', but a feature that has been rightly criticised for decades.[69] How could a 150-year-old way of teaching and learning – designed before telephones, computers, digitisation, globalisation, and the rise of knowledge workers – possibly serve as a meaningful foundation for a career in a world already fundamentally transformed by technology and social interconnectedness?

7.5 PROJECT-BASED LEARNING IN LEGAL EDUCATION

Project-based learning can develop the multidimensional knowledge and skills future lawyers will need: collaboration, design, project management, problem-solving, and lifelong learning. It is one form of a broader pedagogical approach, problem-based learning. Both models put students, rather than the teacher, at the centre of the learning experience and actively engage them in solving real-world problems.[70] In problem and project-based learning, 'students learn content, strategies, and self-directed learning skills through collaboratively solving problems, reflecting on their experiences, and engaging in self-directed inquiry'.[71] Importantly, the problems students tackle should be ill-defined, complex, and without an obvious single answer (just like the challenges lawyers

---

[65] Kerper (n 47); Brown (n 63); Debra S Austin, 'Killing Them Softly: Neuroscience Reveals How Brain Cells Die from Law School Stress and How Neural Self-Hacking Can Optimize Cognitive Performance' (2013) 59(2) Loyola Law Review 791.

[66] Kerper (n 47).

[67] Sullivan and others (n 64).

[68] Brown (n 63).

[69] Jerome Frank, 'A Plea for Lawyer-Schools' (1947) 56(8) Yale Law Journal 1303.

[70] Barrows (n 2); Moens (n 2).

[71] Cindy E Hmelo-Silver, Ravit Golan Duncan and Clark A Chinn, 'Scaffolding and Achievement in Problem-Based and Inquiry Learning: A Response to Kirschner, Sweller, and Clark (2006)' (2007) 42 (2) Educational Psychologist 99.

of the future will face).[72] In the model I propose, the stakes are higher than in a typical problem-based setting because students work for actual clients or community partners.

Project- and problem-based learning is grounded in constructivism, a theory that emphasises the importance of learners actively guiding their own learning.[73] Constructivism is not a theory of how to teach, but a theory of how people learn. The constructivist perspective calls for a fundamental shift in values, turning the traditional model of legal education upside down.[74] Where traditional approaches to law teaching focus on students showing mastery of disciplinary knowledge, problem-based learning begins with student-led (and teacher-supported) acquisition of knowledge and skills in a team-based, problem-solving context.[75] In legal education, problem-based learning holds potential to move students from thinking focused on getting the 'right' answer towards thinking that is creative, iterative, and reflective.

For decades, problem-based pedagogies have been deployed in secondary education, higher education, and in many different professional fields ranging from business, dentistry, engineering, and more, but the model is still relatively rare law teaching.[76] A large body of research has assessed the outcomes and effectiveness of problem-based learning in contexts outside of law school, particularly in medical schools. The findings are mixed and complex, and there are many gaps in the literature, but we do have evidence suggesting that problem-based learning helps students learn conceptual subject-matter knowledge and problem-solving skills.[77] The research also suggests students have higher motivation and willingness to work in problem-based environments, as compared to traditional settings.[78]

This chapter advocates for a project-based learning model within legal education where law students work in teams to wrestle with undefined or ill-defined problems from the real world, in collaboration with community partners or clients. This last factor, the involvement of real community partners, or a client, distinguishes project-based learning from problem-based models that involve simulated or hypothetical problems (albeit based on real-world issues). The substance of each project is driven by client- or community partner-identified goals and needs. Such

---

[72]   Howard S Barrows, *Problem-Based Learning Applied to Medical Education* (Southern Illinois University – School of Medicine 2000); Hmelo-Silver (n 3). For a discussion of how to craft ill-defined problems for law students, see Carpenter (n 2).

[73]   Schwartz and Manning (n 51); Hmelo-Silver, Duncan and Chinn (n 71).

[74]   '[T]he traditional educational technology values of replicability, reliability, communication, and control ... contrast sharply with the seven primary constructivist values of collaboration, personal autonomy, generativity, reflectivity, active engagement, personal relevance, and pluralism.' David Lebow, 'Constructivist Values for Instructional Systems Design: Five Principles Toward a New Mindset' (1993) 41(3) Educational Technology Research and Development 4, 5.

[75]   Hmelo-Silver (n 3).

[76]   Barrows (n 72); Hmelo-Silver (n 3).

[77]   Hmelo-Silver, Duncan and Chinn (n 71).

[78]   Hmelo-Silver (n 3).

high-stakes projects ensure that students are fully committed and accountable. This supports deeper investment, greater lawyer-role assumption, and thus, deeper learning.

Though project-based learning is student-centred and driven, the teacher plays a critical role. It is the teacher's job to identify clients and partners, curate projects for appropriate size and scope, and provide supervision, guidance, and tools to help students learn the cognitive and affective skills they will deploy in their work.[79] For example, in my project-based clinical education course, students represent organisations in complex projects. In the classroom and in team supervision sessions, I introduce them to multidimensional skills as well as the fundamentals of legal practice, such as client interviewing and counselling, negotiation, legal research and writing, legal argument, professional ethics, and case management. The students draw on these classroom and supervision sessions for tools, practices, and methods of thinking over the course of their work for clients.

Through projects, students learn to collaborate by working in teams and navigating collaboration challenges with teacher support.[80] They learn design thinking as a problem-solving and idea-generating methodology and use design to create tools, services, systems, and written deliverables. They also engage in the practices of project management, figuring out how to plan and execute a long-term, complex project, including how to iterate and integrate new information. Throughout the process of working on a project, students are learning complex problem-solving in a real-world context. And finally, with guidance from their teacher, they can hone the strategies and practices of self-directed, lifelong learning.[81]

In closing, I offer one of many concrete examples of what students can achieve, for themselves, the profession, and the communities where they live, through project-based learning. In Tulsa, Oklahoma, a student team completed a project that centred on the challenge of how to help a judge interested in improving how self-represented litigants navigate and experience her housing court docket. This is the docket that handles all eviction cases in the county. Most landlords have counsel, most tenants do not.[82] The students, Leslie Briggs (third year JD) and Kate Forest (second year JD) began their work by meeting with the judge to identify goals. Next, they created a project plan (which they revised in an iterative way throughout the semester), and embarked on a months-long problem-solving process, meeting regularly with a supervisor for support. The students leaned heavily on tools from human-centred design and project management and wrestled with collaboration challenges.

[79]   Ibid.
[80]   Ibid.
[81]   Patience A Crowder, 'Designing a Transactional Law Clinic for Life-Long Learning' (2015) 19(2) Lewis & Clark Law Review 413.
[82]   The students created a webpage, www.tulsahousingcourtproject.wordpress.com, to document their work on the project.

The students ultimately determined their project goal was improving self-advocacy for people without counsel on the housing docket. After meeting with the judge, court staff, attorneys who regularly practise on the docket, litigants, and social service providers, they identified two key problems: self-represented litigants do not know what to expect when they get to court and do not understand that negotiations with attorneys are adversarial conversations. To solve these problems, they created a visual process map, a 'frequently-asked-questions (FAQ)' document, and negotiation guide for self-represented litigants. The visual process map and negotiation guide designed by Leslie Briggs and Kate Forest are shown in Figures 7.1 and 7.2. These products and the work that led to their creation, demonstrates how project-based learning makes it possible to assess a much broader range of skills than traditional law school exams.

Throughout the project, the students collaborated with, and learned from, one another, their teacher, the judge, the court staff, the lawyers who work on the housing docket, the litigants, and many other people and organisations throughout the community. They learned and practised user-centred design and design

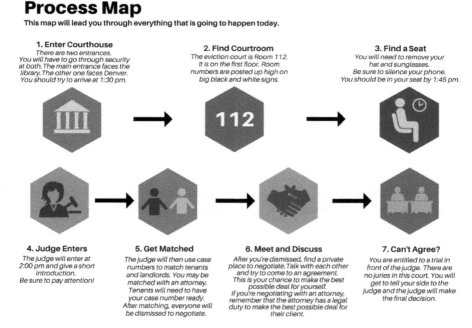

Process Map
This map will lead you through everything that is going to happen today.

1. Enter Courthouse
There are two entrances. You will have to go through security at both. The main entrance faces the library. The other one faces Denver. You should try to arrive at 1:30 pm.

2. Find Courtroom
The eviction court is Room 112. It is on the first floor. Room numbers are posted up high on big black and white signs.

3. Find a Seat
You will need to remove your hat and sunglasses. Be sure to silence your phone. You should be in your seat by 1:45 pm.

4. Judge Enters
The judge will enter at 2:00 pm and give a short introduction. Be sure to pay attention!

5. Get Matched
The judge will then use case numbers to match tenants and landlords. You may be matched with an attorney. Tenants will need to have your case number ready. After matching, everyone will be dismissed to negotiate.

6. Meet and Discuss
After you're dismissed, find a private place to negotiate. Talk with each other and try to come to an agreement. This is your chance to make the best possible deal for yourself. If you're negotiating with an attorney, remember that the attorney has a legal duty to make the best possible deal for their client.

7. Can't Agree?
You are entitled to a trial in front of the judge. There are no juries in this court. You will get to tell your side to the judge and the judge will make the final decision.

FIGURE 7.1 Visual process map developed to assist self-represented litigants in a Tulsa housing court navigate the eviction court process[83]

[83] This work is licensed under the Creative Commons Attribution – No Derivatives 4.0 International License. To view a copy of this license, visit http://creativecommons.org/licenses/by=nd/4.0/ or send a letter to Creative Commons, PO Box 1866, Mountain View, CA 94042, USA.

Negotiation Guide
for Tenants and Landlords

Before the judge will make a decision about your case, she will ask the tenant and the landlord to try to come to an agreement. This is good because this allows you a chance to make the best possible deal for yourself.

What do I talk about?

Here are a few things you could discuss. This list does not include everything so you should be sure to talk about all your concerns.

- Problems with the apartment or home such as plumbing issues, broken locks, etc.
- Payment plans for the tenant to pay back the rent owed.
- If the tenant can move out and the eviction can be dismissed without prejudice.
- Remember to discuss any problems or concerns you may have.

Either party has the right to end the negotiation and ask for a bench trial (a hearing with the judge only, no jury).

What happens next?

There are many possible outcomes to a negotiation. Here are a few options. This list does not include every option available to you. Remember, if you choose to let the judge decide, the judge's decision will be final.

- Tenant will pay back rent on __/__/__ so the eviction is dismissed without prejudice.
- Tenant can stay in the home and has agreed to the following payment plan:

    Tenant will pay _____ every (check one)
    ☐ week ☐ two weeks ☐ month
    until the an amount of $_____ has been paid to the landlord.

    "Without prejudice" means the landlord has the right to refile the eviction if the tenant doesn't pay

- Tenant can stay in the apartment and landlord has agreed to fix the following:

    _____
    _____
    _____

    Landlord will fix all of the above listed problems by: _____ (date)

- Tenant will leave by _____ (date) and the case will be dismissed without prejudice.

- The parties agree to the following:

    Monthly rent going forward   _____
    Back rent due   _____
    Costs   _____
    Fees   _____

Created by The University of Tulsa College of Law, Lobeck Taylor Community Advocacy Clinic

FIGURE 7.2 Negotiation guide developed to assist self-represented litigants in a Tulsa housing court understand the process and adversarial nature of negotiations[84]

---

[84] Ibid.

thinking, testing each of their final products with multiple audiences. They managed a complex, three-month-long project. They stumbled and failed many times, building their resilience along the way, and also achieving small and large successes. In doing so, they practised the process of learning itself – figuring out how to find, synthesise, and apply knowledge. Whilst students also learned the substantive law of the housing court docket, civil procedure, and professional ethics, they did so in the 'real world' rather than the classroom. This context also served to provide them with more holistic insight into how people receive legal services and interact with the legal system – the very challenges this chapter argues tomorrow's lawyers must face.

7.6 CONCLUSION

This chapter has argued law teachers and law schools should take responsibility for giving the next generation of lawyers the multidisciplinary skills they will need to face a changing world. Law schools should teach students how to work with other lawyers, clients, and people from other disciplines; they should be leading the way in introducing law students to the practice of user-centred design and design thinking; they should teach best practices in legal project management; they should challenge students to solve real and complex problems; and they should be imparting the values and practices of a career-long ability and desire to learn new information, develop new skills, and master new technology.

We cannot expect law graduates to successfully dive into a sea of uncertainty if we have not, in some way, prepared them to navigate uncertainty. If we want to train future lawyers to be nimble, creative, entrepreneurial problem-solvers and builders, we need to give them opportunities to create, ideate, and build. In the face of technology-driven change and a growing need for better legal services delivery, it is time to start training the lawyers we need for the future, rather than merely replicating a model of legal education created long before information technology transformed our world. Project-based learning can help build lawyers who will be prepared not only to represent clients, but also to actively shape the future of the profession by harnessing technology and interdisciplinary insights to improve legal systems and create better legal services delivery models for consumers.

BIBLIOGRAPHY

Albiston CR and Sandefur RL, 'Expanding the Empirical Study of Access to Justice' [2013] Wisconsin Law Review 101

Ambrogi B, 'The 20 Most Important Legal Technology Developments of 2018' (*Law Sites Blog*, 2018) www.lawsitesblog.com/2018/12/20-important-legal-technology-developments-2018 .html accessed 12 March 2019

'Utah Nears Licensing of Paralegals to Practice Law in Limited Circumstances' (*Law Sites Blog*, 2018) www.lawsitesblog.com/2018/08/utah-nears-licensing-paralegals-practice-law-limited-circumstances.html accessed 12 March 2019

Areen JC, '2016 James P. While Lecture on Legal Education: Legal Education Reconsidered' (2017) 50(4) Indiana Law Review 1087

Ashar SM, 'Law Clinics and Collective Mobilization' (2008) 14(2) Clinical Law Review 355

Austin DS, 'Killing Them Softly: Neuroscience Reveals How Brain Cells Die from Law School Stress and How Neural Self-Hacking Can Optimize Cognitive Performance' (2013) 59(2) Loyola Law Review 791

Barrows HS, 'Problem-Based, Self-Directed Learning' (1983) 250(22) JAMA: The Journal of the American Medical Association 3077

Problem-Based Learning Applied to Medical Education (Southern Illinois University – School of Medicine 2000)

Barton B, 'A Comparison Between the American Markets for Medical and Legal Services' (2016) 67(5) Hastings Law Journal 1331

Bloom EM, 'Teaching Law Students to Teach Themselves: Using Lessons from Educational Psychology to Shape Self-Regulated Learners' (2013) 59(2) Wayne Law Review 311

Brest P, 'The Responsibility of Law Schools: Educating Lawyers as Counselors and Problem Solvers' (2006) 58(3/4) Law and Contemporary Problems 5

Brown CC, 'The Integrated Curriculum of the Future: Eliminating a Hidden Curriculum to Unveil a New Era of Collaboration, Practical Training, and Interdisciplinary Learning' (2015) 7(1) Elon Law Review 167

Carasik L, 'Renaissance or Retrenchment: Legal Education at a Crossroads' (2011) 44(3) Indiana Law Review 735

Carpenter AE, 'The Project Model of Clinical Education: Eight Pedagogical Principles to Maximize Student Learning and Social Justice Impact' (2013) 20(1) Clinical Law Review 39

Chambliss E, 'Marketing Legal Assistance' (2019) 148(1) Daedalus 98

Chemerinsky E, 'Rethinking Legal Education' (2008) 43(2) Harvard Civil Rights-Civil Liberties Law Review 595

Columbia Law School, 'Columbia Law Expands Experiential Offerings' (2019) www .law.columbia.edu/news/2018/08/new-clinics-experiential-education accessed 20 May 2019

Cox EJ, 'An Economic Crisis Is a Terrible Thing to Waste: Reforming the Business of Law for a Sustainable and Competitive Future' (2009) 57(2) UCLA Law Review 511

Crowder PA, 'Designing a Transactional Law Clinic for Life-Long Learning' (2015) 19(2) Lewis & Clark Law Review 413

Dangel S, Hagan M and Williams JB, 'Designing Today's Legal Education for Tomorrow's Lawyers: The Role of Legal Design, Technology and Innovation' in Antoine Masson (ed.), *Legal and Judicial Innovation: Methodology and Perspectives* (Springer-Verlag 2018)

Derocher RJ, 'What's Going on in Legal Education?' [2012] American Bar Association Bar Leader www.americanbar.org/groups/bar_services/publications/bar_leader/2011_12/ spring/legaled/ accessed 20 May 2019

Flagg BJ, 'Experimenting with Problem-Based Learning in Constitutional Law' (2002) 10 Washington University Journal of Law & Policy 101

Frank J, 'A Plea for Lawyer-Schools' (1947) 56(8) Yale Law Journal 1303

Grimes RH, *Re-Thinking Legal Education under the Civil and Common Law: A Road Map for Constructive Change* (Routledge 2018)

Hadfield GK, 'Privatizing Commercial Law' (2001) 24(1) Regulation Magazine 40

Rules for a Flat World: Why Humans Invented Law and How to Reinvent It for a Complex Global Economy (Oxford University Press 2017)

Hadfield GK and Rhode DL, 'How to Regulate Legal Services to Promote Access, Innovation, and the Quality of Lawyering' (2016) 67(5) Hastings Law Journal 1191

Hagan M, 'A Human-Centered Design Approach to Access to Justice: Generating New Prototypes and Hypotheses for Intervention to Make Courts User-Friendly' (2018) 6(2) Indiana Journal of Law and Social Equality 199

'Participatory Design for Innovation in Access to Justice' (2019) 148(1) Daedalus 120

Henderson B, 'Legal Services and the Consumer Price Index (CPI) (042)' (*Legal Evolution*, 2018) www.legalevolution.org/2018/01/legal-services-consumer-price-index-cpi-cost-going-up-wallet-share-going-down-042/ accessed 20 May 2019

Henderson WD, 'Three Generations of US Lawyers: Generalists, Specialists, Project Managers' (2011) 70(2) Maryland Law Review 373

Hmelo-Silver CE, 'Problem-Based Learning: What and How Do Students Learn?' (2004) 16 (3) Educational Psychology Review 235

Hmelo-Silver CE, Duncan RG and Chinn CA, 'Scaffolding and Achievement in Problem-Based and Inquiry Learning: A Response to Kirschner, Sweller, and Clark (2006)' (2007) 42(2) Educational Psychologist 99

Holland B, 'The Washington State Limited License Legal Technician Practice Rule: A National First in Access to Justice' (2013) 82 SUPRA 75

Kerper J, 'Creative Problem Solving vs. the Case Method: A Marvelous Adventure in Which Winnie-the-Pooh Meets Mrs. Palsgraf' (1998) 34(2) California Western Law Review 351

Knake RN, 'Cultivating Learners Who Will Invent the Future of Law Practice: Some Thoughts on Educating Entrepreneurial and Innovative Lawyers' (2012) 38(3) Ohio Northern University Law Review 847

Kruse KR, 'Biting Off What They Can Chew: Strategies for Involving Students in Problem-Solving beyond Individual Client Representation' (2002) 8(2) Clinical Law Review 405

Kurtz S, Wylie M and Gold N, 'Problem-Based Learning an Alternative Approach to Legal Education' (1990) 13(2) Dalhousie Law Journal 797

Lambreth SR and Rueff Jr. DA, *The Power of Legal Project Management: A Practical Handbook* (American Bar Association 2014)

Lebow D, 'Constructivist Values for Instructional Systems Design: Five Principles Toward a New Minset' (1993) 41(3) Educational Technology Research and Development 4

Miller J, 'Australia's Family Law Crisis Reaches Tipping Point' (*InDaily*, 2018) https://indaily .com.au/opinion/2018/03/22/australias-family-law-crisis-reaches-tipping-point/

Moens GA, 'The Mysteries of Problem-Based Learning: Combining Enthusiasm and Excellence' (2007) 38(2) University of Toledo Law Review 623

Moliterno JE, 'Legal Education, Experiential Education, and Professional Responsibility' (1997) 38(1) William and Mary Law Review 71

'The Future of Legal Education Reform' (2013) 40(2) Pepperdine Law Review 423

Moskovitz M, 'Beyond the Case Method: It's Time to Teach with Problems' (1992) 42(2) Journal of Legal Education 241

Mullan J, 'Legal Project Management: Passing Fad or Here to Stay?' (2012) 12(3) Legal Information Management 214

Nathanson S, 'The Role of Problem Solving in Legal Education' (1989) 39(2) Journal of Legal Education 167

National Association for Law Placement, 'What Do We Know about JD Advantage Jobs?' *NALP Bulletin* (Washington, DC, November 2017) www.nalp.org/1117research accessed 20 May 2019

National Centre for State Courts, 'Civil Justice Initiative: The Landscape of Civil Litigation in State Courts' (National Centre for State Courts 2015) www.ncsc.org/~/media/files/pdf/research/civiljusticereport-2015.ashx

New York Times Editorial, 'Legal Education Reform' *New York Times* (New York, 25 November 2011) A18 www.nytimes.com/2011/11/26/opinion/legal-education-reform.html accessed 20 May 2019

Organ JM, 'Legal Education and the Legal Profession: Convergence or Divergence' (2012) 38 (3) Ohio Northern University Law Review 885

Perrin B, Audas R and Péloquin-Ladany S, 'Canada's Justice Deficit : The Case for a Justice System Report Card' (Macdonald-Laurier Institute 2016) www.macdonaldlaurier.ca /report-card-criminal-justice-system/

Pink DH, *A Whole New Mind: Moving from the Information Age to the Conceptual Age* (Riverhead Books 2005)

Preston A, 'Designing the Australian Tax System' in Richard J Boland Jr. and Fred Collopy (eds.), *Managing as Designing* (Stanford University Press 2009)

Reno J, 'Lawyers as Problem-Solvers: Keynote Address to the AALS' (1999) 49(1) Journal of Legal Education 5

Resnik J, 'The Privatization of Process: Requiem for and Celebration of the Federal Rules of Civil Procedure at 75' (2014) 162(7) University of Pennsylvania Law Review 1793

Rhode DL, *The Trouble with Lawyers* (Oxford University Press 2015)

Ruhl JB, 'The Rise of Legal Project Management' (2015) 19(4) The Young Lawyer 6

Sandefur RL, 'What We Know and Need to Know About the Legal Needs of the Public' (2016) 67(2) South Carolina Law Review 443

Schwartz MH, 'Teaching Law by Design: How Learning Theory and Instructional Design Can Inform and Reform Law Teaching' (2001) 38(2) San Diego Law Review 347

Schwartz MH and Manning PJ, *Expert Learning for Law Students* (3rd edn, Carolina Academic Press 2018)

Silver C, 'Getting Real About Globalization and Legal Education: Potential and Perspectives for the US' (2013) 24(2) Stanford Law and Policy Review 457

Snyder L, *Democratizing Legal Service: Obstacles and Opportunities* (Lexington Books 2016)

Sonsteng JO and others, 'A Legal Education Renaissance: A Practical Approach for the Twenty-First Century' (2007) 34(1) William Mitchell Law Review 303

Stanford University, 'The Legal Design Lab' https://law.stanford.edu/organizations/pages/ legal-design-lab/#slsnav-our-mission accessed 20 May 2019

Sullivan WM and others, *Educating Lawyers: Preparation for the Profession of Law* (1st edn, Jossey-Bass 2007)

Susskind R, *Tomorrow's Lawyers: An Introduction to Your Future* (1st edn, Oxford University Press 2013)

Susskind R and Susskind D, *The Future of the Professions: How Technology Will Transform the Work of Human Experts* (Oxford University Press 2015)

Tashea J, 'California Bar Task Force to Consider Regulatory Changes on Nonlawyer Ownership of Legal Services Firms' *ABA Journal* (Chicago, 27 July 2018) www .abajournal.com/news/article/california_bar_task_force_to_propose_regulatory_change s_affecting_nonlawyer accessed 20 May 2019

The University of Arizona, 'Innovation for Justice: Unlock Change' (2019) https://law .arizona.edu/innovation-for-justice accessed 20 May 2019

Torrey M, 'You Call That Education?' (2004) 19(1) Wisconsin Women's Law Journal 93

University of York, 'Problem Based Learning' www.york.ac.uk/law/postgraduate/llmpro grammes/llm-international-corporate-commercial/problem-based-learning/ accessed 20 May 2019

Wegner JW, 'Reframing Legal Education's "Wicked Problems"' (2009) 61(4) Rutgers Law Review 867

Weinstein J and others, 'Teaching Teamwork to Law Students' (2013) 63(1) Journal of Legal
     Education 36
Weinstein J and Morton L, 'Stuck in a Rut: The Role of Creative Thinking in Problem
     Solving and Legal Education' (2003) 9(2) Clinical Law Review 835
Wikipedia, 'Joshua Browder' (2018) https://en.wikipedia.org/wiki/joshua_browder accessed
     20 May 2019
Zimmerman BJ, 'A Social Cognitive View of Self-Regulated Academic Learning' (1989) 81(3)
     Journal of Educational Psychology 329
    'Becoming a Self-Regulated Learner: An Overview' (2002) 41(2) Theory Into Practice 64

8

Same As It Ever Was?

Technocracy, Democracy and the Design of Discipline-Specific Digital Environments

Paul Maharg

In the field of educational technology there are classic oppositions that shape what we do in our use of technology in higher education (HE) – behaviourism versus constructivism, open versus for-profit, conventional versus innovative curriculum design, technocracy versus democracy. Both sides of the binaries are critical components of what we might determine as the 'social' in HE, and the extent to which their oppositions govern our approach to curriculum design also determines the type of learning that our students undertake in their programmes. In this chapter we explore the effect of these antinomies on the development of simulation software designed and built last decade and still in use at Strathclyde Law School, and adapted elsewhere. The chapter will analyse the assumptions and the history – legal educational, technological and social – that are part of the software build and outline future use and expectations for the software as it develops beyond what might, to date, be characterised as its early beta or *incunabula* stages of development in HE. Above all we shall begin to trace what we hope is one resolution of the classic opposition of technocracy and democracy, a theme that will be developed in future publications.

> The issues raised by the new way of life are difficult and painful, because they strike at the heart of our most complex and intransigent social problems: problems of community, identity, governance, equity, and values. There is no simple good news or bad news.
> — Sherry Turkle, *Life on the Screen: Identity in the Age of the Internet*[1]

8.1 INTRODUCTION

The project of modernising the law school is not itself a modern phenomenon. The first faculties in the new eleventh-century institution in Bologna called a *universitas* were law and theology, founded in part so that the newly-discovered Justinianic codes

---

[1] Sherry Turkle, *Life on the Screen: Identity in the Age of the Internet* (1st edn, Simon & Schuster 1997) 232.

and texts, voluminous, exotic, arcane, could be collated, understood and put into practice, along with the ever-burgeoning, increasingly complex codes of canon law. To cope with the information overload brought about by this data, scholars developed interpretive methods and apparatuses over subsequent centuries that included glosses, commentaries, summaries and much else. Indeed scholarly understanding of canon law and the reception of Roman law would not have been possible without the development of the textual technologies that were to become foundational to our understanding of law and legal method, its reception, structure and migration.

In the millennium since the initial foundations, law schools, law teachers and students have at various points brought about changes, sometimes radical, often-times incremental, by reconstructing aspects of their roles, operations, physical infrastructure, personnel and technologies. Such reconstruction is powerfully affected by context, for law, like any other discipline in higher education (HE), is not a black box. It has been shaped by contexts of politics, history, culture and university practices as well as the practices of law, and the social and material relations arising from those practices.

We can see an example of this in Scottish legal education in the enlightenment period. As Cairns points out, earlier seventeenth century educational practices tended to be highly prescriptive, and emphasised note taking, rote learning and memorisation of principle and case.[2] These were derived in part from scholastic models stemming from Renaissance interpretation of classical rhetorical models. In the eighteenth century enlightenment, however, educators drew upon new models of rhetoric and education. Adam Smith, Lord Kames (one of whose texts had the Deweyan title of 'Introduction to the Art of Thinking'), John Millar, Francis Hutcheson and others focused on reasoning, and moral and ethical analysis. Adam Smith's lectures on jurisprudence, delivered at Glasgow University when he was Professor of Logic and later Moral Philosophy is a good example, in both content and (by many accounts) delivery, the lectures were the opposite of the older style of legal education.[3] Smith took account of new forms of knowledge, new interdisciplinarities, as did Adam Ferguson at Edinburgh University in his Moral Philosophy lectures.[4] Smith's 'Lectures on Rhetoric and Belles Lettres' took a modern turn, for example, eschewing the conventional approach to rhetoric as

[2] John W Cairns, 'Rhetoric, Language, and Roman Law: Legal Education and Improvement in Eighteenth-Century Scotland' (1991) 9(1) Law and History Review 31.
[3] JW Cairns, 'The Influence of Smith's Jurisprudence on Legal Education in Scotland' in Peter Jones and Andrew S Skinner (eds.), *Adam Smith Reviewed* (Edinburgh University Press 1992).
[4] By his own account Ferguson's style of lecturing was relaxed and wide-ranging in its reference. Of his course on Moral Philosophy and Pneumatics he observed to students, with Schönian reflexivity, 'You are at once the Subjects, the Evidence and the Judges of what is to be advanced' (Adam Ferguson, 'Lectures', *Papers of Professor Adam Ferguson (1723–1816)* (Edinburgh University Library Special Collections 1733) 1775, 4 and verso. Ferguson also offered advice on how to study: 'I think it is a hard and unprofitable task to attempt writing the Lectures. They are delivered to be understood not to be written. It may be useful nevertheless to take some short notes in aid of the memory and afterwards compose for yourselves what you conceive on the subject of each days Lecture' (ibid 1775,

comprising forms of persuasion, and defining it as communication in most of its contemporary social forms.[5] He also followed the precepts of Henry Home, Lord Kames, an unjustly neglected figure in the history of legal education in these isles. Kames' emphasis on reasoning in one text[6] was balanced in another that focused on the development of 'sensibility' in legal education,[7] a unique approach that remains to this day still a subaltern focus of study in legal education.

In this example, the social and the literary culture of enlightenment Scotland affected contemporary practices and theories of legal education. Modernising the law school, then as now, is less of an ever-present participle and more of a series of highly local responses to both local and broader changes to social, intellectual and cultural conditions around the activity of learning the law – responses saturated in history and culture. Since we shall be discussing digital technology, in which our own cultures may be said to be saturated, it may be useful at this stage to say what I mean by the phrase 'digital technology'. I take a broad view of technology, defining it not merely as an objective engine or device in the world such as a smartphone or a server but also as a collection of rules, codes, practices and creative initiatives. I follow Lisa Gitelman's useful two-level model of media where 'a medium is a technology that enables communication' but which is also 'a set of associated "protocols" or social and cultural practices that have grown up around that technology'.[8] I also hold with Henry Jenkins' observation that a medium's content shifts according to the delivery technology – he gives the example of television displacing radio as a storytelling medium.[9] Another might be the displacement of the scholarly manuscript by the book in the fifteenth century.[10]

Following this definition, there are classic oppositions in the field of educational technology that shape what we do in our use of technology in HE: behaviourism versus

16.). As I point out, Ferguson expected students to read fairly widely in the texts mentioned on his course, and he also expected coursework to be carried out by students (Paul Maharg, *Transforming Legal Education: Learning and Teaching the Law in the Early Twenty-First Century* (1st edn, Ashgate Publishing 2007) 108).

5 Adam Smith, *Lectures On Rhetoric and Belles Lettres* (JC Bryce ed., Liberty Fund Inc 1762) 133. In Scotland the wider context of this revolution in rhetoric includes the influence of French *philosophes* such as Diderot and Rousseau. It also includes the interest in oral literatures and cultures, in itself the continuation of a historiographical tradition stretching back to the Renaissance (see David Allan, *Virtue, Learning, and the Scottish Enlightenment: Ideas of Scholarship in Early Modern History* (Edinburgh University Press 1993)) and the celebration of common speech in poetry – the work of Robert Fergusson in urban forms and Robert Burns in rural forms and the revival of the song tradition being examples of the latter.

6 Henry Home (Lord Kames), *Introduction to the Art of Thinking* (2nd edn, W Creech and T Caddell 1764).

7 Henry Home (Lord Kames), *Loose Hints Upon Education: Chiefly Concerning the Culture of the Heart* (T Henshall 1782).

8 Lisa Gitelman, *Always Already New: Media, History and the Data of Culture* (Massachusetts Institute of Technology Press 2006).

9 Henry Jenkins, *Convergence Culture: Where Old and New Media Collide* (New York University Press 2006).

10 Discussed in Paul Maharg, 'Disintermediation' (2016) 50(1) The Law Teacher 114.

constructivism, open versus for-profit, conventional versus innovative curriculum design are some of them. One such opposition, the focus of this chapter, is the construct of technocracy versus democracy where the first is marked by arcane expertise, the highly developed artificial languages of code, the development of closed structures of problem-identification and problem-solution; and the second is characterised by practices such as relative transparency, open debate and an aspiration to equality. Technocracy has long been subject to analysis in sociological literatures, particularly as an element in the second or reflexive modernity mapped out by Beck and others.[11] While its effects in HE have been the subject of critique, its effects on legal education and particularly the impact of the digital domain upon legal education, have seldom been analysed; and this chapter is one contribution to that literature.

I argue here that technocracy is a critical component of what we might determine as knowledge constitution, dissemination and reformation in HE. In the extent to which the tensions engendered by technocracy and democracy govern our approach to curriculum design, they also determine the educational conventions that our students experience in their legal educational programmes. Furthermore, if we take seriously Jenkins' assertion that a medium's content shifts according to technology, the question arises whether that can assist us to construct a more radical under-standing of the social and the literate in universities. Can we use the digital to create for our students an environment that facilitates the learning of justice and reflexive awareness of law and social practices? Can it help us to shift from technocratic approaches to democratic approaches in our educational theory and practice? I believe it can, though the processes are complex and, as Turkle observes above, there is no simple good news or bad.[12] To help us focus the argument, in the next sections I shall analyse some aspects of the development of simulation as a heuristic in legal education.

8.2 SIMULATION: THE EDUCATIVE FUNCTION OF ROLE[13]

> A social role can ... be considered as a complex coding activity controlling both the creation and organization of specific meanings and the conditions for their trans-mission and reception.
>
> — Basil Bernstein, *Theoretical Studies Towards a Sociology of Language*[14]

---

[11] Ulrich Beck, *The Cosmopolitan Vision* (Polity Press 2006); Ulrich Beck, Anthony Giddens and Scott Lash, *Reflexive Modernization: Politics, Tradition and Aesthetics in the Modern Social Order* (Stanford University Press 1994).

[12] Turkle (n 1).

[13] Some of this section appeared as an invited blog post written by myself, see Paul Maharg, 'Digital and Simulation in the Teaching of Law: Emerging from the Shadows' (*law-tech-a2j.org*, 2 November 2016) https://law-tech-a2j.org/external-contributor/digital-and-simulation-in-the-teaching-of-law-emerging-from-the-shadows/ accessed 2 November 2018.

[14] Basil Bernstein, *Theoretical Studies Towards a Sociology of Language* (1st edn, Routledge 1971) 14–5.

In the systematic review of the literature on digital simulation in legal education in the period 1970–2012 undertaken by Maharg and Nicol in 2014, the authors traced a shift in educational culture in the early simulations, linked to technology-in-use.[15] Those examples, from the 1970s and 1980s, involved computer-aided instruction and embedded AI programmes in the 1990s they tended to be replaced by interactive video (e.g. laserdiscs) and sims that made use of early video conferencing applications as well as electronic casebooks that provided basic interactivity as well as extensive digital resources. A significant shift in delivery platforms occurred around 2000 with the development of more powerful desktop computing that allowed for the creation and representation of multi-user online environments such as *Second Life*, virtual offices and case management systems, and other custom-made interactive environments.[16]

With the change in medium came a shift in educational approach. By the 2000s there was less instructivist emphasis, and more of a constructivist approach to simulation in law. Abdul Paliwala at Warwick, Paul Maharg and colleagues at Strathclyde, the Dutch projects of RechtenOnline and others elsewhere all worked with varieties of role play and simulation, in online or blended programmes, which were to a greater or lesser extent immersive, and which engaged students in what was for many of them a welcome change to a diet of lectures, tutorials and exams. Students also collaborated with each other in virtual firms and in a variety of online forums.

My work on simulation in legal education began in the mid-1990s at Glasgow Caledonian University in Glasgow where Karen Barton, Patricia McKellar and I met, discussed ideas and practices, and tried out mini-pilots. But it was really the founding of the joint Glasgow Graduate School of Law by Glasgow University and Strathclyde University in 1999 and the merging of a single professional programme – the Diploma in Legal Practice – that shifted the needle. Faced with the choice of either a Strathclyde or Glasgow curriculum as the basis of the Diploma programme, I took neither: with my colleagues, we began to construct our own syncretist pedagogy and practices in learning, teaching and assessing.[17] We drew upon others' ideas, acknowledging and adapting them – the shining example of John Dewey for instance in philosophy of education, the realist movement in legal education in the USA, the progressive education movement in England, the inspirational work by Sherry Turkle on Multiple User Dungeons/Dimensions/Dialogues (MUDs) and the Object Orientated MUD varients (MOOs), by Lucy Suchman on situated learning,[18] Will Wright on SimCity and The Sims, and many others. We learned from kindergartens

15 Paul Maharg and Emma Nicol, 'Simulation and Technology in Legal Education: A Systematic Review and Future Research Programme' in Caroline Strevens, Richard H Grimes and Edward Phillips (eds.), *Legal Education: Simulation in Theory and Practice* (Ashgate Publishing 2014).
16 Julie Cassidy, 'Client View' (2009) 4(1) Journal of the Australasian Tax Teachers Association 55.
17 Karen Barton and Paul Maharg, 'E-Simulations in the Wild: Interdisciplinary Research, Design and Implementation' in David Gibson, Clark Aldrich and Marc Prensky (eds.), *Games and Simulations in Online Learning* (Information Science Publishing, Idea Group Ltd 2007).
18 Lucy Suchman, *Human-Machine Reconfigurations: Plans and Situated Actions* (1st edn, Cambridge University Press 2006).

and primary schools, from medical education, sports coaching and the best of what law firms were doing in professional development. Above all, social and ethical formation was essential: our aim was to prepare students for their possible futures, but to assist society to achieve its best future, too, through our students.

Part of the problem of technocratic and corporatised software is that it is designed to enable conventional pedagogies and assessment practices because there is much more profit in that than in fostering innovation.[19] To define for ourselves and others what we were trying to do required the development of pedagogical principle. Following Dewey and constructivist educators, we developed the concept of trans-actional learning (TL), which we defined in our internal papers and publications as comprising the following seven traits:

> **active learning,**
>   through **performance in authentic transactions**
>   involving **reflection in and on learning,**
>   deep **collaborative learning,** and
>   holistic or **process learning,**
>   with **relevant professional assessment**
>   that includes **ethical standards.**[20]

We used the sim engine to explore new understandings of how it affected learning, and how it changed our roles. Our roles as academics gradually turned into some-thing richer and more expansive. We were compelled to ask foundational questions. Were the sims really 'authentic'? What did 'authentic' mean in the context of TL?[21] Above all, we investigated how students learned in their virtual firms. The work of Karen Barton and Fiona Westwood, for instance, analysed how student learning, trust, ethics and professionalism could fuse to help develop professional, ethical identities. Using a learning/trust matrix, created as a result of their qualitative analysis of the reflective reports produced by students from the experience of work-ing in their virtual firms, student achievement was mapped across four quadrants, measured by quality of learning and quality of trust.[22] Burton and Westwood went on

---

[19] Thus as Boys pointed out, LMSs are generally used to mimic conventional forms of university administration, teaching, learning and assessment LMSs, Boys argues, challenge 'existing pedagogical and organisational processes'; but are ubiquitous partly because they 'enable institutions to avoid difficult questions about how they organise themselves'. It is a form of Bourdieuan *méconaissance*, or deliberate misrecognition by agents – Jos Boys, 'Managed Learning Environments, Joined Up Systems and the Problems of Organisational Change' (Jisc 2002).

[20] I have previously defined TL as a multi-layered concept, comprising Deweyan anti-epistemology (the concept of 'transaction' is at the heart of Dewey's conception of learning and understanding), a Realist educational approach, and a constructivist approach to the use of technology in legal learning. See Maharg, *Transforming Legal Education: Learning and Teaching the Law in the Early Twenty-First Century* (n 4).

[21] Karen Barton, Patricia McKellar and Paul Maharg, 'Authentic Fictions: Simulation, Professionalism and Legal Learning' (2007) 14(1) Clinical Law Review 143.

[22] Karen Barton and Fiona Westwood, 'From Student to Trainee Practitioner – A Study of Team Working as a Learning Experience' (2006) 3 Web Journal of Current Legal Issues 1 www.bailii.org /uk/other/journals/WebJCLI/admin/wjclidex.html accessed 22 January 2019.

to analyse how they realigned teaching practices in key modules to ensure that more students occupied the high-learning high-trust quadrant.[23] And having produced this research, they used it with students to show them how to achieve the benefits of living and working in that quadrant. The result, as they demonstrated, helped to transform our practices and student achievement.

8.3 SIM APPLICATIONS: A CURRICULUM DEVELOPMENT TIMELINE

Our development of the curriculum took place over an eleven-year span, and in three broad phases, during which the splicing of digital choices with educational opportunity was critical to the evolution of the programme. The timeline reveals how modernisation of the curriculum was brought about, and how we dealt with technocratic traits in both software and educational design.

8.3.1 1999–2002: Proto-sims

Our IT manager Scott Walker and I worked with a consultant developer to design a basic sim environment in ColdFusion v.4.5 (CF).[24] This environment allowed us to connect basic HTML pages to a database which, coupled with a basic web editor, enabled online communications to be created and saved, and pages to be attached to basic graphics such as a virtual firm front page, an online map of our fictional town, Ardcalloch, and the like. The CF app was custom-coded using its own proprietary scripting language, CFScript, as well as Java and C++, by the developer from Glasgow University, our partner in the joint Glasgow Graduate School of Law. Figure 8.1 shows an early rendering of our fictional town, Ardcalloch, with no interactivity, and a mixture of student firm and fictional representation (the button bar at the top refers to FAQs for projects, the student virtual office portal, discussion forums for projects). The 'Yellow Pages' graphic is a directory of people and places used in the sims.

The sim educational ecology worked to shift students from law-as-observation to law-as-action. However, custom builds by the developer were expensive and to have the quality of our critical software platform upon which hundreds of staff and students depended outside our direct control was an unacceptable risk. The same applied to our reliance on CF: if the company went down, or was taken over by another corporate and radically altered, we would be faced with major alterations to our software and curriculum. The proprietary scripting language caused us to rely on the developer. Also we needed *more* of a digital environment. Students actually

---

[23] Karen Barton and Fiona Westwood, 'Developing Professional Character – Trust, Values and Learning' in Paul Maharg and Caroline Maughan (eds.), *Affect and Legal Education: Emotion in Learning and Teaching the Law* (Ashgate Publishing 2011).

[24] Adobe, 'Home Page' https://coldfusion.adobe.com/ accessed 19 April 2019.

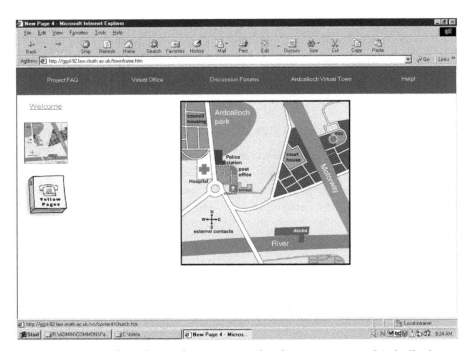

FIGURE 8.1 Screenshot of an early, c.2002, graphical representation of Ardcalloch, our fictional web town

wanted more and better digital spaces, more immersion, and more realia for the projects, as well as more flexibility in use of software and in curriculum design.

8.3.2 *2002–2007: Sim Project Learning Expanded*

In part as a consequence of rising student numbers, we hired more technical staff, both web designers and coders (they were also involved in other projects, e.g. multimedia, webcasts, law-specific content management systems, legal writing projects and induction resources for the law school).[25] We also employed more educational/law staff, and

---

[25]   The Glasgow Graduate School of Law (GGSL) was a unique partnership between the law schools of the universities of Strathclyde and Glasgow. Its ethic was predominantly collaborationist and on its professional programmes it was committed to innovation, which was embedded within the culture and values of the programmes. This was a commitment at the highest level of management within the two law schools. The founding deans, Professors Alan Paterson and Joe Thomson, recognised that if professional learning and digital innovation were to be financed appropriately for the better good of students, the profession and others, then it required the joint resources of a joint graduate school to bring it about. These values, together with success in digital learning resources, ensured that for most of the eleven years of the GGSL's existence there was excellent provision of designers, faculty who were dedicated to educational innovation, and technical staff (web designers, applications developers). For more on the structure and ethos of the GGSL, and a perspective of it as a form of realist

formed the Learning Technologies Development Unit (LTDU), directed by me and with Scott Walker as manager. We went on to dispense with the CF app but retained and enhanced its content for our expanding number of sims. We used various versions of web authoring software e.g. SharePoint, and database apps to reconfigure the environment – substantial design time went into that. On communications, we again stripped out CF, and used Microsoft (MS) Outlook as client-facing sim software.

We used Outlook Public Folders for a basic case management system, embedding links to Ardcalloch Map and Directory of websites; and created many more websites, some more interactive than others. Tools and procedures were much improved, because the process of making and unmaking software and weaving it into the fabric of the curriculum was now much more in our control. Administrative and technical staff worked more closely with educational designers (Karen Barton, Patricia McKellar, Fiona Westwood, leading practitioner tutors, visiting professors and my programme co-director Leo Martin). A key task for us was communicating our developing vision regarding education, professionalism and so forth, to our practitioner-tutors on the diploma.

As a consequence of these efforts there was a major shift in functionality, enabling more complex use of sims in learning, and especially in blended learning. Virtual firm websites began to resemble case management tools. Students and staff liked the implicit link between static content and communications that Outlook Public Folders gave them. But with our move from CF to Outlook we put ourselves more firmly in the hands of corporate software providers. So when MS altered Outlook's Public Folder structure and functionality, it affected much of what we were doing in simulation. Since Outlook was proprietary, the open plugin options for MS were almost non-existent: we had to work around this, again making ourselves vulnerable to corporate code fixes and rethinks.

Our increasing educational and professional learning sophistication was outstripping our hacking of Outlook. We had to constantly patrol the interface between the content management systems we used, our intra-programme communications (e.g. our variety of forums and chat spaces) and our virtual fictional spaces. Sims too became more complex and needed to be managed, with improved communications features, and improved authenticity with regard to transactional data and communications. Student data increased (e.g. questions, answers on forums, feedback), as did our typologies of legal sims, and technical sim data (iterative changes, improvements), and more sophisticated administrative processes were required (e.g. to track the design and development of sims, to pack and unpack sims throughout the year, archive a sim after use, use sims with international partners such as the Netherlands).[26] All this meant that we really needed much more than individual apps and Outlook Public Folders could offer us.

---

legal educational construct, see Paul Maharg, 'Sea-Change' (2011) 18(1–2) *International Journal of the Legal Profession* 139.

[26] Barton and Maharg (n 17).

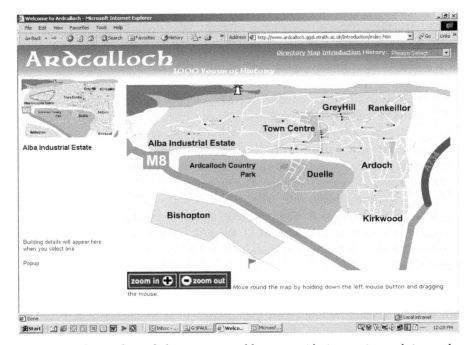

FIGURE 8.2 Screenshot of the now-zoomable map with interactive website nodes (directory, map, introduction to Ardcalloch and town history now separate from legal projects pages)

Figures 8.2 (above) and 8.3 (below) depict the evolution of the platform, demonstrating the addition of new features and changes to the organisation of content.

8.3.3 2007–Present: Sim Learning Deepened

In 2006 we won over £230,000 in grant-funding to develop a simulation engine, called SIMPLE – SIMulated Professional Learning Environment. The LTDU specified, designed, coded and produced alpha and beta versions based on project partners' and our specifications. We also wrote project software, documentation and offered support for implementation during the two-year project which spanned 2006–8, all of which was summarised in the ninety-six-page final report, available from the SIMPLE website.[27] The SIMPLE project, unique in legal education, solved many of the problems we had encountered at the first two stages above.

[27] Michael Hughes and others, 'SIMulated Professional Learning Environment (SIMPLE): Programme Final Report' (Jisc & Higher Education Authority 2008). There were also numerous presentations, publications, and analyses of the learning gains achieved by students. Karen Counsel in the University of South Wales, for instance, recorded a 10 per cent improvement in the Torts examination results of her first year LLB students, when the only significant new factor on the course was the replacement of an essay with a simulation (Karen Counsell, 'Virtual Learning for the Real World: Using Simulation

FIGURE 8.3 Screenshot of the third iteration of a virtual firm law page

After the project the software was adopted by a number of law schools nationally (Northumbria University, University of South Wales and others)[28] and internationally in Hong Kong and Australia.[29] Strathclyde University still currently uses the

with Non-Law Students' in Caroline Strevens, Richard Grimes and Edward Phillips (eds.), *Legal Education: Simulation in Theory and Practice* (Ashgate Publishing 2014) 153.

[28] We also collaborated with the Cyberdam project in the Netherlands, constructing an international simulation between the students at the universities of Utrecht and Strathclyde. Throughout there was a commitment to Open practices – Open-Source Code (see SIMPLE Community, 'SIMPLE Community' (2019) http://simplecommunity.org/ accessed 19 April 2019), Open Educational Resources (see the Simshare project, detailed at Julian Priddle and others, 'Simshare: Project Final Report' (UK Centre for Legal Education 2010) www.researchgate.net/publication/228367047_Project_Final_Report accessed 19 April 2019.), and Open Research.

[29] In Hong Kong University's Faculty of Law, Wilson Chow and Michael Ng have adapted SIMPLE as SMILE, and are achieving significant results- see Wilson Chow and Michael Ng, 'Disintermediator or Another Intermediary? E-Simulation Platform for Professional Legal Education at University of Hong Kong' (2016) 7(1) European Journal of Law and Technology 638. In ANU, SIMPLE has been adapted as VOS, the Virtual Office System, and simulation has been used to great effect on their professional programme, the GDLP. The research that has arisen from the use of simulation is rich and comprehensive, contributing to the exploration of student and professional wellbeing, curriculum design, professionalism, identity and much else – see Anneka Ferguson, 'Creating Practice Ready, Well and Professional Law Graduates' (2015) 7(2) Journal of Learning Design 22; Elizabeth Lee and Anneka Ferguson, 'The Development of the Virtual Educational Space: How Transactional Online Teaching Can Prepare Today's Law Graduates for Today's Virtual Age' (2015) 6(1) European Journal of Law and Technology 1.

software. The SIMPLE platform was upgraded in 2010, but since then there have been no upgrades or bug fixes.

SIMPLE gave us much more control over the core functions of simulation design, student learning and assessment. Technically, it was much easier to have oversight of the many thousands of documents and interchanges between automatic elements, documents, chat and forum exchanges, and to maintain security of student and staff work both during and after a sim. It also gave us much more educational confidence about disciplinary-based learning, and more space (time, energy, strategy, deployment) to research the uses of the application. It enabled much greater flexibility in curriculum design and especially in both formative and summative assessment design. There was also an increase in our dependence upon a single sim platform and our confidence in using it more innovatively. SIMPLE also enabled us to begin sharing sim resources as Open Education Resources (OER). We succeeded in partnering a bid to develop an OER platform, SimShare, to share sim resources across institutions, globally.

However SIMPLE also introduced technocratic issues to sim learning. The SIMPLE tools were complex to use, meaning that academic staff still needed technical staff to assist them in developing and running sims. And while we had a SIMPLE Community, no institution apart from Strathclyde was willing to upgrade the software on a regular basis, despite the software being open-source. Ongoing updates and maintenance were therefore never really solved.

Amongst much else, this very brief history of digital use of sims in a single programme over more than a decade illustrates the extent to which educational innovation can be spurred by digital platforms and apps. We were able to proceed much faster than we thought possible in our development of shadow pedagogies, to adopt Shulman's term, such as simulation.[30] But throughout stages one and two of sim application development, and until the creation of SIMPLE we had to resist the technocratic drag of corporate software. And after SIMPLE we faced the usual problems associated with open-source software communities, those of control, funding and the democratic involvement of the discipline. SIMPLE was a complex and successful app but its complexity, while solving many of the stage one and two problems, introduced traits of technocracy, as defined above. SIMPLE opened up possibilities for students of legal learning unavailable in most other pedagogies; but for staff, in some respects it was still a technocratic platform.

8.4 UNLOCKING THE CODES OF LEARNING

Codes are not directly observable, only speech variants.
                    —Lee S Shulman, 'Signature Pedagogies in the Professions'[31]

---

[30]   Lee S Shulman, 'Signature Pedagogies in the Professions' (2005) 134(3) Daedalus 52.
[31]   Bernstein (n 14) 15.

Can digital affect the frame of learning such that it supports more effective and less technocratic learning? Consider the following exchange between a student, Sarah (anonymised name), and a tutor on a discussion forum that supported the Personal Injury transactional sim, and which was accessible by around 130 other students, or half the year group. Sarah's firm acts for the claimant in the dispute, and she is posting on the subject of medical reports.[32]

> I understand that we can get a report from the treating consultant. If the client can't tell you who that is, is it better to go to his GP or get an independent consultant? If it's the latter, is it a case of contacting the hospital to ask for a consultant or should we identify one in particular? Also, does the client pay for this? He wants to know!

There are some quite complex, interwoven procedural, ethical and client-relations issues here that Sarah has raised; and the tutor answered as follows:

> You would normally instruct an independent consultant of your choice. Most firms have lists of consultants they would use in different cases. The consultant's fee is likely to be about £300–400 and you would want to have your client's agreement to pay this (and his money!) before you arrange it.
>
> In a speculative claim (and this is not a speculative claim) the law firm pays for it itself, and (hopefully) recoups the money when/if the claim is settled.

In addition to giving advice on the specific issue, the tutor also gives advice on what would happen in practice. He also advises the firm on what they should be informing the client about. Several firms had not done this, and had received letters from their clients as a result; and it may be that Sarah's posting was written with knowledge of that.

The student posting and tutor reply is significant rhetorically because it does not conform to the usual pattern of tutor-student communication. The classic modality of classroom exchange between teacher and student is that of initiation, response and follow-up (IRF). Sinclair and Coulthard, for instance, commented upon its use by teachers who initiate an exchange by questioning a student or the whole group.[33] One or more respond, and the response is taken up and elaborated in various ways by the teacher, either by follow-up or evaluation (IRE).[34] As Sinclair and Coulthard observed, in such exchanges teachers rarely ask what we might regard as genuine questions that seek knowledge – what they are trying to do is to start dialogue or test student knowledge.[35] The rhetorical exchange has other characteristics. It enables teachers to control the pattern of interaction with the class, and ensures that classroom talk is organised

---

[32] Discussed in part in Paul Maharg, 'PI Project: Discussion Forum Patterns' (*paulmaharg.com*, 5 May 2005) http://paulmaharg.com/2005/05/05/pi_project_disc/ accessed 2 November 2018.

[33] J McH Sinclair and RM Coulthard, *Towards an Analysis of Discourse: The English Used by Teachers and Pupils* (Oxford University Press 1975).

[34] See also Hugh Mehan, *Learning Lessons* (Harvard University Press 1979); Rupert Wegerif, 'The Role of Educational Software as a Support for Teaching and Learning Conversations' (2004) 43(1–2) Computers & Education 179.

[35] Sinclair and Coulthard (n 33).

along strongly teacher-centred lines, as Edwards and Mercer pointed out.[36] This can have the side effect that teachers cannot clearly discern the pattern of student communications, which might appear beside the point or desultory in comparison to the rhetorical strength of the IRF model.[37]

We need to see IRF in the context of purpose and communicational structure: what are students required to do? What do they perceive that they need to do, and to what purpose? The IRF can be a useful tool of exchange, where close analysis requires tutors to lead, but it can also legitimate interactions that stifle student peer-to-peer interactions.[38] It is true that, as Wells has pointed out, students can control the interaction by literally seizing the initiative in the IRF;[39] but this requires considerable effort to overturn a preexisting discourse pattern where hegemony clearly rests with the tutor.

On simulation discussion forums we planned quite a different mode of interaction. Almost none of the items were initiated by tutors: students raise the issues. The agenda belonged to them. The questions were genuine: students were seeking knowledge that they could not easily obtain elsewhere. Jane's question arises out of a problem she cannot solve, even by checking through the archive of previous years' forums. The tutor responds, with genuine information. There was of course the possibility of follow-ups: either the question had been answered clearly, or else there were subsidiary issues that were raised in students' minds and they too would be answered – and sometimes by students, not tutors. Throughout, it is the issues arising from a transaction that are the focus of discussion, not a tutor's initiating question.

IRF has therefore been reversed, and this is true of most TL environments, where there is genuine information exchange – even between students unmediated by tutors. Nor should this be surprising: as Ravenscroft pointed out students make best use of the web's capacity for information and communication when they interacted through collaborative environments that had been designed, educationally and technologically, for that purpose.[40] And as Rasmussen *et al* pointed out, often IRF will have only a 'limited value for the goal of understanding how and what the students learn' and this is especially true of TL environments where students shift through identities – member of a small virtual firm, novice professional lawyer,

[36] Derek Edwards and Neil Mercer, *Common Knowledge (Routledge Revivals): The Development of Understanding in the Classroom* (1st edn, Routledge 1987).

[37] JL Lemke, *Talking Science: Language, Learning, and Values* (Ablex Publishing Corporation 1990).

[38] Susan Land and MJ Hannafin, 'Student-Centered Learning Environments: Foundations, Assumptions and Design' in Susan Land and David Jonassen (eds.), *Theoretical Foundations of Learning Environments* (Lawrence Erlbaum Associates Publishers 2001).

[39] Gordon Wells, 'Reevaluating the IRF Sequence: A Proposal for the Articulation of Theories of Activity and Discourse for the Analysis of Teaching and Learning in the Classroom' (1993) 5(1) Linguistics and Education 1.

[40] Andrew Ravenscroft, 'Designing Argumentation for Conceptual Development' (2000) 34(3–4) Computers & Education 241.

student, transactional leader, transactional team worker, negotiator, researcher, and the like.[41]

The same can be said for careful design of supporting resources for complex sims; consider a couple of short webcasts of approximately ten minutes duration. Imagine that the cases, legislation, ancillary documents, commentary, graphics and self-testing questions with branching feedback are available, clustered around the central figure of a lecturer, speaking to students, televisually. Time-shifting, replaying, re-thinking, reading, discussing, all at the students' pace, is possible. Students can leave questions under their own names or anonymously, to be answered by a lecturer with the answers available to all. Dialogue is possible there, as is coaching. So is interactivity, amongst students, between students and staff, of a sophistication that is simply not possible *ante-*digital: likes, dislikes, tags, shares, dubs, redubs, extractors, mashups, response-videos, YouTube comments, splicing text with video, re-use of student response, structuring, restructuring and Open textbooks that have video embedded in them. These resources can be sited only a few mouse clicks away from the simulation environment. All this functionality exists out there on the web, but we legal educators still use little of it in our programmes. As William Gibson famously remarked, the future is already with us, it's just not very evenly distributed.[42]

In the above examples of resources, lecturers are the assumed creators. But in a sim approach that fosters active learning, student creativity can also be at the centre of this approach – indeed I would argue that it is essential. Why should students not research and populate resources, under the supervision of staff? It is part of the uniqueness of Open technologies and Open education that students become much more active than in conventional pedagogies.[43] This is also true of simulation itself.[44] One future for simulation is to use vast datasets in our sim design and our communications design – see for example Greaves, who explores how we could use data-rich environments to enable our students to learn from each other.[45] Imagine our students being educated to use Big Data in order to research and critique legal practice. We could go further. Imagine students critiquing legal education theory and practice itself, and thereby helping to dismantle, conceptually, the idea of HE as a common good, as our liberal cultures have it, and reconstructing it as some educationalists have done, as a privileged, gamed system that actually perpetuates

[41] Ingvill Rasmussen, Ingeborg Krange and Sten R Ludvigsen, 'The Process of Understanding the Task: How Is Agency Distributed Between Students, Teachers and Representations in Technology-Rich Learning Environments?' (2003) 39(8) International Journal of Educational Research 839, 848.

[42] 'The Science in Science Fiction', NPR *Talk of the Nation* (30 November 1999) www.npr.org /programs/talk-of-the-nation/1999/11/30/12966633/ accessed 22 January 2019.

[43] For examples in the discipline of history, see Jeremy D Jimenez Jeremy and Laura Moorhead, 'Recasting the History Textbook as An E-Book: The Collaborative Creation of Student-Authored Interactive Texts' (2017) 50(4) The History Teacher 565.

[44] And of course there are many other immense potentials for sim learning in virtual reality, augmented reality, gamification and workplace learning that we do not have the space to discuss here.

[45] Kristoffer Greaves, 'Computer-Aided Qualitative Data Analysis of Social Media For Teachers and Students in Legal Education' (2016) 50(1) The Law Teacher 24.

inequality.[46] Doing so might encourage students to participate in Access to Justice, and Access to Legal Education initiatives where addressing this inequality becomes a core component of the curriculum. In this way legal education could begin to enter its own reflexive second modernity.

8.5 CONCLUSION: TECHNOCRACY AND THE DESIGN OF DIGITAL LEGAL EDUCATION

Digital forms of learning such as sims are still innovative, still disruptive, and they are so because, in Gitelman's terms, digital simulation is both a medium and the set of social and cultural practices that grows up around the medium.[47] We saw this in the timeline of sim development in the Glasgow Graduate School of Law, and in the rhetorical logic of the reversed IRF which was successful because it matched the curriculum heuristic of simulation. It also opened up the space of discourse for more student creativity and knowledge forming, which is key to TL. We also observed how the complexity of its platform could for staff become technocratic. Nevertheless, in Shulman's terms, pedagogies such as simulation are shadow pedagogies;[48] and to that extent they challenge the technocratic aspects of current conventional academic legal education – its formalism, teacher-centredness, highly artificial assessment regimes, its pseudo-accountancy, with perhaps the worst manifestations being league tables and its policy-audit culture. It supports a legal education that is democratically oriented to society – sociolegal, comparative, interdisciplinary in scope, student-centred, imaginative in assessment, focused on learning, not learning tables. It challenges, too, the technocratic aspects of professional legal learning (learn this process, or the content of these documents, memorise these ethical structures and conduct rules to pass this snapshot exam) and can enable it to be democratic in purpose and effect – learning as doing and as being, for future-oriented professional practice in the service of society. And of course it is a heuristic that helps us bind the artificial and damaging divide between academic and professional forms of learning and assessment.

On the creation of digital learning environments, the argument also holds. As we saw in the example of simulation timeline above, corporate apps rarely support innovation and disciplinary specialisms in HE. For emerging heuristics such as simulation we need open, collaborative, disciplinary-based apps that support a wide range of heuristics and discourses. The same holds true, too, for the regulation of

[46] Henry A Giroux, *On Critical Pedagogy* (Continuum International Publishing Group 2011); Ian Stronach, *Globalizing Education, Educating the Local: How Method Made Us Mad* (1st edn, Routledge 2010).
[47] Gitelman (n 8).
[48] Shulman (n 30).

legal education. As we point out in the Legal Education and Training Review Report[49] and as I argue with regard to technology generally in legal education,[50] top-down hierarchical regulation stifles innovation and withers collaborative initiative. We need a regulatory regime that encourages the 'shared space' of collaborative inquiry and joint action in legal education.[51]

Indeed I would go further and argue that a constitution for legal education that emphasises the rights and liberties of students and educators is long overdue. With regulatory pressures increasing, and pressures upon regulators increasing too, it may be that now is the time to seek a form of international *ius commune* for legal education, one that will encourage democratic innovation and collaboration in legal education's second modernity.

BIBLIOGRAPHY

Adobe, 'Home Page' https://coldfusion.adobe.com/ accessed 19 April 2019
Allan D, *Virtue, Learning, and the Scottish Enlightenment: Ideas of Scholarship in Early Modern History* (Edinburgh University Press 1993)
Barton K and Maharg P, 'E-Simulations in the Wild: Interdisciplinary Research, Design and Implementation' in David Gibson, Clark Aldrich and Marc Prensky (eds.), *Games and Simulations in Online Learning* (Information Science Publishing, Idea Group Ltd 2007)
Barton K, McKellar P and Maharg P, 'Authentic Fictions: Simulation, Professionalism and Legal Learning' (2007) 14(1) Clinical Law Review 143
Barton K and Westwood F, 'From Student to Trainee Practitioner – A Study of Team Working as a Learning Experience' (2006) 3 Web Journal of Current Legal Issues 1 www.bailii.org /uk/other/journals/webjcli/admin/wjclidex.html accessed 22 January 2019
'Developing Professional Character – Trust, Values and Learning' in Paul Maharg and Caroline Maughan (eds.), *Affect and Legal Education: Emotion in Learning and Teaching the Law* (Ashgate Publishing 2011)
Beck U, *The Cosmopolitan Vision* (Polity Press 2006)
Beck U, Giddens A and Lash S, *Reflexive Modernization: Politics, Tradition and Aesthetics in the Modern Social Order* (Stanford University Press 1994)
Bernstein B, *Theoretical Studies Towards a Sociology of Language* (1st edn, Routledge 1971)
Boys J, 'Managed Learning Environments, Joined Up Systems and the Problems of Organisational Change' (Jisc 2002)
Cairns JW, 'Rhetoric, Language, and Roman Law: Legal Education and Improvement in Eighteenth-Century Scotland' (1991) 9(1) Law and History Review 31
'The Influence of Smith's Jurisprudence on Legal Education in Scotland' in Peter Jones and Andrew S Skinner (eds.), *Adam Smith Reviewed* (Edinburgh University Press 1992)

---

[49] Julian Webb and others, 'Setting Standards: The Future of Legal Services Education and Training Regulation in England and Wales (Legal Education and Training Review)' (SRA, BSB and CILEX 2013) www.letr.org.uk/wp-content/uploads/LETR-Report.pdf accessed 17 August 2018.
[50] Paul Maharg, 'Shared Space: Regulation, Technology and Legal Education in a Global Context' (2015) 6(1) European Journal of Law and Technology 1 http://ejlt.org/article/view/425/541 accessed 17 May 2019; Maharg, 'Disintermediation' (n 10); Paul Maharg, 'The Gordian Knot: Regulatory Relationship and Legal Education' (2017) 4(2) Asian Journal of Legal Education 79.
[51] Jane Ching and others, 'Legal Education and Training Review: A Five-Year Retro/Prospective' (2018) 52(4) The Law Teacher 384.

Cassidy J, 'Client View' (2009) 4(1) Journal of the Australasian Tax Teachers Association 55

Ching J and others, 'Legal Education and Training Review: A Five-Year Retro/Prospective' (2018) 52(4) The Law Teacher 384

Chow W and Ng M, 'Disintermediator or Another Intermediary? E-Simulation Platform for Professional Legal Education at University of Hong Kong' (2016) 7(1) European Journal of Law and Technology 638

Counsell K, 'Virtual Learning for the Real World: Using Simulation with Non-Law Students' in Caroline Strevens, Richard Grimes and Edward Phillips (eds.), *Legal Education: Simulation in Theory and Practice* (Ashgate Publishing 2014)

Edwards D and Mercer N, *Common Knowledge (Routledge Revivals): The Development of Understanding in the Classroom* (1st edn, Routledge 1987)

Ferguson A, 'Lectures', *Papers of Professor Adam Ferguson (1723–1816)* (Edinburgh University Library Special Collections 1733)

Ferguson A, 'Creating Practice Ready, Well and Professional Law Graduates' (2015) 7(2) Journal of Learning Design 22

Giroux HA, *On Critical Pedagogy* (Continuum International Publishing Group 2011)

Gitelman L, *Always Already New: Media, History and the Data of Culture* (Massachusetts Institute of Technology Press 2006)

Greaves K, 'Computer-Aided Qualitative Data Analysis of Social Media for Teachers and Students in Legal Education' (2016) 50(1) The Law Teacher 24

Home (Lord Kames) H, *Introduction to the Art of Thinking* (2nd edn, W Creech and T Caddell 1764)

Loose Hints Upon Education: Chiefly Concerning the Culture of the Heart (T Henshall 1782)

Hughes M and others, 'SIMulated Professional Learning Environment (SIMPLE): Programme Final Report' (Jisc & Higher Education Authority 2008)

Jenkins H, *Convergence Culture: Where Old and New Media Collide* (New York University Press 2006)

Jimenez, J D and Moorhead L, 'Recasting the History Textbook as An E-Book: The Collaborative Creation of Student-Authored Interactive Texts' (2017) 50(4) The History Teacher 565

Land S and Hannafin MJ, 'Student-Centered Learning Environments: Foundations, Assumptions and Design' in Susan Land and David Jonassen (eds.), *Theoretical Foundations of Learning Environments* (Lawrence Erlbaum Associates Publishers 2001)

Lee E and Ferguson A, 'The Development of the Virtual Educational Space: How Transactional Online Teaching Can Prepare Today's Law Graduates for Today's Virtual Age' (2015) 6(1) European Journal of Law and Technology 1

Lemke JL, *Talking Science: Language, Learning, and Values* (Ablex Publishing Corporation 1990)

Maharg P, 'PI Project: Discussion Forum Patterns' (*paulmaharg.com*, 5 May 2005) http://paulmaharg.com/2005/05/05/pi_project_disc/ accessed 2 November 2018

Transforming Legal Education: Learning and Teaching the Law in the Early Twenty-First Century (1st edn, Ashgate Publishing 2007)

'Sea-Change' (2011) 18(1–2) International Journal of the Legal Profession 139

'Shared Space: Regulation, Technology and Legal Education in a Global Context' (2015) 6 (1) European Journal of Law and Technology 1 http://ejlt.org/article/view/425/541 accessed 17 May 2019.

'Disintermediation' (2016) 50(1) The Law Teacher 114

'Digital and Simulation in the Teaching of Law : Emerging from the Shadows' (*law-tech-a2 j .org*, 2 November 2016) https://law-tech-a2 j.org/external-contributor/digital-and-simulation-in-the-teaching-of-law-emerging-from-the-shadows/ accessed 2 November 2018

'The Gordian Knot: Regulatory Relationship and Legal Education' (2017) 4(2) Asian Journal of Legal Education 79

Maharg P and Nicol E, 'Simulation and Technology in Legal Education: A Systematic Review and Future Research Programme' in Caroline Strevens, Richard H Grimes and Edward Phillips (eds.), *Legal Education: Simulation in Theory and Practice* (Ashgate Publishing 2014)

Mehan H, *Learning Lessons* (Harvard University Press 1979)

Priddle J and others, 'Simshare: Project Final Report' (UK Centre for Legal Education 2010) www.researchgate.net/publication/228367047_project_final_report accessed 19 April 2019

Rasmussen I, Krange I and Ludvigsen SR, 'The Process of Understanding the Task: How Is Agency Distributed Between Students, Teachers and Representations in Technology-Rich Learning Environments?' (2003) 39(8) International Journal of Educational Research 839

Ravenscroft A, 'Designing Argumentation for Conceptual Development' (2000) 34(3–4) Computers & Education 241

Shulman LS, 'Signature Pedagogies in the Professions' (2005) 134(3) Daedalus 52

SIMPLE Community, 'SIMPLE Community' (2019) http://simplecommunity.org/ accessed 19 April 2019

Sinclair JM and Coulthard RM, *Towards an Analysis of Discourse: The English Used by Teachers and Pupils* (Oxford University Press 1975)

Smith A, *Lectures On Rhetoric and Belles Lettres* (JC Bryce ed., Liberty Fund Inc 1762)

Stronach I, *Globalizing Education, Educating the Local: How Method Made Us Mad* (1st edn, Routledge 2010)

Suchman L, *Human-Machine Reconfigurations: Plans and Situated Actions* (1st edn, Cambridge University Press 2006)

Turkle S, *Life on the Screen: Identity in the Age of the Internet* (1st edn, Simon & Schuster 1997)

Webb J and others, 'Setting Standards: The Future of Legal Services Education and Training Regulation in England and Wales (Legal Education and Training Review)' (SRA, BSB and CILEX 2013) www.letr.org.uk/wp-content/uploads/letr-report.pdf accessed 17 August 2018

Wegerif R, 'The Role of Educational Software as a Support for Teaching and Learning Conversations' (2004) 43(1–2) Computers & Education 179

Wells G, 'Reevaluating the IRF Sequence: A Proposal for the Articulation of Theories of Activity and Discourse for the Analysis of Teaching and Learning in the Classroom' (1993) 5(1) Linguistics and Education 1

'The Science in Science Fiction', *NPR Talk of the Nation* (30 November 1999) www.npr.org /programs/talk-of-the-nation/1999/11/30/12966633/ accessed 22 January 2019

9

Ludic Legal Education from Cicero to Phoenix Wright

Andrew Moshirnia

Game-based legal learning has emerged as a topic of intense interest over the last decade as a means of 'modernising' legal education, with game-based learning elicit-ing a wide range of responses from the legal academy. Somewhat unsurprisingly, resistance in the name of tradition has persisted. Yet, the view of game playing as a distinctly modern pedagogical development, and opposition on the basis of tradition is sheer folly. Ludic education has been the dominant teaching method for millennia, with legal game playing traced at least to the time of Cicero. Revealing the rich history of game playing in law, this chapter details ludic legal education from the declamation of Ancient Rome to Nintendo's Phoenix Wright: Ace Attorney. It observes the way in which games can operate as a compelling delivery device for instruction, allow for experimentation, and encourage students to voice their opinions in a field where the sheer breadth of precedent and the relative impenetrability of legal texts may prove intimidating. In demonstrating the potential of game playing to overcome barriers to learning, this chapter considers the modern design principles that have enabled games to emerge as robust and enjoyable content delivery devices in legal education.

9.1 INTRODUCTION

This chapter invites educators and game designers to adopt legal games, both through more creative exploration of legal scenarios in class and the creation of versatile legal simulators outside of class. This approach suggests a pedagogical shift in classroom instruction with a move beyond traditional fact pattern quizzes towards dynamic role-play. Such role-play was a mainstay of legal education in the classical world, and a deconstruction of the practice provides important engagement philo-sophies for modern educators. These same philosophies are reflected in modern game-design and provide additional opportunity for self-directed enrichment.

This chapter proceeds in four parts, comprising a review of: (i) the current tradition-focused approach in legal academia, which frequently leaves students unfulfilled and impedes educational innovation; (ii) the pedagogical support for the use of games-based learning; (iii) declamation, a fantastical game-based form of legal instruction used in the classical world that allowed for social exploration; and (iv) the current state of commercial video games related to the law and the pedagogic principles that may be extrapolated and synthesised from both disciplines.

9.2 THE FAILURE OF THE LEGAL ACADEMY TO ENCOURAGE CREATIVE OR EMPATHETIC LEGAL EXPLORATION

9.2.1 *The Current State of the Academy*

Legal education has been marked by a 'remarkably stable' approach to both curricula and pedagogy.[1] Legal academics frequently note that their field does not prepare newly minted lawyers for meaningful work and is 'tradition-bound and resistant to modernization'.[2] In the face of rampant student dissatisfaction, critics have opined that there 'is so much wrong with legal education today that it is hard to know where to begin'.[3] Though this point need not be laboured, it is worthwhile to give a brief overview of the current state of pedagogy and why it does not encourage a moral or philosophical engagement with the law.

While earlier legal instruction relied primarily on the apprenticeship model, the modern casebook method has been the dominant instructional frame since its inception at Harvard at the end of the nineteenth century.[4] The method spread from the United States to most of the common law world, with widespread adoption in Australia,[5] Canada, and other common law countries. The notion that legal science can be perfected by applying the holdings of appellate decisions to case-specific fact patterns, permeates the modern legal academy. While the legal realist school pushed for greater clinical opportunities and succeeded in reintroducing skills training on the margins, legal pedagogy remains largely impervious to change.[6]

---

[1] James J Brudney, 'Legislation and Regulation in the Core Curriculum' (2015) 65(1) Journal of Legal Education 3.

[2] Lauren Carasik, 'Renaissance or Retrenchment: Legal Education at a Crossroads' (2011) 44(3) Indiana Law Review 735, 736; Margaret Martin Barry, 'Practice Ready: Are We There Yet?' (2012) 32(2) Boston College Journal of Law & Social Justice 247; Harry T Edwards, 'The Growing Disjunction between Legal Education and the Legal Profession' (1992) 91(1) Michigan Law Review 34.

[3] Morrison Torrey, 'You Call That Education?' (2004) 19(1) Wisconsin Women's Law Journal 93.

[4] Robert Stevens, *Law School: Legal Education in America from the 1850s to the 1980s* (University of North Carolina Press 1987) 36. Numerous students have proposed altering this dominant method. See, e.g., Gary D Finley, 'Langdell and the Leviathan: Improving the First-Year Law School Curriculum by Incorporating Moby-Dick' (2011) 97(1) Cornell Law Review 159.

[5] Erwin N Griswold, 'Observations on Legal Education in Australia' (1951) 2(2) University of Western Australia Annual Law Review 197.

[6] Sameer M Ashar, 'Deep Critique and Democratic Lawyering in Clinical Practice' (2016) 104(1) California Law Review 201, 231; Robert R Kuehn, 'Pricing Clinical Legal Education' (2014) 92(1) Denver University Law Review 1, 1.

Legal instruction typically provides limited opportunity for student creativity or meaningful exploration and feedback on legal principles. Students, commentators,[7] and jurists have been complaining for nearly fifty years that legal education too often regresses to a constrictive vocational approach, in which 'knowing the answer is more important than knowing how to arrive at the answer'.[8] This is exemplified by the fact-pattern exam, where students have a single opportunity to apply case law to Byzantine scenarios, with students arriving at answers without synthesising new knowledge or exploring innate conflicts in legal principles. Instead, a premium is placed on recognising analogous facts and memorising legal rules. These exams focus on identifying multiple legal issues in a compressed time limit, a skill set that is ill matched to real world practice with novel questions necessitating creative solutions. Law firms have noted that such an approach fails to impart necessary skills for lawyering.[9]

This method also fails to engage students' philosophical understanding of the law and the morality of current legal structures. As such, it does not afford individual students the opportunity to explore the contours of legal and social bias. The focus rests on the dominant legal rule, not the rule's development, justification, or equitable application. This failure is hugely impactful, as common law countries depend on lawyers for the interpretation and implementation of equal justice under the law.[10]

The difficulty law schools persistently face in recruiting and retaining minority students[11] is also linked in part to this pedagogic deficiency.[12] Members of disadvantaged or underrepresented communities are unlikely to see their viewpoints reflected in case literature or sterile fact-patterns.[13] They may also feel underappreciated or 'otherised' by majority students, who are not asked to think outside of the dominant legal frame. Studies in both the United States and Australia have confirmed that the law school experience is likely to alienate atypical students, including students from 'underrepresented racial groups, women, students with

7   Anthony Daimsis, 'Creative Thinkers Need Not Apply' (*The Law Times*, 26 February 2018) www
     .lawtimesnews.com/author/anthony-daimsis/creative-thinkers-need-not-apply-15393/ accessed 10 March
     2019.
8   Ibid; Francis A Allen, 'The Causes of Popular Dissatisfaction with Legal Education' (1976) 62(4)
     American Bar Association Journal 447, 447–8.
9   David Segal, 'What They Don't Teach Law Students: Lawyering' New York Times (New York,
     19 November 2011) www.nytimes.com/2011/11/20/business/after-law-school-associates-learn-to-be-
     lawyers.html accessed 10 July 2018.
10   See generally Jerold S Auerbach, *Unequal Justice: Lawyers and Social Change in Modern America*
     (Oxford University Press 1976).
11   Gurney Pearsall, 'The Human Side of Law School: The Case for Socializing Minority Recruitment
     and Retention Programs' (2015) 64(4) Journal of Legal Education 688, 689–692.
12   See Jr Derrick A Bell, 'Law School Exams and Minority-Group Students' (1981) 7(2) National Black
     Law Journal 304.
13   These concerns have been present for decades. See, e.g., Henry McGee, 'Minority Students in Law
     School: Black Lawyers and the Struggle for Racial Justice in the American Social Order' (1971) 20
     Buffalo Law Review 423, 427–31.

disabilities, students who are economically or educationally disadvantaged, students whose first language is not English . . . older students, students who are parents, first-generation college graduates, and undocumented aliens'.[14]

In response to these difficulties, numerous reports have challenged legal pedagogy to incorporate more real world lawyering and utilise sociological principles when crafting curricula to include historically marginalised groups. In America, the MacCrate Report of 1992,[15] the Carnegie Report of 2007,[16] and the Best Practices Report of 2007[17] all called for a major curricular overhaul so as to increase skills training and student satisfaction. Similar calls for reform have occurred in Australia.[18] This chapter joins these previous requests, specifically asking for a greater inclusion of dynamic role-play as a means to increase student understanding of legal principles and to cultivate empathetic representation.

9.2.2 *Why Games-Based Learning Can Improve Instruction*

Games-based instruction is a hard sell to the academy. Despite their educational promise, games have had little penetration in traditional legal instruction. The (re) introduction of games to legal instruction faces two distinct challenges: the first is an attitudinal barrier to the use of games in a tradition-bound pedagogy; and the second is disconnect between legal games and modern design principles. To the limited extent that games have been brought into the legal academy, they have consisted of interactive quizzes. For example, the Law Dojo website is a well-designed but fairly restrictive site aimed primarily at law school students.[19] Much like the scenarios deployed in legal exams, these 'games' amount to pattern recognition and rule application simulators. The opportunity for exploration and creativity in arriving at novel solutions to problems is simply absent from these platforms. Moreover,

---

14   Susan Armstrong and Michelle Sanson, 'From Confusion to Confidence: Transitioning to Law School' (2012) 12(1) Queensland University of Technology Law and Justice Journal 21.

15   *Statement of Fundamental Lawyering Skills and Professional Values* in Task Force on Law Schools and the Profession American Bar Association, 'Legal Education and Professional Development-An Educational Continuum. (MacCrate Report)' (American Bar Foundation 1992).

16   The report, *Educating Lawyers: Preparation for the Profession of Law*, ably summarised the disconnect between legal education and student notions of justice, 'In their all-consuming first year, students are told to set aside their desire for justice. They are warned not to let their moral concerns or compassion for the people in the cases they discuss cloud their legal analyses.' William M Sullivan and others, *Educating Lawyers: Preparation for the Profession of Law* (1st edn, Jossey-Bass 2007).

17   For a discussion of the importance of simulations, games and role-plays in effective legal education, see Roy Stuckey, 'Best Practices for Legal Education: A Vision and A Road Map' (Clinical Legal Education Association 2007) 132–8 https://clea.wildapricot.org/Resources/Documents/best_practices-full.pdf accessed 28 September 2018.

18   Nickolas J James, 'A Brief History of Critique in Australian Legal Education' (2000) 24(3) Melbourne University Law Review 965, 973–4.

19   Margaret Hagan, 'Law Games to Learn Smarter Not Harder – Law Dojo' (*Law School Dojo*, 2017) www.lawschooldojo.com accessed 10 March 2019. See also Ulster University Legal Innovation Centre, 'Gamification: Games to Make Learning Law Engaging and Enjoyable' (2017) www.legalinnovation.ai/gamification accessed 4 March 2019.

these games are not taking advantage of their unique opportunity to address socio-logical theory or increase representation of marginalised individuals. This failure is regrettable, as games are an elegant way to increase the knowledge of non-traditional students and non-students alike.

An examination of educational theory provides a motivation for the adoption of a games-based curriculum: games increase subject interest, facilitate philosophical engagement through counterfactual exploration, and encourage knowledge synthesis. At the same time, a deconstruction of classical and modern legal games can provide a template for educators. Classical declamatory play provides a model for fantastical social exploration coupled with skills training, while modern game franchises such as Ace Attorney inform schema to make legal games enjoyable and engaging.

Games have been recognised as a means for fostering creativity, experimentation, and exploration.[20] By freeing participants of common constraints, games invite innovative approaches to complex questions. Moreover, players are likely to re-evaluate outcomes in light of continuous reengagement. Simply put, games can and should be fun, thereby recruiting interest for repeat play. While game theorists have presented various schema for explaining the key components of ludic motivation, these frameworks generally allow for a rule-mediated exploration of one's own abilities in the face of multi-faceted challenges. Educational and motivation theories such as the 'Zone of Proximal Development (ZPD)',[21] 'Self-Determination Theory (SDT)',[22] and 'Adaptive Control of Thought (ACT)'[23] offer insight into the educational potential of games. By encouraging continuous repetition and creative problem-solving, games provide players with declarative knowledge at the same time as providing incentives to synthesise procedural knowledge.

9.2.3 *Games as Interest Recruiter*

Games have an incredible ability to recruit player interest, and as Csikszentmihalyi notes, game players often reach flow. Flow is 'the state in which people are so involved in an activity that nothing else seems to matter, the experience itself is enjoyable that people will do it even at great cost, for the sheer sake of doing it'.[24]

---

[20] It is important here to distinguish between game-based learning and gamification of education. The latter involves the adoption of game design elements in activities that are themselves not games. Thus, gamification may involve assigning points, levels, rankings, and other badge systems common to game leader-boards. This chapter deals with the content and creation of legal games.

[21] Seth Chaiklin, 'The Zone of Proximal Development in Vygotsky's Analysis of Learning and Instruction' in Alex Kozulin and others (eds.), *Vygotsky's Educational Theory in Cultural Context* (Cambridge University Press 2003).

[22] Richard M Ryan and Edward L Deci, 'Self-Determination Theory and the Facilitation of Intrinsic Motivation, Social Development and Well-Being' (2000) 55(1) The American Psychologist 68, 68–78.

[23] John Robert Anderson and Gordon H Bower, *Human Associative Memory* (Psychology Press 1973); John Robert Anderson, *Language, Memory, and Thought* (Lawrence Erlbaum Associates 1976).

[24] Mihaly Csikszentmihalyi, *Flow: The Psychology of Optimal Experience* (Harper & Row 1990) 4.

Flow involves clear goals and immediate feedback, equilibrium between the level of challenge and personal skill, merging of action and awareness, focused concentration, sense of potential control, loss of self-consciousness, time distortion, and autotelic (self-rewarding) experience. Csikszentmihalyi observes that flow occurs in a balance between an individual's skill set and the difficulties of tasks. As the skill set increases, the difficulty of the action also increases, rewarding the player while presenting new challenges. In this way, the game scaffolds to new tasks by employing an ever-increasing zone of proximal development.

The attachment that individuals form with games has been well documented by Lepper and Malone.[25] They described the desire to play games, or ludic motivation, in terms of four main characteristics:

- Challenge – A game is challenging for the participant and that challenge mirrors the development of a player's skill. Games have a winner and a loser. Games without competition are referred to as 'simulations' not games. In some literature, challenge is referred to as strategy, i.e., a game's outcome is not purely random.
- Chance – A game must have some degree of probability, randomness, or chance in order that the player is never bored with automaticity. This lends uniqueness to each game.
- Fantasy – A game asks players to engage in an activity which they normally do not do. Later researchers have argued that this requirement be changed to include 'simulation-games' which have rules, a winner, and satisfy other requirements of a game, but ask the player to do an activity that he or she might normally engage in (e.g. play football).
- Immersion – A game, either through game elements such as story or graphics, or through external elements such as competition, causes game players to focus on the game more than on reality.

Games also allow for the consideration of the fanciful or unreal as a means of better understanding the impact of existing systems and rules. Bunzl[26] and Cowan and Forray[27] have argued that the imagination or consideration of counterfactual scenarios is a powerful tool for the understanding of the abstract principles guiding past

[25] MR Lepper and TW Malone, 'Intrinsic Motivation and Instructional Effectiveness in Computer-Based Education' in RE Snow and MJ Farr (eds.), *Aptitude, Learning, and Instruction: Vol. 3. Cognitive and Affective Process Analysis* (Lawrence Erlbaum Associates 1987); MR Lepper, 'Making Learning Fun: A Taxonomy of Intrinsic Motivations for Learning' in R Snow and MJ Farr (eds.), *Aptitude, Learning, and Instruction: Vol. 3. Cognitive and Affective Process Analysis* (Lawrence Erlbaum Associates 1987).

[26] Martin Bunzl, 'Counterfactual History: A User's Guide' (2004) 109(3) The American Historical Review 845.

[27] Robin Cowan and Dominique Foray, 'Evolutionary Economics and the Counterfactual Threat: On the Nature and Role of Counterfactual History as an Empirical Tool in Economics' (2002) 12(5) Journal of Evolutionary Economics 539.

events. Games allow users to explore the results of those counterfactual realities and compare or retell the newly created narrative.

9.2.4 Games as Skills Teacher and Knowledge Synthesiser

Various educational theories further support games as a means for user-generated skills learning and knowledge synthesis. Vygotsky's ZPD theory marries perfectly with game design. In the social constructivist context, ZPD refers to the interstitial between what a learner can do without help and what the learner cannot do – a zone of development where a learner can achieve the task with guidance. This process is typically marked with struggle and effort, but that work is rewarded by an increase in learner skill with appropriate scaffolding. Games function in identical fashion, presenting increasing challenge in line with player mastery and allowing for repeated failure before success.

SDT also explains how users are motivated to continue playing games. SDT posits that users need feelings of autonomy, competence, and relatedness for the construction and maintenance of motivation.[28] That is, intrinsically motivated individuals feel that they have the ability to make meaningful choices while receiving robust and relevant feedback. Well-designed games give players the creative freedom to change their outcomes, and standard game tropes such as points, high scores, and laudatory exclamations, provide near instantaneous feedback. It is worth noting that legal education, which often consists of a single exam graded anonymously months after the student submits the work commonly fails to give students these same opportunities for curiosity and feedback.

Games frequently encourage players to synthesise knowledge as they must not only memorise game facts, but they must also know when to use and how to combine those facts. Anderson's[29] theory of Adaptive Control of Thought – Rational (ACT-R) provides a cognitive architecture, that is, a theory of how human thought or cognition works. Essentially, ACT-R conceives of rational human thought as algorithmic, with rules, operations, and knowledge used to arrive at an output. ACT-R separates knowledge into declarative knowledge and procedural knowledge.

According to Anderson, declarative knowledge is made up of facts. As I type this sentence, I realise that words are made up of letters, that multiplying two by two yields four, and that the Sun is larger than the Moon. Declarative knowledge is static when compared to procedural knowledge, though declarative knowledge can obviously grow. Procedural knowledge is the knowledge that is used to create or conduct a process. It is the knowledge of how to apply declarative knowledge in order to complete a task. Procedural knowledge is dynamic in that we often reassess

---

[28]   Richard M Ryan, C Scott Rigby and Andrew Przybylski, 'The Motivational Pull of Video Games: A Self-Determination Theory Approach' (2006) 30(4) Motivation and Emotion 344.

[29]   Anderson and Bower (n 23); Anderson (n 23).

the manner in which we do things, or we may know of more than one way to do the same task.

Information processing theory and ACT-R explain why games are such a powerful learning medium. While rote instruction may impart declarative knowledge, games and simulations are excellent vehicles for procedural knowledge. Expert game play is greater than the sum of the facts needed to play the game. Players must also use procedural knowledge to combine those facts into a winning strategy.

9.3 DECLAMATION: A 'TRADITIONAL' MEANS FOR LUDIC INSTRUCTION AND SOCIAL EXPLORATION

While the educational potential of games is apparent, tradition-bound educators are unlikely to embrace a novel approach. Moreover, more progressive educators may balk at adoption of legal games without a clear template for translating gaming principles to legal instruction. Coincidentally, a deconstruction of classical legal instruction assuages both groups by providing a tradition-steeped template for dynamic role-play.

Legal education is often accused of fetishising Latin.[30] Latin terms abound in modern instruction[31] and legal opinions themselves.[32] As late as the nineteenth century legal academic institutions still instructed in Latin, though the practice weakened at the turn of the century.[33] However, this classical obsession is quite useful for the gaming academic since Roman declamatory play was a key component of legal instruction.[34] Thus, an appeal to tradition actually militates in favour of a games-based legal approach. This section deconstructs the declamatory tradition and advocates that educators employ modern games to embrace the social experimentation/exploration that declamatory instruction provides.

---

[30] This may be seen in sporadic efforts to revive classical language instruction as a means to improve legal education. See, e.g., Lynden Evans, 'The Study of Greek and Latin as a Preparation for the Study of Law' (1907) 15(6) The School Review 417.

[31] See, e.g., University of Kent, 'Glossary of Legal Latin' (2019) www.kent.ac.uk/library/subjects/lawlinks/skills-hub/docs/GlossaryofLegalLatin.pdf accessed 4 March 2019.

[32] Peter R Macleod, 'Latin in Legal Writing: An Inquiry into the Use of Latin in the Modern Legal World' (1997) 39(1) Boston College Law Review 235. This is of even greater importance in legal systems based on or incorporating elements of Roman law. See, e.g., Isabel Balteiro and Miguel Angel Campos-Pardillos, 'A Comparative Study of Latinisms in Court Opinions in the United States and Spain' (2010) 17(1) International Journal of Speech Language and the Law 95; Krzysztof Szczygielski, 'Latin Legal Maxims in the Judgments of the Constitutional Tribunal in Poland' (2017) 49(1) Studies in Logic, Grammar and Rhetoric 213.

[33] See e.g., John W Cairns, 'Rhetoric, Language, and Roman Law: Legal Education and Improvement in Eighteenth-Century Scotland' (1991) 9(1) Law and History Review 31.

[34] I do not share Seneca's view that declamation is valuable solely as an instructive tool (see Contr. IX, *Nam si foro non praeparat, aut scaenicae ostentationi aut furiosae vociferationi simillimum est*).

9.3.1 *Declamation: Role-Play as Social Exploration*

Declamation was the primary means through which Roman youths mastered public speaking.[35] Functioning as logic games, declamations allowed students to explore social interactions through dramatic play. A declamation is a short scenario that involves matters of civic virtue or law, often with fanciful, mythical, or historical elements and heightened stakes.[36] Events have conspired to cause a breakdown of the social order; it is up to the declaimer to assume the role of one of the personae and fix the problem. The scenarios are fantastic, roles and categories are 'suspended, created, and reversed ... the process and learning context must be [radical] so that the student relearns and reinterprets his own categories and roles'.[37] This unreality was designed to liberate the declaimer from societal norms and allow him to re-examine social interactions (father to son, man to woman, master to slave) in an effort to arrive at a creative solution.

Declamations invite, and indeed demand, students to investigate social theory through an examination of values and strengths. Just as classical myths force readers to engage in value debate, e.g. familial loyalty versus public duty in Antigone and Agamemnon, these declamatory exercises in theory building are inherently creative. Novelty can force the student into the role of a thinker who 'forms theories about everything, delighting especially in consideration of that which is not'.[38] This process should be familiar to the modern reader. The Western tradition of educating through role-playing is clearly established in the rhetoric training of the classical world, yet this method is now rare in the legal academy.

Moreover, declamations are markedly different from traditional classroom case studies or fact-pattern examinations. Unlike the case method employed in modern legal education, declamations are unresolved and offer no obvious solutions. Take the example of 'Declamation 272 *Orbata Proditrix* (The Bereaved Mother turned Traitor)':[39]

> The punishment for divulging state plans is death. A woman went out by night to recover the body of her son. She was caught by the enemy and revealed, under torture, that relieving troops were on the way. These were caught and crushed. She escaped and warned her city that a mine was being dug. The enemy was defeated. She is accused of divulging state secrets.[40]

---

[35] This should not be read to mean that all classical rhetorical criticism approves of declamation. See Erik Gunderson, *Staging Masculinity: The Rhetoric of Performance in the Roman World* (Cambridge University Press 2003) 17.

[36] I omit deeper discussions of declamatory types (e.g., *controversiae* and *suasoriae*).

[37] Martin W Bloomer, *The School of Rome: Latin Studies and the Origins of Liberal Education* (University of California Press 2011).

[38] Jean Piaget, *The Psychology of Intelligence* (Harcourt, Brace 1947) 148.

[39] Bloomer (n 37) 183.

[40] *Qui consilia publica enuntiaverit, capite puniatur. Ad colligendum filii corpus nocte processit mater. Comprehensa ab hostibus et torta indicavit auxilia venire; quib oppresis de vinculis effugit et nuntiavit cuniculum agi. Oppressis hostibus rea est quod consilia publica enuntiaverit. CD.*

This scenario involves many of the strengths identified by modern positive psychologists. The woman's bravery and fidelity to her son are not in doubt. However, these classical values must be weighed against the woman's responsibility to protect her city's troops. The opportunities for modern students are staggering: discussions of the nature of volition and torture, gender roles, laws in times of war, and many other topics spring to mind.[41]

The successful exercise revolves around empathy, as students assume the various personae needed to resolve the scenario. While Roman students were (in effect) acting out the roles of the individuals with whom they would interact (and eventually socially dominate), modern students can engage in creative play to achieve social understanding of historically marginalised groups. This empathetic embodiment is simply absent from most legal instruction, having been stifled by the nature and high-stakes of pattern-matching exercises.

9.3.2 *Declamations As Means for Teaching Textual and Purposive Statutory Interpretation*

While empathetic exploration is valuable, educators also have concrete curricular goals. A prime goal in legal instruction is to train students on statutory interpretation, with textualist, and purposivist, approaches. While these can be difficult to convey, declamation is rife with examples that force definitional debates of loaded terms. Consider the following example, which touches on the common declamation themes of tyrannicide and paternal privilege:

> A man has two sons, one which makes himself tyrant. The father kills his tyrant-son, but refused to claim the city's standing reward for tyrannicide. The man's surviving son now commences legal action, seeking to have his father declared insane.

Students must explain why civic responsibility trumps familial responsibility in this case, and why the father may be justified in not claiming a reward, which would clearly benefit his surviving son.[42] A response in the legal classroom would almost certainly revolve around the meaning of the word 'insane' and also touch on elements of justifiable homicide.[43] Though this scenario was unlikely to take place

---

[41] Victoria Emma Pagán, 'Teaching Torture in Seneca Controversiae 2.5' (2007) 103(2) The Classical Journal 165; Neil W Bernstein, '"Torture Her Until She Lies": Torture, Testimony, and Social Status in Roman Rhetorical Education' (2012) 59(2) Greece and Rome 165.

[42] Lucian provides a similar textualist versus purposivist exercise: 'A man forces his way into the stronghold of a tyrant, with the intention of killing him. Not finding the tyrant himself, he kills his son, and leaves the sword sticking in his body. The tyrant, coming, and finding his son dead, slays himself with the same sword. The assailant now claims that the killing of the son entitles him to the reward of tyrannicide.'

[43] Tacitus ridicules the overuse of tyrannicide in exercises. See Christopher S Van den Berg, *The World of Tacitus' Dialogus de Oratoribus: Aesthetics and Empire in Ancient Rome* (Cambridge University Press 2014).

in the real world, it reinforced the central tenet of Roman society: personal strengths must be translated into civic virtues.

This subordination of personal desires to civic concerns is best expressed in 'Declamation Minor 246 *Soporatus Fortis Privignus* (The Drugged Brave Stepson)',[44] which would no doubt encourage a modern student to debate the meaning of the term 'poisoning': 'A military hero on the eve of battle was given a sleeping potion by his stepmother. He was accused of desertion. Acquitted of that charge he accuses his stepmother on a charge of poisoning.'[45]

While domestic strife is a popular declamation topic, other topics are more mundane (yet evocative of real world concerns). For example, consider a playwright who introduces characters that are unnamed yet individually recognisable as members of the community due to their masks. Is the playwright guilty of violating a law that forbids satirising subjects by name? The notion of obeying the letter, but not the spirit of the law is one that will cause much debate among modern students.

9.3.3 *Declamations As Logic Tests: Application of False Laws*

Legal students are also inhibited in engaging with the philosophical underpinning of jurisprudence by the very fact that a 'correct answer' exists in terms of precedent. The declamatory player is not so constrained. It is telling that the Romans employed societal restrictions in declamations that were not actually part of Roman society.[46] This makes it clear that declamations are not merely a review of social mores, a sort of perverted guide to etiquette, but are artificial scenarios developed to sharpen a student's grasp of logic.[47] A famous example mentioned by Quintilian exemplifies this point:[48]

A certain father has two legitimate sons: he has one of them adopted and disowns the other. Having then no sons he fathers an illegitimate child and acknowledges paternity. He then makes the disowned son his heir and dies. The laws operating are:

1. Legally made wills should be valid;
2. When parents die intestate children should be their heirs;
3. No disowned son should receive any of his father's property;

Bloomer (n 37) 184.
Quint. DM 246. *Qui fortiter fecerat, bello imminente, soporem ab noverca subiectum bibit. Causam dixit tamquam desertor. Absolutus accusat novercam veneficii.*
Elaine Fantham, *Roman Readings: Roman Response to Greek Literature from Plautus to Statius and Quintilian* (Walter de Gruyter GmbH & Co KG 2011).
Susan Stewart, *Nonsense: Aspects of Intertextuality in Folklaw and Literature* (John Hopkins University Press 1979).
Fantham (n 46) 323–4.

4. An illegitimate child is deemed legitimate if born before legitimi, but if born after then he only has the status of citizen;
5. It should be lawful to give a son in adoption; and
6. An adopted son may return to the family if his father dies without children.[49]

Here, the author has included several rules, which are not valid in Roman law. While rules one, two, and five are common practice, three and four are not.[50] The scenario, impossible under the existing legal regime, has been created so that the student must consider as many issues and relationships as possible. The use of fanciful rules was common. 'He who strikes his father, he will lose his hands.'[51] This rule did not exist in Roman society outside of declamation.

For the scenario in question, each 'son' has different interests, which may conflict with or complement the interests of other actors. And regardless of the persona adopted, the question will revolve around *'Quid sit filius?'* (What may be a son?). The declaimer, like a good chess player, must anticipate the counter arguments of his opponent, and plan several steps again.[52] This exercise would not be out of place in a modern assessment of legal reasoning. Participants must take note of all data, put the problem into perspective, and arrive at a creative solution. More importantly, the fanciful nature frees students to consider alternative outcomes. Unlike test cases studied in modern law school, declamations would not yield any useful precedent. Instead, they exist to strengthen a student's skill in logic and wisdom, while forcing that student to consider the interests of each persona. The educational opportunities for the development of skills, values, and ethics are immediately apparent, especially as invented personae can cover a far broader swath of society than cases typically featuring legally or socially advantaged litigants.

9.4 LEGAL VIDEO GAMES

Declamation provides a superb ideological foundation for legal play, in or out of the classroom: fantastical scenarios, high-stakes cases, low-stakes participation, legal flexibility, and social exploration. However, educators unconvinced by the applicability of classical legal games may look to modern legal video games, which embody the very same design principles. An examination of modern gaming not only reinforces the lessons of declamatory play, but also provides a potential tool for greatly increasing the scope of laymen legal knowledge. The need for scalable learning technologies is apparent: growing student populations and underserved pro se litigants could benefit from independently instructive play. Accordingly, this

---

49 See Quint. 3.6.96.
50 Fantham (n 46) 324.
51 Seneca Cont. 27 (*Qui patrem pulsaverit, manus ei praecidantur*); Quint. DM 358 (*Qui patrem pulsaverit, manus perdat*).
52 Fantham (n 46) 324.

section reviews three commercial video games that provide design templates for legal games.

9.4.1 Ace Attorney Series

The primary legal video game franchise is 'Phoenix Wright: Ace Attorney', for Nintendo consoles.[53] The series has a broad international following and has been referenced in numerous other forms of media.[54] The series, in which the player conducts investigations and takes part in legal trials, began on the Game Boy Advance in 2001. There have been eleven games released in the series, with six games in the main series and five spin-offs. The game franchise has sold over six million copies worldwide. The gameplay style has been widely adopted in other courtroom games. For example, the game 'Harvey Birdman: Attorney-at-Law' has very similar mechanics.

The game is essentially a visual novel, in which the user is a newly barred defense attorney, Phoenix Wright. The player must defend a series of clients from a charge of murder. The game involves two phases for each case, gathering evidence and using that evidence in trial. The gathering of evidence involves travelling to an area, talking to witnesses and the client, gathering evidence, and presenting that evidence to individuals for further clarification. The trial portion involves first reading the testimony of the witness in response to questioning by the prosecution. The player must review the testimony for contradictions, and identify the line of testimony to be challenged. Once the contradiction is identified, the player must present the evidence that supports the player's theory. However, if the player presents the wrong evidence or identifies a statement that is not a contradiction, the judge will become angry. The player is given five exclamation points that function as lives; once five mistakes are made, the client is declared guilty and the game is over.

The game's focus on physical evidence fits the genre of mystery novels and courtroom dramas, but does not comport with actual trial practice. There are no rules of evidence: hearsay and chain of custody issues are not discussed. There is no motion practice and indeed, the entire investigation and trial must be completed within three days. Ace Attorney, therefore, is not a legal simulator that can teach many legal rules.[55] However, its popularity and prominence indicate that elements of the series are worth review for those interested in legal games.

The game design of Phoenix Wright has several elements that encourage in-depth play and thorough exploration. In the first five games, the player is faced with over 1,200 pieces of evidence, with the overwhelming majority of those items being useless in court. The variety in the pieces of evidence prevents the game from

[53]   CAPCOM, 'Ace Attorney' www.ace-attorney.com/ accessed 18 March 2019.
[54]   For example, the anime and light novel of 'Konosuba'.
[55]   The legal system present in the games appears to mix Japanese and American systems, which may account for some omitted or fanciful legal elements.

being a simple matching exercise. The game also involves fanciful cases, with outsized characters and enormous stakes. The relative simplicity of the graphical elements, animations, and user interface also signal that these components may be of lower import to legal game players.

9.4.2 *Papers, Please*

'Papers, Please' is a puzzle game, in which the player assumes the role of an immigration officer at a border crossing in the fictional Soviet Bloc-style country of Arstotzka.[56] The player must review the immigration papers of prospective migrants, with the knowledge that some migrants will be smugglers, terrorists, or wanted criminals, whilst others will simply be undesirable or have deficient documentation. The player earns money for successfully processing migrants in accordance with a set of rules, as well as through bribes. This money is used to feed and clothe the player's family. As relations with neighbouring countries worsen, new rules are added. Scripted scenarios also occur, in which a pleading spouse without papers begs admission, terrorist groups attempt to enlist the player's complicity in overthrowing the government, and other moral dilemmas arise throughout the course of gameplay.

'Papers, Please' has been lauded by critics, winning numerous awards. The game has also been popular despite its low budget and has gone on to sell 1.6 million copies. The game has obvious educational uses as a demonstration of the disparate impact of Boolean rules and the nature of bureaucratic process in the course of dispensing justice. The game has been used in social studies courses, and has been the subject of articles noting, 'the depiction of bureaucracy in Papers, Please closely reflects German sociologist Max Weber's seminal understanding of the modern, rational state'.[57] The game would be well at home in a legislation and regulation course.

9.4.3 *Prison Architect*

'Prison Architect' is a prison simulation game, in which the player builds and manages a private prison complex.[58] The player determines the quality of food, the amount of free time, the use of labour, enrichment programmes, punishment regimes for various infractions, and numerous other aspects of convict life. The player also sets up parole hearings for prisoners, with bonus points awarded for successful parolees. The game has sold more than two million copies.

---

[56] 3909 LLC, 'Papers, Please' (2017) http://papersplea.se/ accessed 18 March 2019.
[57] Jason J Morrissette, 'Glory to Arstotzka: Morality, Rationality, and the Iron Cage of Bureaucracy in Papers, Please' (2017) 17(1) The International Journal of Computer Game Research.
[58] Introversion UK, 'Prison Architect' www.introversion.co.uk/prisonarchitect/ accessed 18 March 2019.

'Prison Architect' may impart many of the same lessons as 'Papers, Please', demonstrating the potentially dehumanising effect of managing large numbers of individuals through broad rules. The creator of the game noted:

> We are putting you in the shoes of somebody who has to build a system that can hold hundreds, if not thousands, of prisoners. And so the net result of that is that players naturally withdraw slightly from any individual prisoner's concerns and start thinking of them as a group, as a whole. I would go so far as to say that was a design aim of the game, to give you that experience of feeling distanced from the humanity of what you're trying to make.[59]

9.4.4 *Key Considerations*

The games examined in this chapter provide elements for incorporation in educational legal games: fantastical scenarios, high-stakes cases, low-stakes participation, legal flexibility, and social exploration. The similarities between declamation and legal video games is apparent. The notions of personae, heightened stakes, fantastical elements, and creativity exploration are shared in both media though separated by thousands of years. A number of additional observations can be made with regard to graphics, choice, stakes, re-playability, opportunities for in-game rewards, and the appreciation of unreal rules.

i. Sophisticated graphics are not necessary – the development of educational legal games is not dependent on powerful graphical engines. The most popular legal game, 'Phoenix Wright', contains very limited animation, and other popular games such as 'Papers, Please' do not depend on realistic graphics. While players no doubt engage with the strong character design of 'Phoenix Wright', players also appear to enjoy games where characters are clearly representational.

ii. Choice is paramount – the popular games outlined above give players a wide degree of choice, either in crafting rules of their choosing ('Prison Architect'), in electing when to deviate from a known set of rules ('Papers, Please'), or in determining relevant information from a very broad field ('Phoenix Wright'). Games have an ability to provide feedback for these choices, be it in a binary lives system, or in a more complex situation in which one choice establishes a path dependent outcome with numerous subsequent choices along the way. At the same time, the meaningful nature of the choices in the narrative can be augmented by imposing a cost for each choice. This trade-off will further train players that not every argument or legal manoeuvre is worth making.

---

[59] Yussef Cole, '"Prison Architect" Has No Room for Political Action' (*Waypoint*, 27 July 2017) https://waypoint.vice.com/en_us/article/d7pw7x/prison-architect-has-no-room-for-political-action accessed 4 March 2019.

iii. Players can engage with high stakes in the face of re-playability – players face elevated stakes, allowing them to engage with the game while mastering skills that might otherwise seem mundane. In 'Papers, Please' and 'Prison Architect' the player is forced to confront the dissonance between seemingly pedestrian choices that precipitate life-and-death outcomes. In 'Phoenix Wright', the defendant faces a murder charge and a ticking clock. At the same time, the player knows the scenario is re-playable, so while the narrative stakes are high, so too is the opportunity for exploration. No two plays of 'Papers, Please' or 'Prison Architect' are likely to be the same, based on random events and player choices.

iv. Players appreciate in-game rewards – consistent with other gamification litera-ture, players enjoy developing a game persona[60] and accumulating in-game acco-lades, with badges, trophies, and high scores. Players advance in legal rank or accumulate more money or are given more responsibility as they progress. This tendency mirrors proximal development – advancement brings rewards but also justifies additional challenge.

v. Fanciful or artificial rules are appreciated – players are happy to address fictional scenarios, involving over-the-top characters, mediated by unreal rules. The games at issue largely use cartoonish graphics, fictional settings and fictional legal systems.

9.5 CONCLUSION

Law students are often fearful to engage in creative risk-taking when faced with high-stakes queries on precedential case law. While the knowledge of existing law is critical, so too is the intellectual ability to engage with how a legal regime has come into existence, how it has developed over time, and the consequences associated with this genesis and evolution. The use of games, whether in the form of exploratory role-play or conventional video/computer, can help students and non-students acquire valuable skills. Following classical pedagogy and modern game-design principles, educators and game creators can effect meaningful change and recruit continued interest in enriching legal play.

It is clear from repeated assessments by multiple stakeholders that legal education needs to change so as to serve students better. While narrow case-method pedagogy may impart legal rules, it risks creating a dissonance within budding lawyers who yearn to serve justice, but who have also internalised repeated instruction to set aside moral or philosophical concerns. Moreover, the case method may alienate students from underserved communities by failing to provide meaningful representation or to

---

[60] See Andrew Moshirnia, 'The Educational Potential of Modified Video Games' (2007) 4 Issues in Informing Science and Information Technology 511, 513.

evoke empathetic understanding from advantaged peers. These deficiencies have persisted despite calls for curricular change.

The literature suggests that games-based learning can help address these shortcomings. Games recruit player interest while facilitating exploration, experimentation, and creativity. Gameplay naturally encourages the adoption of different player roles, either through player choice or through variation of in-game events. The ever-increasing challenge inherent in game design marries perfectly with educational theories of proximal development and learner motivation. Moreover, the freedom to design various game personae presents opportunities for greater social inclusion of atypical students.

While it is entirely predictable that many academics may resist acknowledging the benefits of games, this tradition-centred opposition is farcical in light of the fact that the traditional method of legal instruction was games-based. Declamatory play provides a classical template for robust classroom role-play, which in turn may be further refined by examining paradigms of player choice and fanciful exploration in modern games. Although the adoption of legal games may seem daunting, both classical and modern gameplay sources indicate that simplicity matches well with versatility.

In light of the benefits attendant to games-based learning, legal educators would do well to consider how they can incorporate existing tools in their instruction and/ or assist with the development of new tools. Borrowing from declamation, instructors may refine in-class scenarios and encourage empathetic responses freed from the constraints of narrow precedent. Moreover, legal games may reach a wider audience outside the classroom, facilitating meditation on the nature of justice and concerns of disparate outcomes arising from generalised rules. From Cicero to Phoenix Wright, there are many examples of gameplay capable of inspiring new approaches to legal education; whether ancient or modern, these are examples that educators would be wise to consider as part of any effort made to modernise legal education and empower learners further.

BIBLIOGRAPHY

3909LLC, 'Papers, Please' (2017) http://papersplea.se/ accessed 18 March 2019
Allen FA, 'The Causes of Popular Dissatisfaction with Legal Education' (1976) 62(4) American Bar Association Journal 447
Anderson JR, *Language, Memory, and Thought* (Lawrence Erlbaum Associates 1976)
Anderson JR and Bower GH, *Human Associative Memory* (Psychology Press 1973)
Armstrong S and Sanson M, 'From Confusion to Confidence: Transitioning to Law School' (2012) 12(1) Queensland University of Technology Law and Justice Journal 21
Ashar SM, 'Deep Critique and Democratic Lawyering in Clinical Practice' (2016) 104(1) California Law Review 201
Auerbach JS, *Unequal Justice: Lawyers and Social Change in Modern America* (Oxford University Press 1976)

Balteiro I and Campos-Pardillos MA, 'A Comparative Study of Latinisms in Court Opinions in the United States and Spain' (2010) 17(1) International Journal of Speech Language and the Law 95

Barry MM, 'Practice Ready: Are We There Yet?' (2012) 32(2) Boston College Journal of Law & Social Justice 247

Bernstein NW, '"Torture Her Until She Lies": Torture, Testimony, and Social Status in Roman Rhetorical Education' (2012) 59(2) Greece and Rome 165

Bloomer MW, *The School of Rome: Latin Studies and the Origins of Liberal Education* (University of California Press 2011)

Brudney JJ, 'Legislation and Regulation in the Core Curriculum' (2015) 65(1) Journal of Legal Education 3

Bunzl M, 'Counterfactual History: A User's Guide' (2004) 109(3) The American Historical Review 845

Cairns JW, 'Rhetoric, Language, and Roman Law: Legal Education and Improvement in Eighteenth-Century Scotland' (1991) 9(1) Law and History Review 31

CAPCOM, 'Ace Attorney' www.ace-attorney.com/ accessed 18 March 2019

Carasik L, 'Renaissance or Retrenchment: Legal Education at a Crossroads' (2011) 44(3) Indiana Law Review 735

Chaiklin S, 'The Zone of Proximal Development in Vygotsky's Analysis of Learning and Instruction' in Alex Kozulin and others (eds.), *Vygotsky's Educational Theory in Cultural Context* (Cambridge University Press 2003)

Cole Y, '"Prison Architect" Has No Room for Political Action' (*Waypoint*, 27 July 2017) https://waypoint.vice.com/en_us/article/d7pw7x/prison-architect-has-no-room-for-political-action accessed 4 March 2019

Cowan R and Foray D, 'Evolutionary Economics and the Counterfactual Threat: On the Nature and Role of Counterfactual History as an Empirical Tool in Economics' (2002) 12 (5) Journal of Evolutionary Economics 539

Csikszentmihalyi M, *Flow: The Psychology of Optimal Experience* (Harper & Row 1990)

Daimsis A, 'Creative Thinkers Need Not Apply' (*The Law Times*, 26 February 2018) www.lawtimesnews.com/author/anthony-daimsis/creative-thinkers-need-not-apply-15393/ accessed 10 March 2019

Derrick A Bell J, 'Law School Exams and Minority-Group Students' (1981) 7(2) National Black Law Journal 304

Edwards HT, 'The Growing Disjunction between Legal Education and the Legal Profession' (1992) 91(1) Michigan Law Review 34

Evans L, 'The Study of Greek and Latin as a Preparation for the Study of Law' (1907) 15(6) The School Review 417

Fantham E, *Roman Readings: Roman Response to Greek Literature from Plautus to Statius and Quintilian* (Walter de Gruyter GmbH & Co KG 2011)

Finley GD, 'Langdell and the Leviathan: Improving the First-Year Law School Curriculum by Incorporating Moby-Dick' (2011) 97(1) Cornell Law Review 159

Griswold EN, 'Observations on Legal Education in Australia' (1951) 2(2) University of Western Australia Annual Law Review 197

Gunderson E, *Staging Masculinity: The Rhetoric of Performance in the Roman World* (Cambridge University Press 2003)

Hagan M, 'Law Games to Learn Smarter Not Harder – Law Dojo' (*Law School Dojo*, 2017) www.lawschooldojo.com accessed 10 March 2019

Introversion UK, 'Prison Architect' www.introversion.co.uk/prisonarchitect/ accessed 18 March 2019

James NJ, 'A Brief History of Critique in Australian Legal Education' (2000) 24(3) Melbourne
    University Law Review 965
Kuehn RR, 'Pricing Clinical Legal Education' (2014) 92(1) Denver University Law Review 1
Lepper MR, 'Making Learning Fun: A Taxonomy of Intrinsic Motivations for Learning' in
    R Snow and MJ Farr (eds.), *Aptitude, Learning, and Instruction: Vol. 3. Cognitive and
    Affective Process Analysis* (Lawrence Erlbaum Associates 1987)
Lepper MR and Malone TW, 'Intrinsic Motivation and Instructional Effectiveness in
    Computer-Based Education' in RE Snow and MJ Farr (eds.), *Aptitude, Learning, and
    Instruction: Vol. 3. Cognitive and Affective Process Analysis* (Lawrence Erlbaum
    Associates 1987)
Macleod PR, 'Latin in Legal Writing: An Inquiry into the Use of Latin in the Modern Legal
    World' (1997) 39(1) Boston College Law Review 235
McGee H, 'Minority Students in Law School: Black Lawyers and the Struggle for Racial
    Justice in the American Social Order' (1971) 20(2) Buffalo Law Review 423
Morrissette JJ, 'Glory to Arstotzka: Morality, Rationality, and the Iron Cage of Bureaucracy in
    Papers, Please' (2017) 17(1) The International Journal of Computer Game Research
Moshirnia A, 'The Educational Potential of Modified Video Games' (2007) 4 Issues in
    Informing Science and Information Technology 511
Pagán VE, 'Teaching Torture in Seneca Controversiae 2.5' (2007) 103(2) The Classical
    Journal 165
Pearsall G, 'The Human Side of Law School: The Case for Socializing Minority Recruitment
    and Retention Programs' (2015) 64(4) Journal of Legal Education 688
Piaget J, *The Psychology of Intelligence* (Harcourt, Brace 1947)
Ryan RM and Deci EL, 'Self-Determination Theory and the Facilitation of Intrinsic
    Motivation, Social Development and Well-Being' (2000) 55(1) The American
    Psychologist 68
Ryan RM, Rigby CS and Przybylski A, 'The Motivational Pull of Video Games: A Self-
    Determination Theory Approach' (2006) 30(4) Motivation and Emotion 344
Segal D, 'What They Don't Teach Law Students: Lawyering' *New York Times* (New York,
    19 November 2011) www.nytimes.com/2011/11/20/business/after-law-school-associates-
    learn-to-be-lawyers.html accessed 10 July 2018
Stevens R, *Law School: Legal Education in America from the 1850s to the 1980s* (University of
    North Carolina Press 1987)
Stewart S, *Nonsense: Aspects of Intertextuality in Folklaw and Literature* (John Hopkins
    University Press 1979)
Stuckey R, 'Best Practices for Legal Education: A Vision and A Road Map' (Clinical Legal
    Education Association 2007) https://clea.wildapricot.org/resources/documents/best_
    practices-full.pdf accessed 28 September 2018
Sullivan WM and others, *Educating Lawyers: Preparation for the Profession of Law* (1st edn,
    Jossey-Bass 2007)
Szczygielski K, 'Latin Legal Maxims in the Judgments of the Constitutional Tribunal in
    Poland' (2017) 49(1) Studies in Logic, Grammar and Rhetoric 213
Task Force on Law Schools and the Profession – American Bar Association, 'Legal Education
    and Professional Development-An Educational Continuum. (MacCrate Report)'
    (American Bar Association 1992) www.americanbar.org/content/dam/aba/publications/
    misc/legal_education/2013_legal_education_and_professional_development_maccra
    te_report).authcheckdam.pdf accessed 24 September 2018
Torrey M, 'You Call That Education?' (2004) 19(1) Wisconsin Women's Law Journal 93

Ulster University Legal Innovation Centre, 'Gamification: Games to Make Learning Law Engaging and Enjoyable' (2017) www.legalinnovation.ai/gamification accessed 4 March 2019

University of Kent, 'Glossary of Legal Latin' (2019) www.kent.ac.uk/library/subjects/lawlinks/skills-hub/docs/glossaryoflegallatin.pdf accessed 4 March 2019

Van den Berg CS, *The World of Tacitus' Dialogus de Oratoribus: Aesthetics and Empire in Ancient Rome* (Cambridge University Press 2014)

10

The Gamification of Written Problem Questions in Law

Reflections on the 'Serious Games at Westminster' Project

Paresh Kathrani

Hitherto, hypothetical legal cases in legal education, otherwise known as 'problem questions', have been predominantly presented in written form. Lecturers provide students with a set of written facts and, through the exercise of skills such as research and argumentation, require students to advise a fictitious client. Whilst problem questions are easily accessible and provide useful training in issue identification and legal research, they can be enhanced through the use of novel methods. This chapter explores one such enhancement, brought about by rendering the very same facts within a computer game. It is argued that this environment is important practically and pedagogically as it imports an authenticity that adds to the careful analysis of facts, and expands the environment of traditional problem questions and opportunities for questioning and deduction. This chapter demonstrates the benefits of rendering traditional, written problem-based scenarios into computer game environments (including those using virtual reality) by drawing on work conducted at the University of Westminster.

10.1 INTRODUCTION

Hitherto, hypothetical legal cases in legal education, otherwise known as 'problem questions', have been predominantly presented in written form. Lecturers provide students with a set of written facts, and through the exercise of skills such as research and argumentation, require students to advise a fictitious client. Whilst problem questions are easily accessible and provide useful training in issue identification and legal research, they can be enhanced through the use of novel methods so as to allow for a more immersive and experiential learning process.

Computer games provide a form of hands-on learning that written problem questions (WPQs) cannot facilitate. This lends authenticity to the analysis of facts. The ability to progress through a game, interact with avatars and pursue mappings can naturally expand traditional problem questions. Moreover, this digital environment provides opportunities for instructors to test a wide range of complementary learning objectives, such as questioning, deduction, client interaction, initiative and persistence, in a way that is not possible with WPQs.

In this chapter, I explore the benefits of turning traditional WPQs into games, by drawing on a pilot project I undertook with colleagues Daphne Economou, Vassiliki Bouki and Markos Mentzelopoulos at the University of Westminster from 2013 to 2018. In establishing the motivations underpinning this project and in outlining its execution, I first consider the skills that a law degree is intended to inculcate and the way in which traditional WPQs contribute to the acquisition of these skills. I then map out the development of the University of Westminster projects in greater detail, providing readers with a practical understanding as to how WPQs can be translated into a game environment with the help of experts in the field. I conclude by reflecting upon the benefits and challenges that accompany this process and what these might mean for future efforts of a similar nature.

10.2 THE ROLE OF LEGAL SKILLS IN THE LEGAL CURRICULUM

The work of a lawyer is complex;[1] it draws on general skills such as communication and reasoning, as well as specialist skills that demand marshalling diverse pieces of evidence and researching and interpreting different legal sources.[2] Legal work also demands specialist knowledge of the law. A lawyer must know the minutiae of the legal rules of the field within which they work, the existing pieces of the 'legal puzzle' and how these elements can be used to form new legal interpretations and arguments. Some would not stop here, arguing that traits like empathy and a strong feel for justice are necessary components of a lawyer's skill set.[3] Whilst this may be true, 'hard' rather than 'soft' skills have typically formed the basis of the learning objectives of a law degree, and legal education tends to emphasise the interplay between legal skills and legal knowledge above all else.

To the extent that good lawyering is about having an acceptable proficiency in a range of skills alongside knowledge of law, legal education in England and Wales achieves this via the bifurcation of academic and professional legal studies.[4] The qualifying law degree in England and Wales, such as the Bachelor of Law degree (LLB), performs a valuable role in preparing law students for the world of lawyering.

[1] Sally Kift, 'Lawyering Skills: Finding Their Place in Legal Education' (1997) 8(1) Legal Education Review 43.

[2] Susan Swaim Daicoff, 'Lawyer, Form Thyself: Professional Identity Formation Strategies in Legal Education through Soft Skills Training, Ethics, and Experiential Courses' (2014) 27(2) Regent University Law Review 205.

[3] Charles Halpern, 'The Mindful Lawyer: Why Contemporary Lawyers Are Practicing Meditation' (2012) 61(4) Journal of Legal Education 641.

[4] Solicitors Regulation Authority and Bar Standards Board, 'Academic Stage Handbook' (Solicitors Regulation Authority and Bar Standards Board 2014) www.sra.org.uk/documents/students/academic-stage/academic-stage-handbook.pdf accessed 1 November 2018.

Whilst undertaking a qualifying law degree and studying core and optional modules, law students are placed in different situations from which they learn legal skills and knowledge. 'Situatedness' therefore becomes important; students are asked to consider aspects of the law in a particular place, at a particular time and with reference to a particular perspective. This use of 'situatedness' can be related to phenomenological thinkers such as Maurice Marleau-Ponty,[5] building on the fact that each such situation affords a student a very unique form of learning.[6] Hence, a lecture is situationally different to a tutorial, in the same way that clinical legal education is different from the completion of WPQs at home.

The receipt of information and the learning that this receipt of information begets is contingent upon this concept of 'situatedness'. People store, absorb and draw on information in different ways, and the range of learning situations employed in the delivery of education are intended to leverage these differences and maximise the opportunity for all students to benefit. Historically the law lecture, small group discussion, readings, essay-writing and answering problem questions, have formed the main conduits through which law students have been exposed to 'teachings', and the use of these methods in different contexts have allowed a myriad of different 'situations' to proliferate. A WPQ completed alone at home is situationally different to one that is done by way of group working with peers in a classroom. A discussion in the library between peers takes on a different resonance than one that is facilitated by an expert tutor in class. In the same vein, a lecture delivered by a lecturer in an auditorium to two hundred or more students will have a different influence on knowledge acquisition than an interactive seminar with ten people.

In more recent times, the expansion of clinical work and increased opportunities for mooting have also provided alternative environments or 'situations' within which law students can discuss and apply legal knowledge and legal skills. Technology has also meant that 'blended learning', 'flipped classrooms' and multiple 'virtual learning environments' have increasingly replaced the 'overhead projector' and 'sermon on a mount'.[7] Yet evaluating which 'situation' is most effective to learning remains a work in progress.[8] No one method is necessarily better than another, at least not without regard to context.[9] For this reason there is merit in considering how educators might integrate other 'situations', so as to diversify students' exposure to different learning environments. This objective formed the basis of a number of

[5]   Christopher Pollard, 'What Is Original in Merleau-Ponty's View of the Phenomenological Reduction?' (2018) 41(3) Human Studies 395.

[6]   Steven M Virgil, 'The Role of Experiential Learning on a Law Student' (2016) 51(2) Wake Forest Law Review 325.

[7]   Kylie Burns and others, 'Active Learning in Law by Flipping the Classroom: An Enquiry into Effectiveness and Engagement' (2017) 27(1) Legal Education Review Article 14.

[8]   For example, see Patrick Koroma and Nicola Antoniou, 'Law Students' Clinic Experience: Is It All Hype in Relation to Performance on Black-Letter Law Exams?' (2017) 24(1) International Journal of Clinical Legal Education 58.

[9]   Sue Saltmarsh and others, 'Putting "Structure within the Space": Spatially Un/Responsive Pedagogic Practices in Open-Plan Learning Environments' (2015) 67(3) Educational Review 315.

recent University of Westminster projects, which took WPQs used in the criminal law curriculum and translated these into different games.[10] In doing so, the projects sought to augment one traditional learning 'situation' (the WPQ) and translate it into another.

10.3 WRITTEN PROBLEM QUESTIONS (WPQS)

Legal education, like any other type of formal education, is aimed at achieving learning outcomes (LOs).[11] LOs generally cascade through the specifications of a degree course – general outcomes lead to more specific outcomes, which are then accomplished through the various core and optional modules that students complete. In a qualifying English law degree, the top-level LOs identify the fundamental skills of working with the law, and these give way to more specific skills at later stages such as legal research and communication. All in all, these skills generally focus on what is required for practice in England and Wales as stipulated by the professional bodies and the Quality Assurance Agency (QAA).[12]

The various core and optional modules of a law degree are the means by which these LOs are fulfilled. Students go to lectures, where a lecturer gives information on the relevant legal rules and principles associated with an area of law. This amounts to the transmission of legal information rather than legal knowledge.[13] To acquire status as 'knowledge', this information must progress through several different cognitive machinations in the mind of a student via the processes of application and reflection. In the context of modules on a qualifying law degree, seminars and tutorials provide an example of this process. Questions and answers, group work, debates, mooting and other forms of interactive learning provide the means of 'learning-by-doing' which is crucial for transforming information into knowledge. In this way, there is a close synergy between the 'doing of law' and the 'knowing of law', with these different learning spheres bonded together through reflection.[14]

---

[10] Daphne Economou and others, 'Westminster Serious Games Platform (Wmin-SGP) A Tool for Real-Time Authoring of Roleplay Simulations for Learning' (2016) 16(6) Future Intelligent Educational Environments Article 5.

[11] Jenny Gibbons, 'Exploring Conceptual Legal Knowledge Building in Law Students' Reflective Reports Using Theoretical Constructs from the Sociology of Education: What, How and Why?' (2018) 52(1) The Law Teacher 38.

[12] Quality Assurance Agency for Higher Education, 'Subject Benchmark Statements: Law' (Quality Assurance Agency for Higher Education 2015) www.qaa.ac.uk/docs/qaa/subject-benchmark-statements/sbs-law-15.pdf accessed 1 November 2018.

[13] Karen Jensen, Monika Nerland and Cecilie Enqvist-Jensen, 'Enrolment of Newcomers in Expert Cultures: An Analysis of Epistemic Practices in a Legal Education Introductory Course' (2015) 70(5) Higher Education 867.

[14] Kevin J Brown and Colin RG Murray, 'Enhancing Interactivity in the Teaching of Criminal Law: Using Response Technology in the Lecture Theatre' in Kris Gledhill and Ben Livings (eds.), *The Teaching of Criminal Law: The Pedagogical Imperatives* (Routledge 2016).

WPQs provide a space for this reflection to occur by requiring that students apply knowledge to a particular legal problem. All students who undertake a qualifying law degree in England and Wales will have come across a WPQ, whether in a tutorial, an exam or a textbook. They encompass the core elements that one would find on a lawyer's desk, that is: a client; facts that point to a sphere or field of law; gaps that call forth the need for further legal research; a requirement to analyse the facts; apply the legal rules; advance or communicate a potential solution; and a request to advise a client. As such, WPQs provide an excellent means for teaching, practising and assessing core legal skills, and for students, they also provide an opportunity to experience what lawyers 'do'.

WPQs are also valuable because they facilitate different types of learning, including mobile, distance and asynchronous learning.[15] The lecturer or assessor thinks about the facts or points of law they would like a student to research and analyse and then constructs a scenario that engages those areas. The resulting task is amenable to digital or paper distribution, allowing students to undertake the task at a convenient time and place, independently or with the support of peers. WPQs as a means of practising and assessing legal skills provide all-round flexibility and for this reason it is perhaps no surprise that they remain a favoured method of teaching in law schools around the world.

To this end, WPQs also allow for different forms of 'situatedness'. Whilst the environment within which the WPQ task is completed (such as at home or in class) remains a factor, irrespective of where a WPQ is completed, the task encompasses an element of what it feels like to be a lawyer. Unlike other tasks, with WPQs the client narrative engages the student, allowing for the task to mirror aspects of the real-life client-lawyer relationship. Accordingly, students must consider the practicality of the advice they provide, they must use their legal and communication skills to assist the client, and they must evaluate the merits of different approaches to achieving a particular outcome. In short, WPQs provide a real life simulation through which the effective application of legal skills can be assessed.[16]

In order to enhance the learning potential of WPQs, it is important that the WPQ is written as a lifelike narrative, capable of engaging the student, whilst also maintaining the various twists and turns introduced to test the student's aptitude. Yet, whilst a WPQ ought to strive to incorporate as much realism as possible, it is nevertheless acknowledged that there is a clear difference between reading a case and 'living' a case; in the same way that there is a difference between reading a book about a film and watching the film itself.[17] The senses (situation) that are evoked upon reading about an event are naturally not the same as living it, where one sees, feels and experiences what occurs.

[15] Juliet Turner, Alison Bone and Jeanette Ashton, 'Reasons Why Law Students Should Have Access to Learning Law through a Skills-Based Approach' (2018) 52(1) The Law Teacher 1.

[16] Anna Copeland, 'What Makes a Good Lawyer? Reflection, Clinical Education and Practitioners of the Future' (2016) 43(10) Brief 31.

[17] Lisa M Domke, Tracy L Weippert and Laura Apol, 'Beyond School Breaks: Reinterpreting the Uses of Film in Classrooms' (2018) 72(1) The Reading Teacher 51.

Words on a page are set once the author has written them. They do not allow for forms of engagement or responsiveness that better reflect how the process of giving advice or advocating for a client plays out in the real world.

10.4 ENHANCING THE UTILITY OF WPQS

Whilst the narrative of a WPQ may help facilitate a more immersive environment in terms of applying the law, as well as importing a sense of authenticity,[18] they can only go so far as compared to the more realistic rendering of WPQs in the context of mooting. Mooting actually 'situates' the student in the role of an advocate. Moots can be compared to WPQs in that they both provide law students with the opportunity to experience what it feels like to be a lawyer by making use of a hypothetical client with a set of facts, and requiring the law student to resolve their case through the application of law.[19] However, although a WPQ does better to achieve 'situatedness' than non-narrative approaches, the WPQ arguably achieves less than a moot in terms of simulating an authentic environment.

Moreover, the range of skills that WPQs are capable of testing remains relatively narrow when compared to learning methods such as mooting. Mooting emphasises skills such as written and oral presentation, teamwork, thinking on one's feet, and responding to legal argumentation 'on the spot' in a high-pressure (public) context. In this regard, mooting tests more than a response to a WPQ, however this broader pedagogical value is offset by the relatively resource-intense process of convening a moot as opposed to assigning students a WPQ.

Moots provide a more authentic experience, test a broader skills set and enhance student reflectivity in a way that promotes the acquisition of knowledge. Yet the enhanced value that derives from this 'situatedness' comes at the cost of flexibility, ease of participation and ease of facilitation for both students and instructors. In striking a balance between the two models, there is reason to believe that emerging forms of technology might offer a compromise, maximising learning whilst minimising the difficulties that attend to organising a moot. Just like the authenticity conjured by a moot, there are ways in which gamification technology may enhance and expand the utility of traditional WPQ methods.

10.5 THE GAMIFICATION OF WPQS

The advantages that attach to gamification of WPQs arise for two reasons. First, gamification can encompass a wider range of LOs, designed to test students'

---

[18] This can be broadly related to Adam Jackson and Kevin Kerrigan, 'The Challenges and Benefits of Integrating Criminal Law, Litigation and Evidence' in Kris Gledhill and Ben Livings (eds.), *The Teaching of Criminal Law: The Pedagogical Imperatives* (Routledge 2016).
[19] Luke Marsh and Michael Ramsden, 'Reflections on a High School Mooting Competition: Bridging the Gap between Secondary and Tertiary Education' (2015) 49(3) The Law Teacher 323.

initiative, deductive reasoning, persistence and reactivity. For instance, in a WPQ, events are set sequentially one after another, for example: X stabs Y, Y is then taken to hospital where following medical negligence, Y dies. These sequences provide students with clear cues to help them answer aspects of the question, particularly in this case, aspects of causation, yet in a computer game there is scope to withhold or to prompt information. A student might simply be informed that Y had died, leaving it up to them to fill in the gaps and uncover how Y died though interaction with virtual agents, the collection of facts and the pursuit of relevant lines of enquiry. Where a computer game employs immersive techniques such as virtual reality, a gamified WPQ can further enhance the authenticity of a given scenario.[20]

Computer games can offer variability by incorporating decision-trees so that events unfold in a way that is contingent upon the choice that a lawyer makes at any given moment in time. If, for instance, a lawyer was to use their judgement and chose not to investigate a particular series of facts, then the path of the case and the implications that arise as a result of that choice can vary in a way that reflects the effect of choices made in the real world. Whilst in some instances the choices made will not have a substantive impact upon outcome, computer games permit greater flexibility in this regard.[21]

Second, gamification may operate to better engage students, and make the process of knowledge acquisition and learning more enjoyable. This is partly because game-play stimulates different parts of the brain than other forms of learning, enabling players to reach a peak state of creativity and performance.[22] It is also because a game is, by definition, a challenge. Winning is a gratifying process that increases the brain's release of feel-good chemicals which makes the participant more receptive to learning.[23] Winning requires a person to achieve a certain objective, such as completing a task in a certain amount of time, achieving a goal or beating an opponent, and people develop and apply many strategies to maximise their chances of success. If a 'player' adopts a particular strategy and it brings them success in a particular competition, a reward-pattern is reinforced. They may choose to reapply or consolidate that strategy in an effort to repeat their success.[24] In this way, computer games enable players to accrue smaller successes incrementally in pursuit of a successful longer-term legal strategy.

[20] Gláuber Guilherme Signori and others, 'Gamification as an Innovative Method in the Processes of Learning in Higher Education Institutions' (2018) 24(2) International Journal of Innovation and Learning 115.

[21] Juho Hamari, Kai Huotari and Juha Tolvanen, 'Gamification and Economics' in Steffen P Walz and Sebastian Deterding (eds.), *The Gameful World: Approaches, Issues, Application* (Massachusetts Institute of Technology Press 2015).

[22] See further the discussion on 'flow' in Chapters Nine and Eleven.

[23] See, e.g., Craig Miller, 'The Gamification of Education' (2013) 40 Developments in Business Simulation and Experiential Learning 196.

[24] Karen Robson and others, 'Is It All a Game? Understanding the Principles of Gamification' (2015) 58 (4) Business Horizons 411.

This pursuit of a 'win' means that games resonate well with legal cases.[25] A legal case also consists of a challenge. The lawyer is instructed by a client to achieve a particular outcome. A lawyer naturally knows the law and has to apply it to their client's case to determine the strengths and weaknesses. This may require further questioning or for an evidence or investigation trail to be initiated to collate further facts. Alongside this, the lawyer will need to apply the existing laws, and also think about whether a different interpretation of the law or precedent needs to be set. This demands the application of case theories and strategies, and the possible revision and reconsideration of the approach taken so as to meet the best interests of their client. Put crudely, a case is a quasi-game in which various strategies have to be implemented in pursuit of a 'win'.[26]

For all of these reasons, problem questions rendered into computer games (CGPQs) have various advantages over WPQs. They provide different forms of sensation and learning, and allow for a closer simulation of what actually happens in legal practice. They can incorporate different decision-trees that allow the effects of certain decisions to cascade throughout the case resolution process. They can also reflect the challenges that a real legal case presents and incorporate various tasks that test more than just knowledge or application of the law. Thus games have the potential to facilitate a deeper and more intense form of experiential learning, particularly where virtual reality is used to enhance realness and immersion.

It was with these potential benefits in mind that in 2013 I became involved in a number of projects with Computer Science colleagues at the University of Westminster in which we attempted to translate WPQs into computer games for students studying a module in Criminal law. In the following section I provide an overview of the projects and their establishment, before turning to discuss the considerations that informed design, and the benefits and challenges that arose.

10.5.1 Serious Games at Westminster (SGAW) and Gamifying Criminal Law at the University of Westminster

The University of Westminster holds an annual learning and teaching symposium every summer, which enables staff from different faculties to showcase their innovative teaching methods and share good practice. Several years ago, I went to one such symposium and attended a session delivered by Computer Science and Architecture colleagues who were presenting a computer game that they had developed. In this computer game, a three-dimensional (3D) avatar/character (the protagonist) was shown navigating a park and speaking to other characters within the park

---

[25] Markos Mentzelopoulos and others, 'REVRLaw: An Immersive Way for Teaching Criminal Law Using Virtual Reality', *Communications in Computer and Information Science (CCIS)* (Springer, Cham 2016).

[26] William E Hornsby Jr, 'Gaming the System: Approaching 100% Access to Legal Services through Online Games' (2013) 88(3) Chicago-Kent Law Review 917.

about where to build a skateboard ramp. These characters were offering various bits of information to help the protagonist determine the best location. The decision tree was apparent: unless the protagonist asked the right character the right question, information could not be acquired. This in turn affected the appropriateness of the location selected for the ramp, and the costs and considerations attendant to this choice. The aim of the game was to determine the most effective place to build the ramp.

After this session it occurred to me that 'gamification' would also work well in legal studies. Like the character who was assessing where the best place was to build the ramp, lawyers also engage with many different people and other information sources to piece together the most optimal decision; and like the architect in the computer game, their choices differ based upon who they consult or fail to consult. I also found the various gamified elements of a computer game appealing.[27] Such elements included getting points based upon the completion of certain key milestones and reaching milestones within a particular period of time. I could see the pedagogic value in setting these parameters within a law game, in that not only would it provide students with a method of assessing their progress, but it would also encourage reflection and motivate them to improve and consolidate their knowledge.

This prompted me to contact these Computer Science colleagues to collaborate on a CGPQs project, and these joint efforts culminated in the development of an interdisciplinary research unit at the University entitled 'Serious Games at Westminster (SGAW)',[28] and the production of three law games.

10.5.1.1 Game One: The Virtual Client

The first game involved collaboration between me and colleagues Dr Daphne Economou and Dr Vassiliki Bouki (experts in Computer Science), and Dr Frands Pedersen (an expert in Politics and International Relations). At the time of collaboration, I was the module leader of Criminal Law at Westminster Law School. In this role I was responsible for drafting WPQs on the various crimes taught within the module (including murder, grievous bodily harm and theft) for both tutorials and assessments.

Crimes generally consist of an actus reus, namely the action the defendant must have performed in order to be liable for that crime (the guilty act), and a mens rea, or the guilty state of mind with which that actus reus must have been committed. The

---

[27]   Andrew James Clements, Sajeel Ahmed and Bernadette Henderson, 'Student Experience of Gamified Learning: A Qualitative Approach' in Maja Pivec and Josef Grundler (eds), *ECGBL 2017 11th European Conference on Game-Based Learning* (Academic Conferences International Limited 2017).

[28]   University of Westminster, 'Home – Serious Games at Westminster Research Group' www .westminster.ac.uk/serious-games-at-westminster-research-group accessed 30 August 2018.

typical WPQ involved a hypothetical client who had been accused of a murder. In answering the WPQ, students had to identify whether the full actus reus and mens rea of the murder had been established, and advise their client accordingly. To do so, students had to consider the facts to identify the relevant issues, research the relevant law, apply the law to the facts and then clearly communicate their advice to a client.

This process, known as the IRAC framework, reflects what lawyers do in practice. Whilst there are many different interpretations of IRAC, we relied upon the following definition:[29]

I   read the facts or evidence of a case in order to (i)dentify the (i)ssues;
R   conduct (r)elevant (r)esearch of the legal (r)ules;
A   (a)pply rules to the facts, (a)nalyse facts in light of rules, produce (a)rguments for both sides; and
C   (c)onclude by (c)onstructively advising a (c)lient.

From this, I drafted a law of murder WPQ as usual, and the developers (Bouki and Economou) coupled games platform technology (Unity) with 'Virtual Humans Toolkit' software in order to turn the defendant/client into a virtual character seeking advice from the lawyer/student (the player) in an office environment .[30]

As Figure 10.1 shows, upon logging into the platform, students were presented with a view of their client on their screens. They were then required to type their questions for that client, or speak into a microphone, so as to elicit information pertinent to the 'actus reus' and 'mens rea' of murder. To maximise the learning experience, a range of gamified elements were incorporated, including a timer, set time limits for tasks and targets/key questions based on the 'actus reus' and 'mens rea'. For instance, if the student managed to ask the right question and obtain information about whether the defendant had the intention to kill (mens rea) or were drunk when they allegedly committed the killing (the defence of intoxication), a banner would appear on the screen congratulating the student for identifying a milestone. We hoped that this game would augment the use of WPQs in the course by providing an interactive process that rewarded initiative and curiousness.

10.5.1.2 Game Two: An Interactive Story

Focusing again on the law of murder, the second game drew on the process of 'learning by doing' and was informed by educational theory identifying the narrative,

---

[29]   Christopher N Candlin, Vijay K Bhatia and Christian H Jensen, 'Developing Legal Writing Materials for English Second Language Learners: Problems and Perspectives' (2002) 21(4) English for Specific Purposes 299.
[30]   Daphne Economou and others, 'A Dynamic Role-Playing Platform for Simulations in Legal and Political Education', 2014 *International Conference on Interactive Mobile Communication Technologies and Learning (IMCL2014)* (IEEE 2014).

FIGURE 10.1 Screenshot of the Westminster Serious Games Platform (wmin SGP), a platform that allows the creation of bespoke 3D simulations[31]

enjoyment and reward elements of 'play' as critical to the process of learning. To this end the IRAC methodology was deconstructed into a series of sequential stages by Bouki who used 'Articulate Storyline' software to produce a sequence of mini-games or challenges based upon each stage of IRAC. This is shown in Figure 10.2, which illustrates the sections of the game. This software was chosen because it allowed the project's design experts to be creative with different games. In particular, Bouki's approach to the development of the interactive story was highly creative, using comic-graphics to depict the story. In addition, Bouki integrated gamified elements, such as time limits, reclaiming the learning time, points and rewards throughout the IRAC stages, to engage and motivate learners.[32]

Designing the game around IRAC provided a number of key benefits. Generally, the 'Issue Identification' (or 'I') step of IRAC is important for a number of reasons. Not only do the facts of a case provide the foundation upon which the legal analysis rests and the client is advised, but, from a LOs perspective, it enables a lecturer to determine how good their students are at investigating and analysing a set of facts

---

31 Economou and others, 'Westminster Serious Games Platform (Wmin-SGP) A Tool for Real-Time Authoring of Roleplay Simulations for Learning' (n 10); Economou and others, 'A Dynamic Role-Playing Platform for Simulations in Legal and Political Education' (n 30); Daphne Economou and others, 'Evaluation of a Dynamic Role-Playing Platform for Simulations Based on Octalysis Gamification Framework' in Davy Preuveneers (ed.), *Volume 19: Workshop Proceedings of the 11th International Conference on Intelligent Environments* (IOS Press 2015).

32 See further Vassilki Bouki and Daphne Economou, 'Using Serious Games in Higher Education: Reclaiming the Learning Time' in D Preuveneers (ed.), *Volume 19: Workshop Proceedings of the 11th International Conference on Intelligent Environments* (IOS Press 2015) http://ebooks.iospress.nl/pub lication/39888 accessed 25 April 2019

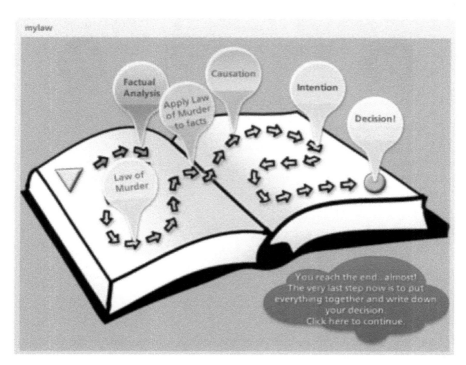

FIGURE 10.2 The Interactive Story educational activities follow the IRAC framework

and conducting further evidential enquiries based on their research. For this reason, it is crucial that students grasp every single fact, particularly where facts are drafted in such a way as to assess if students can spot the relevant grey areas and matters open to interpretation.

Often, students read the facts too fast and do not always identify the nuances of the information provided. In order to emphasise the 'Issue Identification' step of IRAC, Bouki suggested the use of a comic-strip game to present to students the story of what had happened in the case, and to reveal only the first and the last frame of the story. Taking advantage of the momentum of learning, students were required to fill in the gaps in the story and to write out what they believe had happened within a strict time (as shown in Figure 10.3).[33] Students were then required to compare their story and the real one. This ensured that students were alive to the facts. Requiring students cross-reference their assumptions against the real facts was intended to ensure that students appreciated the facts from the very start of the scenario.

Another sub-game required students to separate the 'actus reus' and 'mens rea' of murder into their constituent elements. This game awarded or deducted points based on whether the student placed the appropriate element in the right place. In

---

[33] For an extended description, see ibid.

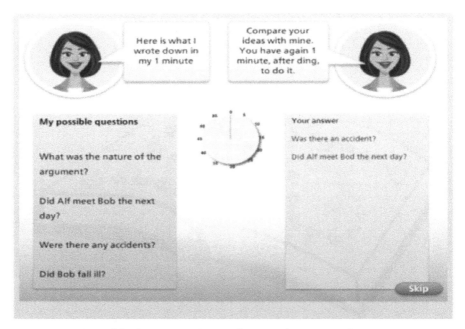

FIGURE 10.3 One of the 'Interactive Story' educational activities where time constraints are used as a motivational element to focus a learner's attention

this way, students were motivated to maximise their reward by completing the task correctly and undertaking the relevant research. Those who answered incorrectly were incentivised to remember earlier errors and modify their answers accordingly so that they could obtain correct results the next time around. This opportunity to reinforce knowledge and correct errors was enhanced by additional functionality, which enabled tutors to be built-in at various stages of game-play to guide students and provide advice before and after each game. Avatars were modelled on actual tutors from the criminal law module teaching team and placed within the game as shown in Figure 10.4.

10.5.1.3 Game Three: REVRLaw – A Virtual Reality Game

Developed in conjunction with Markos Mentzelopoulos (Senior Lecturer in Computer Science) and James Parrish (a final year student in Computer Science), REVRLaw involved the transposing of a murder scenario into a virtual reality (VR) game. A student would be immersed within a physical crime scene with the assistance of a pair of VR glasses. In this environment they would interact with different characters and were provided with different snippets of relevant evidence at various points in time. The scenario revolved around

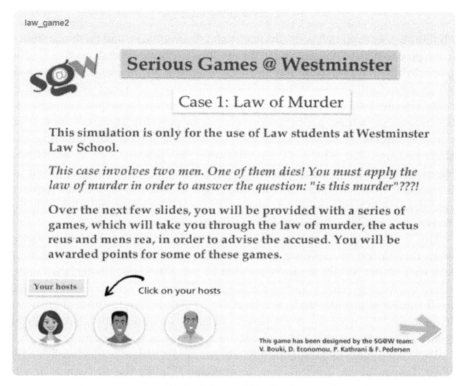

FIGURE 10.4 Avatar tutors provided advice and feedback to students at various points in the game-play

the law of murder, and was based on a narrative in which a killing had taken place in an office block. Different characters and evidence coded into the game gave clues to help students identify whether the 'actus reus' and 'mens rea' of murder were present. The outcome of the game was dependent on how the student navigated the scene, questioned characters, obtained evidence and applied the law.

The virtual environment and map was designed to mirror what happens in an actual murder case. As in real life, the case is rarely linear with various components such as fact-finding turning on who is spoken to and consulted, and what evidence is sought and found. In the real world, the steps an individual takes, as well as the order in which they take these steps determine the narrative trajectory. This involves the use of judgement, learning from experience, memorisation and initiative, all features that the VR game was designed to replicate. In placing the student within the murder scene, and giving them to opportunity to look and walk around the scene, the narrative of the WPQ was dynamically brought to life, producing a particular form of 'situatedness'.

10.5.2 *Evaluating CGPQs*

All three games exhibited both advantages and disadvantages, and these manifested in the process of development and in the resulting user experienced produced by the game. Whilst the first game was relatively simplistic in nature, it arguably took WPQs a step further by presenting students with a virtual character with which they could actually interact. Building in gamified elements such as time counters and targets also augmented the learning experience by providing students with motivations for completion and contextual pressures that roughly simulated the time and target pressures that exist in practice. However, the process of development was laborious, and each character had to be programmed manually so as to include all the possible questions and responses that might be asked or given. This required consideration of the various permutations of natural language and ultimately the decision to curtail the scope of possible responses to a manageable range.

This is not unique to our game, but rather an issue faced by all game designers when they intend on capturing and responding to input text provided in natural language format. Whilst it can be avoided by using prescribed rather than open-ended questioning (such as getting the player to choose between a series of questions to ask), doing so provides students with cues that may undermine student initiative. It reinforces the need for developers to balance ambition with what might be realistic to produce within a given budget, time frame or set of resources.

The second game took a slightly different tact, and relied more specifically on the IRAC framework to structure the game design. Unlike the first game, it also incorporated various methods of reinforcing learning and various tools designed to test student progress. To this end, narrative scripting was combined with drag and drop functionality and tutor avatars designed to reiterate key concepts, aid issue recollection and promote memorisation. Moreover, as with the first game and as with WPQs, students could easily access the game infrastructure. Like a take-home WPQ, as long as students had access to a computer and the Internet, they could participate at a location of their choice. Nonetheless the expanded version of the game also required the design team to consider and more deeply address the policy and moral issues that often arise in a case and which require analysis. For example, we had to consider how we would build in the policy arguments that often arise with issues of legal causation in criminal law whilst striking a balance between simplicity and complexity.

The third game provided a truly immersive experience and one that was capable of incorporating a much wider range of LOs than might be possible through the WPQ alone. Nevertheless, it also required costly, heavy, inflexible equipment and significant effort with regard to coding, development and deployment. The three-dimensional environment required students to play the game using specialist headsets and powerful computer hardware, and this restricted use of the game to locations with the necessary facilities. This meant that whilst the game was immersive and highly innovative, the tools required to produce this game inevitably restrict widespread use or adoption. This may well change in the future as VR systems continue to increase in availability and decrease in size and complexity, democratising access to VR infrastructure and enabling wider use.

10.6 CONCLUSION

All three games offered different incarnations of 'situatedness', giving students the opportunity to meet legal LOs in immersive and highly innovative ways. Legal education is based on ensuring that students acquire competence in the core skills that they will need to work with the law. These include the ability to marshal facts, conduct legal research and analysis and effectively communicate the outcomes. Lectures, tutorials and seminars are directed towards these objectives, and WPQs represent one such variation. Whilst WPQs undoubtedly have their advantages, especially in terms of mobility and other types of convenience, they also have limits as well; particularly with regard to their 'situatedness' and their capacity for immersion, engagement, variability, reinforcement learning and learning by doing.

Thus, there is merit in exploring the potential technology holds as an effective and mobile method by which to enable students to achieve a wider range of LOs and promote sustained interest in a particular subject matter. By using narratives and bringing those narratives to life through game-play, legal problems and principles can be delivered in a way that resonates with students.

Increasingly, software that allows users to design games for education will provide a highly valuable way for legal educators to complement their existing suite of teaching tools. Advances in no-code infrastructure may also enable educators to take their own initiative in this regard and develop methods without technical (coding) expertise. Nonetheless, as the development of these three games at the University of Westminster has revealed, legal educators can enhance their pedagogical materials through collaboration with other faculties. Often, as was the case here, there are those willing to give their time and expertise that are simply in want of a good idea. Given the potential benefits that such collaboration may produce for students, educators and researchers alike, games of the type described here merit further consideration.

ACKNOWLEDGEMENTS

The author would like to acknowledge the contributions of the following individuals who made this project possible: Frands Pedersen and Daphne Economou for funding the development of 'Game 1: The Virtual Client ' which was part of the Comparative Study of the Educational Value of Role Play, Board Games and

Virtual Simulations – (CSEV RBV) project (£8,000 funded by Westminster Exchange, University of Westminster in 2012) and Ioannis Doumanis and Andrey Korubov for working on the development of this project.

BIBLIOGRAPHY

Bouki V and Economou D, 'Using Serious Games in Higher Education: Reclaiming the Learning Time' in D Preuveneers (ed.), *Volume 19: Workshop Proceedings of the 11th International Conference on Intelligent Environments* (IOS Press 2015) http://ebooks .iospress.nl/publication/39888 accessed 25 April 2019

Brown KJ and Murray CRG, 'Enhancing Interactivity in the Teaching of Criminal Law: Using Response Technology in the Lecture Theatre' in Kris Gledhill and Ben Livings (eds.), *The Teaching of Criminal Law: The Pedagogical Imperatives* (Routledge 2016)

Burns K and others, 'Active Learning in Law by Flipping the Classroom: An Enquiry into Effectiveness and Engagement' (2017) 27(1) Legal Education Review Article 14

Candlin CN, Bhatia VK and Jensen CH, 'Developing Legal Writing Materials for English Second Language Learners: Problems and Perspectives' (2002) 21(4) English for Specific Purposes 299

Clements AJ, Ahmed S and Henderson B, 'Student Experience of Gamified Learning: A Qualitative Approach' in Maja Pivec and Josef Grundler (eds.), *ECGBL 2017 11th European Conference on Game-Based Learning* (Academic Conferences International Limited 2017)

Copeland A, 'What Makes a Good Lawyer? Reflection, Clinical Education and Practitioners of the Future' (2016) 43(10) Brief 31

Daicoff SS, 'Lawyer, Form Thyself: Professional Identity Formation Strategies in Legal Education through Soft Skills Training, Ethics, and Experiential Courses' (2014) 27(2) Regent University Law Review 205

Domke LM, Weippert TL and Apol L, 'Beyond School Breaks: Reinterpreting the Uses of Film in Classrooms' (2018) 72(1) The Reading Teacher 51

Economou D and others, 'A Dynamic Role-Playing Platform for Simulations in Legal and Political Education', *2014 International Conference on Interactive Mobile Communication Technologies and Learning (IMCL2014)* (IEEE 2014)

'Evaluation of a Dynamic Role-Playing Platform for Simulations Based on Octalysis Gamification Framework' in D Preuveneers (ed.), *Volume 19: Workshop Proceedings of the 11th International Conference on Intelligent Environments* (IOS Press 2015)

'Westminster Serious Games Platform (Wmin-SGP) A Tool for Real-Time Authoring of Roleplay Simulations for Learning' (2016) 16(6) Future Intelligent Educational Environments Article 5

Gibbons J, 'Exploring Conceptual Legal Knowledge Building in Law Students' Reflective Reports Using Theoretical Constructs from the Sociology of Education: What, How and Why?' (2018) 52(1) The Law Teacher 38

Halpern C, 'The Mindful Lawyer: Why Contemporary Lawyers Are Practicing Meditation' (2012) 61(4) Journal of Legal Education 641

Hamari J, Huotari K and Tolvanen J, 'Gamification and Economics' in Steffen P Walz and Sebastian Deterding (eds.), *The Gameful World: Approaches, Issues, Application* (Massachusetts Institute of Technology Press 2015)

Hornsby Jr WE, 'Gaming the System: Approaching 100% Access to Legal Services through Online Games' (2013) 88(3) Chicago-Kent Law Review 917

Jackson A and Kerrigan K, 'The Challenges and Benefits of Integrating Criminal Law, Litigation and Evidence' in Kris Gledhill and Ben Livings (eds.), *The Teaching of Criminal Law: The Pedagogical Imperatives* (Routledge 2016)

Jensen K, Nerland M and Enqvist-Jensen C, 'Enrolment of Newcomers in Expert Cultures: An Analysis of Epistemic Practices in a Legal Education Introductory Course' (2015) 70 (5) Higher Education 867

Kift S, 'Lawyering Skills: Finding Their Place in Legal Education' (1997) 8(1) Legal Education Review 43

Koroma P and Antoniou N, 'Law Students' Clinic Experience: Is It All Hype in Relation to Performance on Black-Letter Law Exams?' (2017) 24(1) International Journal of Clinical Legal Education 58

Marsh L and Ramsden M, 'Reflections on a High School Mooting Competition: Bridging the Gap between Secondary and Tertiary Education' (2015) 49(3) The Law Teacher 323

Mentzelopoulos M and others, 'REVRLaw: An Immersive Way for Teaching Criminal Law Using Virtual Reality', *Communications in Computer and Information Science (CCIS)* (Springer, Cham 2016)

Miller C, 'The Gamification of Education' (2013) 40 Developments in Business Simulation and Experiential Learning 196

Pollard C, 'What Is Original in Merleau-Ponty's View of the Phenomenological Reduction?' (2018) 41(3) Human Studies 395

Quality Assurance Agency for Higher Education, 'Subject Benchmark Statements: Law' (Quality Assurance Agency for Higher Education 2015) www.qaa.ac.uk/docs/qaa/subject-benchmark-statements/sbs-law-15.pdf accessed 1 November 2018

Robson K and others, 'Is It All A Game? Understanding the Principles of Gamification' (2015) 58(4) Business Horizons 411

Saltmarsh S and others, 'Putting "Structure within the Space": Spatially Un/Responsive Pedagogic Practices in Open-Plan Learning Environments' (2015) 67(3) Educational Review 315

Signori GG and others, 'Gamification as an Innovative Method in the Processes of Learning in Higher Education Institutions' (2018) 24(2) International Journal of Innovation and Learning 115

Solicitors Regulation Authority and Bar Standards Board, 'Academic Stage Handbook' (Solicitors Regulation Authority and Bar Standards Board 2014) www.sra.org.uk/docu ments/students/academic-stage/academic-stage-handbook.pdf accessed 1 November 2018

Turner J, Bone A and Ashton J, 'Reasons Why Law Students Should Have Access to Learning Law through a Skills-Based Approach' (2018) 52(1) The Law Teacher 1

University of Westminster, 'Home – Serious Games at Westminster Research Group' www .westminster.ac.uk/serious-games-at-westminster-research-group accessed 30 August 2018

Virgil SM, 'The Role of Experiential Learning on a Law Student' (2016) 51(2) Wake Forest Law Review 325

11

Virtually Teaching Ethics

Experiencing the Discrepancy between Abstract Ethical Stands and Actual Behaviour Using Immersive Virtual Reality

Sylvie Delacroix and Catrina Denvir[1]

The CAVE experience is an immersive virtual reality (IVR) environment employing high-resolution, 3D video and audio technology. Using the CAVE, researchers at University College London designed an IVR scenario intended to echo the logical structure of a traditional 'trolley scenario' problem, and deployed this activity within an undergraduate Law and Ethics Course. In this chapter we explore how the use of virtual reality can offer students an unparalleled opportunity to reflect on the dissonance between the behaviour they adopt when faced with an ethical dilemma, and the theoretical stance they propose during class discussion. We explore how this personalisation gives rise to sustained student engagement borne out of a desire to understand the discrepancy between principle and practice. Our chapter considers the potential of IVR technology when teaching ethics to future and current professionals. We conclude by considering how such technology can offer more dynamic opportunities for student reflection and how IVR might be sensibly integrated into a broader legal ethics curriculum.

11.1 INTRODUCTION

It has previously been said that the early stages of legal study are designed to divorce legal reasoning from the influence of ethics. Students are expected to 'acquire the ability to think precisely, to analyse coldly, to work within a body of materials that are given'.[2] This is an achievement made possible by learning to 'lop off [one's] common sense, to knock [one's] ethics into temporary anaesthesia' such that an individual's view of social policy, their sense of justice, and any other form of 'woozy thinking' is thoroughly extinguished.[3]

[1] We would like to thank Xueni Pan and Mel Slater who let us use the virtual reality scenario they developed in the context of a prior study (see n 23 below). We would also like to thank David Swapp for his invaluable support when running the above scenario in University College London's CAVE.
[2] Karl N Llewellyn, *The Bramble Bush: On Our Law and Its Study* (Oceana 1960) 116.
[3] Ibid.

Although an individual's ability to see a problem through an ethical lens can safely be rekindled once the skills of legal analysis have been grasped, in England and Wales the study of professional ethics undertaken in preparation for practice tends to maintain a morally detached, rule-based focus. Teaching is orientated around familiarising students with regulatory rules, and requiring students apply this knowledge to a range of scenarios. In some ways this makes sense: if ethical dilemmas are to be resolved by reference to the rules contained in professional codes of conduct, then they ought to remain the focus of instruction. Yet whilst it is agreed that rules are of clear importance, it is also recognised that in the real world, 'they are an incomplete guide to ethical decision-making'.[4]

This is not just because the textual material (i.e. the rule/s) relied upon are often indeterminate.[5] It is also because there is a wide body of research demonstrating the pervasive effect of human emotion and cognitive bias on professional judgements, particularly morally loaded judgements. So whilst legal education sanctifies the objective, mechanistic process of decision-making said to be constitutive of 'legal reasoning', and proposes this form of reasoning as the foundation for resolving ethical dilemmas that arise in practice, this model presents as more aspirational than plausible.

The 'highly instrumental, rule-based character' of teaching and the overemphasis on rule craft to the exclusion of other models of learning also has other effects.[6] It is said to make it difficult to sustain student engagement,[7] as well as appealing to a narrow self-interest by emphasising the avoidance of punishment and liability, over and above encouraging development of mature professional identity.[8] These concerns force us to consider how constructivist approaches may empower educators to deliver training that is truly worthwhile,[9] moving beyond a focus on the 'transmission and temporary

---

[4]   M Robertson, 'Renewing a Focus on Ethics in Legal Education. Australian Lawyers and Social Change' (Australian Lawyers and Social Change Conference, Canberra, September 2004) https://law.anu.edu.au /sites/all/files/users/u4081600/Conference_docs/mikerobertson.pdf accessed 24 September 2018
[5]   Kim Economidies and Justine Rogers, 'Preparatory Ethics Training for Future Solicitors' (The Law Society 2009) 22.
[6]   Julian Webb, 'Taking Values Seriously: The Democratic Intellect and the Place of Values in the School Curriculum' in Michael Robertson and others (eds.), *The Ethics Project in Legal Education* (Routledge 2010).
[7]   See, e.g., Helen Kruuse, 'A South African Response to Ethics in Legal Education' in Michael Robertson and others (eds.), *The Ethics Project in Legal Education* (Routledge 2010); Linda Haller, 'Reading Reported Cases through a Legal Ethics Lens' in Michael Robertson and others (eds.), *The Ethics Project in Legal Education* (Routledge 2010).
[8]   Clark D Cunningham and Charlotte Alexander, 'Developing Professional Judgment: Law School Innovations in Response to the Carnegie Foundation's Critique of American Legal Education' in Michael Robertson and others (eds.), *The Ethics Project in Legal Education* (Routledge 2010) 87.
[9]   Here students are encouraged to take responsibility for their learning, to actively construct knowledge through their own experiences, and derive their own ethical identify through reflective thinking. See further Michael Robertson and others, 'Introduction' in Michael Robertson and others (eds.), *The Ethics Project in Legal Education* (Routledge 2010).

retention of information"[10] so as to produce greater 'ethical literacy by enhancing reflexivity"[11] among law students.

Drawing from previous case studies in the biomedical sciences, this chapter examines one such example, which uses immersive virtual reality (IVR) to enhance the (widely used) 'hypothetical ethical dilemma'. This chapter records the development and deployment of this educational tool, considers the novel nature of the reflective learning experience it facilitates, and details its pedagogical value. Drawing on the reflective post-immersion reports provided by students, it highlights the considerable potential of IVR within the legal curriculum.

11.2 REASONING, ETHICS AND ACTION

Professionals develop their craft by internalising complex cognitive structures and relying upon a mix of habits and intuitive understandings. This 'dual system' accounts for the two different ways in which we perceive and respond to a given situation. While system one (S1) produces fast, instinctive and emotional answers, system two (S2) stands for slower, deliberative modes of thought.[12] S2 is meant to supervise S1's fast, emotional and/or intuitive answers, however, when cognitive load disrupts this supervisory role, intuitions and emotions are given free(er) rein. This can prove problematic, as it can lead to an increase in erroneous judgements. This is particularly so when those judgements proceed from simplifying heuristics rather than applying a skill learned through experience.[13]

It is often assumed that when faced with an ethical dilemma, individuals recognise it for what it is and respond to it intentionally, preferably (in the case of law) by applying the relevant rules of conduct.[14] However, unethical behaviour often arises without intention to act unethically, either because an individual is unaware of the situation or unaware of the contextual influences. These 'blind spots' mean that being taught the rules of conduct is unlikely to improve ethicality. Most people routinely fail to recognise the ethical components of decisions and succumb to

---

[10] David F Chavkin, 'Experience Is the Only Teacher: Bringing Practice to the Teaching of Ethics' in Michael Robertson and others (eds.), *The Ethics Project in Legal Education* (Routledge 2010) 52.

[11] Lynda Crowley-Cyr, 'Towards Ethical Literacy by Enhancing Reflexivity in Law Students' in Michael Robertson and others (eds.), *The Ethics Project in Legal Education* (Routledge 2010).

[12] Daniel Kahneman, *Thinking, Fast and Slow* (Allen Lane 2011).

[13] Daniel T Gilbert, 'Thinking Lightly About Others: Automatic Components of the Social Inference Process' in James S Uleman and John A Bargh (eds.), *Unintended Thought* (Guilford Press 1989); Ellen Menaker and others, 'Harnessing Experiential Learning Theory to Achieve Warfighting Excellence', *Interservice/Industry Training, Simulation, and Education Conference (I/ITSEC)* (National Training and Simulation Association 2006); Swapnil Pawar and others, 'Evaluation of Cognitive Load and Emotional States During Multidisciplinary Critical Care Simulation Sessions' (2018) 4(2) BMJ Simulation and Technology Enhanced Learning 87.

[14] Max H Bazerman and Ann E Tenbrunsel, *Blind Spots: Why We Fail to Do What's Right and What to Do about It* (Princeton University Press 2011) 29.

common cognitive biases; as a result many responses to ethical dilemmas are characterised by ignorance rather than intention.[15]

If we are to assume that instructing students to divorce legal reasoning from ethics is standard practice, then we might see legal education as designed to enhance the dominance of S2. By strengthening students' S2 thinking, the impact of emotion on judgement can (presumably) be minimised. However in reality it does not appear to be quite this straightforward. The 'naturalistic decision-making' tradition (NDM), which owes its name to an endeavour to study how people actually make decisions under conditions (like high stakes or team dynamics) that are not easily replicated in the laboratory,[16] reveals that as experience accumulates it gives rise to 'skilled intuition'. Reliance on skilled intuition dominates under conditions of uncertainty and time pressure, which hamper S2's ability to evaluate a set of options systematically. S2 is not stirred into action unless it acknowledges a situation as 'new', or at any rate one that S1 is not coping well with.

These habits can make us blind to important features of the world we inhabit, since the acuity of both emotional and cognitive responses are blunted by their operation. The social conditioning (or 'habituation') process that shapes 'skilled intuition' may prevent S2 from ever identifying a situation as something demanding of renewed engagement. In a professional context, where the aims of one's practice require constant normative reinterpretation in light of the ethical obligations owed to others, to see past the 'usual client in the usual place', students must be taught to cultivate an ethical sensitivity that is sufficiently aware of its own fallibility. The question is how do legal educators go about the task of reviving the sensitivities of students who have 'knock[ed] [their] ethics into temporary anaesthesia'?[17]

11.3 ETHICS IN LEGAL EDUCATION AND TRAINING

Within and outside of the UK, the use of dilemmas in the teaching of legal ethics is widespread. Typically students are exposed to short written narrative, which describes a particular moral quandary. Having been given information about the quandary, students are then required to discuss how they might hypothetically respond. When used in the context of vocational training, ethical dilemmas provide an opportunity for students to apply professional rules to solve a problem inspired by professional practice, and allow students to apply their knowledge to a particular fact

---

[15] Ibid 37.
[16] See further Caroline E Zsambok and Gary Klein, *Naturalistic Decision Making* (Taylor and Francis 2014); Gary Klein, 'Naturalistic Decision Making' (2008) 50(3) Human Factors: The Journal of the Human Factors and Ergonomics Society 456.
[17] Llewellyn (n 2) 116.

scenario.[18] However, they also bring into question the plausibility of a rules-based approach to learning.

Within the sphere of legal education, practical moral reasoning is wrongly viewed as strictly analogous to theoretical reasoning, the central objective of which is to arrive at correct answers to specific problems. This view of moral reasoning and experience is too narrow, for moral reasoning is not so singularly outcome-determinative. Our evaluations of self and our actions, depend not only on getting our moral sums right, but also on having the appropriate attitudes and reactions to the moral situations in which we act. Yet frequently our ethicality is bounded by belief in our own morality, competence and deservedness, which is said to impede our ability to see the conflicts of interest that give rise to ethical dilemmas.[19]

Admittedly the 'legal problem question' works well when its purpose is to test candidates' knowledge of professional rules. However, students are primed to be on the look out for ethical issues that may more readily go unobserved in the real world.[20] Moreover, in real life, when it comes to dilemmas that amount to morally-loaded judgements, in which non-cognitive skills such as intuition and emotion have been shown to play a role, problem questions involving ethical dilemmas are poor preparation. When used slightly differently, ethical dilemmas have potential as a reflective learning tool. This is the case when students are forced to consider the gap that exists between their abstract stance and their actual behaviour, for it is here where the interplay between reasoning, skilled intuition, habituation and cognitive load is more clearly brought into view. This gives students an opportunity to reflect upon their own ethical identity by confronting the dissonance between their abstract position and their actual behaviour.

The failure of students to see when they are personally prone to ethical blind spots produces a key challenge for ethics education, that of 'inducing students to act in an ethical manner when faced with real challenges'.[21] Simulating the NDM process has the potential to contribute in a substantial way to a student's understanding of the factors (beyond rules) that impact upon ethically loaded professional judgements. NDM usually involves 'in situ' studies, though this is of questionable

[18] See, e.g., Task Force on Law Schools and the Profession – American Bar Association, 'Legal Education and Professional Development-An Educational Continuum. (MacCrate Report)' (American Bar Association 1992) 234–6 www.americanbar.org/content/dam/aba/publications/misc/legal_education/2013_legal_education_and_professional_development_maccrate_report).authcheckdam.pdf accessed 24 September 2018.
[19] Dolly Chugh, Max H Bazerman and Mahzarin R Banaji, 'Bounded Ethicality as a Psychological Barrier to Recognizing Conflicts of Interest' in Don A Moore and others (eds.), *Conflicts of Interest: Challenges and Solutions in Business, Law, Medicine and Public Policy* (Cambridge University Press 2005) 75.
[20] Richard Moorhead and others, 'The Ethical Capacities of New Advocates' (UCL Centre for Law and Ethics 2015) http://ssrn.com/abstract=2849698 accessed 24 September 2018.
[21] Kathleen A Tomlin and others, 'Are Students Blind to Their Ethical Blind Spots? An Exploration of Why Ethics Education Should Focus on Self-Perception Biases' (2017) 41(4) Journal of Management Education 539, 539.

appropriateness where it requires students to be thrust into clinical settings.[22] Alternatively, the use of IVR within education may enable students to gain a better understanding of the factors that impact upon morally loaded judgements, since it allows for those factors to be controlled and replicated with a high degree of precision.

11.4 VIRTUAL REALITY IN EDUCATION

Virtual reality allows for accurate and replicable immersion in a scenario whose ethical implications are not necessarily easily perceived (or dealt with) by professionals. The advantages of IVR as a training tool are twofold: first it allows for the development of the perceptual and intuitive skills that often condition the adequate apprehension of the ethical challenges inherent in a particular professional situation, and second it allows for group discussions aimed at teasing out what factors contribute to the frequent discrepancy between abstract ethical stands and actual behaviour.

IVR has been shown to elicit naturalistic response from individuals on account of two illusions: the illusion of being in a virtual place, and the illusion that the events occurring within that place are real.[23] The more primitive parts of our brain do not know about virtual reality and as a result participants cannot help but display the physiological signs associated with real pressure (e.g. sweat, increased heartbeat etc.). By the time the participant has 'reasoned' that the environment is simulated they have already responded realistically. This remains the case even when the graphics are relatively simple in nature.

The use of IVR for teaching and training is not new and it is already relied on in the context of an increasingly wide range of applications in and outside of the field of ethics.[24] However, the potential benefits of using IVR scenarios in the context of undergraduate legal education remain untested. This formed the impetus for our current investigation, which involved the development of an IVR scenario piloted within a Master of Laws (LLM) and Bachelor of Laws (LLB) Law and Ethics class during

---

[22] Klein (n 16); Zsambok and Klein (n 16).

[23] See, e.g., Xueni Pan and Mel Slater, 'Confronting a Moral Dilemma in Virtual Reality: A Pilot Study', *BCS-HCI '11 Proceedings of the 25th BCS Conference on Human-Computer Interaction* (BCS 2011); Mel Slater and others, 'A Virtual Reprise of the Stanley Milgram Obedience Experiments' (2006) 1(1) PLoS ONE https://doi.org/10.1371/journal.pone.0000039 accessed 19 May 2019; Aitor Rovira and others, 'The Use of Virtual Reality in the Study of People's Responses to Violent Incidents' (2009) 3 Frontiers in Behavioral Neuroscience 59.

[24] Xueni Pan and others, 'The Responses of Medical General Practitioners to Unreasonable Patient Demand for Antibiotics – A Study of Medical Ethics Using Immersive Virtual Reality' (2016) 11(2) PLoS ONE https://doi.org/10.1371/journal.pone.0146837 accessed 20 February 2016; Xueni Pan and others, 'A Study of Professional Awareness Using Immersive Virtual Reality: The Responses of General Practitioners to Child Safeguarding Concerns' (2018) 5 Frontiers in Robotics and AI 80; Pan and Slater (n 23); Slater and others (n 23). For a systematic review, see Mel Slater and Maria V Sanchez-Vives, 'Enhancing Our Lives with Immersive Virtual Reality' (2016) 3 Frontiers in Robotics and AI 74.

the 2016/17 academic year. This pilot exposed students to an IVR environment in which they were presented with a variation on the classic 'runaway trolley-car' dilemma.[25]

11.5 DEPLOYING IVR IN THE LEGAL ETHICS CURRICULUM

11.5.1 *Student Participants*

Although ethics training for aspiring legal professionals in England and Wales is not required until the vocational stage of study, at University College London (UCL) both LLB and LLM students have the opportunity to choose a 'Law and Ethics' module as part of their electives. The undergraduate 'Law and Ethics' subject that ran until 2016/17 was a year-long module made available to third year LLB students. Over the course of twenty-six weeks students were introduced to the process of critically assessing the role of law in dealing with increasingly complex ethical issues, focusing on three broad themes: (1) the ethics of risk; (2) libertarian paternalism; and (3) professional ethics.

The half-year LLM module had a similar focus, though was slightly narrower in scope. Consisting of ten weeks of two-hour seminars, the course aimed to bridge the gap between theory and practice when grasping the ethical challenges likely to shape professional practice. It was structured around two key themes: (1) understanding the factors that contribute to the discrepancy between abstract ethical stands and actual behaviour and (2) the ethical challenges (and opportunities) raised by the growth of artificial intelligence (AI).

11.5.2 *Procedure*

At an early stage within both modules (week three) students were given the opportunity to experience the CAVE – the IVR environment managed by the University's Computer Science Department. The CAVE projects images in real-time onto the surrounding walls and the floor. Specialised eyewear gives users the illusion of 3D objects appearing within and beyond the walls of the CAVE, whilst a head-tracking unit monitors movement to ensure the images displayed remain in the correct perspective.[26]

Students were required to answer two 'pre-CAVE' immersion questions, as detailed in Table 11.1 below. After the IVR experience, students shared their reflections in an online discussion board. This formed the basis of subsequent seminar discussions, which also briefly introduced students to recent findings in behavioural psychology and social neurosciences. In preparation for the two subsequent

---

[25]   Pan and Slater (n 23).
[26]   Technical description from University College London, 'Immersive Virtual Environments Laboratory' (2001) wwwo.cs.ucl.ac.uk/research/vr/Projects/Cave/ accessed 20 October 2018.

TABLE 11.1 *CAVE pre-immersion questions*

QUESTION 1

A runaway trolley is hurtling down the tracks towards five people who will be killed if it proceeds on its present course. You can save these five people by diverting the trolley onto a different set of tracks, one that has only one person on it, but if you do this that person will be killed. Is it morally permissible to turn the trolley and thus prevent five deaths at the cost of one?

Yes ☐ No ☐

QUESTION 2

Once again, the trolley is headed for five people. You are standing next to a large man on the footbridge spanning the tracks. The only way to save five people is to push this man off the footbridge and into the path of the trolley. Is that morally permissible?

Yes ☐ No ☐

seminars, students were required to read select pieces from the moral intuitionist and social neurosciences literature.

Because IVR has been associated with nausea and vision disturbance, the activity was voluntary. Students were given an information statement that warned of these possible side effects and requested that they did not operate machinery for at least three hours after using the equipment. Prior to participating, students were asked to provide written informed consent.

The IVR scenario drew on an adaption of a classic moral dilemma created by Pan and Slater and was used with their permission. Translating paper-based moral dilemmas, such as the trolley exercise that formed the basis of the pre-immersion questions above, raises a number of challenges. The scenario must achieve the same level of clarity as a written description, it has to be new to all participants, and it must not be highly implausible.[27] In order to address these concerns, Pan and Slater changed elements of the scenario and the setting so that:

> The participant is trained to use a lift (elevator) that takes visitors up to the first floor. Eventually an attacker in the lift starts shooting at 5 people who happen to be on the first floor. There is a switch next to the participant that controls the lift. Pushing the switch takes the attacker down to the ground floor, where one visitor happens to be standing. Therefore pushing the switch brings this one person on the ground floor into danger, but the five on the first floor are saved.[28]

Within the CAVE, students were paired together. In these partnerships they were shown this virtual art gallery occupying two floors (ground floor and first floor) with the first floor accessible only by way of a virtual lift.[29] Each student was shown how to operate the virtual lift using a wand so as to take visitors between floors. The

27 Pan and Slater (n 23) 47.
28 Ibid.
29 Screen captures of the scenario are depicted in Figures 1 and 2(a and b) of Pan and Slater (n 23).

TABLE 11.2 *CAVE post-immersion questions*

(A)	Did your reaction in the CAVE fit with your theoretical stance (i.e. deontological v. utilitarian)?
(B)	If it did, do you think your theoretical stance informed your action in the CAVE or was your action mostly influenced by other factors?
(C)	If there was a discrepancy between your theoretical stance and your action in the CAVE, why do you think this is so?

simulation then left the student pairs in control of the operation of the lift. As the simulation commenced, virtual visitors moved around the gallery until eventually five were on the upper level and one on the ground floor. Using the Action Condition (AC) variation of Pan and Slater's simulation,[30] the screen showed a seventh visitor entering and asking the lift operator (the student pair) to go to the upper level. Upon arrival, and while still on the lift, this seventh visitor started firing shots at the existing five visitors, with one visitor immediately injured. A range of audio effects, including loud gunshot sounds and screams, accompanied the scenario. Students were faced with the choice of doing nothing thereby leaving five visitors in peril, or pushing the switch controlling the lift to send it down again, thereby endangering the single visitor on the ground level.[31]

After the experience students were required to answer a series of follow-up questions designed to capture their reactions and thoughts, as shown in Table 11.2.

In the seminar that followed, students participated in a class discussion intended to explore the issues emerging from their IVR experience. This was intended to debrief students and to give them a chance to reflect upon their experiences. Students were encouraged to triangulate between their abstract stances, the actual action they took, and to explain and reason through this by drawing on the themes emerging in the course readings.

11.6 THE PEDAGOGICAL VALUE OF IVR

In order to demonstrate the way in which the IVR experience encouraged students to construct their own knowledge through reflection, in the next section we look at how receptive students were to the IVR experiment, and the pedagogical value of the exercise. As student feedback was anonymous, quotes are not attributed to a specific source.

---

[30]   'The AC involved the scenario described above – the participant has to act to take the lift holding the attacker down to the ground floor, thus saving five but endangering one. In the Omission Condition (OC), everything else was the same except that one visitor was on the first floor and five were on the ground floor. In this case if the participant did nothing, the one would be killed and the five saved.' Ibid 48.

[31]   Ibid 47.

11.6.1 *Student Experience and Reception*

Overall the experience was well received by the students. When asked to indicate their favourite seminar, more than half of LLM students (55.6 per cent) who gave feedback on the course, indicated that this was the most enjoyable seminar of the module. They reported that the experiment was exciting and that pairing the experiment with a seminar was seen as particularly valuable because it enabled 'a deeper discussion and an alternative perspective'. For some, the experience was particularly revelatory, with one student reporting that, '[The] seminar felt like a turning point in the course because the arguments for moral intuitionism were really explored in depth.' The practical element of the course was welcomed, with one student stating 'experiencing relevant themes by different forms, such as experiments, games and literature can attract our interests and help us understand the seminar content better'. For another student, the exercise provided a necessary corollary to the theoretical material covered, addressing the fact that the subject matter 'tends to be a bit abstract sometimes'. Students uniformly welcomed the opportunity to participate in further IVR simulations.

11.6.2 *Student Reflections*

The reflective answers students gave to the post-immersion questions provided evidence to support the view that the IVR exercise stimulated thinking around abstract ethical stands and actual behaviour. Many students were surprised by the effect that the IVR scenario actually had on their behaviour and how this led them to act in a way that did not align with their earlier theoretical stance. As was hoped, this led some students to consider how other factors such as emotion may have impacted upon their decision-making. As one student explained:

> In the pre-CAVE questionnaire I adopted a deontological approach to the two hypotheticals posed . . . The decision I made to move the gunmen away from the crowd however was more in response to [my partner's] reaction than to the simulation itself . . . I remember feeling slightly confused and held off making a decision for 3 seconds or so once [the gunman] started firing. [My partner] however suddenly burst out that I needed to do something and upon the hearing the emotion in her voice I immediately pressed the button to move the [gunman] away from the crowd.

Probing further, the same student concluded that:

> I felt that my behaviour was far more influenced by instinct and emotion than by any other considerations. Whenever a split-second decision is required, you're not so much acting as you're reacting. Therefore although I can rationalise why I think deontology is to be preferred in the abstract, in a situation such as the CAVE 'thinking' doesn't really enter into the equation.

Whilst for some it was the emotions of their partner that prompted action that deviated from their proposed stance, for others the contradiction between proposed action and actual action was a function of their own emotional reflexivity:

> I believe such discrepancy between my theoretical stance and my action was caused by emotion and instinct. Due to the urgency of the incident, the decision that I made was made nearly instantaneously; there was no room for hesitation for that would risk further injury and death. As a result, the decision was made not rationally, but by instinct. And I think instinct would tend to react in a utilitarian way since deep down we all wish to save as many people as we can.

In observing the shift from their deontological approach to the pre-immersion question, some students also considered how their consequentialist 'knee-jerk reaction, based on instinct' was actually misjudged. As one student reflected:

> I certainly wasn't thinking '[oh my god] what should I do, should I move the platform and save 5 people and put only one guy in a predicament'. When I heard the gunshots, I just pressed the button, in an attempt to get rid of the killer. My intuition told me that he'd go away once he's away from the zone in the middle. Sadly, it wasn't the case and he just started shooting the guy on the left.

The same student also went on to observe the difference between the pre-immersion scenario, which was based on an Omission Condition (OC), and the immersion scenario, which was based on an AC. This was also considered by another student, who in exploring how their action departed from their theoretical stance, stated that:

> I do think that the fact that my task was to move the platform made me feel like I should be entitled to some control over the situation, unlike the passer-by and train lever scenario where I one would be 'playing God' and interfering with fate. This likely had a great deal to do with my almost immediate reaction.

Interestingly, the experience also illustrated that students engaged with the concept of bounded ethicality – recognising that they did not appreciate the context of the scenario and its ethical ramifications until all was said and done. A consequentialist stance was often taken in spite of students not really having thought through the consequences of the various choices they could make. Instead, choice was informed by assumption, or as the following student put it, a degree of optimism:

> I immediately moved the platform to the left optimistically hoping the gunman would run off. With hindsight I realise that this was really foolish since the gunman could run off and shoot people outside the gallery. I think I just wanted him to leave the screen. When I saw the people on the sides running to stand up against the walls I realised what the dilemma would be ... I don't think I had a full understanding of the dilemma till after moving the platform.

Importantly, the scenario had the effect of conveying to students how decisions with moral weight may be made without moral consideration in a way that would not have been possible (or at least as tangible) without having participated in the simulation. Thus it encouraged students to reflect on their actions in a way that enriched engagement with the subject's core readings. As one student response demonstrated, 'I am hesitant to classify my reaction to move the gunman away as a moral judgment, because there was no evaluative process of right or wrong going on in my head (as defined in Haidt's article).'

The activity also encouraged a process of philosophical abstraction beyond the initial scenario. Reflecting on the concordance between their initial utilitarian abstract stance and their utilitarian response to the simulation, one student's post-immersion reflections revealed an internal debate in which they questioned whether a utilitarian would still make the decision to kill one person to save five, if 'that one man was a close family member'. They then proceeded to answer the question by exploring each of its two alternatives, stating that if the decision to save the five over the one was not made, then 'utilitarianism either cannot accommodate personal relationships or that it can – in which case are we still maximising utility?' These reflections highlight how students were actively engaging with the difficult theoretical concepts the course and the IVR experience introduced, seeking to make sense of these concepts and to deconstruct their meaning in light of alternative facts. In this way students were exhibiting the behaviour that Sharp sees as critical to identity formation – reflecting on personal values in light of understanding and then transforming these into projections (both personal and professional) of the path that lies ahead.[32]

Games have been identified as effective teaching and training devices not only because they promote student engagement, but also because 'They create dramatic representations of the real problem being studied. The players assume realistic roles, face problems, formulate strategies, make decisions and get fast feedback on the consequences of their actions.'[33] IVR builds upon these benefits superseding the immersive potential of both traditional techniques such as role-play and gameplay by allowing individuals to tap into the 'raw' emotional and intuitive reactions that often escape individual awareness. As with games, IVR can also enable the evaluation of student performance without the costs associated with errors made in real-world try-outs.[34]

In this case, IVR enabled students to tap into raw emotion and intuitive skill. Students reported various physiological responses to the scenario. As one student

---

[32] Cassandra Sharp, '"Represent a Murderer . . . I'd Never Do That!" How Students Use Stories to Link Ethical Development and Identity Construction' in Michael Robertson and others (eds.), *The Ethics Project in Legal Education* (Routledge 2010) 33.

[33] Clark C Abt, *Serious Games* (University Press of America 1987) 13.

[34] Roy Stuckey, 'Best Practices for Legal Education: A Vision and A Road Map' (Clinical Legal Education Association 2007) https://clea.wildapricot.org/Resources/Documents/best_practices-full.pdf accessed 28 September 2018.

described, 'I was influenced by fear and also a rise of adrenaline . . . we lost all of our self-control.' Such was the effect that the student did not remember who was controlling the joystick at the point the decision was made. Interestingly however the same student went on to say, 'I felt that this experience was too virtual to clearly impact my behaviour as a bystander.' This seemed to influence the justification given by some students as to why their abstract stance and their action stance produced such dissonance, with one proposing that their behaviour was influenced by the fact that:

> [Video] games tend to greatly downplay the importance of life and death . . . I think that our brains recognised that we were playing a game and naturally switched to a different set of ethical considerations, which only apply when playing. When arguments regarding the sanctity of life become essentially irrelevant, we tend to look at the sheer quantity of people we could save, thus favouring utilitarian decision-making.

Whilst some students were unconvinced that theirs was a true reaction, the IVR nevertheless served its purpose – enabling students to appreciate the gap between abstract ethical stance and real behaviour in a far more tangible manner than would have been possible through the use of a written hypothetical or role-play scenario. So although students saw this as a limitation, there is less reason for it to be considered a limitation by educators; since in this case, as in others, the narrative exists only to provide a foundation around which students can build their own moral discourse.[35]

IVR facilitated a move beyond the 'agenda to "mould" certain kinds of thinking' that has been said to dominate the teaching of legal ethics to date.[36] Instead, in line with what advocates for change encourage, the IVR experience provided students with the opportunity for decision-making and the opportunity for self-reflection in light of the choices made.[37] The focus on helping students see the gap between abstract stances and behavioural responses, notwithstanding the fact that some students felt that the scenario did not provoke a realistic response, goes some way towards addressing Webb's call for legal educators to provide opportunities for students to critically evaluate and reflect upon their values within a legal context.[38]

11.7 FUTURE APPLICATIONS

The purpose of the LLB and LLM subjects where IVR was deployed was not to meet the regulatory standards that tend to govern teaching at the vocational stage. Rather it

---

[35] For example, Sharp's critical analysis of the value of television texts to teaching ethics, did not identify the fictionality of the narrative as a barrier (Sharp (n 32) 47). So although IVR should strive to be immersive and generate real reactions, its failure to do so does not necessarily thwart its instructive potential, though it may call into question the validity of reactions captured, as is the case here.
[36] Ibid 36.
[37] Ibid.
[38] Webb (n 6) 9.

was designed to develop students' capacity for moral reasoning and by extension, introduce them to the issues that may influence this process. However, there is no reason why the methods we have described here cannot be used to familiarise students with the professional codes of conduct. This could be done through discussions that seek to consider student handling of particular dilemmas with reference to the professional rules, and/or it may take the form of new IVR scenarios that involve moral dilemmas that arise in practice. Given that there have been longstanding calls for pervasive professional ethics training throughout legal education, there is also potential for IVR to be used to prompt consideration of 'blind spots' that arise in practice by simulating legal tasks without drawing specific attention to ethical issues involved.

We recognise however that the practicality of any of these potential applications will continue to be constrained by pragmatic challenges. Central among these are the pressures on educators in higher education institutions that dissuade innovation.[39] Additionally, CAVE environments are costly, require designated space, cannot be moved and require programmers with specific skills; making it difficult for systems such as the CAVE to achieve widespread use in education and limiting the potential of this form of technology.[40]

Whilst creating an environment in which educators are incentivised to innovate is an issue that must be resolved at the institutional level, the issue of access to technology may in time resolve itself. As technology continues to develop, these tools become increasingly accessible, as do the interfaces for programming. The commercial availability and comparative affordability of systems such as Occulus Rift are illustrative in this regard. In time Augmented Reality (AR) tools may well overtake fully immersive ones in the context of professional education, especially given their advantages in group settings.

Separate to this is the question of how IVR might be linked with student performance evaluation. Though students were required to complete the post-immersion questionnaire, they were not graded on their reflections because of the need to maintain the voluntary nature of the IVR experience. However, there may be value in exploring how Kagan's 'Interpersonal Process Recall' approach (where students are videotaped in the simulation, and are then required to view the tape, reliving and verbalising their behaviour), or how other methods of self-evaluation might be utilised for assessment purposes.[41] Appropriate evaluation criteria may also

39 Denise Wood and Carolyn Bilsborow, 'Enhancing Creative Problem Solving in the Higher Education Curriculum through the Use of Innovative E-Learning Technologies', *8th International Conference on E-Learning (ICEL-2013) Proceedings* (Academic Conferences Limited 2013) 416.
40 Laura Freina and Michela Ott, 'A Literature Review on Immersive Virtual Reality in Education: State of the Art and Perspectives', *Conference Proceedings of ELearning and Software for Education* (Universitatea Nationala de Aparare Carol I 2015) 134.
41 See, e.g., Pan and others, 'The Responses of Medical General Practitioners to Unreasonable Patient Demand for Antibiotics – A Study of Medical Ethics Using Immersive Virtual Reality' (n 24); Kimberlee K Kovach, 'Virtual Reality Testing: The Use of Video for Evaluation in Legal Education' (1996) 46(2) Journal of Legal Education 233.

need to look beyond legal ethics so as to capture additional dimensions of competence.[42]

11.8 CONCLUSION

It has previously been said, 'higher education succeeds or fails in terms of motivation, not cognitive transfer of information. It succeeds if it instils in students a willingness to pursue knowledge.'[43] This being the case, our own perception as to the value of IVR is validated by the enthusiasm all students expressed when asked if they would be interested in participating in more IVR exercises in the future, as well as the degree of critical reflection that they engaged in afterwards. Whilst this suggests that there are benefits to incorporating IVR into the ethics curriculum, we would argue that these benefits go beyond just engaging students in the learning process or getting them excited about the subject material.

The approach adopted in this case study highlights the way in which IVR can help educators develop a more constructivist approach to the teaching of ethics. When students articulate, discuss and create stories from observations (simulated or real) they simultaneously give themselves the chance to evaluate, critically, what it is that they value and believe. Far from being just a method of engaging students in learning, the articulation of the students' stories about their own ethical development exemplified the critical process of 'identity in construction'.[44]

The IVR scenario deployed in the LLB and LLM Law and Ethics course provided a unique chance for students to apprehend a difficult situation in a way that allowed for both repetitive immersion and group discussion aimed at teasing out ethical lines of reasoning. It demonstrates how educators might move towards a more reflective curriculum and away from the dominant rule-based approach through which professional legal ethics is often examined. Yet, developing tools to enhance student learning remains a work-in-progress; one that is contingent upon educators being willing to depart from what has been tried and tested, so as to try and test themselves. Whilst IVR is just one tool in the arsenal of educators, for all the reasons we have identified above, it is a tool that merits greater attention.

---

[42] Eg framing the issue using professional knowledge; viewing the problem from multiple perspectives; recognising the possibility for harm, and; identifying analogous cases or scenarios and explaining their relevance. See Ilya M Goldin, Kevin D Ashley and Rosa L Pinkus, 'Introducing PETE: Computer Support for Teaching Ethics', *Proceedings of the 8th International Conference on Artificial Intelligence and Law* (ACM 2001) 98.

[43] Mihaly Czikszentmihalyi, 'Intrinsic Motivation and Effective Teaching: A Flow Analysis' (1982) 10 New Directions for Teaching and Learning 15.

[44] Sharp (n 32) 47.

BIBLIOGRAPHY

Abt CC, *Serious Games* (University Press of America 1987)

Bazerman MH and Tenbrunsel AE, *Blind Spots: Why We Fail to Do What's Right and What to Do about It* (Princeton University Press 2011)

Chavkin DF, 'Experience Is the Only Teacher: Bringing Practice to the Teaching of Ethics' in Michael Robertson and others (eds.), *The Ethics Project in Legal Education* (Routledge 2010)

Chugh D, Bazerman MH and Banaji MR, 'Bounded Ethicality as a Psychological Barrier to Recognizing Conflicts of Interest' in Don A Moore and others (eds.), *Conflicts of Interest: Challenges and Solutions in Business, Law, Medicine and Public Policy* (Cambridge University Press 2005)

Crowley-Cyr L, 'Towards Ethical Literacy by Enhancing Reflexivity in Law Students' in Michael Robertson and others (eds.), *The Ethics Project in Legal Education* (Routledge 2010)

Cunningham CD and Alexander C, 'Developing Professional Judgment: Law School Innovations in Response to the Carnegie Foundation's Critique of American Legal Education' in Michael Robertson and others (eds.), *The Ethics Project in Legal Education* (Routledge 2010)

Czikszentmihalyi M, 'Intrinsic Motivation and Effective Teaching: A Flow Analysis' (1982) 10 New Directions for Teaching and Learning 15

Economidies K and Rogers J, 'Preparatory Ethics Training for Future Solicitors' (The Law Society 2009)

Freina L and Ott M, 'A Literature Review on Immersive Virtual Reality in Education: State of the Art and Perspectives', *Conference Proceedings of ELearning and Software for Education* (Universitatea Nationala de Aparare Carol I 2015)

Gilbert DT, 'Thinking Lightly About Others: Automatic Components of the Social Inference Process' in James S Uleman and John A Bargh (eds.), *Unintended Thought* (Guilford Press 1989)

Goldin IM, Ashley KD and Pinkus RL, 'Introducing PETE: Computer Support for Teaching Ethics', *Proceedings of the 8th International Conference on Artificial Intelligence and Law* (ACM 2001)

Haller L, 'Reading Reported Cases through a Legal Ethics Lens' in Michael Robertson and others (eds.), *The Ethics Project in Legal Education* (Routledge 2010)

Kahneman D, *Thinking, Fast and Slow* (Allen Lane 2011)

Klein G, 'Naturalistic Decision Making' (2008) 50(3) Human Factors: The Journal of the Human Factors and Ergonomics Society 456

Kovach KK, 'Virtual Reality Testing: The Use of Video for Evaluation in Legal Education' (1996) 46(2) Journal of Legal Education 233

Kruuse H, 'A South African Response to Ethics in Legal Education' in Michael Robertson and others (eds.), *The Ethics Project in Legal Education* (Routledge 2010)

Llewellyn KN, *The Bramble Bush: On Our Law and Its Study* (Oceana 1960)

Menaker E and others, 'Harnessing Experiential Learning Theory to Achieve Warfighting Excellence', *Interservice/Industry Training, Simulation, and Education Conference (I/ITSEC)* (National Training and Simulation Association 2006)

Moorhead R and others, 'The Ethical Capacities of New Advocates' (UCL Centre for Law and Ethics 2015) http://ssrn.com/abstract=2849698 accessed 24 September 2018

Pan X and others, 'The Responses of Medical General Practitioners to Unreasonable Patient Demand for Antibiotics – A Study of Medical Ethics Using Immersive Virtual Reality'

(2016) 11(2) PLoS ONE https://doi.org/10.1371/journal.pone.0146837 accessed 20 February 2016

Pan X and others, 'A Study of Professional Awareness Using Immersive Virtual Reality: The Responses of General Practitioners to Child Safeguarding Concerns' (2018) 5 Frontiers in Robotics and AI 80

Pan X and Slater M, 'Confronting a Moral Dilemma in Virtual Reality: A Pilot Study', *BCS-HCI '11 Proceedings of the 25th BCS Conference on Human-Computer Interaction* (BCS 2011)

Pawar S and others, 'Evaluation of Cognitive Load and Emotional States During Multidisciplinary Critical Care Simulation Sessions' (2018) 4(2) BMJ Simulation and Technology Enhanced Learning 87

Robertson M, 'Renewing a Focus on Ethics in Legal Education. Australian Lawyers and Social Change' (Australian Lawyers and Social Change Conference, Canberra, September 2004) https://law.anu.edu.au/sites/all/files/users/u4081600/Conference_docs/mikerobertson.pdf accessed 24 September 2018

'Introduction' in Michael Robertson and others (eds.), *The Ethics Project in Legal Education* (Routledge 2010)

Rovira A and others, 'The Use of Virtual Reality in the Study of People's Responses to Violent Incidents' (2009) 3 Frontiers in Behavioral Neuroscience 59

Sharp C, '"Represent a Murderer . . . I'd Never Do That!" How Students Use Stories to Link Ethical Development and Identity Construction' in Michael Robertson and others (eds), *The Ethics Project in Legal Education* (Routledge 2010)

Slater M and others, 'A Virtual Reprise of the Stanley Milgram Obedience Experiments' (2006) 1(1) PLoS ONE https://doi.org/10.1371/journal.pone.0000039 accessed 19 May 2019

Slater M and Sanchez-Vives M V, 'Enhancing Our Lives with Immersive Virtual Reality' (2016) 3 Frontiers in Robotics and AI 74

Stuckey R, 'Best Practices for Legal Education: A Vision and A Road Map' (Clinical Legal Education Association 2007) https://clea.wildapricot.org/resources/documents/best_practices-full.pdf accessed 28 September 2018

Task Force on Law Schools and the Profession – American Bar Association, 'Legal Education and Professional Development – An Educational Continuum. (MacCrate Report)' (American Bar Association 1992) www.americanbar.org/content/dam/aba/publications/misc/legal_education/2013_legal_education_and_professional_development_maccrate_report).authcheckdam.pdf accessed 24 September 2018

Tomlin KA and others, 'Are Students Blind to Their Ethical Blind Spots? An Exploration of Why Ethics Education Should Focus on Self-Perception Biases' (2017) 41(4) Journal of Management Education 539

University College London, 'Immersive Virtual Environments Laboratory' (2001) wwwo.cs.ucl.ac.uk/research/vr/projects/cave/ accessed 20 October 2018

Webb J, 'Taking Values Seriously: The Democratic Intellect and the Place of Values in the School Curriculum' in Michael Robertson and others (eds.), *The Ethics Project in Legal Education* (Routledge 2010)

Wood D and Bilsborow C, 'Enhancing Creative Problem Solving in the Higher Education Curriculum through the Use of Innovative E-Learning Technologies', *8th International Conference on E-Learning (ICEL-2013) Proceedings* (Academic Conferences Limited 2013)

Zsambok CE and Klein G, *Naturalistic Decision Making* (Taylor and Francis 2014)

12

Paths to Practice

Regulating for Innovation in Legal Education and Training

Julie Brannan and Rob Marrs[1]

Most agree that lawyers of the future will need a greater understanding of how technology can be used to design and deliver legal services. The issue for those involved in setting content for any route to qualification is defining the extent to which this must be regulated, as much as identifying the right level of technological capability. The issue is not merely one of content, but the acquisition of competences. Any accreditation must look beyond simply ensuring capability in relation to discrete tools, looking instead to ensure that future solicitors have the ability to adapt to new technologies. Separately, consideration has to be given to the emerging profession of legal technologists. Whilst some technologists may be legally qualified, those that are not must understand the ethical boundaries and regulatory requirements that lawyers work within. The organisation of the legal profession and the regulatory boundaries shared between various stakeholders require us to consider whether accreditation is the right way forward, where responsibility for accreditation should lie and who should take initiative in this space. This chapter explores these issues by contrasting the approach adopted by the Solicitors Regulation Authority in England and Wales with that of the Law Society of Scotland.

12.1 INTRODUCTION

Over the last few decades legal practice in the United Kingdom (UK) has become, in the words of Van Zandt, 'far more of a competitive business and far less of a traditional guild'.[2] In conjunction with new technological developments it is proposed that 'the legal world will change more radically over the next two decades than over the last two centuries'.[3] These developments raise important issues for

---

[1]   The authors would like to thank Chloe Zeng and Sarah Watson of the Solicitors Regulation Authority for their assistance with earlier drafts.
[2]   David Van Zandt, 'Foundational Competencies: Innovation in Legal Education' (2009) 61(4) Rutgers Law Review 1127.
[3]   Richard Susskind, *Tomorrow's Lawyers: An Introduction to Your Future* (1st edn, Oxford University Press 2013) 13.

regulators in the UK who are tasked with ensuring that lawyers are fit for practice now and into the future. In setting standards for legal education and training, regulators must exercise their responsibility amidst an evolving profession in which the definition of 'competence' is dynamic and not static. Requirements must be stable yet forward-looking, requiring regulators to embrace improvement, exhibit a capacity for change, remain responsive to need and stimulate discussions as to the nature of that need. Further, regulators must determine how they should exercise their regulatory authority. This might involve, on the one hand specifying defined legal technology competences, or on the other, relying on market demand to produce the structural conditions in which educators are motivated to prepare students for a changing profession and incentivised to innovate.

To this end, this chapter considers the role of regulators in defining the scope of professional legal competency, prescribing the route by which competency is to be achieved, setting standards for emerging legal specialisations and promoting innovation in legal education. It does so by contrasting the approach adopted by the Solicitors Regulation Authority (SRA) in England and Wales, and that adopted by the Law Society of Scotland (the Society).

Whilst both organisations are responsible for setting standards for entry into the profession and both employ outcome-based competency frameworks, they differ in their methodology. The SRA recognises that it is not a regulator of legal education. It regulates legal services by reference to statutory objectives, which mean that its core regulatory purpose is consumer protection. Consumer protection requires both proper professional standards and access to justice. Its focus is therefore on assuring solicitors are safe to practise at the point of admission, rather than specifying how professional competences should be taught and acquired. This stands in contrast to the formal qualifying degree and training pathway requirements retained by the Society, which in recent years have been accompanied by the development of specialised accreditation schemes intended to drive forward an innovation agenda and recognise the increasing stratification of professional legal roles. Whilst the Society does set out defined pathways, it does so with a view to retaining room for educational innovation within those pathways.

In contrasting these approaches, we begin in the following section by first setting out the organisation of regulation in Scotland and England and Wales and identifying differences in the nature of the regulatory agencies in each jurisdiction. Second, we examine how professional competence is defined and the extent to which this definition is and should be forward-looking with regard to non-traditional skills such as technology. Third, we contrast the approaches taken by the SRA and the Society to legal education and training, examining the rationale underlying the different approaches adopted, including the approach taken to the accreditation of emerging legal specialisations. Our chapter demonstrates that there is more than one way by which regulators can regulate so as to facilitate innovation and support the growth of a legal education sector that adequately prepares professionals for the future.

12.2 THE REGULATION OF LEGAL EDUCATION

The nature of regulation of legal education differs between jurisdictions in the UK. In Scotland, the route to qualification is set by the Society, a professional body exercising a regulatory and representative function. It acquires the power to set the requirements for entry into the profession under the Solicitors (Scotland) Act 1980,[4] and as per Part II of the same act the Law Society is charged with setting the practical training and legal education requirements upon which entry to the profession is contingent.[5] The Legal Services (Scotland) Act 2010[6] outlines that two of the Society's regulatory functions are (i) setting standards of qualification, education and training, and (ii) admissions of persons to the profession.[7] Accordingly, the Society produces specifications for the vocational stage of training (PEAT 1)[8] and also specifications for the work-based stage of training (PEAT 2).[9] When combined with a 'fit and proper' person's test, successful completion of these stages renders an applicant eligible for entry to the solicitors' profession.

Up until 2007 regulation of the profession in England and Wales was organised in a similar manner to that of Scotland, with regulation overseen by the Law Society of England and Wales. However, following a recommendation that professional bodies holding regulatory and representative responsibilities should separate those functions[10] (later given effect by the Legal Services Act[11]) the Legal Services Board was established as a separate legal regulator. The Legal Services Board in turn devolved regulatory oversight of professional competence to the SRA as the approved regulator of solicitors.

Until recently, this splitting of the representative and regulatory functions achieved by the Legal Services Act 2007 has had little impact upon the training

---

[4] Solicitors (Scotland) Act 1980 (c. 46).
[5] Ibid. § 4–5.
[6] Legal Services (Scotland) Act, 2010 (asp 16).
[7] See further Law Society of Scotland, 'Foundation Programme (Scottish Exempting Degree) – Accreditation Guidelines for Applicants' (Law Society of Scotland 2010) www.lawscot.org.uk /media/359157/foundation-programme-guidelines.pdf accessed 31 October 2018.
[8] See further Law Society of Scotland, 'Professional Education and Training (PEAT) Stage 1: Accreditation Guidelines for Applicants' (Law Society of Scotland 2010) www.lawscot.org.uk /media/9123/peat-1-guidelines.pdf.
[9] See further Law Society of Scotland, 'Professional Education and Training (PEAT) Stage 2: Outcomes' (Law Society of Scotland 2010) www.lawscot.org.uk/media/8913/peat-2-outcomes.pdf accessed 1 November 2018.
[10] See David Clementi, 'Review of the Regulatory Framework for Legal Services in England and Wales' (TSO 2004).
[11] Legal Services Act 2007 ss 29–30.

requirements prescribed in England and Wales. As before the change, the current SRA Training Regulations Handbook[12] continues to require prospective solicitors pass an academic stage by obtaining a qualification covering specified topics set out in a joint statement by the Law Society and the General Council of the Bar.[13] The rules also require prospective solicitors undertake accredited vocational training, followed by a two-year period of workplace training with a recognised training provider capable of providing practical experience across three different areas of law.[14] However, the SRA's decision to introduce a Solicitors Qualifying Examination (SQE) in England and Wales from 2021 onwards denotes a clear step-change in regulatory approach and a significant departure from the existing model.[15]

The SQE is a centralised assessment to be introduced for all prospective solicitors, which will replace the existing academic and vocational stages, and is intended to fulfil the call for rigorous and consistent learning outcomes. It does so by focusing on the assurance of entry standards for the profession intended to protect consumers by testing knowledge of the core competencies needed for safe practice. The SQE will be an independently set, standardised assessment in two parts. The first part ('SQE1') will assess candidates' ability to use their legal knowledge in transactions or litigation. The second part ('SQE2') is an assessment of candidates' practical legal skills including client interviewing, rights of audience, case and matter analysis, legal research and written advice and legal drafting.[16] The assessment focuses primarily on reserved activities.[17] Unflagged ethical questions will pervade the entire exam. In order to be admitted as a solicitor, candidates must also have a degree or equivalent qualification (though not necessarily in law) and complete a two-year period of qualifying legal work experience (QWE). QWE can comprise any work experience in legal services, which enables a candidate to develop the competences needed for practice as a solicitor. In short, the introduction of the SQE is intended to fundamentally reorientate the purpose of regulation in England and Wales towards the objective of assuring competence, rather than specifying how competence should be achieved.

---

[12]   Authorised under sections 2, 28, 79, and 80 of the Solicitors Act 1974 (c. 47) with the approval of the Legal Services Board under paragraph 19 of Schedule 4 to the Legal Services Act 2007 ss 29–30 (n 11).

[13]   Solicitors Regulation Authority and Bar Standards Board, 'Academic Stage Handbook' (Solicitors Regulation Authority and Bar Standards Board 2014) 15–20 www.sra.org.uk/documents/students/academic-stage/academic-stage-handbook.pdf accessed 1 November 2018.

[14]   Solicitors Regulation Authority, 'Student Information Pack' (2017) www.sra.org.uk/students/resources/student-information.page accessed 1 November 2018.

[15]   Solicitors Regulation Authority, 'A New Route to Qualification: The Solicitors Qualifying Examination (SQE) – A Summary of Responses and Next Steps' (Solicitors Regulation Authority 2017) www.sra.org.uk/documents/SRA/consultations/sqe-summary-responses.pdf accessed 31 October 2018.

[16]   Ibid.

[17]   See ibid; Solicitors Regulation Authority, 'Solicitors Qualifying Examination – Draft Assessment Specification' (2017) www.sra.org.uk/sra/policy/sqe.page# accessed 31 October 2018.

12.3 DEFINING PROFESSIONAL COMPETENCE

Whilst the path to admission as a solicitor in Scotland as compared to England and Wales has deviated over the last decade, there remains significant overlap with respect to core areas of knowledge set down by regulators in each jurisdiction. In Scotland, competence to practice requires knowledge of the legal system and legal method; public law; obligations (or contract); criminal law; evidence; procedure; trusts and succession (or equity); ethics and professional conduct; private client; conveyancing; litigation; business; financial and practice awareness; and tax during the academic and vocational stages.[18] The required outcomes for the work-based stage are built around professionalism; professional communication; professional ethics and standards; business, financial, commercial and practice awareness; and substantive and relevant legal knowledge (which will differ from practice to practice). Both the existing academic and vocational stage in England and Wales,[19] as well as the knowledge tested via the SQE,[20] covers the same ground.

Amidst a changing profession, there have been frequent calls for regulators to consider expanding beyond these core domains of knowledge, setting down a broader range of prescribed skills at the academic and vocational stage, including technology-related skills. Similarly, providers of legal education (particularly at the academic stage) have also been encouraged to take the initiative in regard to curriculum innovation. To move away from a focus on knowledge of the law as opposed to knowledge of the practice of law, and to avoid 'provid[ing] law students with the essential content for something which really no longer exists – a career as a solicitor in general practice'.[21] This is notwithstanding the fact that legal educators particularly those in academic settings, may not be best placed to identify the skills needed by practitioners. As has been alleged, 'The essential how-tos of daily practice are a subject that many in the faculty know nothing about – by design.'[22]

---

[18] Law Society of Scotland, 'Foundation Programme (Scottish Exempting Degree) – Accreditation Guidelines for Applicants' (n 7) 18–28.

[19] Sources of law, institutions and personnel, public law (constitutional, administrative and human rights), EU law, criminal law, obligations (contract, restitution and tort), property, equity and trusts, business law and practice, property law and practice, litigation (civil and criminal), wills and administration of estates, taxation. See further Solicitors Regulation Authority and Bar Standards Board (n 13) 15–20.

[20] Principles of Professional Conduct, Public and Administrative law, the Legal Systems of England and Wales, Dispute Resolution in Contract or Tort, Property Law and Practice, Commercial and Corporate Law Practice, Wills and the Administration of Estates and Trusts, and Criminal Law and Practice. See further Solicitors Regulation Authority, 'Solicitors Qualifying Examination – Draft Assessment Specification' (n 17); Solicitors Regulation Authority, 'Statement of Legal Knowledge' www.sra.org.uk/knowledge/ accessed 31 October 2018.

[21] Neil Rees, 'I Look Ahead' (Sir Ninian Stephen Lecture, The University of Newcastle, Newcastle, 10 September 2015) 22.

[22] David Segal, 'What They Don't Teach Law Students: Lawyering' *New York Times* (New York, 19 November 2011) www.nytimes.com/2011/11/20/business/after-law-school-associates-learn-to-be-lawyers.html accessed 10 July 2018.

Reaching stakeholder consensus with regard to the constellation of knowledge, skills, attitudes and values needed to ensure that solicitors are safe to practise remains difficult. This difficulty is amplified by the fact that the profession is not homogeneous: the skills and knowledge required for practice in a global commercial law firm are very different to those needed to advise a child in the police station. For this reason, not all agree that new skills such as technological competency are even relevant for legal practice. Whilst few would deny that technology will profoundly affect the way that legal services are delivered in the future, it does not automatically follow that individual solicitors must be competent in technology as well as the law.

Such skills may be best left to those who have trained specifically in technology and who can bring these skills to bear by working collaboratively with solicitors. In the SRA's consultation on the Statement of Solicitor Competence (which is what the SQE assesses), the vast majority of respondents agreed that it reflected the competency requirements of a solicitor even though no mention was made of Information Technology (IT) skills.[23] Similarly, the 2013 Legal Education and Training Review (LETR) review which focused on preparing lawyers 'fit for the future' in England and Wales, mentioned technology skills only briefly and as a component of broader skills related to commercial awareness.[24] Whilst there is truth to the argument that 'Technology is critical to serving clients at all levels, from legal aid to complex work for corporate entities it is also the case that the specifics of this use differ widely across the profession.'[25]

Added to this is the difficulty inherent in the fact that the development of new technology and the competency such technology demands from users, changes far more rapidly than legal educators or regulators might reasonably accommodate. In 'Educating the Digital Lawyer', Kimbro outlines the core components of a digital curriculum.[26] The topics suggested cover privacy and online networking; internet security and how hackers work; protecting confidentiality; metadata; social media marketing; working virtually with paralegals; SEO and meta-tags; the digital footprint; managing files and e-discovery; unauthorised practice of law (UPL) risks in e-lawyering; cloud-based applications; unbundling legal services; and ethics and the use of technology. In a similar exercise, Canick provides a broader range of

---

[23]   Solicitors Regulation Authority, 'A Competence Statement for Solicitors – SRA Response to the Consultation' (Solicitors Regulation Authority 2015) 2 www.sra.org.uk/documents/sra/consultations/competence-statement-consultation-response.doc.

[24]   Julian Webb and others, 'Setting Standards: The Future of Legal Services Education and Training Regulation in England and Wales (Legal Education and Training Review)' (SRA, BSB and CILEX 2013) www.letr.org.uk/wp-content/uploads/LETR-Report.pdf accessed 17 August 2018.

[25]   Christy Burke, 'Winning the Battle to Teach Legal Technology and Innovation at Law Schools' (*Legal IT Today*, 17 March 2017) http://burke-company.com/wp-content/uploads/2017/04/LegalITToday-Winning-the-battle-to-teach-legal-technology-and-innovation-at-law-schools.pdf accessed 10 July 2018 (quoting Daniel Linna).

[26]   Stephanie Kimbro, 'What Should Be in a Digital Curriculum: A Practitioner's Must Have List' in Marc Lauritsen and Oliver Goodenough (eds.), *Educating the Digital Lawyer* (Lexis Nexis e-Books 2012).

suggestions, including context-based technology training related to e-discovery, presentation skills, communication and collaboration, marketing and social media, hardware and software, and legal research and case management.[27] Were these suggestions (made in 2012 and 2014 respectively) updated for the present year, we might expect distributed ledgers, machine learning, predictive coding and data protection to feature.

If regulators are tasked with producing trained people who can operate as lawyers in their jurisdiction and technology skills are required for lawyers to function competently then the argument that it is incumbent upon regulators to require technology skills of new lawyers, holds some weight. As a result, some jurisdictions have moved in the direction of prescribing a wider range of non-traditional skills. For example, IT skills form an element of professional competence in Canada,[28] whilst the American Bar Association has decreed that proficiency with technology is part of the intrinsic competence of being a lawyer.[29] In a similar vein the Scottish Law Society has incorporated certain basic skills into the solicitors' competency framework since 2009, and more recently, has worked to develop a scheme to formally accredit those who demonstrate additional skills in technology.[30]

Making legal technology a regulatory requirement certainly incentivises legal educators to include the skills specified by the regulator as necessary. However, adding to the core knowledge base is not without difficulty. As already stated, there is the challenge of keeping regulations up to date with technological developments. In addition, law schools in many jurisdictions argue that the curriculum is too full, that regulatory requirements are already onerous, and that it is difficult to find people to teach legal technology skills.[31] In spite of universities coming under increasing pressure to be responsive, agile and differentiated in response to the increasingly consumer-driven market for higher education and rapid changes to legal practice, examples of innovation in higher education remain few and far between. These arguments force us to consider if regulators can encourage legal educators to respond to the changing nature of the profession, without setting down extra knowledge requirements for practice. To this end the approach taken by the SRA in England and Wales offers food for thought. It demarcates a shift away from

---

[27] Simon Canick, 'Infusing Technology Skills into the Law School Curriculum' (2014) 42(3) Capital University Law Review 663.

[28] Webb and others (n 24).

[29] ABA Model Rule 1.1.8: To maintain the requisite knowledge and skill, a lawyer should keep abreast of changes in the law and its practice, including the benefits and risks associated with relevant technology, engage in continuing study and education and comply with all continuing legal education requirements to which the lawyer is subject'. See American Bar Association, 'Model Rules of Professional Conduct' (2018) www.americanbar.org/groups/professional_responsibility/publications/model_rules_of_professional_conduct/rule_1_1_competence/comment_on_rule_1_1/ accessed 1 November 2018.

[30] Law Society of Scotland, 'Legal Tech Assessment' (2018) www.lawscot.org.uk/members/cpd-training/legal-tech-assessment/ accessed 20 August 2018.

[31] Webb and others (n 24).

prescribing more than the essential, core knowledge and competences required for safe practice and from specifying how professional competences should be acquired, and in doing so is designed to allow the legal education market to respond flexibly.

The Society and the SRA provide an interesting contrast in their approach to fulfilling their regulatory duty. Both are charged with ensuring solicitors are fit for practice by instituting appropriate qualification processes, and yet the way in which they go about this substantially differs. For the SRA, innovation in legal education (including emphasis on the acquisition of non-traditional skills) arises when regulators give legal educators greater freedom and flexibility. In contrast, the Society's efforts to prescribe certain non-traditional skills as part of core requirements and to recognise the emergence of professional specialisations through accreditation schemes, suggests adherence to the view that educators and students must be motivated to widen their skill set or, at least, be given credit when they do. Taken together, these approaches illustrate that there is more than one way by which regulators might work to facilitate innovation and support the emergence of a legal education sector that adequately prepares professionals for the future. With this in mind, in the following section we explore the rationale underpinning the approach adopted by each regulator and their associated benefits and limitations.

12.4 CONTRASTING APPROACHES TO THE REGULATION OF LEGAL EDUCATION

12.4.1 *The Law Society of Scotland*

The current legal education and training pathway in place in Scotland has its origins in a full-scale review of the route to qualification undertaken by the Law Society from 2006 to 2009. This review yielded the current model of 'Professional Education and Training (PEAT)' consisting of a first component (PEAT 1) which focuses on vocational study and performance, and a second component (PEAT 2) which encompasses two years of work experience under the supervision of a qualified lawyer.[32] Technology features as a core outcome of professional communication in the PEAT 1 training outcomes, with graduates required to demonstrate:[33]

- The ability to communicate electronically via phone and email
- Use of electronic drafting tools
- Familiarity with electronic case management systems
- Familiarity with speech to text systems

---

[32] Law Society of Scotland, 'Professional Education and Training (PEAT) Stage 1: Accreditation Guidelines for Applicants' (n 8); Law Society of Scotland, 'Professional Education and Training (PEAT) Stage 2: Outcomes' (n 9).

[33] Law Society of Scotland, 'Professional Education and Training (PEAT) Stage 1: Accreditation Guidelines for Applicants' (n 8) 55–6.

- The ability to explain how technology affects current legal practice in Scotland in three areas of legal practice
- The ability to discuss the direction of future trends in legal office technology, and
- Knowledge of the risk posed to client confidentiality by different forms of communication technology.

Additionally, accredited providers of training at the PEAT 1 level are required to exhibit, among other requirements, 'awareness of the state-of-the-art in relation to . . . technology'.[34]

The inclusion of these technology skills as required components of vocational training is intended, in part, to reflect the Society's view (formed in collaboration with academy and the profession) that these knowledge skills are fundamental to the ability to practise as a lawyer. Inclusion of these skills also addresses the erroneous, yet widely held belief, that the new generations of lawyer are 'digital natives' capable of excelling in their use of technology without specific training. As has been recognised by Bates, 'the teaching of research skills to digital natives is actually more important, because a greater level of basic IT knowledge often results in students having a higher opinion of their own abilities than is actually the case'.[35] Whilst the ability to successfully navigate social media may be useful in legal practice, it is unlikely to be a foundation for technological competence. The training requirements also recognise that the focus cannot be solely on higher-level technology skills such as artificially intelligent technologies. As Gayal notes: 'Young lawyers are not always open or motivated to train themselves on the use of legal technology or even basic applications such as MS Word or MS Excel.'[36]

By including basic technology outcomes in PEAT 1, these non-traditional (often-overlooked IT skills) are elevated to a required component of legal education by way of learning outcomes incorporated into specific stages in the route to qualification. Similar requirements are demanded of trainees in the subsequent work-based PEAT 2 stage. As such, these skills are integrated into the training pathway at an appropriate stage depending on the point at which the Society (as regulator), determines that a trainee solicitor needs to know, or should be able to perform certain tasks. Within PEAT 1, up to 50 per cent of content remains elective; the Society does not mandate what is taught and the PEAT 1 provider can offer the elective course it believes will most benefit students.[37] These courses are often designed in collaboration with

---

[34] Ibid 116.
[35] Daniel Bates, 'Are "Digital Natives" Equipped to Conquer the Legal Landscape?' (2013) 13(3) Legal Information Management 172, 177.
[36] Monica Goyal, 'Do Lawyers and Law Students Have the Technical Skills to Meet the Needs of Future Legal Jobs?' (*Slaw*, 29 June 2017) www.slaw.ca/2017/06/29/do-lawyers-and-law-students-have-the-technical-skills-to-meet-the-needs-of-future-legal-jobs/ accessed 20 July 2018.
[37] Law Society of Scotland, 'Professional Education and Training (PEAT) Stage 1: Accreditation Guidelines for Applicants' (n 8) 8–9.

practising lawyers, and numerous PEAT 1 training providers already offer an elective course in legal technology.[38] This means that as well as the minimum standard outlined by the professional body; PEAT 1 offers students the flexibility to learn more about legal technology where this content is offered through electives.

Whilst there are advantages to the incorporation of technology skills as a core element of vocational training, doing so produces a number of challenges. The first is that the incorporation of such skills operates prospectively rather than retrospectively, it therefore does not apply to existing practitioners and sets a higher level of competence for a new generation of lawyers than the existing generation currently in practice. This may not necessarily be a problem since as law and practice changes it is expected that the subjects taught to one generation may be different to that of the next. However, concern might be warranted if the lack of technological literacy amongst the cohort of existing practitioners leads them to undervalue technology skills within the emerging generation of graduates. For this reason mandatory requirements must strike a balance between being basic enough to set a competent standard, without being so specific that they are seen as irrelevant to much of the profession. Finding this balance is not always easy.

Second, in fast-moving fields such as technology, skills move quickly from being novel in nature, to forming a standard part of engaging with the modern world. Regulators must ensure that the requirements keep pace with developments and this demands a commitment to ongoing revision and updating of material. At the same time the academy and practice require certainty from regulators regarding the learning outcomes that students and trainee lawyers are required to meet. Change cannot be constant and outcomes need to be met by trainee lawyers at practices of all sizes. As change has to be negotiated between the Law Society, the academy and the profession, there is a temptation to draft such learning outcomes in a relatively generic way. This can lead to many in the community feeling the outcome is vague and meaningless. Although it is not easy, the view from the Society is that the only solution is to support dialogue between stakeholders so as to arrive at consensus with regard to the specificity of outcomes.

Third, the IT requirements are presently embedded within the vocational stage and therefore focus on technology as a tool to achieve certain legal tasks. However, as the use and application of artificial intelligence in legal practice continues, there is a need to consider the extent to which some topics ought to be studied as part of the academic stage. Such technologies bring the capacity to augment the delivery and constitution of legal knowledge, and as such they raise complex philosophical issues with which practitioners ought to engage.[39] However, the degree stage in most

---

[38] See further University of Glasgow, 'Professional Legal Practice (Diploma)' (2018) www.gla.ac.uk /postgraduate/taught/professionallegalpracticediploma/ accessed 1 November 2018.

[39] See, e.g., Mireille Hildebrandt, 'Law as Information in the Era of Data-Driven Agency' (2016) 79(1) The Modern Law Review 1; Mireille Hildebrandt, 'A Vision of Ambient Law' in Roger Brownsword and Karen Yeung (eds.), *Regulating Technologies: Legal Futures, Regulatory Frames and*

jurisdictions is often lamented as being too full and it is not always immediately clear how technology skills and knowledge can be embedded without seeing something else removed. Yet it does remain possible to teach existing core legal modules differently, to incorporate technology as part of these subjects rather than separate to them. Similarly joint or combined degrees may in time become more common: at least one Scottish university now offers a 'Computer Science/ Law' degree and others may well follow.

Incorporating basic technology skills into PEAT 1 addresses the core requirement for technological competence, though they are not the only way in which the Society regulates for the future. Other measures, such as incorporating the expectation that 'solicitor(s) will regularly look at ways in which technology can support client service(s)' dictated within the profession's standards of service represent a commitment to producing cultural change in the profession.[40] Further, these types of soft requirements also commit solicitors who may not have been exposed to the technology training requirements introduced by PEAT 1, to familiarise themselves with the field. This familiarisation is supported by the Society's provision of a range of Continuing Professional Development (CPD) courses on legal technology and the Society's promotion among members, of a 'Legal Technology Assessment (LTA)'. This is an online training tool intended to improve skills in Word, Excel and PDF, designed by Casey Flaherty and provided by Procertas.[41] These initiatives exemplify efforts taken by a regulator to mainstream legal technology capabilities and to look beyond the tendency to 'generally focus on law students', when discussing 'how people can become more technologically literate or technologically competent'.[42]

These developments go hand in hand with the Society's proactive creation of new membership categories,[43] including an 'Accredited Legal Technologist' classification earmarked for introduction in 2019. The accreditation, developed following more than eighteen months of stakeholder consultation, utilises a 'belted' ranking system in which individuals develop their skills from beginner through to expert, and exhibit competency in both general and applied dimensions of technology. Whilst such initiatives are taken as part of the Society's representative rather than regulatory capacity, they align with the interventionist approach to non-traditional skill acquisition that the Society has exhibited when exercising its regulatory functions. Just as

Technological Fixes (Hart 2008); Mireille Hildebrandt, *Smart Technologies and the End(s) of Law: Novel Entanglements of Law and Technology* (Edward Elgar 2015).

[40] Law Society of Scotland, 'Standards of Service' www.lawscot.org.uk/members/rules-and-guidance /rules-and-guidance/section-e/division-a/guidance/standards-of-service/ accessed 20 August 2018.

[41] See further Law Society of Scotland, 'Legal Tech Assessment' (n 30).

[42] Rob Marrs, 'Technology and the Law: Who, Where and How?' (*Law Society of Scotland News,* 2017) www.lawscot.org.uk/news-and-events/news/technology-and-the-law-who-where-and-how/ accessed 20 August 2018.

[43] John Hyde, 'Law Society of Scotland Opens Door to Non-Solicitors' *Law Society Gazette* (London, 13 August 2015) www.lawgazette.co.uk/news/law-society-of-scotland-opens-door-to-non-solicitors /5050551.article accessed 20 July 2018.

PEAT 1 provides an incentive for educators to take IT skills seriously, the creation of new membership categories encourages educators, students and (solicitor and non-solicitor) professionals to value non-traditional skills by recognising the acquisition of these skills and vetting their obtainment in conjunction with industry experts.[44]

12.4.2 *The Solicitors' Regulation Authority (England and Wales)*

In contrast, the SRA has taken a somewhat different approach in its efforts to produce a legal education environment where regulatory standards do not operate to stifle innovation and creativity amongst education providers. Unlike PEAT 1, the SQE makes no reference to non-traditional skills in IT and such skills are not required in order to qualify as a solicitor in England and Wales under the new SQE model. This reflects the SRA's view that statutory powers to specify the education, training and assessment of solicitors[45] are not an end in and of themselves, but rather a means by which to ensure solicitors are competent. For the SRA, this translates to a requirement that regulators step back from prescribing more than the core knowledge and competences required for safe practise, and from specifying how professional competences should be acquired. The SRA takes the view that while technology undoubtedly is required to enable solicitors to practise effectively, it does not follow that technology skills must be required of all solicitors. It is sufficient that legal businesses can acquire these skills however suits them best. Such an approach, it is argued, strikes the right balance between protecting consumers and promoting access to justice on the one hand and, on the other, freeing up universities to educate law students and meet changing market demands in the ways they think best.[46]

An outcomes-focused regulatory approach to education and training means a shift from regulating educational processes (specifying how candidates are taught), to regulating the outcomes of those processes (assessing what candidates have learned). Such an approach recognises that universities are the expert teachers and gives them the freedom to decide how best to educate their students. Yet the approach taken by the SRA to step back from prescribing educational requirements in detail has been criticised from both sides. For some, the changes are insufficiently prescriptive with

---

[44] This status may be subsumed into a wider type of membership of the Law Society of Scotland. There is an ongoing review of legal services in Scotland. See further: Scottish Government, 'Review of the Regulation of Legal Services' (*gov.scot*, 2019) www2.gov.scot/About/Review/Regulation-Legal-Services accessed 5 February 2019; Esther A Roberton, 'Fit for the Future: Report of the Independent Review of Legal Services Regulation in Scotland' (Scottish Government 2018) www2.gov.scot/Resource/0054/00542583.pdf accessed 20 July 2018; Law Society of Scotland, 'Independent Review of Legal Services Regulation: Response from the Law Society of Scotland' (Law Society of Scotland 2018) www.lawscot.org.uk/media/360006/review-of-legal-services-tp.pdf accessed 5 February 2019.

[45] Solicitors Act 1974 (c. 47) (n 12) § 2–3.

[46] See further Solicitors Regulation Authority, 'A New Route to Qualification: The Solicitors Qualifying Examination (SQE) – A Summary of Responses and Next Steps' (n 15).

regard to certain skills such as technology, whilst for others they 'have the effect of dramatically overregulating legal undergraduate education, with a particular likelihood of inhibiting, rather than promoting, innovation'.[47] Evidently the changes introduced by the SQE are either too prescriptive, or not prescriptive enough, depending on one's point of view, but what support is there for the claim that these changes enhance rather than inhibit educational innovation?

First, changes introduced by the SQE give law schools freedom to decide what to teach. Unlike the previous legal education pathway where a strong division between the academic and vocation stages of training was maintained and where the components of a qualifying law degree were strictly specified, under the SQE it will be up to law schools to decide whether or not to offer a law degree which prepares students for professional practice as a solicitor. Of course, for those who decide to prepare their students to attempt the SQE, the demands of the assessment will inevitably shape the curriculum. Even here however, the SQE is more focused than current knowledge requirements.[48] Universities can decide to orientate their curriculum around SQE preparation, to include a wider range of legal subjects, or to combine law with other subjects (e.g. in business skills, technology or languages). Objectively, the SQE assesses less than the current academic and vocational requirements. Therefore the proportion of space it takes up will depend on choices made by universities, no doubt informed by market pressures. Some may focus their programmes very tightly on the SQE curriculum, whilst others may extend their courses to cover other legal and non-legal subjects.

The SQE therefore goes some way to addressing the familiar trope that the failure of law schools to innovate is down to the inflexible nature of the curriculum and the requirements set down by regulators. It also addresses some of the challenges that might otherwise be produced if a different approach to reform was taken. Whilst the provision of law as a postgraduate degree in the USA invariably produces multidisciplinary graduates, it also operates to extend the length and therefore the cost associated with the legal education pathway. Similarly other approaches taken in Australia, such as the requirement that law can be taken only as part of a double-degree, tends to reduce opportunities for students to undertake interdisciplinary law subjects. Scope for elective subjects is increasingly restricted in order to reserve sufficient credit points to complete the mandatory core without extending the length of a degree.

In addition to greater flexibility with regard to curriculum, a shift away from input requirements leaves educational institutions free to decide how to teach. They can

---

[47] Richard Moorhead, 'Guest Post: Why the SRA's Education Reforms Inhibit Innovation' (*Legal Business*, 2016) www.legalbusiness.co.uk/blogs/guest-post-why-the-sras-education-reforms-inhibit-innovation/ accessed 1 November 2018.

[48] In particular, the requirement for students to study three specialist areas of practice, currently taught as LPC electives, will be removed. This requirement is not connected to any practice restriction. It is not necessary, for example, to have passed a Legal Practice Course (LPC) family law elective to be able to practise in family law as a solicitor.

use their professional expertise to develop pedagogy which best suits their students, to design new programmes of study, to integrate practical and academic elements, or to offer sandwich degrees in which students spend their penultimate year undertaking work placements. In anticipation of these changes, universities are already beginning to look at new, two or three-year degree programmes (both at undergraduate and postgraduate levels) that integrate academic study, professional learning and work experience. Moreover, solicitor-apprenticeships have already been introduced and programmes of study that more actively intertwine clinical and academic learning are being developed.[49] It is expected that these regulatory changes will produce the space and freedom for training providers and the profession to work together to develop bespoke training courses for a range of specialist work areas and practice skills.

Crucially, the removal of the Qualifying Law Degree (QLD) means that universities will not be protected from competition by a requirement, which only they can meet. Despite huge changes to the market for higher education, with far larger numbers of students and higher fees, the core university teaching model centred around lectures and face-to-face seminars and tutorials remains deeply embedded. The revised regulations in England and Wales will no longer hamper new disruptive technologies (emerging within or outside the university sector) from driving change to traditional models of teaching and learning. The SQE dovetails with other initiatives such as the SRA's 'Innovate Educate' initiative, designed to promote and support providers who wish to introduce new ways of training in transition to the introduction of the SQE.[50] This allows the current training regulations to be waived where to do so is compatible with regulatory objectives.[51] Examples in practice include permitting an education provider to use an online learning platform to deliver face-to-face teaching for the Professional Skills Course. The tutor is available to respond to questions online, in the same way as they would be via face-to-face delivery and this provides trainees with greater flexibility and accessibility, whilst still ensuring consistency of standards and the provision of learning support.[52] In the future the changes brought about by the SQE means that no waiver would be required and training providers could adopt new technologies more rapidly.

The approach adopted by the SRA does not address technological training requirements by proscribing the nature of this training or by testing the technological competencies of SQE candidates. Rather, the revised regulatory environment is intended to provide the necessary preconditions for innovation to flourish. Whilst

---

[49] See further Solicitors Regulation Authority, 'Solicitor Apprenticeship Questions and Answers' (2017) www.sra.org.uk/students/resources/solicitor-apprenticeship-qa.page accessed 1 November 2018.

[50] See further Solicitors Regulation Authority, 'SRA Innovate Educate' www.sra.org.uk/solicitors/innovate/sra-innovate-educate.page accessed 1 November 2018.

[51] See further Solicitors Regulation Authority, 'Apply for a Waiver' www.sra.org.uk/solicitors/waivers/apply-waiver.page accessed 1 November 2018.

[52] See the case studies available from Solicitors Regulation Authority, 'SRA Innovate Educate' (n 50).

there is already evidence of this taking place, it is expected that as the changes introduced by the SQE embed, very many more examples of innovation will emerge.

12.5 CONCLUSION

It has previously been said that future lawyers will have to think in new ways, as project managers, as problem-solvers and as information handlers in an information age.[53] In this chapter we have examined the different regulatory approaches taken to the education and training of future solicitors in two jurisdictions and the benefits and limitations associated with each approach. We observe that whilst regulators are not directly charged with a statutory obligation to facilitate innovation in legal education, the objective to protect consumers and promote access to justice means that innovation capable of producing more competent, multidisciplinary, adaptable, future-focused solicitors should be encouraged by whatever means necessary. As is seen with regard to the regulatory approaches exemplified by Scotland, and England and Wales, these means will differ; that they do reinforces the fact that there is no one 'correct' approach to regulation.

Regulating the legal profession and the pathways to qualification in a way that produces professionals fit for the future can take a number of forms. Some jurisdictions such as Scotland, Canada and the USA have taken steps to expose students to new ways of thinking by incorporating non-traditional skills into the requirements for practice. Yet the view that these skills ought to constitute a prerequisite to legal practice varies by jurisdiction and impacts upon the appropriateness of a prescriptive approach.

The issue with which regulators must grapple is whether tech know-how is an essential requirement both for innovation and/or practice. Any perceived advantage believed to attach to lawyers having particular technological skills must be weighed against the additional difficulty, cost and time that a regulatory requirement of this nature would impose. Conversely if it is the view of regulators that lawyers need not have specific expertise in technology given the availability of this expertise elsewhere, there may nevertheless remain a need to consider issues of governance and to delimit the professional responsibilities that attach to each collaborator.

It remains to be seen whether the efforts of regulators in the UK, as described in this chapter, lead to a more innovative legal education sector and/or graduates who are better prepared for the changing nature of legal practice. Such reforms are made

[53] William D Henderson, 'Three Generations of U.S. Lawyers: Generalists, Specialists, Project Managers' (2011) 70(2) Maryland Law Review 373; Kenneth Hirsh and Wayne Miller, 'Law School Education in the 21st Century: Adding Information Technology Instruction to the Curriculum' (2004) 12(3) William & Mary Bill of Rights Journal 873.

with reference to the existing research though their effect in practice can only be assessed after implementation has occurred. The coming years offer an important opportunity for observation as the SQE takes effect, and as Scotland revises its 'PEAT 1 Information Technology' requirements, and launches a legal technology accreditation. Monitoring the impact of this change is a critical step in better understanding the association between regulation and educational innovation, and providing an evidence base for future decision-making. For this reason, ongoing research, data-collection and analysis remains a priority for all stakeholders, and a task to which the Society and the SRA remain committed.

BIBLIOGRAPHY

Legal Services (Scotland) Act, 2010 (asp 16)
Legal Services Act 2007 ss 29–30
Solicitors (Scotland) Act 1980 (c. 46)
Solicitors Act 1974 (c. 47)
American Bar Association, 'Model Rules of Professional Conduct' (2018) www.americanbar.org /groups/professional_responsibility/publications/model_rules_of_professional_conduct/ rule_1_1_competence/comment_on_rule_1_1/ accessed 1 November 2018
Bates D, 'Are "Digital Natives" Equipped to Conquer the Legal Landscape?' (2013) 13(3) Legal Information Management 172
Burke C, 'Winning the Battle to Teach Legal Technology and Innovation at Law Schools' (*Legal IT Today*, 17 March 2017) http://burke-company.com/wp-content/uploads/2017/ 04/legalittoday-winning-the-battle-to-teach-legal-technology-and-innovation-at-law-schools.pdf accessed 10 July 2018
Canick S, 'Infusing Technology Skills into the Law School Curriculum' (2014) 42(3) Capital University Law Review 663
Clementi D, 'Review of the Regulatory Framework for Legal Services in England and Wales' (TSO 2004)
Goyal M, 'Do Lawyers and Law Students Have the Technical Skills to Meet the Needs of Future Legal Jobs?' (*Slaw*, 29 June 2017) www.slaw.ca/2017/06/29/do-lawyers-and-law-students-have-the-technical-skills-to-meet-the-needs-of-future-legal-jobs/ accessed 20 July 2018
Henderson WD, 'Three Generations of U.S. Lawyers: Generalists, Specialists, Project Managers' (2011) 70(2) Maryland Law Review 373
Hildebrandt M, 'A Vision of Ambient Law' in Roger Brownsword and Karen Yeung (eds.), Regulating Technologies: Legal Futures, Regulatory Frames and Technological Fixes (Hart 2008)
  Smart Technologies and the End(s) of Law: Novel Entanglements of Law and Technology (Edward Elgar 2015)
  'Law as Information in the Era of Data-Driven Agency' (2016) 79(1) The Modern Law Review 1
Hirsh K and Miller W, 'Law School Education in the 21st Century: Adding Information Technology Instruction to the Curriculum' (2004) 12(3) William & Mary Bill of Rights Journal 873
Hyde J, 'Law Society of Scotland Opens Door to Non-Solicitors' *Law Society Gazette* (London, 13 August 2015) www.lawgazette.co.uk/news/law-society-of-scotland-opens-door-to-non-solicitors/5050551.article accessed 20 July 2018

Kimbro S, 'What Should Be in a Digital Curriculum: A Practitioner's Must Have List' in Marc Lauritsen and Oliver Goodenough (eds.), *Educating the Digital Lawyer* (Lexis Nexis e-Books 2012)

Law Society of Scotland, 'Standards of Service' www.lawscot.org.uk/members/rules-and-guidance/rules-and-guidance/section-e/division-a/guidance/standards-of-service/ accessed 20 August 2018

'Foundation Programme (Scottish Exempting Degree) – Accreditation Guidelines for Applicants' (Law Society of Scotland 2010) www.lawscot.org.uk/media/359157/foundation-programme-guidelines.pdf accessed 31 October 2018

'Professional Education and Training (PEAT) Stage 1: Accreditation Guidelines for Applicants' (Law Society of Scotland 2010) www.lawscot.org.uk/media/9123/peat-1-guidelines.pdf

'Professional Education and Training (PEAT) Stage 2: Outcomes' (Law Society of Scotland 2010) www.lawscot.org.uk/media/8913/peat-2-outcomes.pdf accessed 1 November 2018

'Independent Review of Legal Services Regulation: Response from the Law Society of Scotland' (Law Society of Scotland 2018) www.lawscot.org.uk/media/360006/review-of-legal-services-tp.pdf accessed 5 February 2019

'Legal Tech Assessment' (2018) www.lawscot.org.uk/members/cpd-training/legal-tech-assessment/ accessed 20 August 2018

Marrs R, 'Technology and the Law: Who, Where and How?' (*Law Society of Scotland*, 2017) www.lawscot.org.uk/news-and-events/news/technology-and-the-law-who-where-and-how/ accessed 20 August 2018

Moorhead R, 'Guest Post: Why the SRA's Education Reforms Inhibit Innovation' (*Legal Business*, 2016) www.legalbusiness.co.uk/blogs/guest-post-why-the-sras-education-reforms-inhibit-innovation/ accessed 1 November 2018

Rees N, 'I Look Ahead' (Sir Ninian Stephen Lecture, The University of Newcastle, Newcastle, 10 September 2015)

Roberton EA, 'Fit for the Future: Report of the Independent Review of Legal Services Regulation in Scotland' (Scottish Government 2018) www2.gov.scot/resource/0054/00542583.pdf accessed 20 July 2018

Scottish Government, 'Review of the Regulation of Legal Services' (*gov.scot*, 2019) www2.gov.scot/about/review/regulation-legal-services accessed 5 February 2019

Segal D, 'What They Don't Teach Law Students: Lawyering' *New York Times* (New York, 19 November 2011) www.nytimes.com/2011/11/20/business/after-law-school-associates-learn-to-be-lawyers.html accessed 10 July 2018

Solicitors Regulation Authority, 'Apply for a Waiver' www.sra.org.uk/solicitors/waivers/apply-waiver.page accessed 1 November 2018

'SRA Innovate Educate' www.sra.org.uk/solicitors/innovate/sra-innovate-educate.page accessed 1 November 2018

'Statement of Legal Knowledge' www.sra.org.uk/knowledge/ accessed 31 October 2018

'A Competence Statement for Solicitors – SRA Response to the Consultation' (Solicitors Regulation Authority 2015) www.sra.org.uk/documents/sra/consultations/competence-statement-consultation-response.doc

'A New Route to Qualification: The Solicitors Qualifying Examination (SQE) – A Summary of Responses and Next Steps' (Solicitors Regulation Authority 2017) www.sra.org.uk/documents/sra/consultations/sqe-summary-responses.pdf accessed 31 October 2018

'Solicitor Apprenticeship Questions and Answers' (2017) www.sra.org.uk/students/resources/solicitor-apprenticeship-qa.page accessed 1 November 2018

'Solicitors Qualifying Examination – Draft Assessment Specification' (2017) www
.sra.org.uk/sra/policy/sqe.page# accessed 31 October 2018

'Student Information Pack' (2017) www.sra.org.uk/students/resources/student-
information.page accessed 1 November 2018

Solicitors Regulation Authority and Bar Standards Board, 'Academic Stage Handbook'
(Solicitors Regulation Authority and Bar Standards Board 2014) www.sra.org.uk/docu
ments/students/academic-stage/academic-stage-handbook.pdf accessed 1 November 2018

Susskind R, *Tomorrow's Lawyers: An Introduction to Your Future* (1st edn, Oxford University
Press 2013)

University of Glasgow, 'Professional Legal Practice (Diploma)' (2018) www.gla.ac.uk/postgrad
uate/taught/professionallegalpracticediploma/ accessed 1 November 2018

Van Zandt D, 'Foundational Competencies: Innovation in Legal Education' (2009) 61(4)
Rutgers Law Review 1127

Webb J and others, 'Setting Standards: The Future of Legal Services Education and Training
Regulation in England and Wales (Legal Education and Training Review)' (SRA, BSB
and CILEX 2013) www.letr.org.uk/wp-content/uploads/letr-report.pdf accessed
17 August 2018

13

'Complicitous and Contestatory'

A Critical Genre Theory Approach to Reviewing Legal Education in the Global, Digital Age

Jane Ching and Paul Maharg

In this chapter we describe a discourse framework for understanding the historical development of modern reports into legal education in England and Wales by analysing the textual features of genre markers. We then apply this framework to a specific subset of *topoi* within such reports, namely the coverage given to digital technologies within legal education. We make three related claims. First, the discourse and rhetorics of reports on legal education has scarcely been analysed in the research literature, and we begin that process here. Second, the culture and context within which digital innovation is reported, analysed and recommended upon in regulatory reports is relatively shallow and 'theory-lite'. We need to draw sophisticated insights into our understanding of digital in a variety of disciplines and discourses (e.g. media, education and discourse analysis generally), and apply those to legal education. Third, the genre-form of reports on innovation inhibit or constrain our ability to develop imaginative, theory-rich and persuasive accounts of digital cultures for legal education. Our case study has implications not just for law schools, but also and more significantly, for regulators and accreditors.

> To consider as potential genres such homely discourse as the letter of recommendation, the user manual, the progress report, the ransom note, the lectures, and the white paper ... is not to trivialize the study of genres; it is to take seriously the rhetoric in which we are immersed and the situations in which we find ourselves.[1]
> ... all discourses of theory ... are ideologically loaded, cultural constructs designed to establish control and a sense of security.[2]

13.1 INTRODUCTION

There is something of a global industry in reviewing legal education.[3] Aside from the internal reviews carried out by institutions and professional bodies, the range of reports

---

[1] Carolyn R Miller, 'Genre as Social Action' (1984) 70(2) Quarterly Journal of Speech 151, 155.
[2] HG Widdowson, 'Discourses of Enquiry and Conditions of Relevance' in James E Alatis (ed.), *Georgetown University Round Table on Languages and Linguistics* 1990 (Georgetown University Press 1990).
[3] This chapter draws on work presented at conferences in Hong Kong, Turkey and the UK, some of which was published. See further Jane Ching, 'The Challenges Facing Legal Services Education in the 21st Century: A Case for Collaboration and Conversation?' in Ayşe Nuhoğlu and others (eds.), *Legal Education*

that is in the public domain is staggering.[4] So, for example, in the period 2010–14 alone, roughly simultaneous reviews were taking place, or reporting, in Australia,[5] Canada[6] (and in particular in Ontario[7]), England and Wales,[8] France,[9] Mauritius,[10] New Zealand,[11] Russia,[12] South Africa[13] and the USA.[14]

    in the 21st Century: Proceedings of the International Conference, Bahçeşehir University and The Union of Turkish Bar Associations (Türkiye Barolar Birliği 2015) http://tbbyayinlari.barobirlik.org.tr/TBBBooks/525 .pdf accessed 15 May 2019; Jane Ching, 'Greener Grass and Re-Invented Wheels: Researching Together' (Society of Legal Scholars Annual Conference, Oxford, September 2016) http://irep.ntu.ac.uk/id/eprint/ 28622/ accessed 20 May 2019; Jane Ching, '"Riding Madly Off in All Directions": Consistency and Convergence in Professional Legal Education' (Directions in Legal Education Conference Hong Kong, June 2016) http://irep.ntu.ac.uk/28240/ accessed 20 May 2019; Paul Maharg, 'The Identity of Scots Law: Redeeming the Past' in Mark Mulhern (ed.), *Scottish Life and Society (A Compendium of Scottish Ethnology): The Law (Volume 13)* (Birlinn Press & The European Ethnological Research Centre 2011); Paul Maharg, 'Shared Space: Regulation, Technology and Legal Education in a Global Context' (2015) 6 (1) European Journal of Law and Technology http://ejlt.org/article/view/425/541 accessed 17 May 2019.

 4   Others, excluded from the scope of this chapter, are not reviews of legal education at all, but reports on the efficacy, wellbeing or anti-competitiveness of the legal professions which, explicitly or otherwise, have implications for education for that profession.

 5   Law Admissions Consultative Committee, 'Rethinking Academic Requirements for Admission' (Law Council of Australia 2010) www.lawcouncil.asn.au/resources/law-admissions-consultative-committee /discussion-papers accessed 17 May 2019.

 6   Council of the Federation of Law Societies of Canada, 'Common Law Degree Implementation Committee: Final Report' (Federation of Law Societies of Canada 2011) http://docs.flsc.ca /Implementation-Report-ECC-Aug-2011-R.pdf accessed 17 May 2019.

 7   Law Society of Upper Canada, 'Pathways to the Profession: A Roadmap for the Reform of Lawyer Licensing in Ontario' (Law Society of Upper Canada 2012) www.lsuc.on.ca/WorkArea/ DownloadAsset.aspx?id=2147489848 accessed 17 May 2019.

 8   Julian Webb and others, 'Setting Standards: The Future of Legal Services Education and Training Regulation in England and Wales (Legal Education and Training Review)' (SRA, BSB and CILEX 2013) www.letr.org.uk/wp-content/uploads/LETR-Report.pdf accessed 17 August 2018.

    Pamela Henderson and others, 'Solicitors Regulation Authority: CPD Review' (Solicitors Regulation Authority 2012) www.sra.org.uk/sra/news/wbl-cpd-publication.page accessed 17 May 2019.

 9   Conseil National des Barreaux, 'Réforme de La Formation Initiale Dans Les Écoles d'avocats' (Conseil National des Barreaux 2014) http://cnb.avocat.fr/Reforme-de-la-formation-initiale-dans-les-Ecoles-d-avo cats_a2071.html accessed 13 February 2019; Conseil National des Barreaux, 'Le Conseil National Des Barreaux s'inquiète de La Qualité de La Formation Des Étudiants, Futurs Avocats, à La Suite de l'avis Du Conseil d'Etat Du 10 Février 2016' (Conseil National des Barreaux 2016) http://cnb.avocat.fr/Le-Conseil-national-des-barreaux-s-inquiete-de-la-qualite-de-la-formation-des-etudiants-futurs-avocats-a-la-suite-de-l_a2592.html accessed 13 February 2019.

10   Jane Ching and others, 'Reform of the Education Structure for the Professional Law Courses in Mauritius' (Tertiary Education Commission of Mauritius 2012).

11   Andrew Tipping, 'Review of the Professional Legal Studies Course' (New Zealand Council of Legal Education 2013) www.nzcle.org.nz/Docs/Review of the PLSC Report .pdf accessed 17 May 2019.

12   Olga Shepelva and Asmik Novikova, 'The Quality of Legal Education in Russia: Stereotypes and Real Problems' (*PILnet*, 2014) www.pilnet.org/public-interest-law-resources/73-the-quality-of-legal-education-in-russia-stereotypes-and.html accessed 17 May 2019.

13   Camilla Pickles, 'Research Report on Mandatory Continuing Professional Development Commissioned by the Law Society of South Africa' (Law Society of South Africa 2010) www .lssa.org.za/upload/documents/Research_report_on_MCPD.pdf%3E accessed 17 May 2019.

14   ABA Task Force, 'Report and Recommendations American Bar Association Task Force on the Future of Legal Education' (American Bar Association 2014) www.americanbar.org/content/

The homogeneity of the phenomenon is, however, misleading. There is a finite repertoire, globally, of structural components of a legal education (e.g. degrees, undergraduate and postgraduate; vocational courses; periods of mandatory clinic or work experience; bar examinations and aptitude tests; Continuing Professional Development (CPD)/Continuing Legal Education (CLE)). There is also a fair degree of commonality in global concerns (e.g. cost of education and numbers of aspiring lawyers; skills; practice-readiness and the nature of 'competence'; the relationships between stakeholders; ethics and global competitiveness). However, the reviews which evaluate these structures and issues are commissioned by stakeholders with widely varying agendas; carried out by people chosen for very different reasons; vary in method from rigorously empirical to benign expert opinion; and, therefore, vary in their conclusions and outcomes. Not only is this problematic for general readers of the reports and the expectations they bring, but it also substantially impedes comparative and follow-up work. This chapter addresses this issue initially by proposing four distinct genres of legal education review, largely derived deductively from the substantial 2010–14 global sample.

Having created a typology of what is present in the field as a whole, the chapter then moves on to problematise a specific and increasingly urgent component of the modern legal education review, that of technology in legal education. When we come to consider how the role of technology in legal education is handled by reviews in the UK in particular, we find quite a different, and very distinct, genre landscape. From an initial base of almost complete invisibility within legal education reviews, legal educational technology reporting has gone through an early phase of information-gathering, followed by a focus upon functionality and specialist investigation, followed by integration into education reviews. The chapter finishes by drawing conclusions as to the history, current status and future of legal education reviews both as a general endeavour and in relation to the specific topic of legal education technology, in the UK and elsewhere.

We shall start by examining how genre theory provides a useful tool for the analysis of legal education reports.

13.2 THE LENS OF GENRE THEORY

Genre theory is familiar in linguistics, cultural and media studies. A genre is a categorisation of text or other cultural artefact by reference to assumptions and conventions that constitute a 'shared code between the producers and interpreters of texts included within [the genre]'.[15] Such frameworks then allow for intertextuality, or, in our context, the potential for viable comparison between legal education reviews. Acting as a benchmark, they can also be used to identify hybrids, and the

---

dam/aba/administrative/professional_responsibility/report_and_recommendations_of_aba_task_force.authcheckdam.pdf accessed 17 May 2019.

[15] Daniel Chandler, 'An Introduction to Genre Theory' (*Visual Memory*, 1997) 5 http://visual-memory.co.uk/daniel/Documents/intgenre/chandler_genre_theory.pdf accessed 17 May 2019.

occasions on which genre conventions are challenged or deliberately ignored which, in turn, may lead to changes in the genre itself, or to new genres.[16]

Genre analysts have developed a range of tools by which texts have been analysed. In the work of John Swales for example, genre analysis is a method by which regularities in and between texts can be explained in terms of their shared communicative purposes within discourse communities.[17] The concept of a discourse community – socially situated, reading and producing genres, and judging texts according to expectations, norms, and agendas of the community – is a key concept to the formation of genre critique as a tool of textual analysis. Swales outlined six descriptive characteristics of discourse communities. They have:

1. a broadly agreed set of common public goals;
2. mechanisms of intercommunication among members;
3. participatory mechanisms primarily to provide information and feedback;
4. one or more genres in the communicative furtherance of its aims;
5. a specific lexis; and
6. a threshold level of members with a suitable degree of relevant content and discoursal expertise.[18]

Genre thus sits within a context of community characteristics that operate upon it, and to which it contributes if the genre is to be perceived as a legitimate genre. In terms of legal education reviews, the discourse communities tend to be more clearly defined than for reports that are addressed to the academic community. Their genre features are more recognisable as a result, and as we shall see in the four genres below, they can be delineated more easily. We shall also see how the diverse discourse communities are served by the four different sub-genres of reviews. And we shall note how the politics of legal education can be enacted in the ways that genres are manipulated. As Bhatia observed, following on from Swales's earlier analyses: 'Most often [a genre] is highly structured and conventionalised with constraints on allowable contributions in terms of their intent, positioning, form and functional value. These constraints, however, are often exploited by the expert members of the discourse community to achieve private intentions within the framework of socially recognized purposes.'[19] Framing the legal education review

---

[16]   See for example the sub-genres of novels, for instance science fiction or historical fiction.

[17]   John Swales, *Genre Analysis: English in Academic and Research Settings* (Cambridge University Press 1990) 24–32. See also John Swales, 'The Concept of Discourse Community' in Elizabeth Wardle and Dough Downs (eds.), *Writing about Writing: A College Reader* (1st edn, Bedford/St Martin's 2011).

[18]   See Swales, *Genre Analysis: English in Academic and Research Settings* (n 17) 26.

[19]   Vijay Kumar Bhatia, *Analysing Genre: Language Use in Professional Settings* (1st edn, Routledge 1993) 13. It is interesting to note that Bhatia, perhaps more than Swales, is sensitive to the ways in which internal switches of point of view can affect meaning within a text. The stance of a researcher, for example, is never only an objective stance: it is constantly changing in subtle ways depending on the topic under analyses, the evidence, the importance of the topic, the views of others in the discourse community around the genre, and many other factors.

in the context of genre, therefore, serves to illuminate characteristics ('the *what*', 'the *who*', 'the *how*', 'the *why*' and 'the *what now*' of the review) and expectations that are, at present, partly obscured for some audiences and purposes, both within and outside the discourse community.

Academic research, without explicitly acknowledging it, also has its genres, where defining characteristics include methodology; origin (grant-funded versus contract research); and format (peer-reviewed; literature review, article, conference proceedings).[20] Not all of the legal education reviews, however, involve research as academics conceive it, and these variables do not alone address the subtleties of the commissioners' agenda or the politics behind the choice of investigators. Perhaps the closest analogy in this context is Rutherford's genre-based analysis of financial accounting reports, governed by accounting standards, socially constructed industry and sector norms, the agendas of those involved in reporting and the 'interrelationships between the expectations of users and preparers'.[21]

13.3 GENRES OF LEGAL EDUCATION REVIEW

13.3.1 *Genre 1: A Collation of Information*

The simplest, conceptually, of the genres is a collation of information about the different structures that comprise a qualification and continuing learning framework. These provide taxonomy and a functionalist overview of the sector.[22] They can provide useful data about trends, such as shifts in the relative significance of university study and workplace apprenticeship in common law countries.[23] Such collations do, however, require resources to keep them up to date and obscure cultural factors such as, for example, the depth of feeling about the value of mandatory pre-qualification work experience (articles, training contracts, internships and similar constructs); concerns about pass rates or cost or the qualitative differences between JDs in the USA, Canada, Australia, Hong Kong and Northern Ireland.[24]

[20] For example, see the genre-based analysis of the structure of articles reporting empirical legal research in Girolamo Tessuto, 'Generic Structure and Rhetorical Moves in English-Language Empirical Law Research Articles: Sites of Interdisciplinary and Interdiscursive Cross-Over' (2015) 37 English for Specific Purposes 13.

[21] Brian A Rutherford, 'A Genre-Theoretic Approach to Financial Reporting Research' (2013) 45(4) British Accounting Review 297, 308.

[22] Konrad Zweigert, Hein Kötz and Tony Weir, *An Introduction to Comparative Law* (3rd edn, Clarenden Press 1998); Ralf Michaels, 'The Functional Method of Comparative Law' in Mathias Reimann and Reinhard Zimmermann (eds.), *The Oxford Handbook of Comparative Law* (Oxford University Press 2006).

[23] David Scott Clark, 'Legal Education' in David S Clark (ed.), *Comparative Law and Society* (Edward Elgar Publishing 2012).

[24] The JD designator is not normally available in the UK. However, the extent of Northern Irish autonomy allows one institution to offer an innovative course that combines the usual UK undergraduate law degree, with a doctoral research degree: Queen's University Belfast, 'Postgraduate

The drivers for such collations are, by contrast with some of the other genres, usually transparent and concrete. Some are designed to provide information for students;[25] or for lawyers wishing to practise outside their home jurisdiction. In these cases the information is likely to be provided by knowledgeable insiders and updated regularly.[26] Others represent attempts by a supranational organisation to collate information about its membership,[27] or by a group of comparative lawyers.[28] These again use data solicited from insiders, which is accurate at the point of collation, but may not be updated. A third subgroup, however, is collated by outsiders for persuasive or political ends, for example, a professional body wishing to demonstrate that a proposed change to policy is a global norm,[29] or conversely that such a proposal could damage the profession by international standards.[30] Here, of course, there is a risk that the information obtained is out of date, misunderstood or mistranslated.

The contribution of this genre, therefore, is a mapping of the scope, 'the *what*', of the field. We need to look to the other genres for evaluation of 'the *how*', 'the *who*' and sometimes 'the *why*', and 'the *what now?*'.

13.3.2 *Genre 2: Expert Review*

It is the second genre that emphasises 'the *who*'. Early reports were necessarily heavily dependent on expert opinions, given the paucity of other data. Twining,

Research Course JD Juris Doctor (JD)' www.qub.ac.uk/schools/SchoolofLaw/Study/JurisDoctor/ accessed 17 May 2019.

[25] For example, LawyerEdu.org, 'Steps to Become a Lawyer/ Attorney in Canadian Provinces/ Territories' (2015) www.lawyeredu.org/canada.html accessed 17 May 2019; National Conference of Bar Examiners, 'Bar Admission Guide' (2019) www.ncbex.org/publications/bar-admissions-guide/ accessed 17 May 2019.

[26] International Bar Association, 'IBA Global Regulation and Trade in Legal Services Report 2014' (International Bar Association 2014) https://papers.ssrn.com/sol3/papers.cfm?abstract_id=2530064 accessed 17 May 2019.

[27] Conseil des Barreaux Européens – Council of Bars and Law Societies of Europe, 'Continuous Training in the CCBE Member Countries: Summary' (Conseil des Barreaux Européens – Council of Bars and Law Societies of Europe 2016) www.ccbe.eu/document/National_training_regime/1_-_Summary_of_national_continuing_training_regimes.pdf.pdf accessed 17 May 2019; European Commission, 'Lawyers' Training Systems in the Member States' (*European e-Justice Portal*, 2018) https://e-justice.europa.eu/content_lawyers__training_systems_in_the_member_states-407-en.do accessed 17 May 2019.

[28] Richard J Wilson, 'The Role of Practice in Legal Education' (18th International Congress on Comparative Law, Washington DC, July 2010) https://digitalcommons.wcl.american.edu/fac_work s_papers/12/ accessed 17 May 2019.

[29] For example, Solicitors Regulation Authority, 'Qualification in Other Jurisdictions – International Benchmarking' (Solicitors Regulation Authority 2016) www.sra.org.uk/sra/policy/sqe/research-reports.page accessed 17 May 2019.

[30] For example, Law Society of England and Wales, 'Report into the Global Competitiveness of the England and Wales Solicitor Qualification: An Investigation into the Potential Impact of the SRA's Training for Tomorrow Proposals on the Global Reputation of Solicitors of England and Wales' (Law Society of England and Wales 2015) www.lawsociety.org.uk/support-services/research-trends/global-competitiveness-of-the-england-and-wales-solicitor-qualification/ accessed 17 May 2019.

for example, describes a report he conducted in the 1970s as 'reveal[ing] how little solid information there existed in nearly all countries about most facets of legal education, even in respect of elementary statistics. We had to proceed and pontificate on the basis of pooled impressions, biases and extraordinarily patchy information'.[31] In this genre, what is critical is the expertise and credibility of the investigators. How and why they are selected is therefore significant to any understanding of their findings. Rarely is the method of selection transparent.[32] It is usually clear that the panel is intended to be representative of insider stakeholders (e.g. the judiciary, academics, the profession). Lay members, representatives of other professions or foreigners may also be recruited for an outsider perspective; students or consumers, lacking in power, less so. What is also less transparent is the extent to which investigators are recruited for their expertise; because their credibility with a particular audience sector is thought to facilitate acceptance of the recommendations; or even because the commissioners know that they can be relied on to take a particular stance in the investigation.

The investigative process may be a form of enhanced quality assurance exercise, a deliberately defensive exercise[33] or something close to a public inquiry soliciting submissions from interested parties and visiting sites.[34] To the extent that the review comes to a consensus on conclusions and recommendations (the 'how' and 'what now'), it may operate in similar ways to a Delphi model, but is unlikely to formalise its activities in quite this way. This type of investigation may expect a great deal of panel members in terms of contribution, including the possibility that they have access to a panacea. It does, however, lend itself to the close, collegiate, discursive, argumentative and persuasive legal habitus. It is also capable of generating strong conceptual and theoretical models that can have traction, because they are at a comparatively abstracted level, outside their own contexts. The three apprenticeships model found in the US Carnegie report[35] – whilst similar in some ways to the three-stage sequential model of the British Ormrod report[36] – is of this kind.

This genre, then, is inductive, setting questions (which may be open, defensive or politicised) and asking the experts to answer them, possibly with the aid of meetings,

---

[31] William Twining, 'Developments in Legal Education: Beyond the Primary School Model' (1990) 2(1) Legal Education Review 35, 48.

[32] There are exceptions: Council of the Federation of Law Societies of Canada (n 6) 6.

[33] See for example the approach of the Australian Law Admissions Consultative Committee in 2010, in asking the legal experts attached to a national project to produce national outcome measures to render the law examples as close as possible to those already promulgated by the Council of Australian Law Deans: Law Admissions Consultative Committee (n 5) 1.

[34] See the approach taken by the ABA Task Force, which conducted meetings and outreach activities, attended public events and solicited submissions and comments from respondents (including students), ABA Task Force (n 14).

[35] William M Sullivan and others, *Educating Lawyers: Preparation for the Profession of Law* (1st edn, Jossey-Bass 2007).

[36] Roger Ormrod, 'Report of the Committee on Legal Education (Ormrod Report) (Cmnd. No. 4595)' (HM Stationery Office 1971).

workshops and submissions. Its strength is as considered advocacy by a group of individuals in whom the audience is able to place a considerable degree of trust.

13.3.3 Genre 3: Deductive Consultation Exercise

By contrast, the principal characteristic of Genre 3 is deductive policy-making where a hypothesis,[37] a policy, a series of options[38] or a detailed implementation plan[39] is put out for consultation: 'the *how*' or 'the *what now*'. There is no necessity that the commissioners contract outsiders to carry out the exercise. The range of consultees may be wider than in Genre 2 although submissions may be solicited and some element of interviewing, survey, workshops or Delphi groups might be used to obtain them. Nevertheless, this form of consultation is not an empirical activity demanding transparency about the method of analysis, nor, unless there is a very clear preponderance of opinion, a quantitative referendum. Indeed, a researcher's analytical approach might produce different results from those articulated by the commissioner.[40] Genre 3 is a feature of regulatory openness and in that it is to be welcomed, but it is only a testing of the water, and there is no obligation on the consultor to act in accordance with what the consultation reveals.

13.3.4 Genre 4: Deductive or Inductive Empirical Investigation

The principal characteristic of the final genre is its approach to analysis of 'the *why*'. Although many professional bodies and academic organisations collect and publish statistics on, for example, pass rates or diversity, quantitative investigation in the legal context is rare.[41] Qualitative empirical investigation may capture similar themes to those uncovered in Genres 2 and 3. Where Genre 4 differs is in matters such as consciousness of the representativeness of samples, of representing the range of opinion as well as the scope of opinion, recognition that what is being investigated is opinion and perception, and in transparently systematic analysis that is usually

---

[37] For example, that the Hong Kong solicitors' profession might adopt a bar examination of some kind: Jane Ching and others, 'Consultation on the Feasibility of Implementing a Common Entrance Examination in Hong Kong' (Law Society of Hong Kong 2014).

[38] Law Society of Upper Canada (n 7).

[39] For example, the detailed proposals and business case for a national examination in Canada: National Admission Standards Project Steering Committee, 'National Law Practice Qualifying Assessment Business and Implementation Plan' (Federation of Law Societies of Canada 2015).

[40] Elaine Hall, 'Notes on the SRA Report of the Consultation on the Solicitors Qualifying Exam: "Comment Is Free, but Facts Are Sacred"' (2017) 51(3) Law Teacher 364.

[41] Evaluation of competences or work types is, however, sometimes quantitative: National Conference of Bar Examiners, 'A Study of the Newly Licensed Lawyer' (National Conference of Bar Examiners 2012) http://flsc.ca/wp-content/uploads/2014/10/admission4.pdf accessed 5 June 2014; Federation of Law Societies of Canada, 'National Entry to Practice Competency Profile Validation Survey Report' (Federation of Law Societies of Canada 2012) http://flsc.ca/wp-content/uploads/2014/10/admission4.pdf accessed 17 May 2019.

thematic in nature. It is also, we suggest, more likely to be inductive and question-based than deductive and hypothesis-based. By contrast with Genre 2, however, the investigators may have been recruited for their qualities as researchers rather than their credibility with the audience, and consequently may have to work harder to achieve a result that is credible for the professional audience.

13.4 INTERTEXTUALITY, MISREADING AND DIGITAL REPORTS

What we have focused on so far is the extent to which a legal education review genre is formed by the organisation of its investigation. There are, however, many other textual features that contribute to our sense of genre, and notably that of intertextuality – the relationships between texts, that is, in our context, the reports that the different kinds of investigation generate. The word was coined by Julia Kristeva as meaning the 'intersection of textual surface' where '[a]ny text is constructed as a mosaic of quotations, any text is the absorption and transformation of another'.[42] Texts always tend to intersect, overlap, spill out into other texts; but Kristeva goes beyond this in her elaboration of the term. It has become associated with a number of critical theorists: Bakhtin (from whom Kristeva derived the concept of 'dialogism' and developed it), Derrida, Foucault, Barthes, Lacan Riffaterre and Greimas, to name a few.[43] It has thus acquired the status of a discourse marker in critical theory across a range of interpretive disciplines. It has generated its own critical lexis, as Fewell and Boal and Mai point out, such as 'echo', 'trace', 'intratextuality', 'inter-autorialité', 'interdiscursivité' and the like.[44] Because intertextuality opens up latent, marginalised or hidden textual meaning this way, it is possible to use it to explain and engage with the ideological complexities of powerful texts and ways of reading within legal education reports – and of course, other legal texts.

A key critical figure in this regard is Harold Bloom. For him, meaning in texts was highly contested, and much of his criticism analyses how that comes about. He agreed with Borges that 'every writer *creates* his own precursors'.[45] He describes how, for writers '[t]o deconstruct a poem is to indicate the precise location of its figuration of doubt, its uncertain notice of that limit where persuasion yields to a dance or

---

Julia Kristeva, *Desire in Language: A Semiotic Approach to Literature* (Leon Roudiez ed., Thomas Gora and Alice Jardine trs., Revised, Columbia University Press 1980) 65, 66.

Earlier critics had similar ideas. TS Eliot, for instance, observed that on account of the 'introduction of the new (the really new) work of art . . . the *whole* existing order' of previous texts 'must be, if ever so slightly, altered', TS Eliot, 'Tradition and the Individual Talent', *Selected Essays* (3rd edn, Faber & Faber 1951). For a semiotic definition of intertextuality, see Algirdas Julien Greimas and Joseph Courtés, 'Intertextuality' in Larry Crist and others (trs.), *Semiotics and Language: An Analytical Dictionary* (Indiana University Press 1982).

Hans-Peter Mai, 'Bypassing Intertextuality: Hermeneutics, Textual Practice, Hypertext' in Heinrich F Plett (ed.), *Intertextuality* (De Gruyter 1991).

Jorge Luis Borges, 'Kafka and His Precursors' in Donald A Yates and James East Irby (eds.), André Maurois and Sherry Mangan (trs.), *Labyrinths: Selected Stories & Other Writings* (New Directions 1964) 201. Cited in Harold Bloom, *Yeats* (Oxford University Press 1970) 4.

interplay of tropes'.[46] He defines as trope 'a stance or a ratio of revision; it defends against other tropes'.[47] One such illustration is the *clinamen* or creative swerve that later or 'belated' poets take around the strong figures of earlier predecessors, for example, Shelley, who was such a 'strong' figure for Yeats. The conflict leads the belated poet to misread the earlier, in an attempt to escape, in the title of one of Bloom's celebrated critiques of poetic canon theory, the 'anxiety of influence'.

Bloom also applies his insight into the process of misreading poetry to a theory of critical interpretive misreading. In a sense, Bloom can hardly avoid moving from a theory of poetic misreading as this is enacted between strong poets, to a theory of reading as this is enacted between strong critics. The reading process and the anxiety of influence are, after all, fundamental to both groups. Bloom went on to define tradition or canonicity itself as a trope within the map of misreading. Tradition thus becomes the effect of misreading.[48]

There are many parallels here to the canon of legal educational reviews. That there is such a canon in each jurisdiction can never be in doubt. In England, the Robbins Report[49] was a powerful education report, created in part by engagement with it by subsequent reports. In legal education in the same jurisdiction, the Ormrod Report[50] was one of the most influential in modern times, and each subsequent report has benchmarked its influence and sought to swerve around it. In Australian legal education, the report on uniform admission requirements based upon prescriptive areas of academic legal study, produced by the Law Admissions Consultative Committee (LACC) is another such example.[51] Misreading, like intertextuality, opens up latent, marginalised or hidden textual meaning in such documents, and it is possible to use it to explain and engage with the ideological complexities of powerful texts and ways of reading within hegemonic legal traditions.

The debates around intertextuality, misreading and the anxiety of influence apply to genres of legal education reviews as much as they do to literary canons. As we shall see, they also apply to the history and current status of legal education technology reports. This also allows us to explore the historical development of reports situated in several of the four basic genres outlined above.

---

[46] Harold Bloom, *Wallace Stevens: The Poems of Our Climate* (Cornell University Press 1980) 386.
[47] Ibid 39.
[48] Harold Bloom, *Kabbalah and Criticism* (Seabury Press 1975) 97. As Alastair Fowler perceptively commented in a celebrated article on the subject, there are a variety of canons existing within any single domain. He identified at least six: see Alastair Fowler, 'Genre and the Literary Canon' (1979) 11 (1) New Literary History: A Journal of Theory and Interpretation 97.
[49] Lionel Charles Robbins, 'Higher Education Report of the Committee Appointed by the Prime Minister under the Chairmanship of Lord Robbins' (HM Stationery Office 1963).
[50] Ormrod (n 36).
[51] Law Admissions Consultative Committee, 'Review of Academic Requirements for Admission to the Legal Profession' (Law Council of Australia 2014) www.lawcouncil.asn.au/files/web-pdf/LACC docs/01.12.14_-_Review_of_Academic_Requirements_for_Admission.pdf accessed 20 May 2019.

13.5 GENRE THEORY AND DIGITAL LEGAL EDUCATION REPORTS

As Maharg points out, the Ormrod Report of 1971[52] makes almost no mention of the use of technology, in spite of the fact that both radio and television had been used for Open University programmes since 1969; and there were earlier examples of distance learning use of technologies in other jurisdictions (e.g. in Australia). The same is true of the Marre Report of 1988,[53] which had a wide remit as a basis for its reporting. As Maharg puts it, however, '[t]he problem lay in how the remit was interpreted by the Committee members. From its absence one can assume that technology was simply not part of a recognisable legal educational landscape worthy of gaze and analysis.'[54] In part this was a function of the genre. Those reports described 'a complex social educational system as if it were a legal system comprising rules, personnel, actions'.[55] There were no debates around educational methods (at a time when there were intense debates in school education reports around the status of the school curriculum in England) or around the emergence of new technologies.

The first reports to take digital learning seriously in the UK were the three British and Irish Legal Education Technology Association (BILETA) Inquiries.[56] The reports were clearly Genre 1 in our categories above, shading into Genre 2, in that they largely presented snapshots of digital provision in law schools. Part of the motivation was political, in that BILETA as an organisation dedicated to the promotion and use of digital technologies, realised that the issue of invisibility and lack of knowledge had to be addressed urgently. The reports also set standards for such provision. However their discussion of educational, media, technological or sociological theory was thin at best, and as Maharg puts it, 'although [the reports'

---

[52] Ormrod (n 36).
[53] Committee on the Future of the Legal Profession, 'A Time for Change: Report of the Committee on the Future of the Legal Profession (Marre Report)' (General Council of the Bar and the Law Society 1988).
[54] Maharg, 'Shared Space: Regulation, Technology and Legal Education in a Global Context' (n 3) 6. This was in spite of the early pioneering work done at Chicago-Kent Law School in 1983, and well-publicised in US legal education. This work was ongoing – each year the law school conducted an annual survey of computer technologies in use by the 500 largest law firms in the USA. In addition to this initiative, a number of conferences sprang up to support the emerging field – for example the international series of Substantive Technology in Law Schools (SUBTECH) Conferences (Richard Jones, 'Second International Conference on Substantive Technology in the Law School' (1993) 7(1) International Review of Law Computers & Technology 237.) Chicago-Kent's work was an inspiration for the BILETA Reports, below.
[55] Maharg, 'Shared Space: Regulation, Technology and Legal Education in a Global Context' (n 3) 6–7.
[56] See British and Irish Legal Education Technology Association, 'Report of BILETA Inquiry into the Provision of Information Technology in UK Law Schools' (British and Irish Legal Education Technology Association 1991); British and Irish Legal Education Technology Association, 'Information Technology for UK Law Schools: The Second BILETA Report into Information Technology and Legal Education' (British and Irish Legal Education Technology Association 1996); Phil Harris and Martin Jones, 'A Survey of Law Schools in the United Kingdom, 1996' (1997) 31(1) The Law Teacher 38.

standards] were seen as minimum standards only, the recommendations arguably did not support those who wished to think more creatively and interdisciplinarily about the relationships between law, education and technology'.[57]

The Advisory Committee on Legal Education and Conduct (ACLEC) Report of 1996 was the first report in England and Wales to take seriously the role of technology in legal education.[58] In the field of technology it made use of the first and second BILETA reports, and cited theoretical overviews such as Abel on legal professionalism,[59] Peter Clinch's work on law libraries,[60] and took account of the detailed fieldwork undertaken by Harris et al.[61] In spite of this, however, there was little integration of education and technology theory; and there was little of the growing sophistication of fusion in new media theory and education generally that was occurring in other educational reports.

Yet in ACLEC we see the emergence of technology as a separate sub-genre in the legal educational report, a process that was continued in the Legal Education and Training Review (LETR) of 2013, an example of Genre 4, where not only was digital theory discussed in some depth, but the literature of adjacent digital educational domains, in education itself and in medical education, were referenced and discussed in the main report[62] and literature review.[63] In addition a separate report was commissioned from Richard Susskind.[64] What we have in LETR is an intertextuality that had not appeared before, and which found the space it did in part because of the BILETA Inquiries, but also because of earlier reports on specific technologies – Paliwala's reports on IOLIS,[65] and a decade later Maharg et al's report on SIMPLE.[66]

More recently, we see new forms of reports arising on technology – *Legal Futures'* roundtable reports on technology, innovation and the professions, for example.[67]

[57] Maharg, 'Shared Space: Regulation, Technology and Legal Education in a Global Context' (n 3) 7.
[58] Lord Chancellor's Advisory Committee on Legal Education and Conduct, 'First Report on Legal Education and Training (ACLEC Report)' (Lord Chancellor's Department 1996).
[59] Richard Abel, *The Legal Profession in England and Wales* (Blackwell, 1988).
[60] Peter Clinch, 'Practical Legal Research the Cardiff Way' (1994) 28(3) The Law Teacher 270.
[61] Phil Harris, Steve Bellerby and Patricia Leighton, *A Survey of Law Teaching* (Sweet & Maxwell 1993); Harris and Jones (n 56).
[62] See for example Webb and others (n 8) para paras 2.99, 3.59, 3.74, 3.86ff. There are many other examples throughout the report.
[63] Julian Webb and others, 'Research Phase Literature Review (Legal Education and Training Review)' (SRA, BSB and CILEX 2013) ch 8, paras 44–63 http://letr.org.uk/literature-review/index.html accessed 17 May 2019. Immediately after this section the authors addressed a subject not hitherto discussed by any legal education report, but of central importance to the use of technology, namely the issue of curricular and technological change processes in legal education (paras 68–81).
[64] Richard Susskind, 'Provocations and Perspectives' (SRA, BSB and CILEX 2012) https://letr.org.uk/wp-content/uploads/Susskind-LETR-final-Oct-2012.pdf accessed 17 May 2019
[65] Abdul Paliwala 'Co-Operative Development of CAL Materials: A Case Study of IOLIS' (1998) 3 The Journal of Information, Law and Technology (JILT) https://warwick.ac.uk/fac/soc/law/elj/jilt/1998_3/paliwala/ accessed 17 May 2019
[66] Michael Hughes and others, 'SIMulated Professional Learning Environment (SIMPLE): Programme Final Report' (Jisc & Higher Education Authority 2008).
[67] Legal Futures, 'Reports' (2019) www.legalfutures.co.uk/reports accessed 17 May 2019.

Such reports focus on specific technologies and though theory-lite, at least try to cover Genres 1 and 2 above. More significant is an initiative such as Dan Linna's Legal Services Innovation Index, based in the USA, which is an attempt to create an index of legal-service delivery innovation, based upon indicia of innovation in law firms and also in law schools – effectively Genre 1. Linna's focus starts not from law schools, but from innovation itself, and by shifting the narrative point of view and the content focus of the report, he creates a new sub-genre of report for digital technologies in legal education.[68] Most of the data was scraped from law school websites, and Linna readily admits there are many more granular innovations within law school curricula that are being missed in his index. Nevertheless, the project is significant as a report in that it sets out data that was otherwise entirely missing from earlier reports such as BILETA or ACLEC. Not only does Linna expose what law schools do in their curricula, but also in the future intends to measure law schools' use of social media.[69] What is missing is the rich genre contextualising of education and technology that is present in the IOLIS or SIMPLE reports (arguably Genre 3), or in sections of LETR. A future direction for technology reports should be the fusion of these genres; and we would argue that until the genre form of reports on technology and legal education become more intertextual and interdisciplinary, until they begin to open to the anxiety of influence and the play of readings and misreadings, they will continue to inhibit or constrain our ability to develop imaginative, theory-rich and analytical accounts of digital cultures for legal education.

13.6 SUMMARY

The march of the legal education review will not be halted.[70] It is true, as a rare comparative review of reports in England and Wales, the USA, Australia and Hong Kong, concluded recently, that, 'Legal education reviews tend to be indifferent in investigating new methods to enhance students' learning.'[71] The point is that it is rarely their remit to do so. The taxonomy of genres developed in this chapter is a first step to dispelling misunderstanding and misplaced expectations amongst the wider audience including in particular those who wish to compare reports with each

---

[68]   Daniel W Linna Jr, 'Legal Services Innovation Index' (*Legal Tech Innovation*, 2019) www .legaltechinnovation.com/ accessed 17 May 2019.

[69]   Ibid.

[70]   Nederlandse orde van advocaten, 'Consultatie Toekomstbestendige Beroepsopleiding Advocaten van Start' (2017) www.advocatenorde.nl/nieuws/consultatie-toekomstbestendige-beroepsopleiding-advocaten-van-start accessed 24 July 2017; Hook Tangaza, 'Review of Legal Practitioner Education and Training' (Hook Tangaza 2018) www.lsra.ie/en/LSRA/20180928 Review of Legal Practitioner Education and Training -Final version
.pdf/Files/20180928 Review of Legal Practitioner Education and Training -Final version.pdf accessed 17 May 2019.

[71]   Wilson WS Chow and Firew Tiba, 'Professional Legal Education Reviews: Too Many "What"'s, Too Few "How"'s' (2013) 4(1) European Journal of Law and Technology http://ejlt.org/article/view/183 accessed 17 May 2019.

other. It may also assist commissioning bodies in understanding the implications and likely outcomes of the kind of investigation that they ask for. It has the potential not simply to inform, but to shape the discourse community.

The taxonomy of the kinds of review that do exist, also serves to highlight the kind of report that is missing. We have, particularly in Genre 1, snapshots. Genre 2 provides us with informed opinion and advocacy on pressing questions of the moment. Genre 3 collates opinions on very specific items of policy. This means that, with rare and honourable exceptions, we lack longitudinal data;[72] data that compares the outcomes of different educational interventions;[73] or the predictive value of different kinds of assessment. Here we are at a considerable disadvantage to our colleagues in medical education who regularly interrogate the effectiveness of what they do, and follow the effects into medical practice. Indeed, there seems to be some reluctance to believe that this kind of activity could, or should be adopted, or adapted for legal practice.[74]

When we turn to the sub-genre of digital legal education reports, we see, historically, the movement for technology of *any* sort, and especially digital technologies, to be recognised as worthy of detailed analysis. We see how thin that analysis is because of the early paucity of interdisciplinary feed-in, and the invisibility that stemmed from the lack of interest in the relationship between education and technology.

Throughout all this, many of the more sophisticated debates around technology recognise the double-edged nature of digitisation. There is no good news or bad: simply better ways to build, and more efficient and ethical ways to use technology educationally. But we also see, as the digital commentary grows in complexity, so too does the necessity to read, misread and read beyond previous reports' treatment of technology. We need to recognise that such technologies are actually

---

[72]   But see Michael Shiner, 'Entry into the Legal Profession: The Law Student Cohort Study Year 4' (The Law Society 1997); Bryant G Garth and others, 'After the JD' (*American Bar Foundation*, 2019) www .americanbarfoundation.org/research/project/118 accessed 17 May 2019; Melissa Hardee and Hardee Consulting, 'Career Expectations of Students on Qualifying Law Degrees in England and Wales: A Legal Education and Training Survey' (Higher Education Academy 2012) www.heacademy.ac.uk /system/files/resources/hardee-report-2012.pdf accessed 17 May 2019.

[73]   And see the comparison between a vocational course and articles in Law Society of Upper Canada, 'Report to Convocation' (The Law Society of Upper Canada 2016) https://lawsocietyontario.azureedge.net /media/lso/media/legacy/pdf/p/pdc-pathways-pilot-project-evaluation-and-enhancements-to-licensing-report-sept-2016.pdf accessed 17 May 2019; and the comparison between two different modes of vocational education in Alli Gerkman and Elena Harman, 'Ahead of the Curve: Turning Law Students into Lawyers' (Institute for the Advancement of American Legal Systems 2015) http://iaals .du.edu/sites/default/files/documents/publications/ahead_of_the_curve_turning_law_students_into_law yers.pdfhttp://iaals.du.edu/sites/default/files/documents/publications/ahead_of_the_curve_turning_law_ students_into_lawyers.pdf accessed 17 May 2019.

[74]   'In contrast with studies about predicting grades, research on predicting attorney effectiveness is limited, particularly with respect to the ways in which success as a lawyer can be defined and measured.' Marjorie M Shultz and Sheldon Zedeck, 'Predicting Lawyer Effectiveness: Broadening the Basis for Law School Admission Decisions' (2011) 36(3) Law & Social Inquiry 620, 623.

institutions:[75] in Swales's powerful description of language, they have the chilling capacity to be at once 'both complicitous and contestatory';[76] and our reports must investigate that ambivalent, protean quality of digital culture and its technologies. They can support neoliberal tendencies in legal education or they can educate ethically and transformationally; they can be used to suppress student agency rather than liberate it. It is in our hands to persuade regulators and others that we need sophisticated reports (at the very least Genre 4) into the nature, current use and future of such technologies if we are to understand how to design and deploy them well for our discipline and our profession; and that such reports require careful attention to genre structure, including many of those aspects we have analysed above.

BIBLIOGRAPHY

ABA Task Force, 'Report and Recommendations American Bar Association Task Force on the Future of Legal Education' (American Bar Association 2014) www.americanbar.org/con tent/dam/aba/administrative/professional_responsibility/report_and_recommendation s_of_aba_task_force.authcheckdam.pdf accessed 17 May 2019

Abel R, *The Legal Profession in England and Wales* (Blackwell, 1988)

Bhatia VK, *Analysing Genre: Language Use in Professional Settings* (1st edn, Routledge 1993)

Bloom H, *Yeats* (Oxford University Press 1970)

  Kabbalah and Criticism (Seabury Press 1975)

  Wallace Stevens: The Poems of Our Climate (Cornell University Press 1980)

Borges JL, 'Kafka and His Precursors' in Donald A Yates and James East Irby (eds.), André Maurois and Sherry Mangan (trs.), *Labyrinths: Selected Stories & Other Writings* (New Directions 1964)

British and Irish Legal Education Technology Association, 'Report of BILETA Inquiry into the Provision of Information Technology in UK Law Schools' (British and Irish Legal Education Technology Association 1991)

  'Information Technology for UK Law Schools: The Second BILETA Report into Information Technology and Legal Education' (British and Irish Legal Education Technology Association 1996)

Chandler D, 'An Introduction to Genre Theory' (*Visual Memory*, 1997) 5 http://visual-memory.co.uk/daniel/documents/intgenre/chandler_genre_theory.pdf accessed 17 May 2019

Ching J, 'The Challenges Facing Legal Services Education in the 21st Century: A Case for Collaboration and Conversation?' in A Nuhoğlu and others (eds.), *Legal Education in*

---

[75] A point made by Giddens: Anthony Giddens, *Central Problems in Social Theory: Action, Structure and Contradiction in Social Analysis* (MacMillan 1979); and quoted in John Swales, 'Genre and Engagement' (1993) 71(33) Revue Belge de Philologie Et D'Histoire 687, 692.

[76] The phrase belongs to Swales, 'Genre and Engagement' (n 75). There, he describes how in structuration theory 'human agency and social structure are implicated in each other rather than being opposed. Human agency constitutes social structure, while social structure is the medium of human agency.' He observes how his own use of standard English reinforces the symbolic orders and forms of communications he analyses – hence his honest acknowledgement of the moment's complicitous and yet contestatory qualities. It is a quality that pertains to most, if not all, regulatory reports, and especially those on, or containing sections upon, digital technologies in legal education.

the 21st Century: Proceedings of the International Conference, Bahçeşehir University and The Union of Turkish Bar Associations (Türkiye Barolar Birliği 2015) www.lawsociety.org .uk/representation/articles/lpc-aptitude-test-report-published/ accessed 7 September 2018

'Greener Grass and Re-Invented Wheels: Researching Together' (Society of Legal Scholars Annual Conference, Oxford, September 2016) http://irep.ntu.ac.uk/id/eprint/28622/ accessed 20 May 2019

'"Riding Madly Off in All Directions": Consistency and Convergence in Professional Legal Education' (Directions in Legal Education Conference, Hong Kong, June 2016) http:// irep.ntu.ac.uk/28240/ accessed 20 May 2019

'Reform of the Education Structure for the Professional Law Courses in Mauritius' (Tertiary Education Commission of Mauritius 2012)

'Consultation on the Feasibility of Implementing a Common Entrance Examination in Hong Kong: Literature Review' (Law Society of Hong Kong 2014)

Chow WWS and Tiba F, 'Professional Legal Education Reviews: Too Many "What's", Too Few "How"s' (2013) 4(1) European Journal of Law and Technology http://ejlt.org/article/ view/183 accessed 17 May 2019.

Clark DS, 'Legal Education' in David S Clark (ed.), *Comparative Law and Society* (Edward Elgar Publishing 2012)

Clinch P, 'Practical Legal Research the Cardiff Way' (1994) 28(3) The Law Teacher 270

Committee on the Future of the Legal Profession, 'A Time for Change: Report of the Committee on the Future of the Legal Profession (Marre Report)' (General Council of the Bar and the Law Society 1988)

Conseil des Barreaux Européens – Council of Bars and Law Societies of Europe, 'Continuous Training in the CCBE Member Countries: Summary' (Conseil des Barreaux Européens – Council of Bars and Law Societies of Europe 2016) www.ccbe.eu/docu ment/national_training_regime/1_-_summary_of_national_continuing_training_re gimes.pdf.pdf accessed 17 May 2019

Conseil National des Barreaux, 'Réforme de La Formation Initiale Dans Les Écoles d'avocats' (Conseil National des Barreaux 2014) http://cnb.avocat.fr/reforme-de-la-formation-initiale-dans-les-ecoles-d-avocats_a2071.html accessed 13 February 2019

'Le Conseil National Des Barreaux s'inquiète de La Qualité de La Formation Des Étudiants, Futurs Avocats, à La Suite de l'avis Du Conseil d'Etat Du 10 Février 2016' (Conseil National des Barreaux 2016) http://cnb.avocat.fr/le-conseil-national-des-barreaux-s-inquiete-de-la-qualite-de-la-formation-des-etudiants-futurs-avocats-a-la-suite-de-l_a2592.html accessed 13 February 2019

Council of the Federation of Law Societies of Canada, 'Common Law Degree Implementation Committee: Final Report' (Federation of Law Societies of Canada 2011) http://docs.flsc.ca /implementation-report-ecc-aug-2011-r.pdf accessed 17 May 2019

Eliot TS, 'Tradition and the Individual Talent', *Selected Essays* (3rd edn, Faber & Faber 1951)

European Commission, 'Lawyers' Training Systems in the Member States' (*European e-Justice Portal*, 2018) https://e-justice.europa.eu/content_lawyers__training_system s_in_the_member_states-407-en.do accessed 17 May 2019

Federation of Law Societies Canada, 'National Entry to Practice Competency Profile Validation Survey Report' (Federation of Law Societies Canada 2012) http://flsc.ca/wp-content/uploads/2014/10/admission4.pdf accessed 17 May 2019

Fowler A, 'Genre and the Literary Canon' (1979) 11(1) New Literary History: A Journal of Theory and Interpretation 97

Garth BG and others, 'After the JD' (*American Bar Foundation*, 2019) www
.americanbarfoundation.org/research/project/118 accessed 17 May 2019
Gerkman A and Harman E, 'Ahead of the Curve: Turning Law Students into Lawyers'
(Institute for the Advancement of American Legal Systems 2015) http://iaals
.du.edu/sites/default/files/documents/publications/ahead_of_the_curve_turning_law_
students_into_lawyers.pdfhttp://iaals.du.edu/sites/default/files/documents/publications/
ahead_of_the_curve_turning_law_students_into_lawyers.pdf accessed 17 May 2019
Giddens A, *Central Problems in Social Theory: Action, Structure and Contradiction in Social
Analysis* (MacMillan 1979)
Greimas AJ and Courtés J, 'Intertextuality' in Larry Christ and others (trs), *Semiotics and
Language: An Analytical Dictionary* (Indiana University Press 1982)
Hall E, 'Notes on the SRA Report of the Consultation on the Solicitors Qualifying Exam:
"Comment Is Free, but Facts Are Sacred" (2017) 51(3) Law Teacher 364
Hardee M and Hardee Consulting, 'Career Expectations of Students on Qualifying Law
Degrees in England and Wales: A Legal Education and Training Survey' (Higher
Education Academy 2012) www.heacademy.ac.uk/system/files/resources/hardee-report
-2012.pdf accessed 17 May 2019
Harris P, Bellerby S and Leighton P, *A Survey of Law Teaching* (Sweet & Maxwell 1993)
Harris P and Jones M, 'A Survey of Law Schools in the United Kingdom, 1996' (1997) 31(1)
The Law Teacher 38
Henderson P and others, 'Solicitors Regulation Authority: CPD Review' (Solicitors Regulation
Authority 2012) www.sra.org.uk/sra/news/wbl-cpd-publication.page accessed 17 May 2019
Hook Tangaza, 'Review of Legal Practitioner Education and Training' (Hook Tangaza 2018)
www.lsra.ie/en/lsra/20180928 review of legal practitioner education and training -final ver
sion.pdf/files/20180928 review of legal practitioner education and training -final version.pdf
accessed 17 May 2019
Hughes M and others, 'SIMulated Professional Learning Environment (SIMPLE):
Programme Final Report' (Jisc & Higher Education Authority 2008)
International Bar Association, 'IBA Global Regulation and Trade in Legal Services Report
2014' (International Bar Association 2014) https://papers.ssrn.com/sol3/papers.cfm?
abstract_id=2530064 accessed 17 May 2019
Jones R, 'Second International Conference on Substantive Technology in the Law School'
(1993) 7(1) International Review of Law Computers & Technology 237
Kristeva J, *Desire in Language: A Semiotic Approach to Literature* (Leon Roudiez ed., Thomas
Gora and Alice Jardine trs., Revised, Columbia University Press 1980)
Law Admissions Consultative Committee, 'Rethinking Academic Requirements for
Admission' (Law Council of Australia 2010) www.lawcouncil.asn.au/resources/law-
admissions-consultative-committee/discussion-papers accessed 17 May 2019
'Review of Academic Requirements for Admission to the Legal Profession' (Law Council of
Australia 2014) www.lawcouncil.asn.au/files/web-pdf/lacc docs/01.12.14_-_review_of_aca
demic_requirements_for_admission.pdf accessed 20 May 2019
Law Society of England and Wales, 'Report into the Global Competitiveness of the England
and Wales Solicitor Qualification: An Investigation into the Potential Impact of the SRA's
Training for Tomorrow Proposals on the Global Reputation of Solicitors of England and
Wales' (Law Society of England and Wales 2015) www.lawsociety.org.uk/support-services
/research-trends/global-competitiveness-of-the-england-and-wales-solicitor-qualification/
accessed 17 May 2019

Law Society of Upper Canada, 'Pathways to the Profession: A Roadmap for the Reform of Lawyer Licensing in Ontario' (Law Society of Upper Canada 2012) www.lsuc.on.ca /workarea/downloadasset.aspx?id=2147489848 accessed 17 May 2019

'Report to Convocation' (The Law Society of Upper Canada 2016) https://lawsocietyontario .azureedge.net/media/lso/media/legacy/pdf/p/pdc-pathways-pilot-project-evaluation- and-enhancements-to-licensing-report-sept-2016.pdf accessed 17 May 2019

LawyerEdu.org, 'Steps to Become a Lawyer/ Attorney in Canadian Provinces/ Territories' (2015) www.lawyeredu.org/canada.html accessed 17 May 2019

Legal Futures, 'Reports' (2019) www.legalfutures.co.uk/reports accessed 17 May 2019

Linna Jr DW, 'Legal Services Innovation Index' (*Legal Tech Innovation*, 2019) www .legaltechinnovation.com/ accessed 17 May 2019

Lord Chancellor's Advisory Committee on Legal Education and Conduct, 'First Report on Legal Education and Training (ACLEC Report)' (Lord Chancellor's Department 1996)

Maharg P, 'The Identity of Scots Law: Redeeming the Past' in Mark Mulhern (ed.), *Scottish Life and Society (A Compendium of Scottish Ethnology): The Law (Volume 13)* (Birlinn Press & The European Ethnological Research Centre 2011)

'Shared Space: Regulation, Technology and Legal Education in a Global Context' (2015) 6 (1) European Journal of Law and Technology 1 http://ejlt.org/article/view/425/541 accessed 17 May 2019

Mai H-P, 'Bypassing Intertextuality: Hermeneutics, Textual Practice, Hypertext' in Heinrich F Plett (ed.), *Intertextuality* (De Gruyter 1991)

Michaels R, 'The Functional Method of Comparative Law' in Mathias Reimann and Reinhard Zimmermann (eds.), *The Oxford Handbook of Comparative Law* (Oxford University Press 2006)

Miller CR, 'Genre as Social Action' (1984) 70(2) Quarterly Journal of Speech 151

National Admission Standards Project Steering Committee, 'National Law Practice Qualifying Assessment Business and Implementation Plan' (Federation of Law Societies of Canada 2015)

National Conference of Bar Examiners, 'A Study of the Newly Licensed Lawyer' (National Conference of Bar Examiners 2012) http://flsc.ca/wp-content/uploads/2014/10/admission4 .pdf accessed 5 June 2014

'Bar Admission Guide' (2019) www.ncbex.org/publications/bar-admissions-guide/ accessed 17 May 2019

Nederlandse orde van advocaten, 'Consultatie Toekomstbestendige Beroepsopleiding Advocaten van Start' (2017) www.advocatenorde.nl/nieuws/consultatie-toekomstbestendige- beroepsopleiding-advocaten-van-start accessed 24 July 2017

Ormrod R, 'Report of the Committee on Legal Education (Ormrod Report) (Cmnd. No. 4595)' (HM Stationery Office 1971)

Paliwala A, 'Co-Operative Development of CAL Materials: A Case Study of IOLIS' (1998) 3 The Journal of Information, Law and Technology (JILT) https://warwick.ac.uk/fac/soc/ law/elj/jilt/1998_3/paliwala/ accessed 17 May 2019

Pickles C, 'Research Report on Mandatory Continuing Professional Development Commissioned by the Law Society of South Africa' (Law Society of South Africa 2010) www.lssa.org.za /upload/documents/research_report_on_mcpd.pdf%3e accessed 17 May 2019

Queen's University Belfast, 'Postgraduate Research Course JD Juris Doctor (JD)' www .qub.ac.uk/schools/schooloflaw/study/jurisdoctor/ accessed 17 May 2019

Robbins LC, 'Higher Education Report of the Committee Appointed by the Prime Minister under the Chairmanship of Lord Robbins' (HM Stationery Office 1963)

Rutherford BA, 'A Genre-Theoretic Approach to Financial Reporting Research' (2013) 45(4) British Accounting Review 297

Shepelva O and Novikova A, 'The Quality of Legal Education in Russia: Stereotypes and Real Problems' (*PILnet*, 2014) www.pilnet.org/public-interest-law-resources/73-the-quality-of-legal-education-in-russia-stereotypes-and.html accessed 17 May 2019

Shiner M, 'Entry into the Legal Profession: The Law Student Cohort Study Year 4' (The Law Society 1997)

Shultz MM and Zedeck S, 'Predicting Lawyer Effectiveness: Broadening the Basis for Law School Admission Decisions' (2011) 36(3) Law & Social Inquiry 620

Solicitors Regulation Authority, 'Qualification in Other Jurisdictions – International Benchmarking' (Solicitors Regulation Authority 2016) www.sra.org.uk/sra/policy/sqe/research-reports.page accessed 17 May 2019

Sullivan WM and others, *Educating Lawyers: Preparation for the Profession of Law* (1st edn, Jossey-Bass 2007)

Susskind R, 'Provocations and Perspectives' (SRA, BSB and CILEX 2012) https://letr.org.uk/wp-content/uploads/susskind-letr-final-oct-2012.pdf accessed 17 May 2019

Swales J, *Genre Analysis: English in Academic and Research Settings* (Cambridge University Press 1990)

'Genre and Engagement' (1993) 71(33) Revue Belge de Philologie Et D'Histoire 687

'The Concept of Discourse Community' in Elizabeth Wardle and Dough Downs (eds.), *Writing about Writing: A College Reader* (1st edn, Bedford/St Martin's 2011)

Tessuto G, 'Generic Structure and Rhetorical Moves in English-Language Empirical Law Research Articles: Sites of Interdisciplinary and Interdiscursive Cross-Over' (2015) 37 English for Specific Purposes 13

Tipping A, 'Review of the Professional Legal Studies Course' (New Zealand Council of Legal Education 2013) www.nzcle.org.nz/docs/review of the plsc report .pdf accessed 17 May 2019

Twining W, 'Developments in Legal Education: Beyond the Primary School Model' (1990) 2 (1) Legal Education Review 35

Webb J and others, 'Research Phase Literature Review (Legal Education and Training Review)' (SRA, BSB and CILEX 2013) http://letr.org.uk/literature-review/index.html accessed 17 May 2019

'Setting Standards: The Future of Legal Services Education and Training Regulation in England and Wales (Legal Education and Training Review)' (SRA, BSB and CILEX 2013) www.letr.org.uk/wp-content/uploads/letr-report.pdf accessed 17 August 2018

Widdowson H, 'Discourses of Enquiry and Conditions of Relevance' in James E Alatis (ed.), *Georgetown University Round Table on Languages and Linguistics 1990* (Georgetown University Press 1990)

Wilson RJ, 'The Role of Practice in Legal Education' (18th International Congress on Comparative Law, Washington DC, July 2010) https://digitalcommons.wcl.american.edu/fac_works_papers/12/ accessed 17 May 2019

Zweigert K, Kötz H and Weir T, *An Introduction to Comparative Law* (3rd edn, Clarendon Press 1998)

Afterword

Elizabeth Chambliss

What will lead to meaningful change in legal education? And what should be the direction(s) of change? In the United States, as elsewhere, law schools are caught between critics who want them to be more responsive to the changing legal market and the needs of private employers, and critics who want them to do more to resist and shape the private market and promote the public good.

These critiques are not wholly incompatible as a blueprint for curricular reform. Increasing students' exposure to new skills and technologies, experiential training and projects, and collaboration with other professions, provides 'opportunities for critical analysis and reflection' as well as making students more employable.[1] Such curricular changes may be (more or less) achieved through local, decentralised efforts by and within individual law schools, as described by several chapters in this volume, and further scaled through collaboration and consortia among schools.

Some promote incremental curricular reform as a theory of change. Henderson, writing in the aftermath of the 2008 recession, offered a 'strategy memo' for law schools, in which he argued that 'not everything needs to change,' but rather 'a portion of us needs to retool (12% to 20%)' to respond to structural changes in the market, 'another portion needs to serve our institutions by doubling down on what they do well (50% to 60%), and a third group needs to agree not to obstruct – or alternatively, to move on'.[2] He proposed forming a consortium of law schools to construct a competency-based curriculum, based on sustained engagement with employers and measurable labour market outcomes. Each school would need to commit only a small fraction of its resources: 'we start with 12% of the curriculum – the equivalent of one course per year – driven by a small subset of faculty, who are willing and able to take up the challenge'.[3]

According to Henderson, this 12 per cent solution could produce significant, sustainable change. 'The process of designing and building a competency-based

---

[1] Introduction 9.
[2] William D Henderson, 'The Lawyer of the Future: A Blueprint for Change' (2013) 40(2) *Pepperdine Law Review* 461, 462, 465–6.
[3] Ibid 504.

curriculum is a profoundly powerful change management tool. With the right leadership, it can also be the basis for a successful law school capital campaign ... [E]ngagement with alumni and the legal industry will lead us out of this maze.'[4] Henderson recently helped to launch such a consortium, the Institute for the Future of Law Practice (IFLP), in which law schools, law departments, law firms and other companies collaborate to provide training bootcamps for law students, focused on 'business, design, project management, technology, and data analytics'.[5] A key feature of the programme is a guaranteed, paid internship for every student, to signal the value of IFLP training.[6] IFLP began in 2018 with twenty-five students from five law schools and an impressive list of company sponsors and, in 2019, expanded to seventeen law schools in the United States, Canada and Europe.[7]

The potential to scale incremental curricular reform is not limited to the private sector. In 2013, riffing on Henderson's 12 per cent solution, Staudt and Medeiros proposed that law schools add a new type of clinical course, an 'Access to Justice and Technology Clinic', in which students 'build tools and write content to help low-income, self-represented litigants' using A2J Author, a widely used document automation software.[8] They estimated that adding their proposed clinic would affect only about 4 per cent of the law school curriculum but, if widely adopted, would 'help law students to learn core competencies needed in an increasingly technological profession' as well as improving access to justice for low-income people.[9] A2J Author hosts centralised, free resources to support the software and clinical project, and law students, legal aid providers and others have produced over 1,100 A2J Author applications.[10]

Yet the transformative potential of curricular reform is constrained by market and political forces. Law students' career intentions are shaped by the job opportunities that are available and students may be sceptical of new forms of training in the absence of a clear path to employment. Since the recession, many have chosen to forego law school training altogether. Between 2010–11 and 2017–18, US law school enrolment fell nearly 25 per cent, to its lowest point in forty years.[11] As for public service, most students who enter law school with public service aspirations cash

4 Ibid 502–3.
5 Institute for the Future of Law Practice, 'Boot Camp: Building T Shaped Professionals' www .futurelawpractice.org/bootcamp accessed 22 June 2019.
6 William D (Bill) Henderson, 'An Update on IFLP' (*Legal Evolution*, 6 January 2019) www .legalevolution.org/2019/01/update-iflp-078/ accessed 22 June 2019.
7 Institute for the Future of Law Practice, 'Get Involved: Law Schools: Give Your Graduates Every Chance to Succeed (2019), www.futurelawpractice.org/law-schools accessed 25 June 2019.
8 Ronald W Staudt and Andrew P Medeiros, 'Access to Justice and Technology Clinics: A 4% Solution' (2013) 88(3) *Chicago-Kent Law Review* 695, 698.
9 Ibid.
10 See A2J Author, 'Welcome to A2J Author' www.a2jauthor.org/ accessed 25 June 2019; A2J Author, 'A2J Clinical Project' www.a2jauthor.org/content/a2j-clinic-project accessed 25 June 2019.
11 See Law School Transparency, 'Law School Enrollment' https://data.lawschooltransparency.com /enrollment/all/ accessed 25 June 2019.

them in when confronted with the realities of the job market and educational debt.[12] Although applications to US law schools have begun to increase in the wake of assaults on civil rights, lawyer independence and the rule of law – the so-called 'Trump Bump'[13] – the question remains: where will these students work?

Many of the chapters in this volume have a transformative agenda and work to connect curricular proposals to public service and social justice ideals. But modernising the JD curriculum (and its equivalent in other countries) will not transform legal education. The transformation of legal education requires the transformation of the legal market through new forms of licensing, service delivery and legal aid funding. It requires collective action by legal educators to challenge untested assumptions about the benefits of professional regulation and to lobby for regulation based on client and consumer interests.[14] This is both a scholarly and deeply political project that goes beyond curricular reform and a focus on student training – and the United States has much to learn from other countries represented in this volume. Fortunately, efforts are underway both inside and outside of legal education to shape the market for legal services to better serve public interests.

BIBLIOGRAPHY

A2J Author, 'Welcome to A2J Author' www.a2jauthor.org/ accessed 25 June 2019
  'A2J Clinical Project' www.a2jauthor.org/content/a2 j-clinic-project accessed 25 June 2019
Bliss J, 'From Idealists to Hired Guns? An Empirical Analysis of "Public Interest Drift" in Law School' (2018) 51(5) *University of California-Davis Law Review* 1973
Chambliss E, 'Evidence-Based Lawyer Regulation' (2019) 97 *Washington University Law Review* (forthcoming)
Granfield R, *Making Elite Lawyers: Visions of Law at Harvard and Beyond* (Routledge 1992)
Henderson WD, 'An Update on IFLP' (*Legal Evolution*, 6 January 2019) www.legalevolution.org/2019/01/update-iflp-078/ accessed 25 June 2019
  'The Lawyer of the Future: A Blueprint for Change' (2013) 40(2) *Pepperdine Law Review* 461
Institute for the Future of Law Practice, 'Boot Camp: Building T Shaped Professionals' www.futurelawpractice.org/bootcamp accessed 25 June 2019
  'Get Involved: Law Schools: Give Your Graduates Every Chance to Succeed' (2019) www.futurelawpractice.org/law-schools accessed 25 June 2019

---

[12] See Robert Granfield, *Making Elite Lawyers: Visions of Law at Harvard and Beyond* (Routledge 1992); John Bliss, 'From Idealists to Hired Guns? An Empirical Analysis of "Public Interest Drift" in Law School' (2018) 51(5) *University of California-Davis Law Review* 1973.

[13] Stephanie Francis Ward, 'The "Trump Bump" for Law School Applicants Is Real and Significant' *ABA Journal* (Chicago, 22 February 2018) www.abajournal.com/news/article/the_trump_bump_for_law_school_applicants_is_real_and_significant_survey_say accessed 25 June 2019; Kaplan, 'Kaplan Test Prep Survey: Nearly 90 Percent of Law Schools Say the Political Climate Was a Significant Factor in Application Increase' (*Kaptest Blog*, 25 February 2019) www.kaptest.com/blog/press/2019/02/25/kaplan-test-prep-survey-nearly-90-percent-of-law-schools-say-the-political-climate-was-a-significant-factor-in-application-increase/ accessed 25 June 2019.

[14] See Elizabeth Chambliss, 'Evidence-Based Lawyer Regulation' (2019) 97 *Washington University Law Review* (forthcoming).

Kaplan, 'Kaplan Test Prep Survey: Nearly 90 Percent of Law Schools Say the Political Climate Was a Significant Factor in Application Increase' (*Kaptest Blog*, 25 February 2019) www .kaptest.com/blog/press/2019/02/25/kaplan-test-prep-survey-nearly-90-percent-of-law-schools-say-the-political-climate-was-a-significant-factor-in-application-increase/ accessed 25 June 2019

Law School Transparency, 'Law School Enrollment' https://data.lawschooltransparency.com /enrollment/all/ accessed 25 June 2019

Staudt RW and Medeiros AP, 'Access to Justice and Technology Clinics: A 4% Solution' (2013) 88(3) *Chicago-Kent Law Review* 695

Ward SF, 'The "Trump Bump" for Law School Applicants Is Real and Significant' ABA *Journal* (Chicago, 22 February 2018) www.abajournal.com/news/article/the_trump_bump_for_ law_school_applicants_is_real_and_significant_survey_say accessed 25 June 2019

For EU product safety concerns, contact us at Calle de José Abascal, 56–1°,
28003 Madrid, Spain or eugpsr@cambridge.org.

www.ingramcontent.com/pod-product-compliance
Ingram Content Group UK Ltd.
Pitfield, Milton Keynes, MK11 3LW, UK
UKHW020355140625
459647UK00020B/2489